DON'T EMBARRASS THE FAMILY

THE TRIAL OF THE HANDLER OF WHITEY BULGER FBI SPECIAL AGENTJOHN CONNOLLY

MATTHEW T. CONNOLLY

♣ ⊩ THE ROCK HILL COMPANY ⊣⊩ ♣

The Twelve Men   G.K. Chesterton

From an essay in Tremendous Trifles, 1909

Now, it is a terrible business to mark a man out for the vengeance of men. But it is a thing to which a man can grow accustomed, as he can to other terrible things; he can even grow accustomed to the sun. And the horrible thing about all legal officials, even the best, about all judges, magistrates, barristers, detectives, and policemen, is not that they are wicked (some of them are good), not that they are stupid (several of them are quite intelligent), it is simply that they have got used to it.

Strictly they do not see the prisoner in the dock; all they see is the usual man in the usual place. They do not see the awful court of judgment; they only see their own workshop. Therefore, the instinct of Christian civilisation has most wisely declared that into their judgments there shall upon every occasion be infused fresh blood and fresh thoughts from the streets. Men shall come in who can see the court and the crowd, and coarse faces of the policemen and the professional criminals, the wasted faces of the wastrels, the unreal faces of the gesticulating counsel, and see it all as one sees a new picture or a ballet hitherto unvisited.

Our civilisation has decided, and very justly decided, that determining the guilt or innocence of men is a thing too important to be trusted to trained men. It wishes for light upon that awful matter, it asks men who know no more law than I know, but who can feel the things that I felt in the jury box. When it wants a library catalogued, or the solar system discovered, or any trifle of that kind it uses up its specialists. But when it wishes anything done which is really serious, it collects twelve of the ordinary men standing round. The same thing was done, if I remember right, by the Founder of Christia.

"SUFFER ANY WRONG THAT CAN BE DONE YOU RATHER THAN COME HERE!"

Charles Dickens in his novel Bleak House wrote that the above inscription should be placed above the door of every court house.

Your children are not your children. . . . You may give them your love but not your thoughts, for they have their own thoughts. You may house their bodies but not their souls, for their souls dwell in the house of to-morrow, which you cannot visit, not even in your dreams. . . . You are the bows from which your children as living arrows are sent forth. . . . He bends you with His might that His arrows may go swift and far. Let your bending in the Archer's hand be for gladness. For even as He loves the arrow that flies, so He loves also the bow that is stable.

Kahlil Gilbran: On Children

ACKNOWLEDGEMENTS

No book can be written without the help and guidance of others. Mention can be made of only a few but I thank all who gave me advice and assistance through the year.

Especial Thanks to:

My Wife : Maria. Ukrainian born - infused with old world values who tolerated my Irish moods and peccadilloes – who successfully raised our three children and tries to follow the advice of Kahlil Gilbran noted above:

My Children:

Matthew — who challenges me to provide support for my ideas; continually enlightens me with his knowledge of matters both esoteric and mundane, foreign and domestic, and nautical.

Teddy — without whom this book would not have been published who encouraged, pushed and assisted me far more than I could ever thank him for and his wife Sharon for helping him and being a good mother to Theo and Cora.

Tatiana – her enthusiasm for my work, her interest in the subject matter, her laughter at my jokes, and her suggestions to make it better from her far off New York lair and John who helps her and us in our many tasks.

My Siblings:

Kathleen and Alice – the bearers of good and bad family news but always there to support me.

Jim, Billy, Neal, and Sammy — we never saw eye-to-eye. The family political disputes are legendary but as we aged we got wiser and mellower but still don't see eye-to-eye. Ask Tom.

Our Friends:

Cal and Jan — who have always been there for us – a great source of inspiration and joy who pitched in with their enthusiasm and suggestions with the book, and, of course, Sydney, who was never far away and never lacking in ideas.

The Arlington Group — it is coming up to a half a century of gathering together for the simple pleasure and enjoyment of each other's company.

The Book Group — four couples on a many decades journey adrift upon a sea of knowledge grabbing handfuls over good wine and fine food.

My Friends:

The Boys in Blue – Brendan, Peter and Steve – three men who did their jobs with integrity.

Brendan I met as a teenager who trained with me getting ready for the Marines. He kept faith with me through the many years that passed, and made cogent suggestions for this book;

Peter who took me by the hand when I went to the DA's office and introduced me to real police work, stuck by me through thick and thin;

Steve a good friend who stood strong on behalf of a fellow trooper when everyone else ran through the briar and the brambles.

The Quincy sub-station guys who called me Fletcher suggesting I'd have benefited from going to the Fletcher School of Diplomacy.

The guys the Drug Task Force who stuck the cognomen of Monty on me suggesting I reminded them of Monty Hall on Let's Make A Deal;

The guys in all the task forces and units who operated with me showing things can be done well and right so that no search or a wiretap is suppressed. We didn't take shortcuts and no one was ever injured.

The DA's Office

WDD — who took many disparate elements, mixed them together in a smooth operating machine; who brought the DAs out of the dark ages. Things we now considered normal were considered shocking when he proposed them.

JK — for the friendship, the many discussion we've had, and the work we did together.

S — for her help while in the DA's office and over the years, maintaining our friendship through thick and thin, and laughing at my inane witticisms.

TABLE OF CONTENTS

Introduction.   10

Chapter One: Opening Statements   24
                       John Durham   29
                       Tracy Miner   38

Chapter Two: The Evidence Begins   46
                       Donald Stern   46
                       Thomas Powers   56

Chapter Three: Masters of Deceit   65
                       John Morris   65

Chapter Four: Stepping in the Mud   107
                       John Martorano   107

Chapter Five: An Officer of Muddleheads   139
                       John Bebbington   139
                       Nicholas Gianturco   144
                       Gerald A. Montinari   148

Chapter Six: A Mucker's Tale   161
                       Kevin Weeks   161

Chapter Seven: The Noose Tightens   204
                       Julie Miskel Rakes Dammers   205
                       Joseph Lundbohm   206
                       Patrick Patterson   209
                       Lynn Tremain   212

Chapter Eight: Memories of the Old Days   217

Francis Salemme   217

Chapter Nine: Limping to the End   248
               Mark Wolf   249
               Jonathan Chiel   258

Chapter Ten: Affixing a Shine to a Sneaker   263
              Dennis Michael O'Callaghan   263
              Thomas J. Daly   282
              Edward F. Harrington   286
              Edward Quinn   292
              Gerald Franciosa   299
              John Connolly (video)   30

Chapter Eleven: Closing Statements   308
                 John Durham   311
                 Tracy Miner   322

Chapter Twelve: Afterwards   334

APPENDIX:
       A: Charts   346
       B: Weeks Weak Tale   347
       C: Title of the Book   357
       D: The Author   364
       E: William "Billy" Bulger   374
       F: Jeremiah O'Sullivan   410
       G: Lancaster Street   420
       H: Myles Connor   438
       I: Crossing the FBI   448
       J: The Prosecutors   459
       K: The FBI   473
       L: John Connolly   502

INTRODUCTION

In the summer of 2011 I pulled into the parking lot of the church where the funeral of Matthew Gallagher, a US Army soldier killed in Iraq, was being held. His father Peter, now retired, was a highly skilled police detective from the City of Quincy. I had worked closely with Peter over many years, so close that Peter told me the son he was then burying had been named after me.

As I was getting out of my car at the church another retired Quincy detective Jack Haines who I had not seen in over twenty years walked over to me. We spoke of Peter's tragedy in losing his son. As I was about to leave he grabbed my arm, a slight smile flickered across his face. He said, "They finally got him." I nodded. I well knew the "him" he was referring to.

It was James "Whitey" Bulger (Whitey). He had been arrested 15 days earlier after sixteen years on the lam. It was an apt time to mention Whitey for it was Peter who got me involved in chasing after Whitey.

In 1976 he all but begged me to go to the Quincy to meet with some other detectives. He knew that prior to becoming a prosecutor I had represented a defendant at a trial in the Commonwealth where for the first time evidence gained from wiretaps authorized by the 1968 federal law was used.[1] Peter figured I had to know

---

[1] Title III of The Omnibus Crime Control and Safe

something about wiretaps. His group wanted to do a wiretap even if it meant disclosing confidential information to a former defense counsel who they didn't completely trust.

Peter took me to what they called the Quincy police sub-station.[2] It was hidden on the second floor in the rear of the old Boston Gear Works building. A small group of detectives who were intent on developing a case against Whitey operated out of there. They had created a huge wall chart showing the organized crime figures in Eastern Massachusetts. Whitey was at the top of a pyramid. Lines emanating from him connected the people controlling various aspects of his operation.[3] I could never have imagined that 35 years after Peter got me involved investigating Whitey I'd go to his son's funeral and I'd hear about Whitey.

Streets Act of 1968 (**Wiretap Act**). 18 U.S.C. §§ 2510-22 authorized states to conduct secret electronic surveillance if certain mandatory procedures were followed.

[2] One day as I was leaving the DA's office I said I was going to the Quincy sub-station. A couple of days later one of my associates approached me with a puzzled look on her face. She said, "I didn't know the Quincy police had a submarine station." Of course, I let her believe it for a while.

[3] The commander of the sub-station was Lieutenant David Franklin Rowell a politically clever officer who knew how to get things done. He had four skillful detectives working under him: Peter Gallagher who excelled at street work and handling informants; Dick Bergeron a master tactician and thinker who created the charts and would eventually get a bug in Whitey's car; Paul Snow superb at surveillance; and Bob Crowley, an independent thinker and actor.

INTRODUCTION

Over the years Peter's group headed by Dave Rowell and other groups of police officers, state and local, worked with me on wiretaps attacking the organization of Whitey and his partner Stephen Flemmi (Stevie). Even though Whitey and Stevie rarely communicated over the telephone, members of their organization, especially the bookmakers, relied on it extensively. Only once did we intercept Whitey and Stevie in a telephone conversation. That call was nothing more than the former advising the latter he was back in the area. Stevie was on the home telephone of a person he would later murder.

In 1976 none of us knew Whitey was an FBI informant. In 1988 when the Boston Globe's Kevin Cullen asked me if I thought he was an FBI informant I told him no. I considered the suggestion preposterous.[4] To me it'd be like the FBI using Al Capone, Myer Lansky or Lucky Luchiano as an informant. It just wasn't done.

Much to my surprise I was wrong. It was done. It continues to be done.[5]

In 1998 Federal Judge Mark Wolf held hearings on motions relating to indictments pending against Whitey and Stevie. During those hearings the FBI was forced to admit that for many years these two

---

[4] I realized later that Kevin without telling me was seeking to verify information for the Boston Globe Spotlight Team. FBI agent John Morris told the Globe reporters that Whitey was an informant and retired FBI ASAC Robert Fitzpatrick confirmed it.

[5] In 2012, at least in Boston, the FBI is still using and protecting high level organized crime figures who are its informants.

INTRODUCTION

vicious criminals had been top level informants for the FBI. In effect this meant the FBI had been protecting them for many years. No wonder law enforcement's pursuit of them had come up empty.

I had retired from my position as deputy district attorney in Norfolk County prior to the time of Judge Wolf's decision. I followed Judge Wolf's hearings by reading the newspapers. Of course the revelations that those men were informants made me shake my head in disgust but I didn't dwell on it. Over time I read about some gangsters turning state's evidence, bodies long missing being unearthed, and the indictment of FBI agent John Connolly who was Whitey's and Stevie's handler. I was no longer in the game so I had only a passing interest in these happenings.

In the spring of 2002 I went to lunch with Brendan Bradley a former Boston police captain and highly proficient homicide investigator who I knew from my teen years. He asked me if I was going to John Connolly's trial. I hadn't even considered it. I didn't relish the idea of going to the Boston waterfront to sit through a trial which I could read about in the newspapers. I said, "probably not." We talked a while about it. He suggested that it'd be good for me to do so. I said I'd give it some consideration.

As I thought about it I figured that if I went to the trial I might learn something about the investigation and indictment of Massachusetts State Trooper John Naimovich. I never understood why he was targeted and indicted by the feds. To explain this, I have to tell you something about him.

I first heard of Naimovich in the mid Seventies from Peter Gallagher who spoke highly of him. This is unusual when you realize local cops don't particularly like state cops. Peter told me that he worked on a wiretap operation in Plymouth County with Naimovich. He said Naimovich was so good that he was able to go undercover and operated a bookmaking office for the mob.[6]

Peter's opinion was not supported by the other detectives in his group. They knocked Naimovich suggesting he was untrustworthy. They didn't point to anything in particular. I was brand new to the world of police intrigue and knew little about the unfounded distrusts, intense jealousies and virulent hatreds among cops. I didn't know what to believe about this Trooper Naimovich but I can't say I wasn't wary about him.

I never suspected that I would meet him soon thereafter. I had finished a wire tap with the Quincy detectives when I was approached by two

---

[6] Naimovich's work in the Plymouth County wiretap resulted in John Martorano's incarceration for six months. Martorano, who testified against Connolly, would have received a greater sentence except he had inside information that allowed him to attack the way the wiretap was conducted. He identified his inside source as State Trooper Richard Schneiderhan who was a life long friend of Stevie. Kevin Weeks, who also testified against Connolly, said Stevie received information from Schneiderhan and Stevie paid him for it on a regular basis. Stevie protected his relationship with Schneiderhan by saying his source was Naimovich.

men outside the Dedham court house. One was Sergeant Charlie Henderson the head of the Special Services Unit of the state police, the unit that did their organized crime investigations, and the other was Naimovich. They liked to avoid the district courts when they got their search warrants so they needed an assistant district attorney (ADA) to bring them before a superior court judge. They were told to seek me out. After talking a while I suggested they consider doing a wiretap rather than a search. Obviously being forewarned about Naimovich I kept up my guard.

I worked with him off and on for over ten years. We were never friends. He was stubborn, gruff and sure of himself, one of those "my way or highway" guys with plenty of rough edges. It became clear that even though he was only a trooper he ran the wiretap operations. He brooked no foolishness. He was easy to dislike. But he was good at what he did.

In the early days we often clashed. He had become used to overstepping into the ADA's area of responsibility and I'd have to push back. He wasn't used to not getting his way but had to put up with me because he realized I could shut down any wiretap at a moment's notice. And, he sensed that I would if I found it necessary to do so. It took him a while to understand that an ADA had an important operational role in a wiretap. Even so, he was adept at cutting me but I put up with it because I respected him highly for his ability and integrity. Despite our rocky relationship we gained good results.

INTRODUCTION

The years mellowed us. In 1987 we began an operation on a low level bookie. It proved productive so we moved from him to his boss and on and on up the ladder to the higher bosses. The operation lasted over six months. Since my other duties were such I could not go out to the wiretap plant like I used to do, Naimovich came to my office early in the morning three or four times a week.[7] We would go over the progress of our investigation, analyze the evidence and prepare the paper work for the raids and other wiretaps.

Eventually we reached the top of this organization. We were on the telephones of a crime kingpin, Abe Sarkis, and his top lieutenant, and had a bug in their office. Abe, although not violent like Whitey and Stevie, was at a level where we thought he might reach out to some other high Mafia figures like Larry Baione who was believed to be Abe's partner which would allow us to swing our operation over against them.

Everything was going along as well as it could. On my son's birthday February 3, 1988, I was in my office early. Aside from the wiretap I had a regular felony case load. I was busy getting ready for court when my private land line telephone rang. Rick Zebrasky, the state police lieutenant in charge of

---

[7] To get a sense of Naimovich I like to tell how one morning a substitute receptionist was at the front desk. She dialed my extension. In a whisper she said, "There's a man here who wants to see you. He says he's a state trooper. I'm sure he isn't. What should I do?" Naimovich's somewhat pudgy figure, his unkempt appearance and gold earring made it difficult for many to believe he was a state trooper.

my drug task force, was on the phone. "Guess who just got arrested by the feds."

I waited.

"Naimovich! For racketeering!"

I was stunned. My immediate reaction was a recognition that we had been doing some outlier things during our investigation and a great mistake had been made by the feds. I called the head of the Federal Strike Force, Jeremiah O'Sullivan, to tell him he'd screwed up. He told me that there was no mistake. He said Naimovich had been giving inside information to organized crime for many years.

Those were the days when the FBI spoke almost everyone fell in line. The local newspapers gushed with its praise. No one doubted the Bureau was on the level. Naimovich's fellow state troopers quickly abandoned him and headed for the bushes. He became a pariah to most in law enforcement.

Two people openly stuck by him, Trooper Steve Lowell and myself. The colonel in charge of the State Police Bureau of Investigative Services, Jack O'Donovan, also supported Naimovich but did it clandestinely through me fearing the repercussions from the FBI if he acted openly. Lowell and I were subpoenaed to testify in his defense at his trial which we did. The jury acquitted him. He was forced to retire. He refused to take his pension. He died not long after that. A good man falsely accused experiencing the inexplicable shredding of his reputation.

It is common knowledge that once a cop is charged with a crime his reputation is pretty much ruined. After Judge Wolf ended his hearings he wrote a 661 page document containing his findings. Stevie had testified before him. He lied by testifying his source of information in the state police was Naimovich. Based on this Wolf called Naimovich corrupt and supported his finding by noting wrongly that Naimovich had been convicted. Wolf didn't bother to check the records in his own court showing Naimovich's acquittal nor to spell his name correctly. Though he had been dead for many years, Naimovich's reputation was still taking a beating.

Here's what else I knew. When Naimovich and I were doing the wiretap of Abe Sarkis some of the state troopers who were supposed to be assisting us were actually working against us. They were working with the FBI investigating Naimovich.[8] They must also have been keeping the FBI apprised of our progress. John Connolly was part of this FBI/state police team as were other agents who received gifts from Whitey. Connolly would also testify for the government at Naimovich's trial.

Connolly had to know not only about our wiretap but also about the investigation by his unit

---

[8] During our morning meetings I would review the intercepted calls and the surveillances. I constantly complained to Naimovich that the troopers seemed not to be doing their job. Important meetings by the targets were not being covered; important conversations were not being highlighted. Naimovich always offered excuses for his fellow troopers. The truth was the investigation had shifted from the criminals to Naimovich and the wiretap was being neglected.

of Naimovich. Whitey and Stevie were still being handled by him. The Connolly trial would show he was adamant in demanding that any information pertaining to them be given to him so he could protect them.[9]

I did not think it would be possible that Connolly would let Naimovich be targeted by his unit if Naimovich was Stevie's source of information. Whitey and Stevie would want to protect their state police source. Connolly could guarantee that the FBI would not interfere with Whitey and Stevie's insidious actions. They still needed protection from the state police. If they were getting that from Naimovich they would want to insure that continued. That meant they would not have let Connolly investigate him nor would he have done so.[10]

But they would be delighted to let the state police with the FBI's help identify the wrong person as their source. Using the FBI to destroy Naimovich allowed them to accomplished three things: incapacitate a man who had been a thorn in their side; provide protection for their true source of information; and shut down my wiretap operation which Connolly would have known had penetrated high into their network.

---

[9] The trial would show that he asked O'Sullivan not to indict them in a race fixing case; he tipped them off as to investigations against them; he told them who was informing on them, and he became irate if he knew someone in the FBI office was not disclosing all they knew about them to him.

[10] The evidence would show that Connolly was not handling Whitey and Stevie, it was more that Whitey and Stevie, but especially Whitey, were handling Connolly.

I later came across an FBI report which stated that Stevie was asked to identify his source in the state police. Stevie refused to tell saying that he was a life long friend. Stevie grew up in Roxbury a part of Boston. Naimovich grew up in Chelsea north of Boston. They had no such connection. I reasoned the real source had to be someone from his neighborhood. It would turn out that I was correct.[11]

I thought attending Connolly's trial I had a chance to discover more about what was behind Naimovich's indictment. I believed if the FBI knew Naimovich was innocent, yet brought about his prosecution, it would be a pretty sordid act.[12]   It turned out it would be nothing compared to what I heard at the trial.

Aside from my interest in Naimovich I had little interest in the case. I could take Connolly or leave him. He may have compromised some of my investigations but I could not prove it. I knew he poisoned the Boston FBI agents against my office

---

[11] Prior to the trial I did not know about Schneiderhan. Schneiderhan was later indicted and convicted on matters relating to attempting to compromise an investigation. He testified he and Stevie were life long friends and grew up together in Roxbury. At one point when he thought he was dying he asked his family to make sure Stevie sat in the first row at his funeral.

[12] This would not have been unusual for the Boston FBI office. It let four men get convicted for a murder, two were sentenced to death and two to life in prison, while hiding exculpatory evidence that showed their innocence. It would end up costing the taxpayer over one hundred million dollars. It cost the FBI agents nothing. See: House Report 108-414: Everything Secret Degenerates

by filing scurrilous reports about us in an attempt to protect Whitey and Stevie who felt threatened by us because they had no way to get information from our office. Connolly wrote reports that had Whitey complaining about the Norfolk DA and the Quincy police having a vendetta against him as if there was something wrong with targeting the top criminal in the New England.

As far as I was concerned, what Connolly did was in the past. I had pretty much let it go. When I thought that he used these two gangsters as his informants, I questioned his judgment but less so when I learned more experienced agents encouraged him to do this and that his superiors approved his actions over the years. His actions did not endear him to me but I figured he was doing what the job wanted him to do.

At the time of his trial I considered him in the same way I had always felt about him. I had interacted with him either in person or on the telephone less than a dozen times. He was a likeable and pleasant man who worked on the prosecution side as I did. We did very little business together. If I met him on the street, we would exchange pleasantries and pass on. After the trial and as time passed I've thought more about him. My feelings are set out in the last section of the Appendix.

What was brought out at the trial only gives part of the picture. Without understanding how the Bureau operates it is difficult to understand as Paul Harvey would intone, "The rest of the story." To fully understand Connolly I hope at some point to discuss the FBI environment in which he leaned and operated. That is beyond the scope of this writing.

Here I deal with my experiences attending John Connolly's trial. I took copious notes of the testimony in long hand. The testimony of each witness is set out from what I wrote and remembered. It is like a transcript but better. I combine the answers of each witness to the direct and cross-examination into a continuous narrative. This was easy because the testimony during direct or cross-examinations varied slightly because of factors unique to this case.[13] To keep the flow of the trial I insert corroborative testimony by a minor witness following or within the main witness's testimony. This is italicized and underline. I also put in my thoughts and speak of the happenings I am witnessing in court to add flavor to the testimony, also italicized and underlined.

Because I grew up in South Boston and Savin Hill, I have a sense of these neighborhoods on my skin. It was in these areas that much of the happenings occurred. I personally knew some of the characters involved. I was friendly with people who knew the ones I did not.

I cut my teeth as a trial lawyer doing general trial work in all the courts and administrative agencies and a heavy dose of criminal defense

---

[13] Neither the prosecution nor the defense wished to blacken the FBI. The prosecution wanted the jury to believe Connolly was a rogue agent; the defense did not think it helped him if it proved he worked for a rogue outfit. The FBI skated through untouched which frustrated my attempt to learn the truth.

work in a small but high powered firm that also represented Mafia leaders. Most of my career I spent as a prosecutor. I actively investigated organized crime groups. There is much I knew about the matters that arose in this case that would not be known to others. To provide my insights, I have used footnotes throughout the testimony and included an appendix.

Whitey operated so long because of his involvement with FBI agent John Connolly. Connolly saw it as his job to protect Whitey. Connolly thought the FBI would protect him if he did his job. He was wrong. It needed a scapegoat.

Whitey's capture totally consumed the local news for over a week. The media flocked to the courthouse to see him. Every aspect of his life was touched upon and examined. The Boston Globe brought out its old stories. Old gangsters became new celebrities. New reporters became instant experts. Hyperbole ran amok trampling over facts. Facts were not allowed to stand in the way of a good story. Major errors crept into many tales.

I have been sitting on this book about John Connolly's trial for many years. Seeing how ill informed people appear about the past I hope that I might be able to straighten out many of the misconceptions that have floated about since Whitey's arrest. To toss out an old saw this is my attempt to set the record straight.[14]

---

[14] I started a blog, www.thetrialofwhiteybulger.com.

CHAPTER ONE

OPENING STATEMENTS

When I arrive in Boston at 9:00 a.m. on the opening day of the trial fifteen people are standing outside the courtroom door. Within 30 minutes the number swells to over fifty. After waiting another half an hour and after a little pushing and shoving I am allowed into the court room. I sit in the left front row at the aisle immediately contiguous to the jury box. The first two rows of the seating area in the center section of the court room are packed with police officers. The members of the media sit in the rows behind them.

I notice that the defendant, John Connolly, is talking to his attorney, Tracy Miner. He's about 5' 9" tall. His hair is full, dark and well groomed. His face is full, round, wan and puffy. He has put on weight since I've last seen him, adequately filling out his dark business suit. I watch him as he returns to the front row on the right side directly opposite me. He sits in the aisle seat. He is with his wife and their three young boys aged between eight and fourteen. There will be much courthouse chatter over the appropriateness of Connolly bringing his sons to court, or as his detractors say 'hiding behind his kids.'[15] Connolly leaves the

---

[15] I saw nothing wrong with Connolly bringing his sons to court. My experience taught me it is wise. I was certain that those who were the loudest in their denunciation of Connolly would be the first to bring in their own spouse and kids.

It helps a defendant for a jury to see his family. As a prosecutor I wanted a defendant to leave his family at

courtroom with his boys as the prosecution team comes in.

The lead prosecutor, John Durham, is smiling. He's carrying a folder in his left hand. He's medium height, slight, owlish looking with eyeglasses and a baby walrus type moustache. With him is Cynthia Shepherd of the Justice Department in Washington, DC. She is well-dressed, very petite hardly reaching the five foot height mark. Durham

---

home. I did not want a jury having to concern itself with the effect its decision may have on innocent individuals like a defendant's family.

I recall an arson case that I tried twice, each time for over a week. Both times the jury deadlocked: 6 for guilty, 6 to acquit. My evidence of the defendant's guilt was circumstantial. I had clear motive evidence. This usually tips the scale in an arson case. My case was weakened when the defendant showed up in court with his attractive wife and well-dressed, well-behaved, and comely children. You'd be happy to have them as friends and neighbors or have your kids play with his kids. I could never get all the jurors to bite the bullet. Despite the evidence some did not want to hurt the nice family that sat in court every day supporting their father and husband.

On the other hand, I was facing an extremely difficult circumstantial arson trial against two defendants who were represented by two highly skilled defense counsel who had well credentialed expert witnesses to testify against me. The motive evidence was sketchy. This case lasted several weeks. The first day of trial both defendants showed up without any family members. I clearly recall sitting at counsel desk and looking over as the courtroom door opened and the two defendants walked in. Each was dressed in a leisure suit, the style everyone associates with "wise guys." When I saw them I breathed a sigh of relief. I knew my chances for conviction had increased markedly.

speaks amicably with Tracy Miner and then moves
forward to his desk where he speaks with the court
stenographer. Connolly returns with his boys and
sits down in the aisle seat he had previously left.
He will sit there throughout the trial.[16]

---

[16] I expected Connolly to leave his family and sit in the enclosure at counsel table. I thought it unusual that he sat in the spectator section. I wasn't alone,

On the next morning a Boston Herald newspaper columnist Peter Gelzinis had an article in which he wrote: "For some strange reason, Judge Joe Tauro allowed the defendant to vacate his seat at the defense table, to be with his wife and kids on the other side of the rail, where the rest of us who weren't facing multiple counts of racketeering and obstruction of justice were sitting."

Judge Tauro in an obvious response to that article explained to the jurors that by tradition only lawyers, court personnel and those with the permission of the judge could sit within the enclosure. He said a defendant may enter the enclosure and sit at counsel table but only with the permission of the judge and that most defense counsel make that request and it is routinely granted. Here no request was made so the defendant can sit wherever he wants in the courtroom. The only caveat is that if a defendant elects to sit among the spectators, he must sit in the same spot every day.

Defendants were never allowed within the bar enclosure (the railing separating the front area of the court room from the spectators) when I first started practicing as a defense lawyer. Back then some defendants were kept in cage-like structures; others were shackled to the bar or to the benches placed immediately outside the bar. Court officers usually stood behind them. This all inured to the benefit of a prosecutor. At the start of a jury trial, a clerk would state to the defendant, "You are now set at the bar to be tried" which was literally true.

In the early 1970s, the courts expanded many of

OPENING STATEMENTS

The prosecution team consists of three attorneys, John Durham, Leonard Boyle, Cynthia Shepherd and an FBI agent Gary Bald. Durham is the lead prosecutor. Leonard Boyle will assist him with some of the major witnesses. Shepherd will present the less important corroborating witnesses. Bald will handle the evidence. [17]

---

the rights afforded to defendants including the right to counsel. At that time the lawyers started to have their clients sit next to them. Today, few defense counsel, if any, request such permission from the court. They assume it is the defendant's right to sit at counsel table.

As a young lawyer I worked for JJ Sullivan. He had developed his acerbic personality to an art form. At the start of one particular trial, during the days when things were changing, the judge came into the court. He saw the defendant was sitting at the bar. He said, "Mr. Defendant, you may sit at counsel table."

JJ stood up slowly from his seat at counsel table, held up his hand toward the defendant like a cop stopping traffic, took off his reading glasses, then turned his scowl on the judge and irascibly stated, "The defendant may not sit at counsel table."

JJ believed that a defendant's place was to be as far away from him as possible. JJ considered himself a professional hired to represent an amateur who if near him would only be a distraction. He would tell me, "A surgeon does not ask his patient for advice during an operation."

[17] For his work in Connolly's case, he was promoted to Special Agent in Charge (SAC) of the Baltimore FBI office. Five months after this trial Bald will be seen on national television almost nightly in his dark suit towering silently behind Chief Moose during the two to three week period when the snipers terrorized the Washington, DC area. He eventually rose to head the FBI's National Security Branch before retiring in 2006 for a job with the Royal Caribbean Cruise Lines.

As the hand on the clock ticks closer to the ten o'clock hour, the tension of starting a major case permeates the courtroom. I notice the joviality of the prosecution team has abated. They stand grim faced with their arms crossed tightly across their bodies. FBI Agent Bald stands with his hands in his pockets. Miner sits at her desk reading through some papers. Sitting next to her is Jay Tangney who will work closely with her during the trial.

The door behind the judge's desk opens. Judge Joseph Tauro enters. All in the courtroom rise. I haven't seen him since I testified in front of him in 1988 in the Naimovich case. I'm amazed at how good he looks. He appears younger than back then. He exudes a strong energy, a marked alertness and a confident demeanor. There's no doubt that, like a captain on a Royal Navy war ship, he's in command. He greets everyone with a smiling and confident "good morning" while gesturing that we should sit back down. His impressive manner will be maintained throughout the rest of the trial. I'll come to believe that it would be of great benefit to our state judicial system if many of the judges now presiding in the Commonwealth's courts spent a week or so watching him.

Durham returns the good morning, introduces himself and his team to the judge. Miner does likewise. Tauro says one juror has been excused so they will continue with seventeen.

The jurors are brought in. All are white except for one who appears to be Asian. The jury is about evenly split between men and women. The ages are between 30 and 50. Judge Tauro says "good morning" to them. He gets no reply. So he stares, friendly-like, at them for a second or so while indicating with a movement of his hand that he's expecting a return salutation. He finally gets a halfhearted "good morning." He'll go through the same routine in the afternoon. He'll eventually receive a robust greeting each morning from the jurors in response to his salutation.

John Durham rises to makes his opening statement. He stands facing the jury at its center point behind a podium situated about three feet from the jury rail. He speaks in a controlled calm voice, gesturing with his right hand and keeping his left hand in his pocket. For almost an hour, he will stand in front of the jury keeping good eye contact. His voice will be forceful, his mannerism effective, but he will exhibit little emotion. He has an outline of his argument on paper. He rarely looks at it showing he is well prepared.

DURHAM'S OPENING STATEMENT:

The defendant John Connolly is a retired FBI special agent. He was known by various nicknames among the criminal element such as Zip. This shows he has a different relationship than would be normal for a FBI agent.

Back in December 1994 the US Attorney for Massachusetts, Donald Stern, was planning to indict James Whitey Bulger, Steven Flemmi and others. Before doing that, he wanted to learn if Whitey Bulger was an FBI informant. In order to find out, Stern held a meeting on December 22, 1994, with FBI agents from the Boston office during which he told these FBI agents that he would return indictments against Whitey Bulger, Steve Flemmi, Frank Salemme, John Martorano and others around January 10, 1995.

OPENING STATEMENTS

On January 5, 1995, Stern secured arrest warrants and went looking for these men. Whitey Bulger was nowhere to be found. He had fled from the area. He remains a fugitive to this date. Frank Salemme also fled but he was later captured.

After their indictment, in hearings before the court, Flemmi filed motions stating that he could not be prosecuted because the FBI Special Agents John Connolly and John Morris authorized him to commit the crimes for which he had been indicted.

FBI Agent Morris will testify he did not give such an authorization to Flemmi. Morris will also tell you that while he was an FBI agent he accepted bribes and engaged in other dark and sordid acts like getting money and cases of wine from Connolly. Morris will tell you that he asked Connolly to get money from Bulger and Flemmi for him. On one occasion Connolly got Morris a thousand dollars so that Morris's girlfriend could meet him in Georgia without his wife knowing. Morris will tell you that Connolly gave him a case of wine with a thousand dollars secreted in it that came from Bulger. He will also tell you that in June 1988 he learned of a wiretap in which Flemmi was the target. He told Connolly about it. In return he received five thousand dollars.

Morris will testify about a 1979 race fixing case that was being readied for indictment. A criminal gang led by Whitey Bulger and Stevie Flemmi known as Winter Hill was involved in fixing horse races on the East Coast. The prosecutor investigating the case was AUSA O'Sullivan. He was ready to return indictments against this gang.

Connolly and Morris told him Bulger and Flemmi were their informants. They asked him not to indict them. O'Sullivan did as asked and kept them out of the indictment.

You'll hear that the defendant John Connolly was the FBI handler for Bulger and Flemmi. John Morris will tell you he went to Connolly and asked him why they were informants. Morris said to him, "What do they want?" Connolly replied: "All they want is a head start." That is, they wanted a chance to escape if they were going to be charged with a crime.

You'll hear about a Brian Halloran. He told an FBI agent that Bulger, Flemmi and a guy named Callahan asked him if he was interested in the job of killing a man named Wheeler. He said he would cooperate with the FBI if he received protection. When Morris learned about this, he told Connolly. Halloran was murdered shortly after that. A witness Kevin Weeks will tell you how William Bulger, I'm sorry, James Whitey Bulger, killed Halloran.[18]

In June 1988 the FBI planned a wiretap on John Bahorian who was connected to Flemmi. Morris told Connolly to tip Flemmi and Bulger about this. Later that day or the next, remembering that after

---

[18] I thought this a significant slip of the tongue. William Bulger is Whitey's brother. William, or Billy as he is commonly called, for many years wielded enormous power in Massachusetts as president of the state senate. At the time of the trial he was president of the University of Massachusetts. His name will be mentioned again during the trial. See Appendix for more on William "Billy" Bulger

he previously told Connolly that Halloran had become an informant and Halloran ended up being killed, he went back to Connolly and said, " I don't want another Halloran."

You'll also hear that Morris leaked to the Boston Globe that Whitey Bulger was an FBI informant.

There will be evidence that at the end of 1976 Connolly told Bulger that Richard Castucci was informing on Joseph McDonnell and James Simms. McDonnell and Simms were in the Winter Hill gang but hiding out in an apartment in New York City. Castucci was providing information against them. Castucci ended up being murdered by John Martorano.

Johnny Martorano will be a witness. He was also part of the Winter Hill gang. Martorano will say that Whitey Bulger met with John Connolly. He will tell you that Whitey gave a diamond ring from the Winter Hill gang to Connolly for the information he was providing to them. To corroborate this, Connolly's ex-wife will testify that in 1976 Connolly, a government employee, gave her a $5,000 ring for her graduation from nursing school.[19]

---

[19] FBI agents enter at grade 10 and move to grade 13 in a non supervisory level. They also receive additional pay for availability. The rates of pay under the General Schedule beginning on October 1, 1976, in grade 10 went from $15,524 up to $20,177 and in grade 13 from $24,308 up to $31,598. No evidence was introduced to show Connolly's pay at the time although a secretary testifies she saw pay checks in the amount of two thousand dollars in his desk drawer that he had not bothered to cash.

Johnny Martorano has pleaded guilty to the murder of over 20 people. Martorano will testify that Bulger and Flemmi tipped him off that an indictment was coming down against him in the race fixing case. This led him to flee to Florida. Martorano will tell you that at the request of John Callahan he killed Oklahoma businessman Roger Wheeler shortly after arriving in Florida.

Right after the murder of Roger Wheeler, Martorano will testify that Connolly told Whitey Bulger that the FBI was planning to put a lot of pressure on Callahan. Connolly did not think Callahan could take the pressure. Bulger feared Callahan would talk. He told Martorano to murder him.

Kevin Weeks, the right hand man of Whitey Bulger will testify. He will tell how he gave five thousand dollars to Connolly. He will say that Connolly met with Bulger on a regular basis. Weeks will tell you that they referred to Connolly by the nickname Zip. He will say that Bulger was worried that Connolly was showing too much flash.

You will hear from Joseph Lundbohm, a Boston police detective, who went to Connolly to tell him that Bulger had extorted a liquor store from his niece and her husband. He asked Connolly if he could do anything to help them. Connolly asked him if either his niece or nephew would wear a wire. Lundbohm said no. Connolly told him that there was nothing he could do about it. Later Lundbohm was told by his nephew to back off because Bulger did not want him pushing the issue. Weeks will tell you that after this happened, Bulger said to him that it was a good thing Lundbohm went to Zip.

Francis Salemme will testify. He was boss of the New England Mafia.[20] Salemme has admitted to killing seven people. The Justice Department will help him get out of jail earlier than scheduled for his testimony. He'll testify that he was involved with Bulger and Flemmi. He'll tell you Flemmi took five thousand dollars from him to give to Connolly.

He'll also tell about an accidental meeting in 1994 that he had with Connolly at the Prudential Center in Boston. He will testify that Connolly told him about the grand jury investigation into his activities. He will also tell you that Connolly spoke to him about a book he was writing.

---

[20] The FBI calls the Mafia the LCN, or La Cosa Nostra. J. Edgar Hoover, the first FBI director, who served in that capacity for 48 years, adamantly maintained for many years there was no Mafia in the United States. When the New York State Police raided a meeting at Apalachin, New York in 1957 they discovered a nationwide network of Italian criminals that walked, talked and looked like a Mafia. Congress demanded that the FBI do something about it. (Perhaps the last time Congress demanded anything from the FBI.) Hoover, embarrassed, reluctantly had to admit the Mafia's existence.

There's an old canard that having denied there was a Mafia Hoover had to save face. He decided to have his FBI underlings call the Italian gangsters a name he made up, La Cosa Nostra or the LCN, rather than Mafia. Salemme testified he was a boss and a 'made man' in the La Cosa Nostra.

Salemme after talking to other people became concerned that Connolly's book would make it looked like he was an informant. Figuring out that as a Mafia boss that would not look too good, he decided to return to Connolly's office to make sure his integrity among his fellow criminals would not be besmirched.

When he arrived uninvited at his office, Connolly was talking with a person named John Ford, a close friend of Connolly's. Ford was employed by the Suffolk District Attorney's office. Ford and Connolly's secretary will testify that Salemme was at the office. Ford felt apprehensive seeing Salemme so he quickly left leaving Connolly and Salemme alone. Connolly and Salemme talked. Salemme will testify Connolly promised him that he would tell him when the indictments against him were coming down. Salemme will testify that he did get a heads up on January 5, 1995. On that date he met with Flemmi who told him the indictment was to be returned on January 10, 1995. Salemme then fled.

Kevin Weeks will testify that after Flemmi was indicted he was incarcerated at the House of Corrections in Plymouth.[21] Weeks will tell you he visited him regularly. He will say Flemmi asked him to meet with Connolly. Connolly had retired from the FBI in December 1990. Flemmi wanted Connolly to help him on the case pending against

---

[21] After Whitey Bulger was captured, he also was incarcerated here. Unlike Flemmi, Whitey would be escorted to court in a caravan of police vehicles and even at times flown in on a helicopter.

him. Just before a hearing in the federal court in front of Judge Wolf, Connolly tried to do that. Judge Wolf received a letter on Boston police stationary allegedly sent by three Boston police officers on March 31, 1997. The letter said the evidence gained against Flemmi was illegally intercepted by the state police who had done gypsy or illegal wiretaps.

Weeks will testify that he helped Connolly send the letter to Judge Wolf. If Judge Wolf believed the letter's allegations, the government's case against Flemmi may have been dismissed. The letter was an act of obstruction of justice for which Connolly is charged. Weeks will testify that Connolly gave information to Flemmi and Salemme identifying the four informants who gave him information to place the bug in the Mafia induction ceremony.

Weeks will most importantly testify that Connolly told him about the meeting between Donald Stern and the FBI officers that took place in December 1994 that I already mentioned. At that meeting Stern sought to learn if Whitey Bulger was an informant. He also told the participants at the meeting that indictments were coming down in January.

When Flemmi testified before Judge Wolf he said it wasn't Connolly but Morris who told him when the indictment was coming down. Records will show Connolly called the FBI on the day of the meeting. There will be evidence that Connolly used his calling card and home phone to call Flemmi's lawyer at his office, home and car.

There will be bad people who will testify for the government. You should not be repelled by their testimony.

With that statement Durham finishes his opening and sits down

Tracy Miner rises and has two charts with her. She puts them up facing toward the jury. One is a chart of the Mafia hierarchy and the other of the FBI. (See Appendix 1) There is a stark similarity between the organizational structures of these two groups. Miner leans with both hands clasping the outer edges of the podium. She speaks softly at first but then quickly comes up to stride as her voice gathers more strength and assertiveness. She refers to her three-ring notebook that sits on the same podium that Durham used. Her opening is typed in large black letters on the right hand page which she turns as she moves along. She's not captured by the notebook. She moves from it to the charts and back again. She maintains good eye contact. The jury is attentive.[22]

MINER'S OPENING STATEMENT:

Connolly grew up in South Boston, went to Boston College, and after leaving college joined the

---

[22] Miner has an extremely difficult task. She is walking gingerly through a treacherous minefield. Her goal is to muddy up the FBI by showing its complicity and culpability in everything Connolly did. But in doing this she recognizes that the mud she smears on the FBI also sticks to Connolly. Go too hard she hurts her client; go too softly she hurts her client. She is also restricted in her ability to cross-examine by the limits put on her by Connolly who believes he was justified in what he did.

FBI as a special agent. The FBI is a hierarchical organization in the Department of Justice controlled from the top of its pyramidical structure, as is shown on the chart, by the director. Connolly is on the bottom rung of the organization.

Connolly started in the Boston FBI office November 1973. He was assigned to the organized crime squad. During his time with the FBI he dedicated his life fighting the LCN, or as it is also called, the Mafia. This was an important fight for the FBI which urged its agents to recruit informants so that they could get information against the Mafia.

As you know, most of the informants are criminals themselves. Connolly demonstrated a superior ability to seek out and develop informants. The FBI recognized this. It encouraged him to do it. His strength was the development of informants.

The LCN or Mafia has a similar pyramidical structure to the FBI. To be a member of the Mafia, you must meet its basic requirements. These are that you be a male, be of Italian descent, and have killed someone. If you meet these requirements you can join and become a made man or a soldier. A candidate then goes through a secret ceremony at the conclusion of which he is inducted into the Mafia. We know what happens at the secret ceremony because Connolly was instrumental in having such a ceremony bugged. It was the only time ever that such a ceremony was recorded on tape.

There is a third organization that you will hear about. It is the Winter Hill Gang. Unlike the FBI and Mafia, it is organized differently. There was no central control. There were seven equal bosses. These bosses of Winter Hill were Howie Winter, James "Whitey" Bulger, Steven "Stevie" Flemmi, John Martorano, Jimmy Martorano, Joseph McDonald, and Joseph Simms.

Like the Mafia, Winter Hill was engaged in bookmaking, shylocking, extortion and similar behavior. Winter Hill, a local gang, was much smaller than the nationwide Mafia. It had to learn to co-exist with it. It had to be particularly careful not to take out any members of the Mafia for fear of retribution.

Connolly enlisted Whitey Bulger to be an informant. He pitched a line to him, the basis of it being that he could help the FBI take down the local Mafia group. That would leave the field open for Winter Hill. Connolly knew that this would appeal to Whitey Bulger since he, like all criminals, was only interested in his own welfare.[23]

There will be evidence from witnesses that money went to Connolly. That is untrue. These criminals, especially in loosely connected gangs like Winter Hill, were all in it for themselves. Any

---

[23] Flemmi's asserted that Bulger and he were told they could commit any crime they wanted except murder. Connolly's offer to Bulger, according to Miner, is that he help the FBI take down the Mafia and in exchange the FBI will let him take over the Mafia's business. Every subsequent action taken by Connolly, the FBI, Bulger and Flemmi appears to confirm this understanding.

money one criminal gave another usually never made it further than the pocket of the receiving criminal. These gangsters continually stole from each other.

The relationship between Bulger and Connolly was that Bulger gave Connolly information. Connolly gave him nothing. But to protect himself, Whitey Bulger had to let Winter Hill believe that Connolly was giving him information. He knew if he were ever seen with Connolly by any members of the gang he'd be thought of as a rat unless he had a reason for being with him. So he lied to them to protect himself.

Everyone in the FBI knew that Whitey was Connolly's informant. The FBI knew that Whitey Bulger and Stevie Flemmi were murderers but encouraged Connolly to use them. Bulger and Flemmi were instrumental in helping the FBI plant a bug in the headquarters of the local Mafia at 98 Prince Street, Boston.

Connolly was not aware of the full extent of the criminality of his informants. There were rumors of their involvement in killings. Everyone heard the rumors. But the FBI chose not to terminate either Bulger or Flemmi as informants. Why weren't Bulger and Flemmi closed? It was because they were needed and no one else could control them except for Connolly.[24]

---

[24] Here's an example where Miner faced a difficult balancing act. The evidence will show that Bulger and Flemmi were notorious murderers. She wants the jury to believe that the FBI knew this, did not care, and kept using them as informants. On the other hand she wants the jury

When Connolly left the FBI, Bulger had grown older. He had become out of touch with things. That's when the FBI terminated him. That was in the early 1990s. At that time, the Mafia was in shambles because of Connolly's work. Bulger was no longer needed. So the government decided to go after him. Bulger was indicted in January, 1995. He fled and went into hiding. Connolly had nothing to do with his flight.

The whole issue about Flemmi and Bulger being informants arose when Flemmi said that he was authorized by the FBI to commit the criminal acts he was charged with. At that time the U.S. Attorney did not know that Flemmi was an informant. That is because the FBI doesn't tell the federal prosecutors the identity of its informants. The FBI hoped never to disclose Flemmi and Bulger were informants. The FBI never expected them to raise the authorization defense. The disclosure of the identity of Bulger and Flemmi as informants was entirely unexpected by the FBI.[25]

---

to believe Connolly was a skillful, clever, street-wise agent handling Bulger and Flemmi but unlike others in the FBI he was naïve and did not know they were stone killers. I thought she would have been better off acknowledging Connolly also knew they were murderers but was told by the FBI to continue to deal with them. Then I realized that perhaps Connolly would not let her use that defense. He seemed to cling to the belief that despite what everyone else knew he had no evidence they were murderers.

[25] Throughout its history, the FBI rarely has had to disclose an informant's identify. Traditionally it protects it by providing affidavits setting out the information received from an informant. The FBI feared having its agents testify

You'll hear from Martorano, Morris, Salemme, and Weeks. These are people with bad backgrounds. All are liars, cheats and murderers. They will come in here and lie to you. They are evil people but good liars. You'll hear from Agent Morris. He just traded down. He was Connolly's boss but he gave Connolly up to help himself.

---

under oath about dealings with informants. It knew that if live testimony from agents subject to cross-examination is offered, the FBI could lose control as it did here.

In an affidavit you can tell the truth but not the whole truth. An affidavit can be constructed to fit a desired story. It may provide a picture of the events that omits things detrimental or embarrassing to the FBI or its case.

For instance suppose it was alleged that Gangster Smith was told to stay away from a bug installed at Business X by FBI Agent Jones. To rebut this allegation, the FBI may file an affidavit stating, "Agent Jones did not tell Smith anything at any time about the bug." What happened is he passed him a note. In other words, affidavits can tell the truth (he didn't tell him) but not the whole truth (that he gave him the note). That is why an accused person has the right to confront the accuser and subject him or her to cross-examination. It is the only way that we can come close to the full truth.

In this case Connolly's right to confront the witnesses against him was severely restricted. That is because much of the evidence against him came from one gangster testifying as to what another gangster said. Such hearsay evidence is permissible in a conspiracy prosecution. Martorano never met Connolly. When Martorano says Whitey said he gave Connolly the diamond ring it is almost impossible to get beyond that. We can't even begin to search for the truth. Whitey is not there to be cross examined. All we know is what Martorano decides to tell us. We don't know what really happened and have no way of finding out.

Martorano is going to do 12 ½ years in jail for over 20 murders, less than one year per murder. Weeks admitted to killing 5 people and he is going to do about one year for each of his murders. Salemme has spent 11 years in jail and he has filed a Rule 35 motion that will allow him to get out much sooner than scheduled. No one knows how many murders Salemme had committed but to be a member of the Mafia you had to commit one murder just to enter. Imagine how many you have to commit to become boss. You may be assured he's had lots and lots of murders on his hands to rise to the top spot.

This prosecution is narrowly focused on Connolly. The government is not interested in what really took place and does not want to know what really happened. FBI agent Morris took money from other informants, but the government didn't want to know about it. The government did not ask Salemme about all the murders he was involved in. The government let Weeks keep his deal even though he failed a polygraph and was never polygraphed again.

Connolly was writing a book. Salemme worried that he might be identified as the one who informed about the Mafia ceremony that was recorded on tape because all the local Mafia members attended except Salemme. Any indication he had ratted out the ceremony would be very detrimental to him. When he went to see Connolly, it was to be sure that Connolly's book was not going to give anyone the idea that he was an informant.

Remember, to get information from informants you have to ask questions. When you ask questions, you give out information. If you ask about anyone or about a telephone number, the informant knows that you are looking at that person or planning to do something in connection with his phone. So any information that Bulger or Flemmi picked up from Connolly was merely as a result of the normal police officer/informant relationship. Through all his dealings with informants, Connolly kept his supervisor informed of his actions. They were written up and justified.

Agents routinely exchanged small Christmas gifts with their informants. They use these gifts to gain the confidence of an informant. The agents were instructed by the FBI not to treat informants like informants, but like friends. They were told that you get more information from people who think that they are your friends.

John Morris's unit was planning to do a wiretap on a man named Bahorian. Morris approached Connolly and told him to tell Flemmi to avoid the telephone that was going to be tapped. Connolly told Morris to tell Flemmi himself. Morris did that.

The actions of Bulger and Flemmi after the indictment were inconsistent with them being tipped off. Bulger was returning to Boston when he heard on the radio that he had been indicted. He had been in New Orleans where he had registered for rooms under his true name. Flemmi was arrested coming from his son's restaurant so obviously he was not tipped off.

The letter to Judge Wolf was not written by Connolly but by Weeks.[26] There will be no evidence that the letter was sent from any of Connolly's computers. All computers retain even deleted files.

Connolly loved the FBI. He loved to take down the LCN. Connolly never did anything that was criminal. He did not like criminals. He did not want to associate with them. But he was directed by the FBI to associate with, to befriend, and to get their information from them.

Miner ended with that.

Judge Tauro gave us an opportunity to stretch after Miner's opening statement ended. He then asked the prosecution to call its first witness.

---

[26] In her closing statement Miner will tell the jury that the letter was sent by a Boston Police officer. I wondered if any juror picked up the contradiction.

45

CHAPTER TWO

THE EVIDENCE BEGINS

DONALD STERN

FORMER UNITED STATES ATTORNEY FOR MASSACHUSETTS.

Stern is dressed in a gray suit, white shirt and red checkered tie. He has graying black hair and looks all the part of a lawyer. At first he appears unprepared. He uses his calendar to refresh his memory as to the date of an important meeting that was to be the crux of his testimony. He puts Martorano into the wrong group of criminals. But after a few minutes of direct testimony he settles down into a matter-of-fact recitation of his memory of events. During his cross-examination he becomes somewhat hostile to Miner.

Durham in his questioning of Stern and later throughout the case with his other witnesses used extensive leading questions to elicit testimony.[27]

---

[27] As a general rule you do not ask your own witnesses leading questions, one that suggests an answer to a witness and is generally answered yes or no. For instance Durham in his direct examination asked Stern, "It is not permissible for an FBI agent to accept money, is it?" The question should be: "What are the rules about FBI agents accepting money?"

A judge will allow the use of leading questions if opposing counsel does not object to them. Miner will not object to Durham's leading questions. There is nothing wrong with leading questions on peripheral matters. You move quickly to the essential matters. When you near the crux of the matter they should cease.

My name is Donald Stern. I went to Hobart College in Long Island and Georgetown Law School. I now practice law with one of the larger Boston law firms. I was the United States Attorney for Massachusetts during the Clinton years, from November 1993 until June 1, 2001.

During 1994 we had a grand jury sitting that was investigating certain RICO offenses. A grand jury listens to the evidence put in by the Justice Department attorneys and decides whether a person or group of persons has committed a crime. Evidence before a grand jury is supposed to be secret. During this grand jury sitting there were continuing leaks of grand jury information. I requested an investigation of these leaks. I was unable to determine from where they had come because too many people had access to the information. These people included the witnesses who knew what they were asked about, the attorneys for the witnesses, any people who would be on the 13th floor of the old federal court house who would see who was coming and going into the grand jury room as well as the numerous investigators involved in the investigation.

We had indicted Robert DeLuca, and Frank Salemme, Jr, the son of LCN boss Frank Salemme, in October 1994 for RICO offenses. We planned to return superseding indictments to the DeLuca indictments against Bulger, Flemmi, Salemme,

---

Durham asked leading questions so extensively he was like a ventriloquist and the witnesses his dummies sitting on his lap moving their heads up and down in agreement with his assertions.

Martorano and others. A superseding indictment adds other charges or people to an indictment that has already been returned where they arise from the same events charged.

After the DeLuca indictment, the surveillance on Whitey Bulger, Stevie Flemmi, and Frank Salemme intensified. As the date of their indictment neared, there was a concern that these men might flee so we tried to keep closer tabs on them. We increased the surveillance around Christmas.[28] That was why the decision was made to obtain complaint warrants rather than wait for indictment warrants.

A warrant for an arrest can be obtained on a criminal complaint before the return of the indictment. This is done by going before a judge and showing some of the evidence you have against a person. If a judge after reviewing it determines there is probable cause to believe the person committed the crime then the judge may issue a complaint warrant. If we did not secure a complaint warrant then after the indictment returned we would get an indictment warrant.

By filing the complaint and getting a complaint warrant fewer people know about the warrant. Only the prosecutor, the law enforcement officers involved and the judge will be aware of it. Persons waiting for an indictment warrant, such as

---

[28] No surveillance evidence was introduced at trial. A major issue was what happened around the time of Whitey's flight just before Christmas. It seemed that surveillance evidence would have a been relevant to a crucial meeting at Whitey's liquor store.

witnesses before the grand jury, persons watching the courthouse, and others would not know a complaint warrant issued.

As we were getting ready to indict Bulger in December 1994, some people in my office thought that he might have been an FBI informant. If so, they believed legal problems might arise if Bulger raised the defense that he was authorized to commit certain of the crimes for which we planned to indict him. I decided that it would be best to inquire of the FBI regarding Bulger's status.

On December 22, 1994, two people from my office, James Farmer and Jonathan Chiel, and I met with FBI Agents Dick Svenson and Dennis O'Callaghan. FBI agent Quinn might also have been there. We told them that the grand jury had sufficient evidence to indict Bulger. We wanted to know if he was an informant. We also advised them that an indictment against Bulger, Flemmi and others was coming down in January. I'm not certain of the exact words I used on that date about the planned date of the indictment. I may have said it was being returned in mid-January. I have had no specific memory of the date I mentioned.

It was not the practice of the FBI to identify informants to the US Attorneys or their legal staff. That especially was the case if the informant was a top echelon informant. A top echelon informant is a person with high access to the leadership of organized crime families. The FBI relied heavily upon these informants since they are crucial to its work especially in doing electronic surveillance.

The meeting concluded with Svenson telling us he'd take our request to learn whether Bulger was an informant under advisement. He asked to see the prosecution memo that is prepared for every case but usually held in-house by the US Attorney. This memo is sometimes called the pros memo. It sets out the facts of the case, the legal issues, and an analysis of the strengths and weaknesses of the evidence.

In a RICO case, a prosecution memo has to go to Washington, DC, for approval. On December 22 we had not yet received the approval but we expected it to come down within a week or so of that date. I don't remember if the date that it was approved was December 30 or whether just a preliminary draft memo had been sent at that time.

We sent the FBI the prosecution memo it requested on January 4. On January 5 the complaint warrants were issued. At the meetings to prepare for the execution of the complaint warrants, there were officers from the FBI, DEA, IRS, and Massachusetts State Police who knew about the issuance of the complaint warrant. When we got the warrants, we sent out arrest teams. I don't remember how many people were arrested on January 5. I know Flemmi was arrested on that date. Salemme was arrested 6 months later in Florida. Bulger is still on the loose over 7 years later.

On January 5 I did not know that Bulger or Flemmi were informants. I did not learn this until I met with FBI officials on January 9 the day before the indictment was returned. These agents told me that Whitey Bulger and Stevie Flemmi were informants but they had been closed out. We discussed our concern that Bulger and Flemmi would raise the authorization defense. It was the strong view of the FBI people at the meeting they would not do it. At that time, on balance, I agreed with them. This was because in the past other informants had been indicted and did not raise it. They did not want it disclosed that they were informants. The others from my office who were there agreed the FBI prediction was probably accurate. Ultimately, we got their informant files to review. Sometime later I learned Connolly was their handler. He was the FBI agent who they dealt with and who was responsible for their activities.

Flemmi did not raise the authorization issue until two years after he was indicted. When he raised it, he did it through a motion to suppress the evidence accompanied by four affidavits wherein he asserted he was an FBI informant who had immunity from the crimes charged in the superseding indictment. Flemmi stated he was authorized to commit those crimes by FBI Agent Morris who told him he could commit any crime he wanted to do except for murder. When this claim was made we had to respond to it. We reviewed Bulger's and Flemmi's informant files. My office concluded they were not authorized to commit crimes.

At the time Flemmi's claim was an explosive admission. It resulted in great adverse publicity for the FBI and in court hearings in front of Judge Wolf that lasted for a year. The bad publicity was often played up in the local press

We went to FBI Agent John Morris. At first he wouldn't be interviewed. He then made a proffer of his testimony. A proffer is a statement setting forth the evidence a person possesses and will testify to in exchange for the government's promise not to prosecute the person or in some other way to help the person. This is done so that the government will know what evidence may be expected from a person before it decides whether to make a deal with the person. The government wants to know all the information a person has about the matter. Even so it is rare to get everything the person knows in the proffer.

In making these deals with criminals we agree to make a lower sentence recommendation than the guidelines if the person will cooperate and testify. When a person in his proffer admits to committing crimes and an agreement is not consummated then what the person said cannot be used against him. In other words, the information given in a proffer cannot be used against the person giving it unless we come to an agreement.

I accepted Morris's proffer. The court granted him immunity from prosecution. When a person is given immunity, there are still adverse consequences that can happen to that person. He can be prosecuted for failing to tell the truth in his testimony.

We did communicate with John Connolly about Flemmi's assertion of authorization to commit crime. I don't remember whether Connolly was inquired of about Flemmi's assertion prior to Morris's proffer or whether this was done prior to December 1997. I knew Morris was Connolly's supervisor. I believe Connolly was also given the chance to make a proffer but it was my understanding that Connolly's attorney rejected it.

Two other persons entered into cooperation agreements with us before January 10, 1995. They were two bookies, Chico Krantz and James Katz. They testified before the grand jury that issued the indictments on January 10. I don't know what deal they were given for their testimony.

During the Wolf hearing the government made deals with some of the defendants. One was with Martorano. He was willing to cooperate if the government made a favorable recommendation allowing him to spend as little time in jail as possible. We negotiated with Martorano over a year, from June 1998 to August 1999, before reaching an agreement.

In the RICO indictment of January 5, 1995, Martorano was not indicted for murder. He revealed to us a number of murders that he committed. He also admitted to murders in Florida and Oklahoma. These are death penalty states. He did not give up the location of any bodies. Martorano had not been indicted for his involvement in the murders in Florida and Oklahoma at the time he confessed to his participation in them. His lawyer and the Justice Department agreed that they would recommend that he be sentenced to 150 months in jail. Martorano also made separate agreements with the states of Florida and Texas where he had murdered people. That agreement was that he will plead guilty, be sentenced to between 12 ½ to 15 years, but in no event will he have to spend any more time in jail than that given by the federal court. This was a joint recommendation so the court will most likely follow it.

Kevin Weeks also had a deal. He is a known extortionist and is suspected as an accessory to murder. He made his proffer on December 20, 1999. We signed a plea agreement on July 6, 2000. Weeks provided information about murders and the burial places of some bodies. Prior to his admission there was no basis for charging him with any murder. With Weeks's help we recovered five or six bodies. Weeks's agreement is not like Martorano's. There is no agreed upon recommendation. Weeks's agreement is not binding. If the court did not agree to sentence him in a certain range, not less than 60 months or not more than 180 months, he could get out of it.

Salemme also became a cooperating witness. Salemme was the head of the New England La Cosa Nostra. It is the usual procedure that in getting one person to testify against another you do not use some one like Salemme, the head of such a group, but someone in a lower position. You usually want to work your way up.

Salemme agreed to plead guilty to everything pending before Judge Wolf. He would get a two level downward adjustment for pleading guilty. That adjustment would be provided if the government determined Salemme cooperated properly. Salemme was doing a sentence when we entered into an agreement with him. We agreed to file a Rule 35B motion that would allow the court to reduce his sentence that had been imposed. We will return to the court at some later date to seek the reduction in his sentence dependent upon the extent of the cooperation.[29]

The FBI has new guidelines on the use of informants. These were made effective after 2001. They made it clear that socialization with informants is not allowed. They require the US Attorney's office be notified if the informant commits a crime. This was the first time that the FBI was required in writing to notify the US attorney's office of this. I don't know if there were written guidelines about socialization before this. It is not permissible for an FBI agent to take money, or to convey money, or to disclose the identity of informants or the identity of persons giving confidential information to the FBI.[30]

---

[29] Salemme was released from prison in January, 2003. A short time later he was charged with perjury and again incarcerated. The last I heard he was back on the street.

[30] In the middle of Stern's testimony, we take our noon recess. I walk toward the elevators. As I round the corner I meet John Connolly. He puts out his hand and thanks me for coming to give him support. His handshake is soft, mushy and halfhearted. He seems nervous. He's not as tall as I remember him to be. I don't tell him I'm there to observe. Instead, I utter some inanity like "how's it going." We quickly depart. I think of how Connolly's bravado is gone. He's acting like any other person would act in these circumstances, nervous and worried.

I speak to Stern briefly over the noon recess. He laments that he'd much rather ask the questions like he was used to doing as a litigant rather than to be answering them. I always felt the same way when I had to testify.

THOMAS POWERS

ASSISTANT AGENT IN CHARGE OF BOSTON FBI OFFICE

He is a man of small stature. He wears a work-a-day off-the-rack suit. He looks like a prototypical accountant.

My name is Thomas Powers. I am an assistant agent in charge in the Boston FBI office and a CPA. In my years with the FBI I have investigated international terrorism and I have been on the hostage rescue team. I came to Boston in September, 1991 after Connolly left the office. I will explain the different types of forms we use in the FBI. They will be referred to during the trial. We use Airtels. These are forms used to communicate between offices. We use a form 302 that contains the results of an investigative effort.

We have a form 209. That is used in conjunction with a 209 insert. The insert contains information from informants. Informant files are kept in a separate room. In the informant file there is a checklist called the pink sheet. That sets forth what an informant can and cannot do. The FBI relies upon the integrity of the person filing the information to insure its accuracy.

I have reviewed the files in the Boston office. One of these shows that Richard Castucci was a top echelon informant who provided evidence to the FBI about the location of McDonald and Simms during September and November 1976. Castucci's 209s were placed in his informant file and were also sent to other files located in a rotor file. The rotor file is accessible to all FBI agents including Connolly.

When a 209 insert goes to another file, the informant's name is not provided. The information is listed as coming from the number that has been assigned for that informant. That is so the other agents may learn of the information but not the informant's identity. Even though only a number identifies an informant it still may be possible to figure out his or her true identity from the information that is provided. If only two or three people know that information, one may be able to figure out who gave the information. An ASAC[31] is not required to review informant files on a regular basis. On occasion he will do this. Sometimes headquarters will review an informant's file.

James Whitey Bulger was first opened as an informant on May 13, 1971, and closed on September 10, 1971. He was reopened on September 18, 1975, and became a top echelon informant on February 4, 1976. For a short period in 1978 he was closed. He remained open from May 4, 1979, until December 3, 1990.

Stephen Flemmi first became an informant on November 27, 1965. He was closed in December

---

[31] Assistant agent in charge.

1967, but reopened in September, 1980. He stayed open until 1982, was closed until 1986 and thereafter remained open until December 1990.

Connolly joined the FBI in 1968. He was in Baltimore in 1969, in San Francisco in 1971, in New York in 1972, and in Boston from 1973 through 1990. In March 1988 he became a supervisor. He started in the organized crime division on October 29, 1973; he opened Bulger on September 18, 1975 and opened Flemmi on October 12, 1980. He closed both of them on December 3, 1990 when he left the FBI.

The personnel records of Connolly show he was rated as a good agent. He got incentive awards. Overall Connolly was rated as good but was not exceptional. In the early years he received excellent ratings up until 1981. In 1983 he received superior ratings, the highest being exceptional. The record shows that throughout the period he received the highest rating, exceptional, in his handling of informants. In one year, he was marked truly exceptional. In the early years outstanding was better than excellent. In the later years exceptional beat all the other ratings.

In 1984 Connolly was praised for developing informants who provided information for electronic surveillance affidavits, the affidavits used in wiretaps or in placing bugs in places. He lectured to new agents at the FBI academy about dealing with informants and contained many commendations and awards as an agent. In January 1973 he received a cash award for catching Frank Salemme in New York City.

I reviewed a document about the meeting that the FBI office had with Donald Stern on December 22, 1994. It showed that Svenson, O'Callaghan and Quinn were the FBI participants. It stated that Stern advised these men that Bulger was to be indicted in January and that those present did not believed Bulger would use the authorization defense. If he did, it was expected that the judge would accept affidavits from the FBI regarding the issue. No live testimony would be required.[32]

The FBI manual on informants requires an agent to control the informant's activities to insure the conduct is consistent with legal restrictions. The reliability of informants must be constantly checked. Agents are to report everything about the relationship accurately and completely.

Informant guidelines promulgated by the Attorney General have changed over the years. They were first promulgated in 1976. In 1980 they were changed by Attorney General Levy. In 1990

---

[32] There was never any benefit for an arrested or indicted FBI informant to admit he was a rat, The consequences of doing so were twofold. He'd be in danger of great physical harm from those he informed against, and more importantly, the FBI would not lift a hand to help him. The FBI extorted his silence. Usually, the indicted informant must sit quietly while the FBI worked in the background to ameliorate his punishment. The FBI and the U.S. Attorney were counting on the usual occurring.

Even in the extremely unlikely event Bulger or Flemmi admitted being an informant, the FBI still banked upon handling that problem with affidavits. The FBI never thought its informant files would be opened and its agents called to testify.

Attorney General Stivelletti relaxed them. They were tightened in 2001 by Attorney General Reno. Her guidelines were the first to mention socialization with informants. They forbid socialization. The reason for prohibiting socialization is to help agents avoid the likelihood of corruption.

Since Reno instituted these guidelines, the number of informants had declined. This is a concern for the FBI. I do not know if new guidelines are being drafted to meet this problem.

The Attorney General's guidelines in 1988 said the use of an informant is a permissible investigative technique. It said an informant cannot engage in acts that an undercover FBI agent could not do. Other Attorney General guidelines said agents shall not allow informants to participate in acts of violence nor can an agent initiate or plan to commit criminal acts with an informant except if the FBI determines their necessity.

The guidelines also state an FBI agent upon learning an informant violated the regulations should discourage such acts. An agent must not take any actions to conceal the informant's criminal activity. Other guidelines require an agent to tell his informant that the relationship will not protect him from criminal prosecution unless the FBI determines otherwise. The informant is to engage in no violence or other criminal actions without approval and must be told this on a yearly basis.[33]

---

[33] I inwardly smile at these provisions. They are Kafkaesque. They sound like they prohibit acts but they

Approval to engage in violence or other criminal activity can only be done by a supervisor who must make written findings. The SAC[34] is to review such approval every 90 days and file documents indicating this was done. If the criminal conduct authorized is extraordinary, then the SAC must get the concurrence of the Attorney General. Connolly filed reports over the years stating he was aware of the guidelines and had advised his informants about them.[35]

---

don't forbid anything. They use terms as, "except if the FBI determines their necessity," or "discourage such acts," or "unless the FBI determines otherwise," or "without approval." These are big loopholes that do away with the prohibition. In sum, agents may give their informants carte blanche to do anything.

[34] Special agent in charge.

[35] Witnesses in this case including a federal judge will testify that informants such as top echelon informants like Bulger and Flemmi must be involved in serious criminal activity to be effective informants. The game is for the FBI agents to know and accept this but not to openly acknowledge it, especially not to explicitly approve it in writing. The tacit acceptance of this requires no supervisor to stick his neck out nor puts anyone at headquarters in DC in jeopardy. When Flemmi was an informant, an investigation against him was started. On paper the FBI terminated him as an informant. In fact he continued as usual. Nothing changed except the written termination statement in Flemmi's file which Flemmi knew nothing about but it protected the FBI. It would rather live a lie than expose itself to embarrassment.

There is an FBI expression, "If it is not in writing, it doesn't exist." These allegedly grown-up agents think that by failing to put down in writing something that happened allows them to pretend it didn't. Or, alternatively, putting

The FBI refrains from disclosing the identity of informants to other people. A review of Bulger's and Flemmi's files showed no written finding that they were authorized to commit criminal activity. There was no indication that FBI headquarters was advised of any such activity by Bulger or Flemmi. The rules provide that if an informant participates in an activity not authorized, there must be a written determination whether to continue him. If a serious crime is committed by an informant, then headquarters in Washington, DC must be notified. At that time, a determination will be made whether or not to notify the state authorities.

The FBI can authorize a person to engage in criminal activity. On line 5 of the informant pink sheet it sets out whether such an authorization has been given. You'll note on the pink sheet there are several boxes that may be checked. One box asks whether person is authorized to commit a crime. If authorization is given, the special agent who gave the authorization to commit a crime must be identified. There is no showing on Bulger's pink slip that he was authorized by the FBI to commit crimes. The only box checked off by Connolly indicates that Bulger received certain warnings about what he could and could not do.[36]

---

an untruth in writing makes it true. Witness Powers was quick to point out there is no indication in writing FBI headquarters was advised of Bulger or Flemmi's activity. Even if they knew because it was not in writing they pretend they didn't. One can only think of Lewis Carroll's Alice's adventures.

[36] I think "of course there is nothing in the file that says Bulger is authorized to commit a crime." I doubt if

There are two types of informants, regular and top echelon. The top echelon informants have access to the leaders of organized crime groups. It is probable such a person would also be involved in criminal activity because it is unlikely that a high Mafia official would reveal any of his criminal operations to persons other than those known to him to be criminals.

The power is in the ASAC to decide if an informant is to be closed. If an ASAC closes an informant the agent cannot use him or her. Neither a supervisor nor a line agent could overrule the ASAC. I have had no personal experience with top echelon informants. You may direct an informant to do something for you. The guidelines make no mention about the everyday life habits of the informant. Informants are always important in organized crime and terrorist investigations. FBI

---

any pink slip in the file of any top echelon informant has a check in the box saying the informant may commit a crime. It's not like the high placed gangster won't commit crimes if the box isn't checked or the FBI doesn't know he is committing crimes which one must do to be a high echelon informant.

We are dealing with bureaucrats. Their nature is to act to protect themselves and their pensions above all other things. Which one of them in his right mind would put his fate in the hands of a major criminal? If an informant had been given permission by an agent in writing to commit a heinous crime and it became public, that agent could kiss his career and pension goodbye. Agents avoid this by not checking the box and by giving the informant a wink and a nod. I'm sure no informant ever asked to see if the box on the pink slip was checked.

Agents cannot take money from a top echelon informant.

CHAPTER THREE

MASTERS OF DECEIT

JOHN MORRIS

RETIRED FBI SPECIAL AGENT

It's the morning break of day 2 of the trial Thursday, May 8, 2002. I remain in the courtroom. While chatting with another lawyer I see retired FBI Agent John Morris enter the courtroom. He takes a seat at the end of the bench against the back wall on the opposite side from me. He's a small thin man with a mouse-like appearance. The color of his clothing mirrors his aspect: a gray suit, gray tie, gray socks, and receding gray hair. The black band of his watch that edges out beyond his cuff and a gold wedding ring stand out starkly against his drabness.

He is speaking with Assistant U.S. Attorney Fred Wyshak. Wyshak is the person most responsible for the January 10, 1995, RICO indictments and bringing to light the sordid dealings surrounding this case. They speak in a friendly manner.

I'm always surprised when I see things like this. Wyshak a pillar of integrity knows Morris's actions as an FBI agent were reprehensible. In some ways as corrupt as those for which Connolly is charged. Yet he sits next to him and engages in friendly banter. Is he forced by the needs of his job to overlook Morris's criminality and humor him because he's his witness? Or is there something in human nature that makes it difficult to maintain the

65

appropriate response to a person you are forced to associate with for what you believe a greater good?[37]

I'll see this throughout the trial. During the breaks in their testimony, the depraved mobsters and the upright cops will smile and waive at each other like long lost friends. Why does a murderer like Martorano suddenly become a 'good guy' in their eyes? I don't understand it.

Retired FBI Agent John Morris is sworn in. He will testify through the remainder of this day and most of Friday, May 9, 2002. Morris will answer Durham's leading questions quickly and succinctly. He will prove difficult for Miner to handle on cross-examination because he will give rambling answers. At one point Judge Tauro feels compelled to admonish him saying that as an FBI agent he should know how to answer the questions that were being asked. Despite this, Morris continued to give discursive replies. Later Tauro again admonished him telling him that during his cross-examination he "must answer the question as asked. If it requires a yes or no answer, you must only say yes or no, or, if you can't answer with a yes or no, then you must state that. I don't want to hear any more speeches." Morris replied that he did not testify much during his career as an FBI agent and continued his evasive rambling.

---

[37] Wyshak will participate in a Florida murder prosecution of Connolly. He and Connolly will engage in a heated battle of words during Connolly's sentencing hearing. Seeing his great animosity toward Connolly and remembering this friendly interchange with Morris, two FBI agents who are like peas in a pod, seemed strange. I was never comfortable with the Florida prosecution of Connolly which seemed a far overreach.

My name is John Morris. I am testifying pursuant to an immunity grant given me by Judge Wolf. I won't be prosecuted for any of my crimes as long as I testify truthfully. Not only won't I be prosecuted, I'll keep my FBI pension. If I had been convicted of a crime while an agent I may have lost the pension.

If I make false statements, I may be prosecuted for perjury. The immunity order protects me from the crimes of bribery, conspiracy, and obstruction of justice that I engaged in as an FBI agent. In the past I have not always been truthful. I lied when it suited my purpose. In the past I lied to stay out of trouble. Now to stay out of trouble I must tell the truth. [38]

I graduated from the University of Miami. I gained a master's degree at Northeastern University. I spent three years in the army as an officer. I joined the FBI in 1970 and came to Boston in the spring of 1972. I first met Connolly in 1973

---

[38] Truth is a stranger to Morris who led a life of lies. He moves between truth and lies as easily as flipping a light switch. Morris says he lied to benefit himself but now must tell the truth to benefit himself. Morris told the government a story it wanted to hear to save himself. No one knows whether it is true or not since much is uncorroborated. All Morris must do is stick with what he told the government and which the government has opted to believe. His alleged fear of being prosecuted for perjury is far fetched. He knows the government would never do that. He has the government in a bind. It made its bed with him. To undermine him by charging him with perjury would also undermine its case against Connolly. That is the last thing it would ever do.

or 1974 when I worked in the major theft unit. He was in the organized crime unit. I associated with Connolly on a daily basis in the office. Outside we had a limited association. The friendship I developed with Connolly in 1973 continued until I left the organized crime squad. In 1975 Connolly and I worked together. There were two groups of 15 men each in the organized crime squad, the old group and the new group. I did not fit in any of the groups. Connolly befriended me.

Early in my career in Boston I was the case officer in a case involving Eddie Miani who associated with an organized crime group. I tried to get him to cooperate in an investigation I was doing. Miani refused.

On July 19, 1975, I placed an explosive device consisting of batteries, wires and a blasting cap on the gas tank of his car. I was with another agent when I did this. I don't remember if it was Connolly or not. After I did it I called the Revere police. It was an anonymous call. I reported there was suspicious activity near Miani's car. I wanted them to find the device.

When they responded I was about three or four blocks away. The Revere police filed a report. It said they found that the cap of the gas tank had been removed and an active explosive device had been connected by wire into the gas tank. It said that if the car had been moved an inch the device would have exploded and any person in the car severely hurt. The report called the act an attempted murder. I disagreed with part of the report since I don't think the device would have gone off.

I did this because I wanted Miani to think someone was attempting to murder him so I could scare him into cooperating with me. It was my idea to do this but I'm sure I talked about it with Connolly. This was 27 years ago. I don't remember if I mentioned the Miani incident when I first made a proffer to the government. I know the report of my interview doesn't mention this.

In late 1974 I worked on a loan shark case and a stolen stamp case involving Joe McDonald, James Simms and John Martorano. They were part of the leadership of Winter Hill. This was a not a Mafia group of criminals but it was involved in the same thing as the Mafia such as gambling, committing extortion and loan sharking. The other leaders were James Whitey Bulger, Howie Winter, Stevie Flemmi, and Jimmy Martorano. In that case I had a witness against Martorano who ended up dead. I suspected that Flemmi and Martorano killed him.[39]

McDonald was indicted and became a fugitive. He was believed to be living in New York City. He was on the FBI's top ten fugitive list for killing a witness in the state of California. In the office McDonald's status as a fugitive was discussed at

---

[39] Morris believed Flemmi an FBI informant had killed a government witness. Incredibly, rather than going after him he befriends him. AUSA O'Sullivan testified in December 2002 that he knew Bulger and Flemmi were murderers in 1978 but he did nothing to stop them from being used as informants. As we heard in Durham's opening statement, he saved them from being indicted

our group meetings. I'm sure I discussed the case with Connolly even though the Simms and McDonald case was assigned to another agent.[40]

In 1975 I worked on a case involving an organized crime figure, Peter Pallata. He was willing to cooperate with us. Because he was willing to work with us, we accepted him as a cooperating witness. A cooperating witness is different from an informant. An informant will only give the information and will not testify since he does not want his identity disclosed. A cooperating witness not only provides information to the FBI, he is willing to testify. A cooperating witness knows that his identity will become public.

Pallata was the victim of loan sharks. Whitey Bulger was believed to be a loan shark and was one of our targets. With a cooperating witness like Pallata who has a criminal background we wanted some good corroborative evidence. We weren't able to get it.[41] Pallata never gave us enough information to indict Bulger.

---

[40] This is an attempt to link Connolly to the Castucci murder. The theory was that Connolly may have discovered Castucci was informing. The jury was supposed to believe because the opportunity was there Connolly took advantage of it without more. It is a stretch.

[41] Former AUSA O'Sullivan offered the same excuse in his testimony before a Congressional Committee for his failure to indict Bulger and Flemmi. Both he and Morris assert lack of sufficient corroborative evidence as a reason not to go after known violent gangsters. My experience taught me differently. I believed you always wanted to try to put a career criminal in jail. If a cooperative witness would testify against such a criminal in

At that time I had no informants myself. Connolly came to me. He asked if he could use the Pallata case to try to convince Bulger to become an informant. I agreed to let Connolly develop him.[42] I did not meet Bulger at that time. It was later that Connolly came to me and asked me to become the alternate agent for Bulger. I did it as an accommodation to Connolly. I got no credit from the FBI for assuming that role.[43]

Bulger was opened in 1975. He became a top echelon informant. This type informant usually can provide information against organized crime groups especially the Mafia and will have access to policy level information at the capo level or above. This is the highest level informant.

Informants were crucial to the effort against the Mafia. As I said, informants provide information but do not plan to testify. The identity

---

a non-capital case you would charge that person rather than walk away from the case even if your corroboration is weak. If you bring the charges and lose, nothing changes; if you bring the charges and win, you've locked up a career criminal.

[42] In effect Morris was letting Connolly tell Whitey that Pallata was informing against him. At a maximum he was jeopardizing Pallata's life, at a minimum undermining his investigation.

[43] Morris was pressed on this point on cross-examination. He became quite agitated. He testily raised his voice to a whine lamenting he did not get credit for being an alternative agent. He appeared pathetic like a child seeking to get approval for everything he did. I wondered what he thought was the reason behind the government giving him a regular pay check. It was an interesting look into his dark soul.

of an informant is normally only known to the agent, the alternate agent if any, and the supervisor of the agent.[44]

As an agent you never ask an informant what type of criminal activity he is involved in. I know most informants are engaged in criminal activity. If an agent receives credible information of serious criminal activity by his informant he should report it.

In getting information from an informant, you've got to remember that you also give them information. Like when asking for a telephone number, you're indicating your intention to do something about a telephone; or when you ask about a murder, they know you may be investigating it.

In December 1977 I became the supervisor of the organized crime squad. This group was composed of fifteen agents. I remained in that position until January 1983. My squad just worked on organized crime matters. Our goal was to take down the New England Mafia. It was the near exclusive focus of my group. After that were Winter Hill, Asian gangs, and the Hell's Angels.

---

[44] John Ford who worked for the FBI as a civilian clerk from 1978 until 1988 will testify that he overheard the civilian staff talking in the office about Whitey Bulger being an informant. He became concerned. He went to Connolly to tell him this. Connolly thanked him for his concern. Connolly confirmed to him that not only Bulger but also Flemmi was an informant. The knowledge of the identity of informants is much more widespread than Morris would have us believe.

Connolly was in my squad. It was my duty to direct him, to appraise the reports that he filed and to set the goals of the group. Connolly had quite a few informants. Some of them were top echelon informants. He was judged on the number and the quality of the informants he handled. He received the highest marks for his performance.

It was within the first year of becoming supervisor that I had dinner at my home in Lexington with Bulger, Flemmi, and Connolly. It was at my home because it's difficult for FBI agents to be seen having dinner with top level gangsters. We needed a secure place. So we picked my home. My wife was never happy about this. At that meeting we may have talked about the activities of Peter Pallata.

This first meeting was a social meeting. It was a lengthy dinner. Bulger was the outgoing one, very sociable. Flemmi was more quiet. Only the four of us were present. There were other dinners between December 1977 and December 1979 at which the four of us were present. Connolly always set up the dinners. The last time we met was in the spring of 1988. Over a period of ten or eleven years we met somewhere between eight to ten times.

Over the years, I met with Bulger and Flemmi three times at my house in Lexington, once at my girlfriend Debbie's, once at Flemmi's mother's house, once in a hotel, once to tell them about the Boston police investigation and at other times to get information from them. I was always with

Connolly when I met them. At times, I would file 209s about the meetings.

Although I was designated the alternative agent for Bulger, I always contacted him through Connolly. Whenever Bulger or Flemmi called the informant telephone number at the Boston FBI office, they would only speak with Connolly. Connolly was very good at dealing with them. Bulger and Flemmi never asked me for authorization to commit any crimes. Therefore I did not follow the procedure to grant them permission to do so.

Bulger and Flemmi made it clear that they never wanted it disclosed that they were informants. Even if arrested, they wanted no one to know they were providing information to us. One day I asked Connolly what do these guys want for giving the information. He responded, "All they want is a head start." I understood that to mean that if they were about to be indicted, we should tell them about it so that they could flee.[45]

I had phone conversations with Bulger and Flemmi but I never initiated any calls to them. I was closer to Flemmi than Bulger. I gave Flemmi a picture of Korea where he served in the army. Bulger and Flemmi gave us lots of information on

---

[45] If you believe Connolly told Whitey and Flemmi to flee when the indictments were coming down, and you believe the quid pro quo for them being informants was to be so advised, then Connolly never should have been found guilty of doing what he was bound to do by this agreement which he had the right to make. Had this defense been raised and accepted, they'd have been no bribery conviction.

people other than the LCN like the information they gave on Joe Murray.[46]

I supervised a case involving a Myles Connor. Bulger and Flemmi provided information that helped in that case. Connolly received a commendation in March of 1981 for his work on the Connor case. It came in the form of a letter from an official in the Commonwealth of Massachusetts praising Connolly and FBI Agent John Clougherty for their work that resulted in the conviction of Connor.[47]

In 1978 I knew about a horse race fixing investigation being conducted by FBI Agent Tom Daly. The targets of the investigation were the leadership of Winter Hill including Bulger and Flemmi. The witness, Tony Ciulla, implicated Bulger as a target. Because of this the FBI closed Bulger as an informant. I wanted to continue to use Bulger. Both Bulger and Flemmi were aware of the race fix investigation. I may have discussed it with them. They steadfastly maintained their innocence. I was aware that all targets of investigation protest their innocence. I really didn't think a target would admit to me his involvement in a crime. They told me they tried to discourage the others in Winter Hill from being involved in the race fixing. So Connolly and I went to Assistant

---

[46] Joe Murray was a big scale marijuana dealer who had to buy his way out of the clutches of Bulger for five hundred thousand dollars. Later he wanted to give information to the FBI about Connolly taking payoffs from Bulger and Flemmi. He is discussed later.

[47] Myles Connor is discussed in Appendix H.

United States Attorney, Jeremiah O'Sullivan, chief of the Federal Strike Force who was in charge of the race fixing prosecution. It was up to him to decide whether or not to indict Bulger or Flemmi. O'Sullivan and I shared the same goal at that time which was the destruction of the New England Mafia. We told O'Sullivan that Bulger and Flemmi were our informants.

We also told O'Sullivan that Bulger and Flemmi had value in the investigation we were doing together with him in the North End. We told him they denied being involved in race fixing and had tried to stop the others from fixing the races. O'Sullivan listened to us. He said he wanted to talk to Agent Tom Daly about our request.

O'Sullivan agreed not to indict them. He named them as unindicted co-conspirators along with about fifty other people. Twenty-one persons were indicted. Howie Winter went to jail. Martorano fled after Bulger and Flemmi told him the indictment was coming down. It did not bother me at all that Martorano fled.

The race fix case destroyed the leadership of Winter Hill leaving only Bulger and Flemmi. It was appropriate to help out Bulger and Flemmi because they said they were not involved in the race fixing. I knew they would be valuable down the line.[48]

---

[48] O'Sullivan initially testified before a Congressional committee that he believed Bulger and Flemmi were involved in fixing races but he lacked corroborating evidence to convict them. He was then confronted with his 1979 report that showed he had

In 1980 there was an investigation going on by the Massachusetts State Police into Bulger's and Flemmi's activities at the Lancaster Street Garage in Boston's North End. Bulger and Flemmi believed the state police had a bug in there. I called Sergeant Ryan at the Boston Police Department and told him that Bulger knew there was a bug in Lancaster Street.[49] When Colonel O'Donovan of the Massachusetts State Police heard about my conversation with Sergeant Ryan he filed a complaint with the Justice Department saying that Connolly and I had tipped off their bug. He demanded a meeting over this issue. This caused friction between me and the state police. At the meeting I denied Bulger was my informant because I had to protect him. The FBI policy is to maintain the confidentiality of informants. There are strict rules against disclosure.[50] I would do it again if I had to.

---

excellent corroborating evidence. He was forced to admit he did Connolly and Morris a favor. Apparently he did not see anything wrong with having the two top non-Mafia gangsters in New England as informants and going out of his way to protect them.

O'Sullivan also testified Connolly and Morris asked him if they could ingratiate themselves with Bulger and Flemmi by telling them they saved them from being indicted. O'Sullivan said it was fine. I assume once these criminals heard that they now had the chief of the organized crime task force working for them, they had to believe the door was open for them to do anything. In retrospect they were correct.

[49] Morris did not call Sergeant Ryan. He was at a Friday after work get together having a few wines when he blurted out this information to Ryan

It was in the interest of law enforcement that I mislead the state police even though at the time I regretted doing it.   What I did concerning Lancaster Street was stupid.   Bulger and Flemmi told Connolly about this and Connolly told me.[51] They had the absolute details on how it was done. I gave the information I had obtained from the Winter Hill group to Detective Ryan.   I told Bob Ryan that if he had a bug in Lancaster Street, Bulger and Flemmi know about it.   The techniques the state police used in putting in the bug sounded risky to me so I was concerned with the safety of the police involved.[52]

---

[50] The FBI policy not to disclose the identity of an informant to anyone outside the Bureau seems to be more honored in the breach.   Morris told O'Sullivan the identity of two top echelon informants. O'Sullivan testified he knew the identity of many FBI informants.   Morris will testify that he disclosed to the Boston Globe that Bulger was an informant.   He did not tell the truth to the Massachusetts State Police about Bulger's status but he did tell a newspaper.   Morris tried to hide the identity of another informant who gave him money from the federal prosecutors.   Morris protected or revealed an informant's identity to suit his convenience.

[51] The investigation at Lancaster Street by the Massachusetts State Police was compromised.   Former AUSA O'Sullivan and the hierarchy of the state police blamed Morris or Connolly for compromising it.   A successful state police operation would not only have taken out the prize FBI informants, Bulger and Flemmi, but more importantly the state police would have beaten the FBI to its goal, the destruction of the Boston Mafia.   See Appendix G.

[52] If this were true Morris should have gone to the

78

I told Connolly what I had done. He was upset about it. He thought that by me doing that I was revealing Bulger was an FBI informant. Connolly told Bulger that I might have disclosed his informant status. I knew that they had to be upset by my blunder. I testified before Judge Wolf that they were furious that I would take information from them and pass it back through other law enforcement authorities.[53]

The FBI interviewed Bulger about this. Both Bulger and Flemmi were asked if they wanted to continue being informants. Bulger said he wasn't concerned. No one would believe he was an informant. I don't recall talking to either one about this.

Six months after Lancaster Street was compromised during January to April 1981 we did a Title III by putting a bug in the Mafia headquarters at 98 Prince Street in Boston's North End where the Boston LCN group's under boss, Gennaro 'Gerry' Angiulo, his brothers, and Larry Zannino conducted their illegal businesses. I was the supervisor for this operation. To do this we needed probable cause. That meant we had to include as much information as possible into an affidavit.

---

state police and not the Boston police.

[53] Morris's testimony reverses the flow of information. It went from the FBI to Bulger and Flemmi. The gangsters were far from furious at Morris. Shortly afterward they began to give Morris gifts. Connolly told Morris they would do anything for him.

Connolly asked me if Special Agent Ed Quinn had used any information from Bulger or Flemmi in his affidavit. I went to Quinn and asked him. Quinn was the case agent for the 98 Prince Street wiretap. He developed the probable cause to get the authority to put a bug in Angiulo's office and signed the affidavit. I asked Quinn if he had included Bulger and Flemmi as informants in his affidavit. He said no. Being Quinn's supervisor I directed him to put them in the affidavit. Quinn said if that was what I wanted, that was what he would do.

Two affidavits were written for the planting of the bug at Prince Street. The first one written without listing Buger and Flemmi as informants was withdrawn at my request. In the second one we added information from them. This allowed us to say that they participated in the probable cause for the bug.

If informants give information for a wiretap, it is standard practice to protect them. If an informant went into 98 Prince Street and was intercepted talking about criminal activity and we did not indict him, then it would be a dead give away that the person is an informant. If we did not list Bulger and Flemmi in the affidavit, we would not have told them to avoid 98 Prince Street. But once their information was included, they were told to stay out of there. I wanted them included as much as Connolly did.

Bulger's and Flemmi's involvement in the 98 Prince Street affidavit was to get the physical layout of the office inside that address. This technical stuff they provided was as difficult as the other information provided. Both of them were reluctant to do this. They were afraid they would be in physical danger if they went into the Mafia's headquarters. Their information was not necessary for the probable cause to do the wiretap but it was helpful in a technical sense. Bulger and Flemmi also gave substantial other information on Angiulo so I would say these informants were important for the probable cause at 98 Prince Street.[54]

We routinely tell informants that a Title III[55] court authorized electronic surveillance has been installed so that they will avoid being intercepted. If a place is under surveillance, we will tell them to avoid it. We trust that the informant will not tell others about the information we give to them.[56]

---

[54] AUSA O'Sullivan testified before a Congressional Committee that that there was no need for including the information from Bulger or Flemmi in the affidavit.

[55] The use of the term Title III refers to the federal law that governs the issuance of electronic surveillance orders which allow federal agents to put listening devices into places or to surreptitiously listen to telephone conversations.

[56] This is a remarkably naïve if not corrupt policy. It is against the law to make such a disclosure. Moreover criminal informants by nature are untrustworthy. After all, they are squealing on their friends. Yet the FBI tells them about electric surveillance operations hoping these stool pigeons won't tell others. Once you tell a criminal about a wiretap the results you get will not accurately reflect the activity that has been occurring. You don't know who that criminal might be protecting or trying to set up. We never told an informant we were doing a tap since we never

As a result of the Prince Street bugging the under boss and a good number of the LCN hierarchy were indicted and convicted. After this my squad transcribed the intercepted tapes. We had a problem deciphering one part of the tapes. I sent Connolly with the tape to Bulger and Flemmi to have them listen to it and to decipher it for us.[57]

After the successful bugging of 98 Prince Street the Boston Mafia was just about wiped out. A new SAC came to the Boston FBI office named Sarhatt. He was here two years. He expressed concern about Bulger and Flemmi being used as informants. He made me provide a memorandum justifying their continued use. Connolly wrote out a three page justification. I added a one-page attachment supporting Connolly's position.

In that memorandum which I have in front of me Connolly wrote that the 98 Prince Street Title III operations established that Bulger is not a hit man. That was only technically true. No one explicitly stated that Bulger was a hit man. But Under Boss Gerry Angiulo and Larry Zannino did say the Mafia could get Bulger and Flemmi to do anything they wanted them to do. SAC Sarhatt did not

---

trusted our informants. Our intercepts showed the wisdom of our policy.

[57] Because neither counsel in court asked what part of the tape needed deciphering, I began to realize that a lot of the inside information I hoped to hear was not going to come out. I should point out that allowing criminals access to wiretap interception material is a violation of Title III's prohibitions since disclosure of this information is strictly limited to authorized persons. It seems our FBI agents believe the laws were not intended for them.

know this because he didn't review the transcripts of the intercept. He did not know that Connolly was dissembling in this memorandum. But I knew of the deception and went along with it.

Connolly decided to apply in 1981 to the Harvard School of Government as a full time student in the prestigious Master of Public Administration program. This was a very busy time for my squad. I opposed the request. I didn't want to take a man out of the squad at such a time. Despite my opposition, Connolly went there. I did not think that it was fair.

Connolly attended Harvard for the school year. During that time he was around the office from time to time more frequently than occasionally. Connolly continued to work with his informants. During this time I did not socialize with him. When we interacted, it was just a working relationship. I don't think Connolly and I ever stopped being friends. I don't recall him being upset or angry at me because I tried to stop him from going to Harvard.

During 1981 the FBI office in Oklahoma City asked for help in following up on some leads. They were investigating the murder of Roger Wheeler. He had been gunned down in cold blood at a country club in Tulsa, Oklahoma. Wheeler was a legitimate businessman who owned the Miami World Jai Alai. We received a teletype in the Boston office from the Oklahoma City FBI asking us to check our indices and sources to see if we had any information that would assist them.

I assigned this to Connolly to pursue the leads. In August 1981 we received a follow-up request asking that the work be expedited. I again gave this to Connolly to perform.[58]

When I first met with Bulger, Flemmi, and Connolly small gifts were exchanged. Bulger and Flemmi brought a bottle or two of wine. I would normally reciprocate with a gift in the early days but after a while I could no longer do it because the gifts became too expensive.

The first case of wine I received from them was part of a practice that I had with Bulger and Flemmi of exchanging gifts. After receiving a case of wine I would buy a half a case to send back. I'm not sure when exactly the first case came whether it was around Christmas or not.

I first viewed the wine as a gift. I liked to drink wine. I drank about three bottles a week. On occasion I would buy a case of inexpensive wine.

Shortly after assigning the investigation request from Oklahoma to Connolly he came up to me at the FBI office in Boston. He said he had a case of wine for me in the trunk of his car that was in the FBI garage. Even though I was a wine aficionado I did not want to take it. I told Connolly to take it back. Connolly told me "You

---

[58] Connolly sat on the requests and then after doing nothing closed out the files. The Boston FBI never helped the Oklahoma FBI. Oklahoma and Connecticut detectives who were investigating Wheeler's murder were given a run around. Detective Mike Huff from Tulsa after a trip to Boston wrote in a report that he thought Special Agent Connolly was a member of the Winter Hill mob.

got to take it back yourself. If you don't take it they'll think you don't trust them." So I went there, took it out and put it into my car. The garage isn't a clandestine place. Anyone passing through there could have seen me. I took it because I did not know how to give it back. I also took it because I wanted the case of wine. It was valued at somewhere between $300 and $400. Connolly did not force me to take it.[59]

I don't recall discussing the case of wine with Bulger or Flemmi. They never asked me to do anything in exchange for giving me the wine. I viewed it as a gift although I was uncomfortable with it. I testified in front of Judge Wolf that I did not feel compromised until later when I received the wine with the thousand dollars.

Around that time two FBI agents in the Boston office, Brenner and Montanari, were receiving information from Brian Halloran about the murder of Roger Wheeler in Oklahoma. The first time I

---

[59] Morris, in telling this, shows he was aware at that time that he was corrupting himself otherwise why would he not want the wine. He'll testify that it was not until much later that he realized he was violating the law. But his own words about his thoughts and actions at that time condemn him. He says he did not know how to give the wine back when it was still in Connolly's car. He simply could have refused to take it. But he says he couldn't do that because Connolly told him that the gangsters wouldn't trust him if he refused to be bribed so he had to take it. This is absurd on its face. If he actually believed that, he could have taken it and reported it. Morris wants us to believe that any agent offered a bribe by an informant must secretly accept it to keep the informant's trust.

knew Halloran was cooperating was when Agent Brenner came to the office to ask me about Halloran's credibility. I told him I thought Halloran was not credible. I knew that Bulger and Flemmi did not like Halloran. They blamed him for an earlier investigation against Jimmy Martorano. They also did not like that he was involved in doing cocaine.

When Brenner discussed Halloran's credibility with me, he told me that Halloran had been offered a contract by Bulger and Flemmi in the presence of a John Callahan, former president of World Jai Alai, to kill Roger Wheeler. He said Halloran declined the contract to kill Wheeler. He asked me if I thought Bulger or Flemmi would trust Halloran to do anything like this for him. I told him that I did not think so.

At that time I knew Halloran along with Jackie Salemme, the brother of Frankie Salemme, a high LCN figure, had been indicted for the murder of George Pappas. Halloran was facing a life sentence in prison for this killing. Halloran wanted the FBI's help. He wanted to get into the witness security program where he would get a new name and identification.

I did a threat assessment on Halloran saying there was a clear and present danger to Halloran's security. I recommended he be admitted into the program. In my report dated October 2, 1981, I stated that Jackie Salemme was in hiding and the Mafia wanted Halloran hit in the head. I reported that the Mafia believed Halloran was making a deal for himself and would give up Salemme. I was aware the Mafia used violence and murder to protect itself. I didn't know other people had tried to attack Halloran before he was killed.

All the information I had about the Mafia wanting to kill Halloran came from Bulger and Flemmi. In a sense I was using their information as a basis for getting Halloran into the witness security program. A person in that program has certain obligations. I didn't know if Halloran would play by the rules.[60]

Connolly provided me with some information for that assessment. I told Connolly that Halloran was giving information on the Wheeler murder. Connolly told me that Halloran was not credible. At that time I did not know if Connolly went to Bulger or Flemmi to determine this. A little later Connolly came to me to find out what was going on. I was reluctant to tell him but my resistance crumbled when Connolly said, "If someone's saying something about my informants, I have a right to know." I told him what Halloran had told the other agents.

Connolly later told me that Bulger and Flemmi knew what Halloran was doing. He told me as far as they were concerned Halloran was pulling a Pallata. Pallata was the cooperating witness I

---

[60] It was somewhat surreal watching Morris carrying on with this façade with a straight face. Halloran was prepared to give evidence against Bulger and Flemmi. These were the people who presented a threat to Halloran. Morris using their information files a misleading report saying that the danger Halloran faced came from the Mafia. Bulger and Flemmi are delighted to throw the suspicion away from themselves onto the Mafia.

mentioned. He went to Winter Hill and told them he was informing on them. But he said he would not testify against them if they gave him money. When Connolly told me this, I understood it to mean Halloran was trying to shake down the Winter Hill people. He was not planning to testify against them.

But I also realized that Connolly had talked to them about Halloran's statements. I felt that in doing this Connolly had compromised Brenner's and Montanari's investigation. It was shortly after that I learned that Halloran had been murdered. I never told anyone that Bulger and Flemmi knew Halloran was informing against them. Connolly never told anyone, either. [61]

I learned Halloran told a Boston police detective at the scene that he was shot by Jimmy Flynn. I felt relieved hearing this. Flynn was not part of Winter Hill.[62]

I went to Glencoe, Georgia between June 2 and 17, 1982. At the time I was married but I was involved with my secretary, Debbie. Before I left I had made plans to have Debbie come down and join me. My relationship with Debbie was the

---

[61] We will later hear testimony that Halloran was wired by the FBI. Incredibly, Morris sat back knowing two agents were putting a wire on Halloran while at the same time knowing that Connolly had already compromised the investigation.

[62] Morris was relieved when he heard this but knew it was false. He was quite certain that Halloran had been killed by Whitey and Stevie because he said a little later when he gave information to Connolly to pass on to Whitey and Stevie that he didn't want another Halloran.

worst kept secret in the office. Connolly was well aware of it. Immediately prior to Debbie coming down I called back to Boston and spoke with Connolly. Connolly had told me that Bulger and Flemmi liked me and would do anything for me. I asked him if they would spring for a ticket for Debbie to fly to Georgia. I may have spoken twice with Connolly about this.

Connolly was able to get me a thousand dollars. I remember that I specifically requested that Connolly get the money from Bulger and Flemmi. Connolly and I schemed up the story to tell Debbie that the thousand dollars came from my desk.[63]

Halloran also gave us information about John Callahan. Callahan was connected with the Winter Hill people and was president of World Jail Alai in Miami. In August 1982 three months after Halloran's murder Callahan was found in the trunk of a car in Miami. After hearing this my concern

---

[63] Halloran was killed on May 11, 1982. His blood is still fresh on a South Boston waterfront street when Morris is asking the people he should have known killed him for money to fly his girlfriend to Georgia.

Morris's girlfriend, Debbie, testified she was a typist in the FBI office in Boston and started dating Morris in 1973 shortly after he arrived at the Boston office. When Morris went to Glencoe, he wanted her to come down. She remembered him speaking with Connolly and shortly after that Connolly came up to her and gave her a thousand dollars. Connolly said "Isn't it nice you have the money to visit John," stating the money came from Morris's desk. She had access to his desk and never saw any cash in it. Morris was divorced in 1998 fifteen years after he started his affair with Debbie. He subsequently married her.

about Bulger and Flemmi increased but I did not take any action or communicate about it to anyone.

Connolly also did not take any action against Bulger and Flemmi. I knew the SAC Sarhatt was concerned about Bulger and Flemmi being informants. But I did not convey my thoughts to him that they might have been involved in these murders.

After Callahan's killing, maybe around Christmas time a year or two later, Connolly told me he had something for me from Bulger and Flemmi. He told me to come to his house. Connolly lived at Thomas Circle in South Boston. I don't recall how much longer after the conversation I went there. I don't remember where and when I opened the case of wine. It was not at FBI headquarters. When I did open it, there was an envelope with a thousand dollars sitting on the second level of the wine box. I don't remember what I did with the thousand dollars.

Connolly called me that afternoon or the next day to be sure I received the envelope. I didn't want the wine or the money but I didn't know what to do. I didn't want to tip them off that I had been compromised. I didn't believe I was compromised. I thought it was just a gift. But in retrospect, I realize I was compromised.

I really didn't know if I had concerns. I knew I didn't want to rock the boat. I did not discuss the wine and the thousand dollars with Bulger or Flemmi. They never asked me to do anything for them. I really thought it was a gift. Later I found out it wasn't.

It was in 1983 or 1984 that I first suspected that Connolly may have been taping the calls between us. I was concerned. I know my suspicion and beliefs are not consistent with my testimony that we were good friends.[64]

As supervisor I could close out an informant. If an informant is a target he can be closed. If I wanted Bulger or Flemmi closed out, I could have suggested to ASAC Ring that it be done. But it would be difficult to do after having received two payoffs from them.[65]

On January 11, 1983, I moved off the organized crime squad to become a the task force coordinator. In 1984 I was temporarily assigned to the Miami FBI office.

In 1986 I became supervisor of the public corruption squad. Special Agent Robert Jordan

---

[64] Morris was not threatened by Connolly's possession of the tapes. He couldn't use them because they would likewise incriminate Connolly. But he knew the tapes in Bulger's and Flemmi's hands made him vulnerable. He had no idea when the taping began. Realizing this his ultimate goal became the protection of himself at all costs. To do this he had to insure neither Bulger nor Flemmi would be put in a position where to save themselves they would want to disclose his corrupt actions which would be supported by the tapes. He now had to work doubly hard to protect them from other law enforcement agencies. If he couldn't protect them he had to silence them.

[65] Morris stated he was never asked to do anything by Bulger and Flemmi. They no longer have to ask Morris to do anything because he became a witting collaborator. He had to protect them to protect himself. They were now handling him.

who was assigned to the squad had developed a police corruption case. Jordan was working on the case hoping to use it to get Flemmi. The first part of the investigation was to be a Title III intercept on a telephone being used by John Bahorian, a bookmaker, and a Boston police detective he was paying off for protection, Peter McDonough. I never told Jordan about my relationship with Bulger and Flemmi.

I realized the planned intercept might capture Flemmi. I was fearful that if it did then Flemmi would roll over against me. So to protect myself I sought out Connolly to tell him that Flemmi was a target and listed as a person who we expected to intercept. Connolly knew nothing about it before I told him. Bulger had no connection to it. I told Connolly to pass the information about the tap to Bulger and Flemmi. As the supervisor, I could decide whether to alert informants about wires or bugs.

Connolly came back to me and said he told them. He said they wanted to hear it from me. He told me I must meet with them myself. I made arrangements to meet them at Debbie's house. I told Bulger, Flemmi, and Connolly about Jordan's investigation. Flemmi put his hand out to thank me for the information. I feared they were recording the conversation. Flemmi thanking me was unusual. I don't remember whether I had ever given him information like this before but he never thanked me before that time. Flemmi, Bulger, and Connolly arrived together, as they always did, and left together

After telling Connolly, Bulger and Flemmi about the Bahorian wiretap I was concerned about what they would do. I sought out Connolly and told him, "I don't want another Halloran."

Morris stammered and reddened when he said this.

I didn't know if they killed Halloran or not but I thought just in case I'd warn them off. I did not want them to kill Bahorian like I believed they did to Halloran. I recognize the situations between Halloran and Bahorian are not totally similar. Halloran was cooperating with the Government. Bahorian was a target.[66]

After telling Flemmi of the tap I was concerned that Flemmi would tell Bahorian and compromise this important investigation. It had been going on for a number of years. My concern was unnecessary. It turned out Flemmi did not tip off the wire.[67]

---

[66] Morris knew the situations were quite similar. Bahorian as a target once caught could easily decide to cooperate with the government and give information against Flemmi. It was imperative that Morris take steps to undermine the Bahorian wiretap.

[67] Morris had no way of knowing whether Flemmi told others about the tap. All he knows is that during the tap some evidence was uncovered and some persons were implicated in criminal activity. Morris does not know how many people Flemmi told not to use the phone. Nor does he know whether Flemmi alerted Bahorian to the tap who then tailored his conversation to minimize his exposure. Nor whether Bahorian and Flemmi knowing the FBI was listening conspired to mislead the listeners or to set up innocent people such as cops to expose them to criminal liability. There are so many things one does not know when the criminal is made the show's producer and

I spoke with Connolly about trying to get Peter McDonough to cooperate. Bahorian had been paying McDonough for protection from the police. I felt Bahorian would not cooperate but thought perhaps McDonough would. I asked Connolly whether he thought McDonough would cooperate. Connolly said not to worry about McDonough. He said he's taken money from them so that means he's one of them. [68]

When Connolly said that, I realized I was also one of them. I realized I could not go to the SAC with this information, for to do so, would be for me to fall on my own sword.[69]

---

director. However one thing is guaranteed: you won't get the same information you would have gotten had you not alerted the criminal of the tap.

[68] Morris presents himself as a naïve waif understanding nothing except what Connolly tells him. This statement rings particularly false. Why would Morris ask Connolly whether McDonough would cooperate? He testified Connolly knew nothing about the Bahorian investigation. He knew it was routine for cops who were caught taking bribes to become cooperating witnesses to save their pension and avoid jail. Morris worked on cases where this happened and became one himself.

[69] Morris is spinning a line. He wants the jury to believe that after taking all the money and other gifts and covering up the activities of Bulger and Flemmi the first time he became aware of his criminality was when Connolly made that statement. The true reason Morris did not want McDonough to cooperate and prevented him from doing so is if McDonough was taking bribes then he could give them Flemmi which may have endangered Morris.

In 1986 I was going through a divorce. I had health and personal family problems. Connolly approached me and said Bulger and Flemmi wanted to get together with me. We made arrangements for another dinner, this time at Debbie's apartment in Woburn. Connolly, Flemmi, and Bulger arrived and departed together. It was a social dinner. Not much business was discussed. After eating, Connolly and Flemmi left the kitchen. Bulger headed for the door but trailed behind. Just before walking out he stopped and turned. He reached in his jacket and gave me an envelope. It contained five thousand dollars.

Before saying "five thousand dollars," he flushes a brilliant pinkish red in marked contrast to his usual drab gray aspect. He stammers as he speaks.[70]

That was the last money I received from them. I never told Connolly I received that money.

It wasn't Connolly's fault that I took the money. I don't blame him for my decision to accept the money. That was my decision and my decision alone. From the late '70s up to 1986 I received from Bulger and Flemmi a total of seven thousand dollars, two cases of fine wine, isolated bottles of wine, a silver bucket, and a bottle of wine or two when I had them over for dinner.

---

[70] He was overwhelmed with an enormous sense of self-pity at having been forced to reveal his grave inner turpitude. He was not concerned about the enormity of his conduct other than how it affected him. His aspect flared red only when he realized that in taking the five thousand he had hurt himself. He didn't reddened when he testified about betraying his fellow agents by tipping off a wiretap or when telling how he revealed an informant's identity.

In 1988 I opposed Connolly's promotion to supervisor. It was well known that Connolly was upset because of this. At that point we had no friendship at all. In 1988 I told Boston Globe reporter Dick Lehr of the Boston Globe's Spotlight Team that Connolly was living beyond his means.[71]

Also at that time I decided that I had to try to shut down Bulger as an informant. I could have gone to SAC Potts to ask him to close them out. All I had to do was say they were targets. They would have been closed.

Rather than confessing about my involvement I planned to leak to the press that Bulger was an informant . I felt sure that once it became public knowledge then the FBI would shut him down. I told the Boston Globe that Bulger was an informant. I hoped the information would be printed in the newspaper. I knew I was putting Bulger's life in jeopardy. There had been little bits of information out on the street before that time that had caused a suspicion to arise that Bulger and Flemmi were informants. I knew that if the LCN believed that they were informants, they would take action against them. I did care if Bulger got hurt. But I was not concerned enough that it stopped me from disclosing Bulger's identity as an informant. I didn't care enough to warn him that I had told the Globe he was an informant. I

---

[71] Morris true to his colors and long before he was in jeopardy was undermining his fellow agent Connolly. Yet he testified he considered Connolly a friend. He has no shame.

recognized there was a danger of harm to Bulger or Flemmi as a result of my leak to the Globe.

My leak to the Globe did become a concern for others in the FBI at higher levels. I told the Globe that Bulger was an informant. I also leaked other information to the Globe. When the investigation into the sale of 75 State Street that involved Senate President William Bulger was ongoing, I told the Globe about it. When Senate President William Bulger was re interviewed by the FBI, I told the Globe. These were closely guarded secrets that were known only to a handful of people. I leaked that to the Globe knowing that they would print it.[72]

After the leaks to the Globe, the Office of Professional Responsibility, OPR, conducted an investigation. The OPR can recommend criminal prosecution or non-criminal sanctions. I became the subject of the investigation. I filed an affidavit containing several lies about my role in the leak. Among the lies in my sworn statement are that I talked only with O'Sullivan, the SAC and ASAC about the investigation and that I told Gerry O'Neil of the Boston Globe I could not discuss it. I lied to protect myself. I refused to take a polygraph.

A month later I filed a second statement under oath that I personally wrote. That also contained many false statements. But my statement that I

---

[72] Morris follows a time honored FBI tradition of agents selectively leaking confidential information to newspapers to advance a specific agenda. The most notorious, Mark Felt, Deep Throat, the second in command of the FBI did it hoping he would be made director. It is a tradition lacking in honor and full of deceit where trust is betrayed for personal gain.

considered Mr. O'Neill of the Boston Globe a friend was not false. I consider him to be a friend.[73]

I also talked to Globe reporters O'Neill and Lehr about other things. I don't recall if I leaked information to them about the McCormick investigation. I remembered discussing the case with them. They printed a lot of information about the case including information about the grand jury. I agree that someone had to tell them that the grand jury matters were coming down. I had the information about it but I can't recall whether I did or did not release it to the Globe.

After the OPR investigation I was suspended for three weeks without pay and censored. I lied to the FBI investigators when I denied leaking the information. I also lied about other matters because I wanted to protect myself. Even so they concluded I was the person who leaked the information.

For punishment I was placed on probation for a year. At the end of the year in 1991 I left the Boston office. I spent two years in Washington, DC. I then was promoted to an ASAC and sent to Los Angeles. I spent two years there. I then went to the FBI academy at Quantico, Virginia, where I became a section supervisor. My FBI record is

---

[73] Gerry O'Neill and Dick Lehr of the Boston Globe's spotlight team wrote an excellent book about Bulger's relationship with the FBI called *Black Mass*. They gained much of their information from Morris and another agent Fitzpatrick. Their book is shaded in their favor. Morris without friends in the FBI sought to find them in the Globe by undermining his fellow agents.

spotless except for the leaking of the identity of the informant.[74]

I had left the Boston FBI office in January 1991. I retired from the FBI in December 1995 when I was a section chief at the FBI school in Quantico, Virginia. I was having some health problems. But the immediate impetus for my decision to retire was a telephone call I received on October 13, 1995, from Whitey Bulger at the FBI school at Quantico.[75] He was a fugitive from the January 1995 indictment. Bulger called and told me that I took money from him. He told me that if he went to jail he would take me with him. He demanded that I call the Boston Globe to have it retract some of the things the Globe had said about him. He told me to use my Machiavellian mind to figure out how to get the pressure off him.[76]

---

[74] Only an FBI agent could say he had a spotless record which included placing explosive devices on a car's gas tank; covering up for and protecting murderers, taking bribes, compromising FBI and state investigations, putting informant lives in jeopardy, filing false affidavits, imprisoning others for what he was doing, and endlessly lying to his boss and associates to mention a few acts.

[75] Debbie Noseworthy Morris testified she picked Morris up at work on October 13, 1995, the day Whitey called him. He was leaving his Quantico office and he appeared quite upset.

[76] Twice during the trial Morris mentioned that Bulger said he had a Machiavellian mind. He seemed proud of it. In telling us this he failed to understand how this damned him. I can not imagine what he did to so impress the master Machiavellian criminal mind, Bulger himself. He testified as if he was led around by the nose by Connolly. This gives lie to that portrayal. Morris was

The call from Bulger unnerved me. I reported it to the OPR but in the report I lied. I lied when I said I didn't take money from Bulger. I lied when I said I played no part in the Boston Globe stories about Bulger. If I didn't lie, I would have lost my job and my pension. I would have embarrassed myself and my job so I just lied. After filing my OPR report I began the process of retirement.

Before this call in 1995 I had not spoken to Bulger since 1988. That was the time when I tipped off Bulger and Stevie about the Bahorian wiretap. It was also around that time I told the Boston Globe that Bulger was an FBI informant.

I knew Bulger and Flemmi were indicted in January 1995. I learned about that investigation while I was at Quantico from Ed Quinn of the Boston office. The next thing I knew they were indicted. I didn't know when they would be indicted. I heard Flemmi said I tipped them as to the January 1995 indictment. I didn't do it.

I found out in late 1997 or early 1998 that Flemmi made a claim that he had been authorized by me to commit any criminal act except murder. Flemmi hoped I would support this false affidavit. I wouldn't do it. Flemmi's claim made me realize I had not left the past behind me.

After Flemmi made the claim I was approached by other FBI agents. They wanted to know whether Flemmi's assertion was true. Initially I didn't talk. I knew no one in the FBI

---

pulling the strings to such an extent that Connolly ended up taking the rap and he walks away scot-free with a pension. Bulger was right; he has a Machiavellian mind.

except Connolly was aware that I had been taking money. I knew if I talked to the investigators I would have to tell the truth which would incriminate me.

You could say Bulger's call made me get religion.[77] I decided to make a deal for myself. I made a proffer to the government. I dealt with Assistant U.S. Attorneys Wyshak and Kelley and also with some FBI agents.

I had a relationship with another informant, an old big time bookie I'll call Mr. X. I had been assigned to Mr. X in 1977. I held him as an informant through 1990. He also gave me five thousand dollars but that was a loan. Mr. X was my only top echelon informant. Mr. X provided information to me about Gerry Angiulo and Vinny Ferrarra of the North End LCN. Connolly had nothing to do with him. I received gifts from Mr. X such as periodic deliveries of pizzas, sneakers, tennis shoes and periodic gifts of clothing. I had him to my house a few times for dinner. He was in the clothing business. I also used Mr. X's condominium in Florida at times with my wife, my daughter, and also with Debbie. Throughout the time when I dealt with Mr. X I received gifts from him and used his place in Florida. I was the FBI agent responsible for handling him as an informant.

---

[77] It had to be a slow conversion. It took two years after that call before he came forward. His seeing the light truly came when he realized he was in a race with John Connolly to the Justice Department's immunity locker.

In 1986 I asked Mr. X to use his vacation house in West Palm Beach, Florida. I also got the five thousand dollars that I mentioned from him at that time. I lied to my wife that Debbie had loaned me the five thousand dollars when I listed my assets for my divorce. I did so because I needed the cash to make a down payment on a car for my wife. I paid that money back. I paid twenty-five hundred dollars sometime in 1992 or 1993 after I was transferred to Washington, DC. I still had not paid back the other twenty-five hundred dollars at the time of the Wolf hearing last year when I testified under a grant of immunity. I paid it back sometime after that. I never reported any of this. I never felt compromised by these gifts. The state police did a wiretap on Mr. X at one time but he was authorized by the FBI to engage in bookmaking.[78]

Throughout the entire time I was debriefed by the government agents, I never mentioned anything about my relationship with Mr. X. I was

---

[78] It is unclear what happened to the state police wiretap. Everyone in the courtroom seemed to know Mr. X's real name is Berkowitz. I suggest there is something wrong with the FBI when it permits a person to engage in ongoing, daily criminal activity such as bookmaking from at least 1977 through 1990. I wondered what laws allow the FBI to give certain people a life long right to commit crimes while prosecuting the rest of us if we commit one crime. How many people are committing crimes and being protected by the FBI? Isn't it important to our democracy that there be some check on the FBI's ability to give people a carte blanche to violate the laws? Is there no term limit on the time a criminal can continue his career under the FBI protection?

debriefed on December 16 and 17, 1997, on April 20, 1998, the day before I testified in front of Judge Wolf, and on April 26, 1998, after my testimony. I met with prosecutors on March 29 and 30, 1999 to prepare for my grand jury testimony. Over nine times I had meetings to discuss my testimony. The government agents would ask questions and I would answer them.

The reason why I didn't disclose the money and gifts that Mr. X gave me was that maintaining the secret identity of an informant is important to me. Once an informant's identity is out, it is out. If I told the Justice Department of the gifts from Mr. X, I would have compromised him.[79] I did not think that telling of more gifts would affect how the government treated me.

Between the time I first made my proffer and then I was concerned about protecting Mr X's identity. My concern changed in 2002 because the prosecutors asked me if there was anything that I hadn't told them. It was on April 10, 2002 less than a month before the trial started that I first told the government about the money and other benefits I received from Mr. X. I knew at that time the defense team planned to talk to my first wife, Rebecca. I did not reveal the information because I feared my ex-wife would disclose it. It's just I was

---

[79] Morris testified how he revealed Whitey's identity as an informant to AUSA O'Sullivan as well as the Globe. Here he says it was important to him not to reveal Berkowitz's identity to the AUSAs. The difference is that revealing the latter may have hurt him.

not asked whether there was anything else the government should know until April 2002.

I remember at the Wolf trial denying that I ever took any money before I took it from Bulger or Flemmi. I was not asked if I took any money at anytime. I was not concerned about being asked about it.

If they asked me the right question at that trial, I would have told about the money but not have disclosed the name of the informant.

I'm aware that I could have been forced to disclose his name. All I can say about the Wolf hearing is that I was on the witness stand for eight days and I was overwhelmed. Most of that time is blurry.

I received things of value from Mr. X. It's true I assisted in the prosecution of Boston police officers who had received much less than I got. I knew I lied in affidavits filed in court. I knew I had taken things of value from Bulger and Flemmi.

When Judge Wolf began his hearings, I was only concerned about myself. I knew I had committed some serious crimes. That was why I made the proffer to the government.

I recognized over time it became clear there were strings attached to the gifts. As I said, it came to a head with Bulger's call telling me, "I go to jail, you go to jail. Get the Globe to back off! Put your Machiavellian mind to work!"

I also realized what I received were not gifts when some unusual events occurred. One was when Connolly asked me if Lieutenant James Cox of the Boston Police was cooperating with the FBI.

Another was when Connolly and I had the conversation about Boston police detective McDonough where Connolly told me McDonough was one of the bad guys saying McDonough is "one of them."

I knew the taking of the money had affected me. I tipped Bulger and Flemmi about the wiretap in the Bahorian case. I knew I was compromised. I would not have tipped them off if I had not taken the money.[80]

---

[80] Long before Bulger's phone call Morris knew he was at great risk. It was when he learned Whitey and Stevie were indicted in early 1995. He feared that the Justice Department may deal with Bulger, Flemmi, or Connolly. He after all was the supervisor. They may have him on their tape recordings. He had no cards to play. He could only sit and pray.

When Flemmi testified the agreement he had with Morris and Connolly was that he could do whatever he wanted except hit someone, Machiavellian Morris saw his golden opportunity. The Justice Department (DOJ) needed one of them to say there was no such agreement. Morris acted with resolve. He gave the DOJ what it wanted to hear in exchange for his pension and freedom.

The strangest thing about Morris's testimony was how little information he gave about his dealings with Connolly. They had associated together over fifteen years. Listening to Morris's testimony it seemed they barely talked. Neither the prosecution nor the defense sought to get into their conversation. Wouldn't these two men who worked side by side for many years have discussed the wine, the money, the criminal activities of Bulger or Flemmi, or a million other things? Wouldn't Morris have asked Connolly what he was getting? Did he ever see Connolly flashing a roll of money? Didn't he see Connolly driving expensive cars, boats or wearing expensive suits or

---

jewelry?

So much of the interaction between Morris and Connolly was left out that I was baffled. I wasn't alone. At the end of Morris's testimony an attorney attending the trial who represents the family of one of Bulger's victims asked me, "Is this case fixed?" He sensed like I did that much of what went on is still kept hidden. The Justice Department's complicity in hiding the FBI's part in this affair is as offensive as Morris's total venality.

CHAPTER FOUR

STEPPING INTO THE MUD

JOHN MARTORANO

LIFE LONG CRIMINAL, SERIAL MURDERER

It's Monday, May 13, 2002. A couple of minutes before 10:00 am, Judge Tauro enters. His judicial robe as usual is open. It hangs loosely from his shoulders. He wears a dark blue shirt and a blue and yellow checkered tie. After a short bench conference with counsel he says to the marshal, "You can bring him in."

Two marshals enter through a side door on the right side of the courtroom with a man who looks around sixty years old. He has dark kempt hair with no gray, heavy set, 5' 7" with a bishop's stomach wearing a white shirt and dull dark blue tie. His buttoned blue suit jacket stretches anxiously over his paunchy waistline. He slowly and deliberately walks around the witness stand which is against the wall on the opposite side of the courtroom facing the jury box and which can be entered only from one side. It is elevated about a foot off the ground. Its front is enclosed so that only the upper body of the seated witness is visible to the jurors and the court spectators.

The witness steps onto it, pulls back the chair, but remains standing in front of the chair for a few seconds looking around the courtroom. His demeanor is neither threatening nor retiring. I recognize him from his pictures. It is John

107

Martorano, reputed stone cold killer of at least 20 people, a Winter Hill boss. He seems to want to send a message that for him this is just like another day at the office. I suppose after having killed so many people that testifying in court is no more than that.

I reflect upon him thinking he doesn't look like a person who has killed at least twenty people. But then again I remind myself that serial killers do not have a particularly sinister aspect that would disclose the depravity in their hearts. One American whose appearance fit his crime came to mind, Charles Manson.

Martorano sits down and leans back in the witness chair with an expression of disdain and boredom.

The jury is brought in. Its loud "good morning" response causes a bright smile from Judge Tauro. Martorano puts on a pair of sun glasses with clear bottoms. He leans forward, his left hand on the desk in front of him.

Martorano in jail since January 1995 does not have the prison pallor that most people develop who have been incarcerated for this many years. His appearance shows his incarceration has been easy. He speaks in a deep unemotional voice. I feel as if I'm in the theater of the absurd watching the government put forth a killer of twenty people to testify against an FBI agent who it will turn out he never met or talked to.[81]

---

[81] The jury will totally disbelieve every essential element of Martorano's testimony.

STEPPING INTO THE MUD

He has moved his hands to below the façade of the stand where they are no longer visible. He is obviously fidgeting with the sleeves of his suit jacket as he answers the questions about the deal he has reached with the Justice Department. The fidgeting continues as Durham leads him through the questioning involving his immunity agreement.

Durham picks up speed as he reads through the list of people Martorano admits to killing, as if by rushing through it, the blood that drips from the hands of Martorano will be less noticeable. My notes read: "Michale Milans, Al Plumber, Wm O'Brien, Jas____, James O'Keefe, A____, James Sousa, Tom King, Edward Connors, Castucci." I'm unable to catch even half the names.

Durham recites the evidence and Martorano's role is to agree with all of Durham's assertions. As Durham recites his testimony, Martorano answers with a simple "yes."

My name is John Martorano. I am here because I made a deal with the government. I have pled guilty to charges against me that were contained in an indictment that came down in January 1995. I've been in jail about seven and a half years.

The indictment that I was arrested on charged me with racketeering, conspiracy involving gambling, extortion, and loan sharking. I've also pled guilty to two-second degree murder charges in Tulsa, Oklahoma, and Miami, Florida. I'm awaiting sentencing on all of these cases.

It took me over a year to get my deal with the government.[82] I started back in 1998. First, I had to deal with the US Attorney in Boston. Then I had to deal with the prosecutors in Oklahoma and Florida. Those two states are death penalty states. At the time I decided to cooperate, I knew Flemmi could give me up on the murders. So I got there first. I had that in mind when I made the deal to testify.[83]

I didn't want to be executed for the murders I committed in those states. It's not that I worried about it when I murdered the people there. It's just I thought it a good idea to include those murders in my deal and wrap up everything at once. I wasn't charged with those murders, but I knew if I didn't make the deal, someone may have tied me to them down the road. I didn't want to take a chance of that happening.

To get my agreement, I dealt with DEA agent Dan Doherty and state troopers Steve Johnson, Tom Duffy and Tom Foley. If convicted on the charges under the 1995 indictment, I could have faced between 24 to 30 years. I'm 61 years old. If I didn't get that time reduced, I'd spend the rest of

---

[82] Martorano's lawyer was Frank DiMento. I worked as an associate to Frank for eight years before becoming an ADA. Frank's brilliance as a criminal defense lawyer is well known and is shown by what many said was Martorano's deal of the century.

[83] Martorano has the same mentality as Morris, 'get there first' to make a sweetheart deal for himself. Tell the government what you think it wants to know. The goal is not to tell the truth but to get the deal and that means saying whatever it is necessary to get it.

my life in jail. So I made the deal. The government and my lawyer originally agreed to recommend that I go to prison between 12 ½ to 15 years. But now they've agreed to lower the recommendation. The government will recommend 12 ½ years. What I'd like it to do is to recommend 3 years.

When Martorano said this some spontaneous laughter erupted in the courtroom [84]

It was important to me to get the 12 ½ year recommendation and wrap all my cases up at one time. I'll serve all my time in the federal prison system although, to be frank, I don't care where I do time since a prison is a prison.[85]

What's important to me is the 12 ½ year recommendation. That means I'll actually be in prison for 10 ½ years from the date I was arrested. That was in January 1995.

I knew Joe Barboza got himself out of jail by cooperating. I knew that Barboza did not testify

---

[84] I found myself repulsed by this degenerate man talking in such a cavalier manner. The laughter emboldened Martorano. Thereafter at every opportunity he tried to play the role of a stand-up comic. It was strange listening to this multi-murderer trying to be a comedian and hearing some laugh at him.

[85] This was far from the truth. These guys do care where they do their time. The prisons in Florida and Oklahoma have few of the amenities of the federal prisons. As a protected witness in the federal system, Martorano looked comfortable and well cared for. Had he spent any time in the jails of those sunshine states I dare say he would be a lot less chipper.

truthfully after agreeing to cooperate. But that's not something I'd do. I don't think that way. At the time of my arrest, I was in business. What type of business, I guess you would call it monkey business.

When he said this, he looked around with a smile on his face showing that he thought he was really being funny. His handlers, the policemen in the first row, and a few spectators laughed. Judge Tauro remained poker faced. None of the jurors appeared to see any humor in the remark. I felt physically uncomfortable experiencing this.

I'll tell you one thing that I was concerned with was protecting my brother Jimmy. Not only him. I wanted to protect everyone except Whitey Bulger, Stevie Flemmi and corrupt officials. But I'll tell the truth about anything I'm asked, even about my brother, if I have to.

Oh, yeah, my agreement with the government says that I forfeited all my property. That's accurate but what it doesn't say is that I got rid of everything before I signed the agreement except my house in Florida. But I should say about the house, well the government gets none of that. You see my second wife, Carolyn Wood, had a two hundred thousand dollar judgment against me for child support. So the money from the sale of that house will go to pay off that judgment.

I used illegal funds to buy the house. I really don't know how much I paid for the house. You could say I really never owned it because it was not in my name. I guess I put ten thousand into buying the house with a friend of mine. Well, then again, if you really want to know how much I really put in, I'd say in the ballpark between thirty to forty thousand dollars.

So basically I forfeit nothing to the government. When I was arrested in 1995 and brought back to Boston, I only had about forty thousand in my name at the time and a handful of people who owed me money. All the assets I had in 1995 are gone. The van, the trailer, and the Mercedes that I had when I was arrested, I disposed of before the agreement. I got about 25,000 for them. I sent the money to my family or my lawyer.

While I'm in prison, the Justice Department gives me money. To date I've received between $2,000 and $3500. I don't keep track of it. Every so often the Justice Department puts $300 to $400 into my commissary account for food and soda. Whenever I need the money, I call DEA agent Dan Doherty but I don't call that often.

In exchange for the deal I got I've told of my role in several murders. The Justice Department would not have known about many of these murders if I did not tell them. When I was helping the Justice Department, I discussed up to 40 or 50 murders. There were 80 murdered people I knew. I went through a list to see what I knew about each of the killings. I told them about the ones I did, I told them what I was told about others. I told them about the ones I had heard nothing about, but I did know about the vast majority of them.

STEPPING INTO THE MUD

I will testify for the Justice Department against retired State Police Lieutenant Richard Schneiderhan and FBI Agent John J. Connolly, Junior. If I don't tell the full truth and fully cooperate, the Justice Department will tear up the agreement. When I get out of prison, I'm going to be put into the witness security program. I'll receive government protection and a new identity.

I grew up in Boston. My father had a business called Luigi's. I hung around with Joseph Barboza in the 1960s. I committed a lot of crimes with him, no murders but many extortions. I can't remember one from the next. I hung around a lot with my brother Jimmy. We had a garage. Jimmy did some illegal stuff. Mostly it was shylocking. Jimmy would lend money to people sometimes at more than a point a week. You know if he lent a guy $10,000, the guy would have to pay at least $100 a week interest.

Jimmy was in jail from 1970 to 1976. After he got out he operated a lounge in Boston called Chandlers with Howie Winter. I had nothing to do with Chandlers. I would get a paycheck for hanging around there but Jimmy took care of the business end. I don't know who came up with the money for the business. Jimmy couldn't put his name on the business because of his criminal record. He didn't have good credentials with the banks.

I don't know if Jimmy's a member of the Mafia or not. I'd be the last person to know. I was not a Mafia lover.

STEPPING INTO THE MUD

During the 1960s I got to know some of the Winter Hill people. Those were the days of the gang wars. We were with Stevie Flemmi, Frankie Salemme, and Winter Hill. My brother Jimmy never did anything illegal with Winter Hill.

I never sold cocaine but I did buy it for my own social purposes. I used it once or twice a week in the 1960s and 1970s. In those days, I socialized with prostitutes, singers, bar maids and waitresses because those were the people I hung around with. I'd give them gifts on occasion but I never paid any of them for sex.

I've killed a lot of people in my time. In all, I've killed 19 people. I was with the guys when we killed the 20th, Eddie Connors. The names of the people I killed, let me see. Before joining Winter Hill, I killed Bobby Pallidino, John Jackson, Tony Veranis, Herb Smith, a woman named Elizabeth and a guy named Douglas, Robert Hicks, and John Banno. After joining, I killed Al Nostrangelli, Milano, Plumber, William O'Brien, John Leary, Joe Nostrangelli, Jimmy O'Toole and Eddie Connors.

When he's asked whether he murdered a specific person, he scratches his chin and indifferently answers "Yes I did".

I usually had good reasons to kill them. They were going to be witnesses for the government against me or my friends or they beat up my friends. I killed people to prevent them from testifying against me. I killed for money. But my freedom means more to me than money.

STEPPING INTO THE MUD

Whitey Bulger came to me in 1972. I did not really know him prior to that time. He was having a dispute in South Boston. He wanted me to introduce him to Howie Winter. He wanted Winter to settle a dispute between two gangs in South Boston, the Killeens and Mullins. After the dispute was patched up, Whitey wanted to join Winter Hill with me.

We joined Winter Hill in 1972. Howie Winter, Joe McDonald and Jimmy Simms were then running the operation. Before then I was involved in my own illegal stuff but not with Winter Hill. In the 1960s, I was involved in selling hot goods. After joining Winter Hill I never received any money from hijacking because I had nothing to do with that stuff. McDonald, Simms and Winter were involved in hijacking trucks with the Charlestown or Somerville gangs.

Winter Hill had also been involved in horse betting, the numbers, and race fixing. We wanted to run a sports betting operation with them. When they agreed, it then became five guys who were partners. We decided to split the money from the illegal gambling business. Bulger got one third of the proceeds because he had to cut his share among some other guys from South Boston. We agreed to take a lesser share. Bulger also had a side operation. I had part of the Winter Hill action and nothing outside except sometimes I would loan money.

Before joining Winter Hill, I had already killed several people. In November 1965 I killed Bobby

Pallidino who had information about the murder of Margaret Silvestri. My brother Jimmy was charged as an accessory after the fact to that murder. The investigation was also focusing on me. Stevie Flemmi told Bobby to talk to me to straighten some things out. When Bobby showed up we never had a chance to talk, he pulled his gun first. He wasn't as quick as me so I killed him. I guess you could call this some kind of self-defense. But Bobby did have information on Margaret Silvestri's killing, so I had to kill him.

In April 1966 I killed Tony Veranis. Tony was bragging about beating up my brother. I heard about it indirectly. I went to see him. Tony pulled a gun on me in an after-hours joint in Roxbury. As he reached for his gun, I shot him. Tony was another guy I was faster than.[86]

In September 1966 I killed John Jackson. Flemmi told me he planned to testify against my brother Jimmy. Jackson was the last person with my brother Jimmy before Silvestri disappeared. Joe Barboza may have also told me about this. I did

---

[86] No one was faster than Tony with his fists. I knew Tony and attended many of his fights. He held a New England boxing title. His punches landed like sledge hammers. The reports on his death indicate that he was shot in the back of the head. Many believe Martorano snuck up behind Tony and shot him. Telling the truth would lessen the tough guy aura Martorano likes to put on. Unless the Massachusetts AG signed off on Martorano's deal, he can still be prosecuted for Tony's murder.

not want him to testify against Jimmy so I killed him.

I also killed Robert Hicks in March 1969. He was going to be a witness against someone. He came to the restaurant and we had a few drinks together. I really didn't like him so I took him out. I shot him in the head.

I killed Herbert Smith, a bouncer at Basin Street. Al Cincotta and Rocco Lamatina ran the Basin Street lounge business at the time. Herbie beat up Stevie Flemmi the night before. So I killed him.

Herbie showed up at 2:00 a.m. in the middle of a snowstorm. There were two other people in the car with him. I didn't get a good look at the other people because they were bundled up. I was a foot away from Herbie when I killed him. I thought there were three men in the car but one turned out to be women. I would not have killed the other person if I had known she was a woman. But then again I couldn't leave any witnesses behind.

I had nothing to do with killing Billy Kearn's girlfriend. If I did, I would remember it even if it was done in the 1930s. If I had killed a single girl, I would admit it. If I didn't, I'd spend the rest of my life in jail. I've got to tell you one thing. Them 1960s and 1970s were tough times.

Around 1974 Stevie Flemmi joined Winter Hill. He had been a fugitive from justice up to that time. When he joined, we began to split things six ways. We started the sports business by identifying independent bookies. We would approach them and tell them to either join Winter Hill or get out of business. Eventually all of the bookies joined Winter Hill or the Mafia. Bulger's part of the operation was to go about and intimidate people. I had the same job. Bulger was intelligent, charming, and scary. I killed several people when I was with Winter Hill. At each killing either Howie Winter, Whitey Bulger, Jimmy Simms or Joe McDonald was present or a combination of them.

Both Winter Hill and the Mafia were in the same business. Because of that we tried to negotiate a co-existence agreement. Me, Howie Winter, and Gerry Angiulo, the local Mafia boss, negotiated the agreement. Under it Winter Hill said it would not hit any of the Mafia people without getting clearance from Angiulo. The Mafia had more people, money and guns. Even so, it's possible, it's probable we could have beaten the Mafia if a war broke out.

When he said this, a smirk crossed his face.

I was involved with Flemmi in killing Eddie Connors. Connors was shooting his mouth off about Spike O'Toole. O'Toole was involved in a deal with me. Connors should not have been talking about it so he had to be killed.

In November 1975 I planned to kill Buddy Leonard. But before I could do it others in South Boston got him. I killed Tommy King. Tommy was talking about killing Boston police officer Eddie Walsh.[87] Tommy and I had been in on some murders together. Bulger wanted to kill Tommy King earlier. I told him not to do it. But when I thought Tommy King would kill Walsh, I had to kill him. I knew that if a cop were killed, that would cause Bulger a lot of trouble in South Boston.

I never knew what they did with Tommy's body until one day when I was driving over the Neponset Bridge with Whitey Bulger, and he said to me, "Tip your hat that's where Tommy is." Tommy's body was recovered near the spot Bulger indicated after I turned state's evidence and began to cooperate.

I killed James Sousa to protect Billy Barnowski. I was in a score with Sousa in the early 1970s. Sousa was selling gold bars. He was connected with Tony Ciulla and Billy Barnowski. They would give Winter Hill a cut of their proceeds. One day Tony Ciulla kidnapped a kid. Some thought Ciulla should be killed. I decided it was better to kill Sousa.

You know back at that time the Mafia was not so strong. I never really hated the Mafia. I just had nothing to do with them. One day Gerry Angiulo was indirectly looking for help and he approached us. He wanted the Notorangelli brothers killed.

---

[87] Eddie Walsh was said to be John Connolly's first cousin but he wasn't. They continually drove around and hung out in bars together. Tommy King was a very tough guy. Street talk was that Bulger was afraid of King and he was hit because he was after Bulger rather than Walsh.

We planned to kill Al Notorangelli in the beginning but by mistake we killed his brother who looked like him.

Al Notorangelli tried to buy himself out of his problem. He went to Howie Winter and to Bulger. They went to see Jerry Angiulo. Al offered to pay $50,000 to save his life. Angiulo took the money and then we killed Al. It was something like that. After the killing, Angiulo gave me $25,000 for expenses and equipment.

I didn't get $50,000 from Angiulo for killing Notorangelli as some people said. Angiulo gave me $50,000 on another matter involving a bet with a bookmaker. We assessed a bookmaker $100,000 for putting out a bad line.[88]

We split that with Gerry Angiulo. The $25,000 I got was for guns and walkie-talkies we needed to kill Notorangelli. We never kept many guns around so the $25,000 was not for the killing but for expenses. It was not a fee for killing.

Flemmi was involved with me in a lot of the murders after May of 1974. We killed Pallidino and Jackson in 1965. From 1969 to 1974 Flemmi was on the lam. Of the 20 murders I committed, aside from Pallidino and Jackson, Flemmi helped me with Smith, Dickson, Barrett, and Douglas. He was not involved with me in the Veranis and Hicks

---

[88] A line is what bookies give to their customers. It consists of the odds on each of the athletic contests that will be played. A bad line is one where the odds are changed to give some people a greater advantage of winning.

murders. In the Notorangelli murder, he provided the machine gun.

Winter Hill was always looking for sources of information in law enforcement. At that time we had some local cops, state cops, a state cop in the attorney general's office,[89] and at one point someone in the FBI who gave us information. We usually paid the cops in cash except for the time we gave Connolly the diamond ring.

I remember it was in the mid-seventies when Whitey Bulger approached me and Howie Winter saying an FBI Agent named Connolly called him and wanted to meet with him. Whitey told us about his planned meeting with Connolly. He knew that if anyone in our gang was seen talking to an FBI agent, he would probably end up dead.[90] We positively agreed that Whitey should meet since we'd be able to get information.

When Whitey returned from the meeting, he told us that Connolly would keep his ear to the grindstone.[91] Connolly would let us know what he could find out. We received information about FBI investigations over a period of time.

---

[89] Schneiderhan worked in the AG's office. Naimovich never worked there.

[90] Stevie, an informant since 1965, never told them or thought he was in danger. It is doubtful Whitey who was first opened in 1971 had to do this. This is pretty much tough guy fiction

[91] He said ear and not nose confusing ground with grindstone.

STEPPING INTO THE MUD

I asked Whitey why Connolly was doing this. Whitey said that Connolly owed his brother Billy a favor. Billy helped him go to college and get into the FBI.[92]   Connolly wanted to return the favor. Connolly said he went to Billy and asked him what he could do. Billy told him to keep Whitey out of trouble. Sometime between 1973 and 1976, probably in the middle of 1976, but before McDonald and Simms went on the lam we decided to give Connolly a gift. We called Connolly Zip. Whitey came to me and said Zip was looking for an anniversary present for his wife. We decided to buy a diamond from Joe McDonald who dealt in hot diamonds and give it to Connolly as thanks for his help. We paid for a two carat diamond in a man's setting that Joe had.

Mary Ann Hockery, Connolly's ex-wife, would testify she married Connolly in 1970. Her engagement ring had a small diamond. She said Connolly gave her a two carat ring in 1976. It was for her graduation from nursing school and not an anniversary present.[93] A

---

[92] This statement produced sensational headlines in the Boston newspapers linking Billy with Whitey.
Again, like much of Martorano's testimony it seems a fiction. Billy had no clout to help Connolly get into the FBI. The Speaker of Congress, John McCormick from South Boston was a friend of Connolly's father. He wrote a letter to J. Edgar Hoover. That is how Connolly get into the FBI.
[93] It's the little things like this, a present for an anniversary rather than a birthday, or help from Speaker McCormick rather than Billy Bulger that show most of Martarano's testimony is false when it relates to things Connolly did with Whitey.

jeweler, Harry H. Solomon, would testify the ring was worth about five thousand dollars at that time.

We gave it to Whitey. I'm aware Whitey wore lots of jewelry and had many girlfriends. I never saw him give the ring to Connolly so I can't say for sure he did. All I can say is he told us he gave it to Connolly and that he said Connolly thanked him. We had other discussion about giving things to Connolly. Bulger and Flemmi always said they took good care of Connolly.

(Connolly at this moment was sitting with his arms tightly crossed across his chest. The side of his mouth slanted sharply downward. He looked as if he was about to become sick.)

I never met Connolly. I never spoke with him.[94] All the information I had about him came from Bulger or Flemmi. They were supposed to get the information from Connolly and not to give any to him.

I was getting information from Dick Schneiderhan, a Massachusetts State Police officer. Others in Winter Hill knew that I was getting information from him because I told them he was

---

[94] Keep this statement in mind. Connolly only dealt with Bulger. Martorano had no direct conversation with Connolly. He can't say from his first hand knowledge that Connolly ever met Bulger. Everything he knows about Connolly is what other people told him. This is hearsay information. We do not know where these other people got their information from or even whether they are just plainly making it up. It is notoriously unreliable. The jury was smart enough to pick up on this.

my source.[95]   I never met Schneiderhan alone. Howie Winter was always with me. Every time we talked with him we left an envelope with cash. He got cash for information. I never gave him any information in return, just cash.   Me and Schneiderhan used real names. I'm not sure if Bulger or Flemmi met Schneiderhan. When I left for Florida, I gave them Schneiderhan's phone number.[96] I first met him with Howie Winter. We called Schneiderhan, Eric.

I knew Richie Castucci. He wasn't a bookie. He was a gambler and involved in other illegal activities. Castucci was involved in past posting bets on race track events. Doing that to Winter Hill wasn't acceptable.   One consequence was you wouldn't get paid.[97]

---

[95] Another lie. Schneiderhan testified at his own trial that he and Stevie were close friends from their teenage years. He highly admired him.

[96] Hardly did Stevie have to get the number from Martorano.   Schneiderhan idolized his boyhood friend Stevie. Martorano was debriefed by the government before the evidence against Schneiderhan was discovered. When it was clear Schneiderhan was Stevie's friend and source, Martorano was stuck with this falsehood. The government went along with it. Probably because of this Martorano wasn't used to testify against Schneiderhan even though he testified that was part of his original deal with the Justice Department. Martorano's lies about this will be used to impeach his testimony at Whitey's trial.

[97] Past posting occurs when a bet is placed with a bookmaker after the results of the race are known. This is what occurred in the movie "The Sting."

STEPPING INTO THE MUD

I don't recall if Castucci ever won big. I know we never borrowed money from the Mafia to pay him. Look! Castucci was not a bookie. He was a swindler. But I'll tell you one thing. He'd never try to swindle Winter Hill.

Castucci met a guy Jack in New York City. Jack was our source to wash gambling money through. We ran many tens of thousands of dollars through him. We owed Jack large amounts of money. We managed to pay him $400,000 over a period of some months shortly before Castucci died. When Castucci died, we still owed him $150,000. Castucci was affiliated with the LCN but he did business with Winter Hill. Yeah, he was with the LCN but they didn't protect him so good.

At the time we were paying off Jack, Joe McDonald and Jimmy Simms, our partners in Winter Hill were hiding out in New York City. They were fugitives from state and federal charges. They were holed up in a rented apartment in Greenwich Village. I paid Jack to get it for me. I paid a year's advanced rent for it. I didn't know at the time that Jack was with the LCN.[98]

One morning Whitey Bulger comes to me and says, "Zip says Joe McDonald's got to move. Richie Castucci told the FBI where the apartment was." When I heard that, I told Joe McDonald to move. Then Whitey and Stevie went to New York to meet with Joe to tell him why he had to move. They also

---

[98] Jack was also an FBI informant working with the New York City FBI.

told him not to tell anyone they got the information from Connolly.

This was within a week of Richie Castucci getting killed. In December 1976 Richie was supposed to deliver money to Jack. I spoke with Whitey, Howie Winter and Stevie Flemmi. We decided to take Richie out. I killed him to solve the problem. We put his body in a sleeping bag, into the trunk of a car, and left the car in Revere.

When Castucci died, we still owed Jack $150,000. Shortly after that, the LCN out of New York City came to collect on the debt. We refused to pay the money because Jack was a rat.[99] Jack gave up the location of the apartment to Richie where McDonald and Simms were hiding. The LCN agreed not to try to collect it. They agreed not to collect it because they couldn't collect it. We said we wouldn't pay. They said all right. After that we never heard another word about it. I didn't learn until later that Jack was an informant.[100]

---

[99] It is doubtful Martorano would have known that at the time.

[100] There is a more probable explanation for Castucci's death and the New York City LCN backing off. Winter Hill killed him so it could keep the $150,000. It then used his death as an excuse for not paying that money. When NY City LCN showed up to collect Winter Hill said it had given the money to Castucci and that whoever killed Castucci took their money. They may have suggested it was the Boston LCN suggesting it was not them because they would never hit a made man. Winter Hill would not care if Castucci was giving up Simms and McDonald. If they were caught there would be two less mouths at the

STEPPING INTO THE MUD

Around that time we learned from Connolly that Howie Winter was being investigated by the Feds for trying to extort money from people who owned pinball machines. Some guy complained to the FBI that Howie was moving in on his operation. I told Howie to straighten the problem out. Howie dragged his feet and got indicted.

In 1977 or 1978 I was indicted and did time for setting up a gaming operation that took bets on sporting events. I received assistance on that case from Dick Schneiderhan of the Massachusetts State Police.[101] I pled guilty before Judge Wolf to the

---

trough.

[101] This surprised me. I knew the cops who did this investigation. I believed it was an extremely successful operation done by Plymouth DA Bill O'Malley. It resulted in Martorano's incarceration and the destruction of his operation. I knew it was not compromised. To check my recollection I called Detective Peter Gallagher who worked the investigation and participated in the raids. He told me it wasn't compromised in any manner. They found everyone where they were supposed to be. Naimovich was also part of the investigation again showing he was not a source for these people. If Martorano were getting information from Schneiderhan, Naimovich could not have run an office nor would Martorano have been arrested with contraband. I thought Martorano, as Peter Gallagher would say, was not letting "the truth stand in the way of a good story."

But it turned out Schneiderhan did give out information but it was after the raids. Schneiderhan did not know about the wiretap. But after the arrests and before the trial, Schneiderhan learned that the officers monitoring the wiretap had listened to conversations

race fixing case. It involved fixing horse races all over the country. I knew about the investigation because it was common knowledge that Tony Ciullo was talking to the FBI about the case. I didn't know when I knew it. I knew Connolly went to Jeremiah O'Sullivan and kept Bulger and Flemmi out of the indictment.

This happened shortly after I got out of jail in 1978 after serving three months for my conviction on the sports bookmaking case out of Plymouth. Whitey told me that about 20 people, including me, were to be indicted in the race fixing case. We were all Winter Hill people and associates. When the indictment was coming down, Whitey told me about it. When I learned that, I went on the lam fleeing to Florida.

Before I took off, I had a conversation with Whitey and Stevie. They told me I'd be a fugitive for six months and then I could come in and get a separate trial. I headed for Florida. I stayed there 16 ½ years until the Massachusetts State Police arrested me for the RICO charge in January 1995.

While in Florida, I was in contact with Winter Hill and considered myself to be partners with Stevie and Whitey. Mostly I talked with Stevie. He and Whitey kept telling me not to come back north. I think it's probably because they knew I would find out about them being informants. After I fled I

---

outside the times allowed by the warrant. He passed that information on to Stevie who gave it to Martorano who was able to use it to gain a lighter sentence for himself.

only met with Whitey twice. Once after my father died and one other time. I met Stevie in New York at least ten times to pick up money from him. I always tried to find out how much he was holding for me but I never could. I learned they had been cheating me but there was nothing I could do.

I was supposed to get one-third of the Winter Hill operation. Before the 1990s I received whatever I needed probably around $10,000 a month. I never really knew where the money was coming from. Stevie told me they were ripping off drug dealers. After the 1990s I received less and less. I gave $20,000 toward buying the Marconi Club. When it was sold, all I got back was my $20,000. I figured they sold it for a lot more so I should have received more but I didn't. I couldn't monitor the profits from Florida.

Look, I was a fugitive so in a sense anything I got I was thankful for. Money would be sent to me by mail or friends would bring it down. George Kaufman would mail it to me. John Callahan, a friend of my brother, Jimmy, and Howie Winter, would get money from my friend George Kaufman and bring it to me in Florida.

Whitey and Stevie never liked John Callahan. They thought he was a plant and a suspicious character. But I liked him. I stayed at his apartment a few times and even used it when Callahan was not around. One time Callahan brought me $25,000 in cash.

Martorano is leaning back into the witness chair appearing very relaxed. He speaks in a deep unemotional voice as if chatting with some close friends over a cup of coffee at a diner. Sometimes he would clasp his hands together. When the court took a recess, Martorano looked over to some of the police officers in the front row and gave a big smile to them. They returned the greeting.

When I first knew Callahan, he was president of World Jai Alai in Miami. But a new owner, Roger Wheeler, took over that business. He was from Tulsa, Oklahoma. After that Callahan either resigned or was fired from the business.

One day Callahan came to me and told me that he and his friend, Richie Donovan, were going to buy World Jai Alai from Wheeler. They were going to offer between sixty and ninety million for it. Once he owned it, Callahan said he would give Winter Hill ten thousand dollars a week for protection. I spoke to Stevie Flemmi about this. He was in favor of doing it. Winter Hill would protect him from any wise guys bothering him. I met with Callahan, Donovan and Paul Rico, the ex-FBI agent from Boston, to talk this over. Rico had retired and was working for World Jai Alai.[102]

Wheeler refused their offer to buy the business. He said he was more interested in prosecuting the

---

[102] Paul Rico had been an FBI agent in Boston for many years. He was the partner of Agent Dennis Condon. They first developed Flemmi and Bulger as informants and arranged for the turnover to Connolly. They framed four men for murders they did not commit to protect an informant. Rico was indicted for Wheeler's murder. He died in jail in Oklahoma while waiting trial.

people who were stealing from the company. Callahan told me that he and his friends were worried about being indicted.

Callahan asked me to kill Wheeler. He knew of my reputation for being ruthless. I'm not one to be reckoned with. Callahan said after Wheeler was dead he planned to make another offer for the World Jai Alai business.

At first I said no. Wheeler was a legitimate guy and it's more difficult to kill such a person. Callahan then asked me to talk to Stevie who said it was all right with them if I killed Wheeler. Stevie told me to ask Joe McDonald to help and get some help from Paul Rico. McDonald was also a fugitive and was living in Florida since 1976. I had been in touch with him off and on.

Rico urged us to do it. Rico asked Flemmi to have me do it as a favor. McDonald agreed to help me because he said he owed Rico a favor because Rico did Buddy McLean,[103] McDonald's friend, a favor when he was in Boston.

We told Callahan we would kill Wheeler if Callahan defrayed expenses. I received $50,000 for our expenses and for the killing. Callahan gave me a slip of paper with Paul Rico's handwriting on it with all the information about Wheeler.

Of course, I was interested in killing Wheeler for my own benefit. If Callahan could buy the place, I'd get the original ten thousand dollars a

---

[103] McLean was the original leader of the Winter Hill group.

week deal. McDonald and I flew to Oklahoma City where we rented a car and drove to Tulsa. We had no weapon with us but had made arrangements with Stevie for a gun to be sent in a package to the bus station. I picked up the gun and went to the golf course where I shot Wheeler who was sitting in his car. [104]

After I got back to Florida I let Whitey and Stevie know I had carried out the murder. They probably already knew about it. I passed the message through Stevie. I remember I complained to them that the gun they sent me in the package

[104] Wheeler's son who was 29 years old when his father was killed gave very emotional testimony before the congressional hearing in December 2002. He told how his father had been shot in the face and of his dread in going to the funeral parlor with his mother and seeing her kiss his father on the face while fearing the makeup would fall off. He put a human face on the tragedy brought about by Martorano to his family. One could only think of the many other families that likewise suffered by his depraved actions and think of how little consequences Martorano received for the suffering he has caused. I thought an effective way to rebut the testimony of these killers is to bring the families of the victims to the court room during to the trial to tell of their sufferings. Other than that we're just listening to names and cannot possibly understand the enormity of a murder. To paraphrase the cruel Joseph Stalin: "One death's a tragedy, twenty's a statistic."

Martorano would have a book written about his killings. He cooperated with the author. It would be nice if any profits from this went to the estates of the victims rather into the pockets of the author or the aggrandizement of Martorano.

exploded when I shot Wheeler. I was told one of Bulger's men prepared the package.

From my days with Winter Hill I knew Brian Halloran. He was a cocaine user. Sometime in 1975 to 1977 Peter Pallata was involved in an extortion. Because of that extortion my brother Jimmy was indicted. Halloran was a co-defendant. Pallata cooperated against Jimmy who was convicted. Halloran was acquitted. I blamed Halloran for my brother's problems. I didn't hate him. I just didn't like him. But I had nothing to do with his murder.

After Halloran got killed Stevie called me. They were concerned that Callahan had been hanging around with Halloran. Whitey sent me a message through Stevie that Callahan might have been wearing a wire. I knew I had talked with Callahan on the phone. He had my personal phone number. But I didn't remember talking to Callahan about Halloran's murder.

They wanted to meet with me. We met about two to four weeks after Halloran's murder at the Marriott at LaGuardia airport. It wasn't unusual for me to go to New York. I had been traveling at times back and forth from Florida to New York to meet my family. I would stay in a trailer park in New Jersey.

At the Marriot I had a room under an alias. The purpose of the meeting was to bring me up to date on Halloran. Bulger did most of the talking. He said Callahan had been hanging around with Halloran and told Halloran I had killed Wheeler.

Halloran had gone to the FBI with it. Zip told them what Halloran had been talking about. So they had to kill Halloran.

They said that Zip said that the FBI would want to talk to Callahan. They would put a lot of pressure on him. Zip said Callahan couldn't handle the pressure and he wouldn't hold up. They spent time trying to convince me Callahan would fold under pressure from the FBI. They knew Callahan was a friend of mine. They told me if I didn't kill him, we would all spend the rest of our lives in prison.

I wanted to protect myself. They had to convince me to do it but it did not take long. They told me to kill him in Florida because they were still getting a lot of heat in Boston because of Halloran's murder. They kept emphasizing that I had to get to Callahan before the FBI did.

I kept calling Callahan on the telephone trying to convince him to come down to Florida. I didn't think he would be suspicious because he had visited me before. We had plans to make Callahan's murder looked like a robbery. We would take his watch and leave it in the Cuban section of Miami. On the 1st or 2nd of August 1982 I met Callahan at Fort Lauderdale Airport with Joe McDonald. Callahan got into a van with me and as soon as I could, I shot him in the head. McDonald followed me in Callahan's car. The next morning we transferred the body to the trunk of his car and brought it to the Miami airport. McDonald again followed me. Later Stevie and I went to meet Paul

Rico. We asked him what had happened with regard to the sale of World Jai Alai. Rico said nothing was going on.

I continued to live in Florida after Callahan's murder in 1982. I had a bookmaking business I operated in Boston. Neither Bulger nor Flemmi wanted part of that because they would have had to pay if they lost. My bookmaking business was run by Joey Yerardi.

It was expensive to live as a fugitive. I took trips to Hawaii several times. If anyone wanted me, they would leave a number and I would call them back. In 1983 Flemmi told me that Zip called him to say I had been spotted in Florida and I should move. I did move. I moved again after I killed Callahan. I had other people who helped me out and gave me false identifications that I used. I never knew Stevie Flemmi was passing information on to the FBI.

I had a friend, Jeffrey Jenkins, who used to launder money for me. I purchased a few cars from Jenkins, somewhere between 10 and 20. All the cars had dealer plates on them. I purchased them but never was listed as the owner.

As a fugitive, all one can do is lie. I used a lot of aliases and had false identifications. I usually paid for things in cash. The only way I could survive was to lie and pay cash. I was able to get my Florida license because I had a false identification that was made up from a stolen Massachusetts Registry of Motor Vehicles license machine. I had family and friends in the Boston area holding cash for me. I also had some friends in Hawaii

When I was arrested in 1995, I was incarcerated in the Plymouth House of Corrections. I had contact with a bookmaker named O'Brien who was in there for contempt. He refused to disclose who he was paying rent to in order to run his gaming operation. It was to Flemmi. I had done my bookmaking business with O'Brien. Flemmi wanted me to test the waters. We wanted to see if O'Brien would be a problem. It turned out he wasn't.

Stevie Flemmi may have suggested to O'Brien that he purge himself of contempt by testifying. He told him that rather than telling the truth he should say that he was paying rent to George Kaufman who at the time was dying. Kaufman was a friend. I did illegal business with him. He kept my bankroll. There would be no way the grand jury would know O'Brien was lying. I wanted O'Brien to lie to the grand jury because I did not want O'Brien to give information against me. It's possible, even probable, I told O'Brien to lie to the grand jury. I just don't remember.

When I was in jail in Plymouth, Kevin Weeks came to meet with me. I didn't know Weeks prior to that time. I was in that Plymouth jail when I first learned that Flemmi was an informant. I saw reports filed by Connolly stating that Bulger and Flemmi had been informing on everyone they could including the Mafia and their friends.

When I first learned this, I was disgusted, furious, and very upset. I wanted to kill Flemmi.[105] I could have done it if I wanted even though we were both in jail. I didn't have a gun but I didn't need one. But instead I decided to settle the problem legally and that's what I'm doing now. All the information I got from Bulger and Flemmi over the years that they said came from Connolly proved to be accurate.

---

[105] Martorano's reaction to learning Flemmi was an informant is what one would expect. He felt absolutely betrayed and wanted to kill him. Salemme, who will testify later, will have a strange, different reaction.

CHAPTER FIVE

AN OFFICE OF MUDDLEHEADS

Martorano started off the fifth day of the trial, Tuesday, May 14, 2002, finishing up his cross-examination. The government then produced six witnesses to add to or corroborate parts of Morris's or Martorano's testimony.

Two of them, Connolly's ex-wife and a jeweler testified about her receiving a ring as a present and the value of the ring.

The other four witnesses were all connected to the FBI. One, Susan Ratyna, an administrator with the FBI, testified about the FBI forms called 209 and explained some of the codes used on them. She repeated Morris's testimony that informant files were located in a separate room while all the rest of the files were kept in a rotor file in the main area. The rotor file contained thousands of documents that all the staff could access. Information in the rotor file from an informant did not include an informant's name, only his or her identification number. Testimony from the other three witnesses, all FBI agents, follows.

JOHN BEBBINGTON

FBI AGENT

My name is John Bebbington. I am a special agent in the FBI out of Washington, DC. I had been working in the Washington field division when I was temporarily assigned in 1999 with agents from other parts of the country to this investigation.

When Martorano told us he murdered Richard Castucci because he learned he was an informant, I checked our records to see if we listed Richard Castucci as an FBI informant. The records showed the following:

On January 30, 1970, he was designated a top echelon informant. The records show Castucci provided information to FBI Special Agent Tom Daly.[106]

Daly filed a report on September 30, 1976, in which he stated he received information on September 16 and 28 from Castucci, identifying him by his informant number. Daly wrote that Castucci had information from an excellent source who said that Jimmy Simms and Joe McDonald were living in Manhattan and that the people in the Winter Hill group were supporting them. Daly cautioned that Castucci's information is extremely singular. That meant that Castucci's identity could be easily discovered just from the information he provided. Daly noted because of this care should be taken in disseminating it. The report on Castucci's information was distributed to the Winter, Simms, D'Agostino, and general intelligence files.[107]

---

[106] Daly was the agent on the race fix case where Bulger and Flemmi were pulled from the indictment. He will testify for the defense.

[107] Note the haphazard manner these singular

AN OFFICE OF MUDDLEHEADS

Daly filed another report a little over a month later on November 4, 1976 again identifying Castucci by informant number and stating the information is singular. Daly reported that Simms and McDonald were in an apartment outside Greenwich Village in New York City which they had rented for six months for $1000 per month. This information was distributed to the Winter and Simms files.

On November 11, 1976, a Teletype was sent from the Boston FBI to the New York City FBI saying Boston's source has information that McDonald and Simms are in the vicinity of Christopher and Gay Streets and that they are getting assistance from the Irish gang. It also said that Boston's source will remain in contact with contacts in New York and Boston.

On November 26, 1976, a Teletype went from New York FBI to Boston FBI stating that in the spring of 1976 the New York source had been requested by Flemmi, Martorano, and Howie Winter to rent an apartment for McDonald and Simms.[108]   It went on to state that extensive

---

reports relating to a specific topic were placed helter-skelter in other files. The 9/30 to Winter, Simms, D'Agostino and general intelligence; the 11/4 to Winter and Simms; early December to McDonald and Simms; and on December 27 to Simms, McDonald and Donovan. I wondered why there was no "Winter Hill" file or why no copies went to Whitey's or Stevie's file. It is a sloppy system designed for muddleheads.

141

surveillance of the apartment disclosed no individual resembling either McDonald or Simms

A November message went from Boston to Washington, DC. It stated that an intensive investigation by the New York FBI had not placed McDonald or Simms at the residence. It added that the New York FBI office said it would maintain the surveillance.

In December Agent Daley filed a third report that related to information he received from December 2 to December 10 containing the cautionary statement that the information is singular. He stated Castucci, identified by number, said the apartment was empty at that time but he expected to hear from his source whether Simms and McDonald are in the New York City area or have left. It was distributed to the McDonald and Simms files.

On December 27, 1976, Daly distributed a final report to the Simms, McDonald, and Donovan files stating that according to sources in New York and Winter Hill, McDonald and Simms will be returning to the apartment after the holiday. The report also stated that the apartment is located at the corner of Christopher and Gay streets and that

---

[108] The New York source is "Jack" who was washing money for Winter Hill through Castucci according to Martorano. He was an FBI informant for the NY FBI office. Sometimes it seems all the big criminals are FBI informants.

someone else wanted to use the apartment while it was vacant but Bulger said no.[109]

I next found a report of a meeting that was held on January 3, 1977, two days after Castucci's body was found. It was a weekly intelligence report to Gerry McDowell, the then head of the Federal Strike Force. It said Connolly doesn't think the Winter Hill people did the Castucci hit. Connolly said it is not their MO.[110] He suggested it may have been a rip off by an independent bookie.[111] The report notes other people speculated that Castucci had been killed for past-posting bets, for borrowing heavily, for being involved in drug dealings, and or it was a rip off.

The next relevant document that I found was a Teletype dated January 4, 1977. It said Richard

---

[109] These reports present the picture of one hand not knowing what the other hand is doing. FBI New York's source has actually rented the apartment for Simms and McDonald but Daly's reports show an ongoing attempt to find out the location of the apartment. FBI New York surveillance never showed McDonald or Simms there.

[110] MO, of course refers to modus operandi or method of operation. Every kid knows that from the cops and robber movies. Twenty-nine year FBI veteran Agent Thomas Daly who testified for the defense initially said he did not know what MO meant. It was hard to listen to such answers.

[111] Connolly was repeating the Winter Hill line which as I previously suggested was that Castucci had been paid the $150,000 and then had been killed (ripped off). It saved them the money and retribution from the New York City LCN.

AN OFFICE OF MUDDLEHEADS

Castucci was murdered on December 29 by someone who he knew well who shot him at close range. It went on to say the Bureau is sure his killing had nothing to do with his relationship to the FBI in Boston.[112]

I found other reports. One was dated January 3, 1977. This report was an insert to a 209. It said Castucci introduced Bulger to Jack, a New York Bookie. Another report showed that Castucci's wife tried to sell his share in a lounge to Angiulo. Then we have a report that someone talked to Howie Winter. He said he had not seen McDonald for two or three days. The reports show the FBI had multiple sources who were giving it information to track down McDonald and Simms.

NICHOLAS GIANTURCO

RETIRED FBI AGENT

Nicholas Gianturco is of short stature. He has a classic movie-type Italian appearance. He looks like he'd

---

[112] At the meeting the day before the January 4 teletype law enforcement officials speculated on the reasons for Castucci's murder. None thought it may have been because he was set up by Winter Hill to avoid paying money owed to the NY City LCN. They were at a loss to figure out the reason. Yet it didn't stop the FBI from sending a Teletype to Washington clearing itself of any involvement in his murder. Ironically over twenty five years later it sought to implicate itself or at least its Agent Connolly in his murder.

AN OFFICE OF MUDDLEHEADS

be at home in the Corlione household or a staple in the
Soprano's series. He appears to be in his late 50s. He
wears a white shirt, blue tie with red stripes, and an FBI
looking suit. Leonard Boyle conducts his examination.

My name is Nicholas Gianturco. I am a retired
FBI agent. I worked in Boston from 1977 to 1993
and was assigned to the organized crime squad. I
worked with Connolly over the years. I considered
him to be a friend. In March 1979 I had finished an
undercover assignment when Connolly came up to
me and said that Bulger and Flemmi wanted to
meet with me.

We met at my home in Peabody. We talked
about the undercover case that I had just finished. I
met with them in June or July 1979 and probably 4
or 5 more times after that. At one point after
Connolly asked me I became an alternate agent for
Flemmi. An alternate agent is available for an
informant to contact in an emergency. I met
Flemmi once a year. I never met him alone nor
spoke privately to him. If he had to reach me for
any reason, he would go through Connolly. I
didn't know Bulger's alternate agent.

I met three times at my house with them and
once at Flemmi's mother's house. Each time it was
over dinner. These were social meetings. No
business was transacted. Bulger was a bright
person, charming, well-read, and well-versed on
things. Flemmi was more quiet, fairly intelligent
and well-read.

AN OFFICE OF MUDDLEHEADS

What we sought to do was to minimize the risks by meeting at someone's home. There's no perfect place to meet. We used the homes for the dinners because it was easier not to be spotted. It's better to have three people in one car and not in four cars going to a location. These were individuals everyone was chasing and were well known.[113]

Bulger and Flemmi always brought wine. I received Christmas gifts from them such as cognac, a statue, and a briefcase. The first time I met them they gave me a wooden truck. I never received the gifts directly from Bulger or Flemmi. They were always conveyed back and forth through Connolly.

I never received any gifts through John Morris. They never asked for anything in return for the gifts. At the time I was exchanging gifts with them they were informants. I didn't think that exchanging Christmas gifts was a major event. I never received cash nor asked for cash. Taking cash would be illegal. It would be a bribe. There were no strict restrictions in the FBI against this.[114]

---

[113] Gianturco attempting to justify these home dinners admits knowing that Whitey and Stevie were top level criminals sought after by other law enforcement agencies saying "everyone was chasing" them. It doesn't bother him that he is protecting them, socializing with them and accepting gifts from them.

[114] Gianturco suggests it's all right for FBI agents to take gifts from gangsters as long as it is not money. It's all right to take a $5000 ring as long as it isn't cash. There's the story of a rich man saying to a beautiful actress, "If I

AN OFFICE OF MUDDLEHEADS

A top-level informant is very important and is more difficult to acquire than an ordinary organized crime informant. He deals with a high level of criminal activity and must have an idea of the intent and philosophy of high-level organized crime figures. Sometimes a regular informant can be moved up to become a top echelon informant.

The investigation of the LCN was the number one priority mandate from the Attorney General's office. In the 1980s when an agent was evaluated, one-third of the rating was based on the agent's interaction with informants. It is critically important to develop trust with the informant. You get more information if the informant is treated with respect. You are asking a lot of a person. He could be killed. You need to protect the safety of the informant and have a good relationship with him.

All informants have a code name and number. These are given to protect their security. When they receive money or make a call or are written about, their code name is used to protect their identity. Informants do not always tell you the

---

offer you a million dollars, will you sleep with me?" She consents. He then says, "What if I offer you ten dollars?" She reddens and retorts, "What do you think I am?" He replied, "We've already established that. Now we're just determining the price." Once an FBI agent takes an unreported gift from a gangster, we've already determined what his is.

truth. You never get the 100% truth from informants.

You want to corroborate what information informants give you. They can give you bad information either intentionally or unintentionally. It is important that an agent not get too close to an informant. If informants are involved in crime they are supposed to be closed down.[115] Informants are critical to the success of an investigation. You need them for affidavits if you plan to do wiretaps and capture organized crime figures.

Bulger's and Flemmi's contribution to the Boston office was significant to its investigation of the Mafia. They were top echelon informants. The Boston FBI did not have a lot of top echelon informants. Connolly not only had Bulger and Flemmi as informants, but many others beyond them.

GERALD A. MONTANARI

RETIRED FBI AGENT

He is dressed in a brown suit, He is tall and distinguished appearing with a square jaw which gives him somewhat of a bulldog-like aspect. His gray hair is nicely groomed. Unlike Gianturco, he looks and carries

---

[115] Gianturco said this with a straight face while at the same time telling us everyone was chasing after his informants.

AN OFFICE OF MUDDLEHEADS

himself like the Hollywood portrayal of a FBI special agent..

My name is Gerald A. Montanari. I am a retired FBI agent. I was in the FBI from 1968 through 1998. I came to Boston in June of 1978. I spent my time in the C2 squad. Connolly was on the C3 squad it seems like forever. I never worked with Connolly. I would see him at the office and nod to him.

In early 1982 my partner in the FBI office was Agent Leo Brunnick. Brunnick died in August, 1996. In January 1982 Brian Halloran became our informant. Halloran was a mid-level strong-arm type of gangster who worked with Winter Hill. He had an extensive record. It included bank robbery, extortion, and other crimes of violence. He told us he had participated in murders and he would tell us about his murders if he could work out a deal.

Before he came to us he had two or three attempts made on his life. He was under indictment for the murder of George Pappas in Suffolk County. He told us he had several enemies on the street.

He wanted to give us information about a businessman named Wheeler who was murdered in Tulsa, Oklahoma. We interviewed Halloran at length. He sought protection and our help with the pending murder charge.

Halloran told us that in January 1981 John Callahan called him to come to his apartment at Commercial Wharf. When he got there, Whitey

Bulger and Stevie Flemmi were also there. During the course of the meeting Callahan said that Roger Wheeler, the new owner of World Jai Alai in Miami, had uncovered some improprieties in the records of that business. Wheeler fired some of Callahan's people and replaced them with his own people. Callahan feared he was going to get caught and would end up doing time. A million dollars or more was missing. Callahan wanted Halloran to kill Wheeler.

Halloran said Callahan also told him that Paul Rico, a former FBI agent in Boston, would help set it up. Callahan bragged that Rico was in his employ and Rico would find out Wheeler's habits. Callahan said John Martorano would also be involved.

Halloran told us Callahan did most of the talking. Halloran never attributed anything directly to Bulger but would say Whitey and Stevie said something rather than attribute the statement to one or the other. He did say that Flemmi expressed a concern that if the police were called in their people may not stand up.

Halloran said he offered an alternative plan as to how to take out Wheeler. Neither Bulger nor Flemmi seemed to like it. They said they would get back to him. Two weeks later Callahan called Halloran and asked him to come to his office. This was located downstairs on Commercial Wharf underneath his apartment. Callahan gave him $20,000 in $100 dollar bills. He told him that Bulger and Flemmi talked it over and decided not to involve him in the matter.

Shortly after Wheeler's murder on March 27, 1981, Halloran ran into Callahan at a bar in Boston. Callahan told him "Johnny had done it" implicating Martorano in Wheeler's slaying. He said Flemmi was the driver of the car and Bulger was in a back up car. He told him a witness had seen Martorano run away from Wheeler's car after he shot him and get into the getaway car. He said Martorano was wearing a baseball cap, sunglasses and a fake mustache. Brunnick wrote up a report about this on January 8, 1982.

Halloran and Jackie Salemme had been indicted for the murder of George Pappas. Halloran denied he killed Pappas. He said he wanted physical protection because about 2 or 3 attempts had been made on his life by Winter Hill before he walked into our FBI office to be debriefed. He said Richie Ford, a Winter Hill associate, shot at him. Patrick Nee of Winter Hill was trying to set him up to be killed. He said the LCN also posed a threat to him because Jackie Salemme was the brother of the LCN's Frankie Salemme. He did not mention any specific threat but he was concerned about Salemme. Halloran also mentioned Connolly but I don't recall what he said about him.[116]

---

[116] Apparently he filed no report about what Halloran said about Connolly. FBI agents seem to have memory failures when asked to remember something an

AN OFFICE OF MUDDLEHEADS

Halloran told us that if Bulger or Flemmi knew he was cooperating, they would go to any length to kill him. I knew that Bulger and Flemmi were FBI informants. I was aware that Connolly was their handler.[117]

On April 28, 1982, a document was filed that mentioned certain people who were looking for Halloran, including Bulger and Flemmi. On May 11, 1982, Halloran told Brunnick that he heard that Jimmy Flynn was looking around for him. Halloran had previously provided information to the FBI for a search warrant against Flynn.

We wanted to corroborate what Halloran was telling us. We developed a plan to target Callahan to get a case against him. This involved putting a wire on Halloran and having him talk generally with Callahan about other crimes he was involved

---

informant tells about another FBI agent even though in the normal course of things it would seem that would be the thing you would most remember. We'll see this later when the FBI interviews Joe Murray for the precise purpose of finding out what he knew about Connolly taking money for leaking information and nothing about it was in the report.

[117] According to *Black Mass*, O'Neill's and Lehr's book, Halloran became quite upset during his debriefing when he learned that Bulger was an FBI informant. This makes no sense. There is no reason to believe either Brunnick or Montanari would disclose that information to Halloran. O'Neill and Lehr depended upon Morris for their information. Morris's had no problem defaming his fellow agents by suggesting they were also releasing names of informants to other informants.

in.   If we acquired enough incriminatory information, we would squeeze Callahan for information on the Wheeler murder.   Halloran wouldn't wear a wire against Bulger or Flemmi because he thought Flemmi was out to kill him.

Halloran wore a wire three times against Callahan and two or three times against other people. [118]   We summarized these recordings. Some may have been made over the telephone. Most were general conversations that were not very productive.   We did not get the results we hoped for even though he met with Callahan two or three times.   Halloran was not able to engage Callahan in any talk about criminal activities.   He thought Callahan was avoiding him.

John Morris was aware of Halloran's cooperation because Brunnick spoke to him to find out what he knew about Halloran.   I suppose that

---

[118] Unfortunately for Brunnick and Montanari everyone in Boston except the nuns at St. Clair's convent and the kids at the Home for Little Wanderers knew Halloran was wired. Morris told Connolly who told Bulger and Flemmi.   Agent Daly and other agents filed reports saying the word on the street was he was cooperating.   It seems strange the agents didn't tell their fellow agents who had a wire on him.   Brunnick and Montanari should have figured this out especially since Callahan tried to avoid Halloran and none of the expected information was obtained.   It may have been that Halloran was double-crossing the FBI by telling the people he was speaking to that he was wired.   He wanted the FBI's help but did not want to hurt his friends.

a number of people knew Halloran was talking to the FBI. Let's see, Agents Morris, Brunnick, Fitzpatrick, Sarhatt, and I knew, as did Jeremiah O'Sullivan, the Strike Force chief, and Detective Bob Hudson of the Boston police. Tom Mundy, the Suffolk assistant district attorney, would have known because we would have needed help from Mundy to get him into the program.

Whenever Halloran would wear the wire, we would have other agents provide security for him. These agents, members of my squad and of Morris's squad, would also know of his cooperation. They may not have known the specific information that was being given out. The people in headquarters in Washington, DC would know what was going on. Also, Halloran told us his lawyer knew he was cooperating.

FBI agent Daly filed a report and in it he said that people on the street had seen Halloran talking to the FBI. He stated these people believed he was cooperating with the FBI. After Halloran was killed I learned the word on the street was that he was cooperating. Certain informant reports indicated people believed he was cooperating with the FBI. One report indicated Halloran was cooperating with the state police.[119] I don't recall

---

[119] This may have been from Connolly. His MO was always to foment trouble against the Massachusetts State Police. He filed one report trying to protect Whitey saying that a state police colonel did not like the FBI which served its purpose. The FBI's ire turned toward the colonel

specifically what these informants told the other agents about the word on the street nor whose informants they were.[120]

After receiving the information from Halloran about the Wheeler murder I checked our office's files to see if anything about it had been reported. I saw that an inquiry came from Oklahoma the previous summer because Callahan had worked at World Jai Alai. It was a request that Callahan be interviewed. The request went to Supervisor Morris who had assigned it to Connolly. The matter was in a closed status.

I re-opened it. At that time we had no supervisor so I went to ASAC Bob Fitzpatrick. We wrote a 302 concerning our interview with Halloran for Fitzpatrick. In the 302 we did not identify Halloran by name. We decided to treat him as an informant so we gave him a number. Today we would call Halloran a cooperating witness.

I did not put the file on the rotor file that is available to all the personnel. I kept it in Fitzpatrick's office. After Halloran's murder we contacted the Oklahoma City FBI office to determine the details of Wheeler's murder. We

---

and away from Whitey. He filed a report saying Halloran was hit because he was a state police informant.

[120] I didn't understand why he did not have this material in court with him. The FBI has great difficulty with openness like other secret societies.

spoke with agent Ron West. The Tulsa case agent was Bob Mitendi.[121]

Halloran wanted to enter the witness protection program. Before a person is admitted to that program you must see if a threat exists to the person's life. We did a threat assessment on Halloran. We concluded there would be a continuing threat to his life which would allow him to be admitted to the program. As part of the assessment, Brunnick asked Agent Morris to what degree he thought Halloran was threatened.

Morris agreed he was in danger. Yet Halloran was not admitted into the program.[122] All Brunnick and I could do was put him in a secure location outside of the city. We told him to stay at that location, not to tell anyone about it, and to stay out of the City of Boston. He was there from mid-January until the day he died.

The week before he died we had a problem with him. He told his attorney he had been

---

[121] Montanari's actions in hiding the file show that back in 1982 he suspected there was a problem in the Boston FBI office. ASAC Fitzpatrick concurred. He was obviously keeping the file from Connolly. Strangely believing Connolly was a cancer in the house he did nothing about it.

[122] AUSA O'Sullivan testified he was not admitted because Tom Mundy, the first assistant in Suffolk County, who was prosecuting Halloran for the Pappas murder, refused to cooperate with him. Mundy, a prosecutor's prosecutor, died a young man. The truth here is elusive since O'Sullivan offered other explanations at other times.

working with the FBI. He resisted taking a lie detector test. He was waffling about going into the witness protection program.

On the day he was killed, May 11,1982, I took a call at my office from Halloran. We did not know where the call had come from. Later that afternoon at about 3 or 4 Brunnick called him back. He told us that he was in Boston. This bothered us. After he died we learned that the call came from a particular establishment on Northern Avenue.

During that call Halloran did not ask us to take any specific action. In order to bring Halloran back into line, as a reality check you might say, we told him we were done with him. We did not intend to cut our ties with him but we were getting fed up with him. He was running around Boston when he was not supposed to be in the city. We hoped by telling him we were not going to have any further dealings with him we would wake him up to the danger he faced. We wanted him to start getting with the program, to get religion, to begin following our directions and be more serious about cooperating. Because we told him we were cutting our ties with him we did not go to get him out of the bar. Later that night he was murdered.

Connolly never spoke to me about Halloran's cooperation. I did not expect that he would. I did not know he knew about it. He had no need to know about it nor was he supposed to know about it.

AN OFFICE OF MUDDLEHEADS

After Halloran's murder we kept the Wheeler investigation open. We worked with the people from Oklahoma. On May 27, 1982, there was a meeting with ASAC Fitzpatrick, Brunnick, Morris, Connolly and me. We told Connolly that Bulger and Flemmi were targets of our investigation based on Halloran's statement that Bulger and Flemmi were involved in Wheeler's murder. Connolly said he did not believe it.[123] We discussed getting Bulger and Flemmi through Callahan.[124]

At that meeting neither Morris nor Connolly mentioned that prior to Halloran's murder Connolly had alerted Bulger and Flemmi about Halloran's cooperation. I told them the Tulsa police wanted Bulger and Flemmi interviewed. I asked Connolly to arrange a meeting with them.

Because they were targeted we discussed FBI policy that required them to be closed out as informants. ASAC Fitzpatrick or someone above him made the decision not to close them.[125] The

---

[123] The pattern of Connolly rushing to the defense of Whitey and Stevie and his willingness to spread false information to protect them makes it difficult to attribute his actions to naiveté.

[124] Montanari and Brunnick's stated intention to squeeze Callahan and Callahan's death within two months sure should have raised some eyebrows.

[125] Connolly may have gone to great lengths to protect Whitey but he is aided and abetted by many others in the FBI. Montanari is running into a stone wall as he tries to stop the reign of terror. He is bucking the Bureau that wants to protect Whitey and Stevie despite the

AN OFFICE OF MUDDLEHEADS

meeting concluded with the decision that Brunnick and I were required to coordinate our investigation with Bulger and Flemmi through Connolly. I was astonished when we were told to coordinate information that way. They were targets. Why would we want to coordinate our investigation of them with them?[126]

---

probability that they had killed Wheeler and the almost certainty they just killed Halloran. Even after Callahan is killed making their involvement beyond all doubt the FBI will keep them as informants. You can't put all this on Connolly as has been done.

[126] In <u>Black Mass,</u> ASAC Robert Fitzpatrick, who along with Morris cooperated with Lehr and O'Neill in their research for that book, was portrayed as deeply concerned because O'Sullivan was keeping Halloran out of the witness protection program to the extent that Fitzpatrick took the extraordinary step of going over O'Sullivan's head to the U.S Attorney, William Weld, to try to help Halloran. Not only had he gone to Weld, but he had cooperated with Montanari in keeping Halloran's file locked up in his office.

Fitzpatrick having taken these steps attributed to him then one is left to wonder why he did a total about face after Halloran's murder. Rather than allowing Montanari a free hand in investigating the Wheeler murder, Fitzpatrick not only didn't close out Whitey and Stevie who were now targets, but he put them in charge of the investigation into their activities.

Fitzpatrick wrote a book about this in 2011. I searched it looking for the answer. All I found was he had a dismal understanding of what happened in the Boston FBI during that time. He never mentions Montinari or Brenner, rather he steals the credit from them to himself

AN OFFICE OF MUDDLEHEADS

A report setting out this decision went from ASAC Fitzpatrick to SAC Sarhatt. After that Connolly made the arrangements for Bulger and Flemmi to be interviewed. Callahan was murdered on July 31, 1982, about two months after the meeting.[127]

---

saying he flipped Halloran. Inexplicably he doesn't explain why he put Whitey and Stevie in charge of his FBI agents investigating them.

He labels himself as "the FBI agent who fought to bring [Whitey] down" when he actually acted to empower him. He maligns Jeremiah O'Sullivan. He credits himself for taking down Mafia boss Gerry Anguilo when all he did was a ministerial function of serving arrest warrants. The evidence against Anguilo had been wrapped up prior to Fitzpatrick's arrival in Boston by O'Sullivan. I could go on but sadly his book adds little to our knowledge.

[127] I felt Montanari came closest to telling the truth than any other agent who would testify but even he could never escape from the FBI code of not reporting in writing what someone says about a fellow agent. He was welcome little light in a very dark world.

CHAPTER SIX

A MUCKER'S TALE

KEVIN WEEKS

A SMART, TOUGH, VIOLENT WISE GUY

Weeks appears to be in his mid-forties. He has a stocky, bully-boy aspect like a person whose days are spent lifting free weights at an expensive gym. His black hair shading into gray is close cropped. He s wearing a dark shirt and no tie. His voice is deep. He speaks in a soft-spoken matter of fact manner. He seems less arrogant than Martorano, less afraid of associating with the truth and almost believable.

He sits comfortably with his hands loosely clasped. His elbows rest on the arms of the chair. His quiet voice belies his life as a gangster. I'm surprised how relaxed he seems until I again remember testifying pales in comparison to beating and killing people.

He responds like a well trained seal barking out his yeses in agreement to the endless leading questions that AUSA Boyle asks during direct examination. His facility for understanding how to give one word answers vanishes during cross-examination. He gives little speeches in response to Miner's leading questions that could have been answered, like those of Boyle, with a yes or no. In these answers I see the soul of a wise guy hoodlum. But don't for one instance think this is a dumb guy.

At one point after bobbing and weaving his responses, Miner pressed him about a point. He quietly but with an edge responded: "I'll write the names down if you think I am lying." Judge Tauro who rarely interrupts a witness remonstrates with him telling him to answer the question. He does for the next two or three questions. Then Miner asks an important leading question requiring a yes or no answer. If she got the no answer which she expected, she would have made a nice point. But Weeks again rambled on taking away any good she could have gained.

When under examination by Miner, Weeks noticeably keeps his eyes firmly fixed on her. He never once looks away. He eyes her as a cat watching prey ready to pounce. His gaze turns defiant when giving his answers as if daring her to disbelieve him. It is strange that there appears to be no sign of invention or avoidance in his testimony even though in answering her questions by giving speeches that is exactly what he is doing.

My name is Kevin Weeks. I was arrested on November 17, 1999 in South Boston on a federal indictment. I was charged with racketeering. The underlying offenses were money laundering and extortion. The original indictment was only the tip of the iceberg. The government was not aware of many of my other crimes at the time I was indicted.

A little over a month after my arrest on December 20 I made a proffer to the government setting out my criminal activities.[128] Nothing in the proffer could be used against me but it could be used for other investigations. I agreed to testify about my criminal activities in exchange for a deal.

Before I was arrested I had spoken a lot with Stevie Flemmi who was in jail in Plymouth. He told me that if I were charged with a conspiracy offense, I could be convicted on crimes that other people in the conspiracy committed even though I did not do them. That meant I could be charged with murders others had committed.

When I made the proffer, I knew Johnny Martorano was already cooperating with the government. I didn't think he could implicate me in any crimes but I really didn't know what he knew about me or what he was telling the government. I knew that both Bulger and Flemmi could implicate me in murders. But I wasn't really worried about them. I had enough to worry about. The charges I was facing called for me to spend life in prison.

After being arrested I was put in jail for the first time in my life. I didn't mind being in jail when I first got in. It was like being in the Boys' Club. But given the choice I'd rather not spend the rest of my life there. I made the proffer so that I could get a lesser sentence.

---

[128] The people in Southie refer to him as "Two Weeks." That's how long he was in jail before he decided he'd have to talk and give up his good friend Whitey. Weeks will be the one who will most damage Whitey when he comes to trial because of his intimacy with him.

After the proffer, government agents interviewed me. The time between when I gave the proffer to the time I entered into the agreement was seven months. During my negotiations with the government I told them how I had been involved in 5 murders. Later I pleaded guilty to a superseding indictment charging me with those murders. It also charged me with trafficking in narcotics and some additional extortion counts.

I also made an agreement with the Suffolk County authorities and with the Oklahoma and Florida authorities since I had information about the Wheeler homicide and Callahan's murder. I didn't participate in either one but I knew what took place after the fact. Cops from Oklahoma and Florida interviewed me. They said I had no culpability but my lawyer insisted that I get agreements from them. Everyone agreed that the only time I will do in jail will be the time the federal court gives me.

To get my deal I've got to fully cooperate with the Justice Department and to testify truthfully. I'm not concerned if the government is not happy with my testimony. I'm going to tell the truth. Only by telling the truth will I be able to get a lesser sentence than the guidelines call for. If I could avoid spending time in jail, I'd lie. If I were granted immunity, I would confess to killing President Kennedy. I'm only being facetious. I'm committed to telling the truth or not saying anything. I admit I did not tell the truth when first asked about the Rakes case, but I did after the government caught me in the lie.

I expect the sentence that I get will be between 5 to 15 years. The Justice Department is committed to recommending somewhere between those time periods. I don't know the exact recommendation that will be made but I know the Justice Department's recommendation matters greatly with the court. My lawyer can recommend less than five years.

The agreement provides that I'll testify against any persons charged with a crime within three years of July 6, 2001, the date of signing the agreement. There are no limitations on the number of cases in which I'll be required to testify. I'm also scheduled to testify against Richard Schneiderhan and Steven Flemmi.

What I really hope is that I get out of jail at the time I'm sentenced. I'm hoping to do even less than five years in prison as a result of my cooperation. If I get five years with parole I may only have to do 52 months. As part of my cooperation, I helped in recovering bodies for the State Police and DEA. I realize that the final sentence will be up to the judge regardless of what anyone recommends although I can't get more than 20 years. To get the most favorable recommendation I must testify and fully cooperate.

At the time of my arrest my assets were my car, some jewelry and a lottery ticket. Even though my home was in my name, I did not consider it an asset since it belonged to my wife and kids. I did not live there. It was not forfeited.

I had property in New Hampshire with my brother, Jack. In the summer of 1995 I transferred the property to Jack. At that time I was worried I might be indicted but I did not do the transfer because of that. I did it because Jack felt he was being placed in a difficult position between my wife Pam and me because I used to bring girl friends to that property for weekends. It was not forfeited.

My friend Mike Linskey won the lottery. We learned he had a winning ticket. We bought it from him. We didn't extort if from him. With the lottery ticket I receive $119,000 a year before taxes. It now goes into an escrow account. My ex-wife gets 75% of it and I get 25%. The Justice Department did not require me to forfeit it.

I testified in a prior case that I gained no benefit from the lottery. That's true because I didn't have any benefit from the lottery because everyone is suing me. I'll have nothing left when it's over.

My plea agreement with the government states I agreed to forfeit my interest in the South Boston Liquor Mart, the Columbia Wine and Spirit, the Rotary Variety, and some real property on Columbia Road. That's what I agreed to do. But I had no interest in those places to forfeit.

I once went to Boston Police Headquarters with Mr. Bulger. He wanted a firearms identification card so he could have a gun. Mr.

Bulger learned that if he ever was found with a weapon his parole would be violated. Because I was with him, out of the blue, I had my permit to carry a weapon revoked. I gave my guns to a friend in New Hampshire. I did not have to forfeit them because my friend owned them.[129]

I once threatened Janice Connolly. I told her I would throw her body into a landfill. But that was in the heat of the moment. Sometimes I say things to someone like I will kill them but when I cool down I don't intend to do it. But sometimes I mean it. Janice Connolly was my girlfriend. I made the threat to her during a domestic dispute. I had a long-term relationship with her after that.[130]

At one time I had interests in some bars with Mr. Bulger who had a 50% interest in everything I had an interest in. In 1981 I lied during a deposition in a civil suit when I said I was the sole owner of a bar. Mr. Bulger couldn't be put on the

---

[129] The government was so anxious to do a deal with Weeks that he forfeited nothing.

[130] Miner brought out the threat Weeks made to Janice. The prosecutor in an attempt to rehabilitate him brought out that Janice was his girlfriend and it was a domestic dispute. Apparently the prosecutor believed this somehow mitigated Weeks's threat. He seemingly slipped back in time twenty or so years to the days when it was all right to beat up and threaten women as long as they were your property such as a wife or girlfriend. There is little doubt Kevin and his girlfriend maintained a long term relationship after that threat. Her choice was Kevin or the landfill.

license. Mr. Bulger had an interest in the South Boston Liquor Market. I couldn't let anyone know about it because Mr. Bulger had no legal right to be involved. What I was doing was illegal but at the time I was not going to admit it. I didn't take the Fifth Amendment when asked the question because my lawyer told me to answer the questions.[131]

I dealt with another guy from South Boston named Timmy Connolly. I had a conversation with him but I thought that he was wearing a wire. He asked me questions. I gave him answers. I told him that the government had to give him immunity if he didn't say a word. I told him if he got immunity, he was to tell the truth, that he never gave me, Mr. Bulger or Stevie Flemmi any money. That was a lie because we had extorted money from him. But I knew Timmy was wired. I wasn't going to admit on the tape that I had extorted him.

I know how to coach people to lie. Look, if I wasn't concerned Timmy was wired, I wouldn't have spoken to him at all. The only reason I felt that I had to speak with him was I thought he was wired.[132]

---

[131] Weeks throughout his testimony will refer to Bulger as Mr. Bulger or Jim. He never called him Whitey. Apparently Bulger never liked to be called Whitey, although he did refer to himself as Mr. White when he was seeking to reach Morris at Quantico. Persons close to him in Southie used the term Mr. White. This insured they did not slip when in Whitey's presence but also bought into the neighborhood patois.

A MUCKER'S TALE

I was born in 1956 and graduated from South Boston High School in 1974. After graduation, I worked as an aide at the high school and a bouncer at a bar called Flicks. I knew of Mr. Bulger's reputation from the time I was about 13 years old. My older brother told me about him one day when we saw him entering an apartment building. I've been committing crimes since I was 18 years old. I've gotten into hundreds of fights. Yes, sometimes I enjoyed fighting. I became very good at it.[133]

I worked for 6 months at Flicks. Then I worked at Triple O's, a neighborhood bar in South Boston owned by the O'Neil brothers, Kevin, William and Jackie. I was a bouncer and then a manager there. Mr. Bulger would come in on weekends. Stevie Flemmi came in on occasion. Mr. Bulger thought I should get 20% of the Triple O's business. Jackie O'Neil said no. So I left that job and started driving around with Jim Bulger.

In 1979 I went to work for Mr. Bulger. After working with him, I got involved in more universal criminal activity. Jim Bulger was a control person.

---

[132] Miner finds it useful to bring out the occasions when Weeks has lied in the past. She did the same thing with Martorano showing he filed false insurance claims. Her theory is that if they've lied so much in their lives you can't believe a word they said. I assumed the jury would understand that these men who were involved in killing people would also have little difficulty lying anytime but Miner had so little ammunition she fired what she could.

[133] Weeks in his book "Brutal" describes his many fights as a skillful amateur boxer.

He was very disciplined and street smart. He taught me never to talk in cars or in buildings or over the telephone. He said all conversations about business should be outside. He told me to read. He even gave me some books. Some were on the Mafia. They weren't required reading but I read them and discussed them with him. I read a book about Joe Barboza. I read some of the book Underboss but not all of it. I read Murder Machine, that was a good book. But I didn't really learn too much from the books. What I knew was that it was important to plan out your crimes. The idea of committing a crime is getting away with it. I did my extortion in private places.

I carried a pistol. I was Jim Bulger's right hand man. I committed crimes with Mr. Bulger and Stevie Flemmi. In 1980 Jim Bulger was part of Winter Hill and he collected money from dope dealers. When working for Mr. Bulger, I did whatever was asked of me. I beat some people up at times. When we drove around, Jim Bulger always drove. Mr. Bulger would tell me what was going on at Winter Hill and also what he and Flemmi were doing.

Mr. Bulger kept away from the LCN. Neither Stevie Flemmi nor Jim Bulger was afraid of the LCN. They just didn't deal with them. I didn't deliberately stay away from the LCN. I also didn't deal with them. I wasn't intimidated by anyone in my circle. Let's say I had a healthy respect for some people but I wasn't intimidated by them. We always believed that everyone was weaker than we were. What I tried to do was to intimidate in secret as much as possible. Of course I was concerned that people could implicate me.

I never killed a bookmaker. I really didn't deal with bookmakers anyway. That was Mr. Bulger's business. I was concerned with drug dealers. I did think of killing Jackie Cherry but he was a drug dealer not a bookmaker.

As I said, I was involved in five murders. I was there when Bucky Barrett was killed. It was supposed to be a shakedown. We got forty-seven or fifty-seven thousand dollars from him. Jim Bulger and Stevie Flemmi went to the house to get the money. I wasn't there when they counted it because I had to go into town to pick up ten thousand dollars from another guy who owed Barrett money.

I was present when John McIntyre was killed. McIntyre was one of the people on the Valhalla, a gun running ship for the IRA. McIntyre had been associated with many ships aside from the Valhalla. He could have given information about Jim Bulger's involvement in the gun running.

---

[134]Miner brought the McIntyre matter up on cross-examination. It shows the difficulties she faced in representing her client. On one hand she needed to undermine Weeks's credibility by showing his evilness. But in doing this she ends up having her client portrayed as part of the evilness surrounding Whitey. He was giving Whitey information about people who were being killed yet he kept doing it.

Connolly told Mr. Bulger that McIntyre was cooperating with the government. We brought McIntyre to a house. He admitted that he was cooperating. Initially the plan was that McIntyre would go to South America or he would testify to what Mr. Bulger told him to testify to. But in the end Mr. Bulger decided it was best to kill him. He did so because Connolly told him he was an informant.[134]

I knew about the murders of Debby Hussey, Buckie Barrett, and John McIntyre. I was there when they were killed. I knew where they were buried. I led the police to their locations.

When I extorted money, at times I would threaten people with taking their lives unless they paid up. At other times I would just threaten them with a beating. It depended on the person. Some were easy to extort but others took a little more persuasion.

We extorted twenty-five thousand dollars from Ray Slinger. I was there only for backup. I would do anything Mr. Bulger asked me to do. If he wanted me to make my presence known, I would do it. He didn't need me for intimidation since he did it very well by himself. Basically I was with Jim Bulger all the time. So I was there whenever he extorted people.

I was there when he threatened Slinger with his life. We were upstairs over a barroom. There was a story on the street that when Jim Bulger was threatening Slinger, he told me to get a body bag. That wasn't true. Jim Bulger didn't have to say things like that to scare people because he would tell them straight out he was going to kill them. What Jim told me was to get him a bottle of beer. He never said get him a body bag. We were in a barroom. Barrooms don't usually have body bags in them. He sent me downstairs to get a beer.

I got ten thousand dollars from the extortion of Timmy Connolly. My share of the extortion of Michael Salomando was sixty thousand dollars. We got a total of four hundred eighty thousand to six hundred thousand dollars from him. I didn't participate in the extortion of Richard Puccieri. I was outside in the car. Mr. Bulger did it and gave me fifty thousand dollars.

I don't remember anything relating to Shillinger. I don't recognize the name. If he was a bookie, I wouldn't know about it. As I said I didn't do the bookie stuff since that business was established before I came on board. I didn't extort Billy Shea.

I got fifteen hundred a month from drug dealers Paul Moore and Jackie Sherry. Joe Murray gave us money over time. He paid us five hundred thousand dollars as a severance package to be able to leave our grasp. Jim Bulger did the dealings with Murray.

We didn't extort Arthur Intardo. His younger brother had been shot by the Charlestown people. He wanted us to settle the problem. We told him we'd help him out. He paid us sixty five thousand dollars to do this. In the end we just took the money and sat back and watched. The extortion of

Frank LaPere was before my time. I shook Kevin Hayes down.

Bobby Ford ran the South Boston booking office for Jim Bulger. Bobby would keep a percentage of the profits. Bulger would get a percentage.

I had twenty to twenty-five customers in my own loan sharking business. I lent sums between one hundred dollars and twenty five thousand dollars. I charged 2½ to 5 points a week. I dealt directly with these persons. They understood if they did not pay I would hurt them. I never hurt any of my customers. I did get in a fight with one. It wasn't over the money he owed, it was because he said to me, "Go fuck yourself." I knocked the person out. As far as I'm concerned, when someone says that to you, that's as good reason as any to knock the person out.

I was familiar with Connolly. I first met him when Johnny Pretzie was training me to be a boxer.[135] Connolly was hanging around the gym, he seemed friendly enough. I purchased a car from him after Pretzie told me Connolly's car was a good car.

At that time I also worked for the MBTA laying track. I worked from 8:00 in the morning to

---

[135]Pretzie was a South Boston legend. A tough boxer who fought Rocky Marciano and Jake LaMotta, losing to both. As a youngster, I knew of him because he was friendly with my mother's siblings. He got in a bar room beef at age 69 with a thirty something year old who he beat up. His victim went home, sulked and then returned and gunned him down.

4:20 in the afternoon. After work I'd go to the appliance store at the corner of F Street and West Broadway where I'd meet Kevin O'Neil, Jimmy Bulger and Stevie Flemmi. They were usually there in the late afternoon.

We had nicknames for Connolly. We called him Neighbor or Zip. I knew he was an FBI agent. I knew that Jimmy Bulger and Stevie Flemmi had a relationship with Eric, a Mass State Police officer. Eric's real name is Richard Schneiderhan. Bulger and Flemmi gave gifts and cash to the FBI, the state police, and the Boston police. A large number of cops got cash.

Brian Halloran was a friend of Howie Winter.[136] He hung around with some of the Winter Hill people. Mr. Bulger had an interest in Halloran. He always told me he thought he was a bully. I had heard on the street that people had made attempts to kill Halloran. James Flynn, a Charlestown bank robber, was one of them. Jimmy Manville, a South Boston hood from back in the 1960s, was another.

In 1982 Mr. Bulger told me he wanted to embrace Halloran. That meant he wanted to confront him. Jim Bulger told me that Zip told him Halloran was cooperating with the FBI about a murder. I didn't know what murder he was

---

[136]According to my cousins from Southie, Halloran had a great singing voice. He used to croon with the world famous South Boston music group called the "Irish Volunteers." I think my cousin's had some connection with it.

talking about. He said the FBI would not let him into the witness protection program. He said the FBI was divided into two camps, one that believed Halloran and those that didn't.

Jim Bulger said he would flush him out. We looked for him for a month or two. We'd spend the weekends looking for him. We weren't carrying guns. We heard Halloran was hanging around in the bars. We made efforts to find him to confront him with his dealings with the FBI and make him leave town.

One day at the appliance store John Hurley came by. He told us he had just seen Halloran at the Pier Restaurant. Jim Bulger told me to meet him at the Club located on O Street between 2nd and 3rd. I drove to the Club and met him. Jim was looking for some people including Flemmi and Pat Nee to go with him.

Jim then told me he was going to go to Theresa Stanley's house and would meet me back at the Club. A short time later, Jim Bulger pulled up in a blue Chevy. We called it the tow truck because the engine was souped-up. It was a hit car. The car could lay down a smoke screen.

Jim was wearing a light brown wig and a mustache. He told me to drive to Jimmy's Restaurant on Northern Avenue to wait for him. I was driving my sister's Delta '88. I wasn't concerned being in my sister's car because I wasn't going to be involved in the shooting. Her car would be one of a thousand in the area.

I positioned myself near Jimmy's Restaurant. Mr. Bulger pulled up beside me in the tow truck. A person was in the back seat. He waved to me. I really didn't know who it was because he had a ski mask on.[137] I figured it was either Jimmy Mantville or Pat Nee. I never told DEA that I thought Manville had nothing to do with it. The guy in the back seat was in a ski mask so I really didn't know who it was. Manville went around telling people he had something to do with it but I never believed him.

I had never met Halloran but had seen him once or twice from a distance. Jim Bulger pointed him out to me the night he was killed. He was sitting in a booth by the window in the Pier restaurant. Jim gave me a police scanner and a walkie-talkie. He told me to wait there and to radio him when Halloran came out of the restaurant. I was to say "The balloon is in the air." Jim Bulger referred to Halloran as balloon head.

I sat in the car and watched. I saw Halloran come out of the restaurant. He got into the passenger side of a small blue car. Someone else was driving it. Bulger pulled up next to it, passenger door to passenger door. Jim Bulger leaned across to the passenger door. He called to

---

[137] Weeks's answer here is hard to believe. He's obviously protecting a friend. He'd have us think that after the gunning down of Halloran no one again discussed it. I have a good idea who it is. I could tell by the way Weeks talked about him.

177

Halloran, "Brian!" Then he started shooting at him. Then he made a U-turn with the car and started shooting into the car again. The last thing I saw was Jim Bulger still shooting Halloran. I left the area. I went over to the Capitol Market. I later contacted Bulger. He was at Theresa Stanley's. He told me to go get something to eat and he'd contact me later.

As I said, Jim Bulger was looking to embrace Halloran. I didn't realize anything more was going to happen until he showed up in the hit car with a wig and mustache. After Halloran's killing I took the guns to my mother's house where I disassembled them. I then went to Marina Bay and dumped the parts into the ocean.

Later that night we went back and picked up a hubcap. It was not near the shooting but down a way at Atlantic Ave and the Viaduct. We didn't go back to the scene. We then went to Steve Flemmi's mother's house where Jim Bulger and Stevie Flemmi discussed what happened. I watched television in another room. Jim and Stevie often had conversations when I was around that I did not want to participate in.

A short time later I heard that Halloran told one of the cops before he died that James Flynn shot him. I didn't know at the time that the cops had executed a search warrant at Flynn's house two days prior. After I heard that I spoke to Jim Bulger about it at midnight outside his condo. He told me that when he put on the wig and mustache he did look a lot like Flynn. He also told me that he sometimes used the name Jimmy Flynn as an alias.[138]

I was supposed to take the tow truck to a garage. The speedometer was not calibrated to the engine and it wasn't working right. Jim Bulger beeped me. He told me not to move the car. He said that FBI agents Morris, Connolly, and Newton were at his house drinking Beck's beer and sitting around talking. Morris had a few beers too many. He told Bulger they had gotten the license plate on the car that was involved in the hit. Jim Bulger said to me, "Thank God for Beck's beer."[139]

I believed Mr. Bulger when he told me that Morris inadvertently told them about the license plate. I didn't ask him any questions about it. If you knew Jim Bulger, you'd know you didn't ask him questions about what he said. He only tells you what he wants you to know. He said Morris had told him the FBI had the plate number of the car and they were waiting for the car to show up because it was a bore job. Morris said the FBI knew that the engine had been worked over. When Jim

---

[138] Jimmy Flynn was tried by the state for Halloran's murder. The FBI did nothing to discourage that trial. Flynn was acquitted no thanks to the FBI. Apparently the FBI is not bothered if innocent people are tried for crimes they probably didn't commit.

[139] It is a sad commentary that no one is shocked at this revelation that within days of having one of its informants murdered three FBI agents were drinking beer at Whitey's house, the person he was informing against and the one who most likely murdered him, and talking about the murder.

Bulger said that to me, I thought Morris was corrupt because he revealed the FBI had the plate number to Bulger.

Shortly after Halloran's murder, I knew that Bulger and Flemmi planned to go to New York to see the Cook. That's what we called Johnny Martorano. They were going to meet at the airport.

Jim Bulger was concerned about John Callahan. I had seen Callahan twice when he came to Triple O's with John Hurley. Jim Bulger wanted to see if Martorano thought Callahan would stand up to the FBI's pressure. When he got back, he told me about his visit. He told me they agreed Callahan wouldn't do ten to twenty years in jail so he had to go. Martorano was against it in the beginning but finally agreed. I knew Callahan was the subject of a grand jury investigation but did not know what it was about. At that time I wasn't aware of the Wheeler murder in Oklahoma.

I remember around that time a meeting at the Club at O Street and Third Street between Jim Bulger and Stevie Flemmi. They were upset about something George Kaufman did when he sent guns down to Florida. Kaufman was the liaison between the Jewish bookies and Bulger. Jim was also upset because they left Callahan's body at the airport and did not bury it. That was when he told me that Martorano and Joe McDonald killed Callahan.

I met Johnny Martorano sometime after Halloran was killed but before we killed Bucky Barrett. I heard that Johnny's brother Jimmy was a businessman. Martorano, Bulger and Flemmi were in a partnership that existed a long time before I came around. They were partners in Winter Hill and they shared their proceeds. I only knew about some of what they did from what they told me.

I didn't share in any Winter Hill dealings. My primary concern was South Boston as was Jim Bulger's. Stevie Flemmi was concerned with Mattapan and Dorchester. All the things I did Jim Bulger knew about. I shared the profits from my extortion with him but I didn't share my loan shark money with him.

After Halloran's killing FBI agent Montanari was hanging around in the area of the Club. Bulger and Flemmi disliked Montanari since he was out to get them.[140] Bulger told me Montanari was investigating Wheeler's murder. He told me what it was all about. He said he was against Wheeler's killing because his family had zillions of dollars and would never let it rest until they found the murderers. He thought they would never survive that murder.

Bulger and Flemmi decided to start collecting rent from the drug dealers, a percentage of their profits to let them stay in business. You ask me what would happen if anyone balked at paying. All I can say is no one ever balked.

---

[140] You would think that all the FBI agents would have been out to get them rather than socializing with them. Connolly filed reports complaining that people were investigating Whitey. Whitey came to believe that no one had the right, never mind duty, to investigate him.

A MUCKER'S TALE

I had a bar at F and 2nd street. One day Mary O'Reilly, Steven Rakes' sister, came in to see us. Jim Bulger was there. We spoke with her. We knew her brother, Steven Rakes, who we called Stippo, had just opened a liquor store. Mary said Stippo, his wife, and her parents are frightened because Stippo has been getting some bomb threats at the liquor store. She asked us if we could look into it. We liked Stippo's mother and father so we said we'd see what we could do even though we hated Stippo.

We went around and grabbed a few people to try to see who was doing it. We were having no luck finding out. One day we were talking to an old time bookmaker, Tommy Musico, who owned a bar in Andrew Square. Tommy asked us if we heard about Stippo. We asked, what about him? Tommy said he had been scaring him by making bomb threats. We both laughed when we found out Tommy was the guy doing it. We asked him to stop.

We then went to Stippo at the liquor store to talk to him to find out if he was interested in selling it. We had heard he was in over his head. He said he'd listen to us. We discussed the price. Stippo wanted one hundred fifty thousand dollars. We finally agreed on one hundred twenty five thousand. We paid one hundred thousand dollars and wrote out a twenty-five thousand dollars note to make it look legitimate. Up to that point in the negotiations, there was no threat used against Stippo. We counted the 100,000 dollars and so did

Stippo. Stippo ultimately accepted the cash and signed the store over.

We found out later he misrepresented the inventory and the store had a higher debt than he told us about. So we only paid eight of the remaining twenty-five thousand. He used to ask for the rest but I reminded him about the inventory problem.

Later that night as we were negotiating on the price, we met Stippo at his house. He had agreed upon a price. Stippo's wife, Julie Rakes, was not in the discussion. We went over the books to see what business the store was doing. When we were there, two of his kids and his sister-in-law were there.

While doing the transaction, Stippo said he changed his mind. Mr. Bulger was upset. We thought he was trying to hold us up for more money. I took out my pistol and put it on the table to let him know he didn't have the option of backing out. The deal was going through. While the discussions were going on, Jim Bulger was holding one of Stippo's kids in his lap. She reached out for the gun. Jim pushed the gun away from her toward me.

We ended up with the package store and owned it for about four or five years. When I first told the story of the meeting with Stippo, I denied there was any extortion. But later I admitted it.[141]

---

[141] Weeks in first telling his story to the Justice Department presented the happening with Stippo as a

After getting the money Stippo left for Disney World with his family for a vacation. Jim Bulger and I started to hear all sorts of weird stories about Stippo: that he had been killed, that he had been hung by his feet from some bridge, that we stuck a gun in his mouth or his kid's mouth. We had to find out where he was from his sister. We called him in Florida and told him to come back. We made a show of him being back.[142]

After we took over the store a Boston police detective named Joe Lundbohm, the uncle of Stippo's wife Julie Rakes, came around. He was questioning about how we got the liquor store. Bulger told me that Lundbohm was stirring up trouble saying his niece Julie and her husband had been extorted out of the store. He said to me, "Thank God he went to Zip." The FBI never conducted an investigation of how we got the store.

One time in the early 1980s, Connolly came into the store and asked me "What's up" or "What's going on." I felt he was trying to get some

---

straightforward business deal. After he flunked a lie detector test the Justice Department was going to walk away from its deal with him. As the FBI agents would say, Weeks got religion.

[142] Stippo interrupted his family vacation and flew back to Boston. He met Bulger and Weeks at his former store called the South Boston Liquor Mart. It is located at a busy traffic rotary circle. Weeks and Stippo stood outside the store for several hours like politicians running for office waving at many of the passing cars to show that Stippo was still alive.

information from me. I was offended by the remark. When Jimmy Bulger and Stevie Flemmi came in later, I was still mad. I told them that "Zip was in and he asked me what's up." I told them I was offended about him asking me questions. Mr. Bulger said "Don't talk about the guy like that, he's a friend of ours."[143]

I never gave Connolly any information. I had no idea that Jim Bulger and Steve Flemmi were giving Connolly information. I thought Connolly was giving them information. I was never with Jim Bulger when he was giving information to Connolly. I sometimes drove with him to meet with Connolly. I would drop Jim Bulger off. I'd then drive away so the car would not be seen near Connolly's place. I was not involved in the meetings with Connolly. They were usually only between Jim Bulger, Steve Flemmi, and Connolly. I was not Mr. Bulger's driver.[144]

It was not until the late 1990s that I first learned Steve Flemmi and Jim Bulger were

---

[143] Weeks had no relationship with Connolly nor did any of the other hoodlums, only Bulger. That's why his later story of Connolly confiding in him rings false.

[144] Weeks seemed highly sensitive to the suggestion he was Bulger's driver reacting as if it were a slap in the face. His response markedly differed from his other answers. I thought that would be a good place to go after him during cross-examination since he was so bothered by it. Nothing of evidentiary value might be gained, but it was a chance to shake his composure.

informants for the FBI. It was when Flemmi first admitted it in court.[145]

Jim Bulger and Steve Flemmi told me they gave "Vino", that's what we called John Morris, five thousand dollars because he was having some financial trouble. I knew that Bahorian was a bookmaker agent for Bulger and Flemmi.[146] We called him Dirty John. One day Lieutenant James Cox of the Boston Police pulled up at the liquor store to talk to Flemmi. Bulger said to Flemmi, as he went out to talk to him, "Remember Cox is wired up." They had information from the FBI that Bahorian and Cox were wearing wires. Later they told me they got the information from Morris.[147]

---

[145] Once arrested Weeks quickly moved for a deal. To get it he had to turn on Whitey. I suppose realizing Whitey was an informant made that easier. Whitey still remained larger than life to Weeks. Talk during the trial said the word on the street in Southie was that Weeks cleared his testimony with Whitey. I tended to doubt it. Whitey was smart enough to know Weeks would be the most credible witness against him if he were ever captured.

[146] Morris never mentioned Whitey was also involved with Bahorian.

[147] Morris did his utmost to protect himself by protecting Flemmi. It follows that not only would he tell Flemmi about the Bahorian wiretap but he would also have told him what other investigative methods his FBI group was using. When it wired Cox and sent him to meet Flemmi, Flemmi knew he was wired as did every person Flemmi decided to tell. That Cox, a police officer caught in compromising situations, was wired makes nonsense of Morris's testimony about Connolly telling him McDonough was "one of them" and unwilling to cooperate.

A MUCKER'S TALE

I had been at Theresa Stanley's house when the envelopes were made up around Christmas time. She was Jim Bulger's girlfriend. She lived on Silver Street in South Boston. Jim used to say to me "Christmas is for cops and kids." We sometimes had as many as 30 or 40 envelopes for the cops. Jim kept the list of cops' names on a small piece of paper. It contained symbols and nicknames. I would go around with Jim shopping before Christmas. We'd buy crystal and expensive clocks.

I saw four names on the list of FBI agents. They were Pipe, the nickname for FBI agent James Ring; Vino, who is John Morris; Nickie, the nickname for FBI agent Nickie Gianturco, and

---

Cox was an example of a cop saving himself and cooperating even though he had become "one of them." There were many others. Cox did arrange to meet with Detective Joe Lundbohm who grew up in the same neighborhood, Savin Hill, for lunch.

When Lundbohm's indictment was pending I ran into him at Linda Mae's Coffee Shop in Dorchester. He swore to me that Cox set him up by putting words in his mouth. He expected to be acquitted. He wasn't. Cox kept his job as a Boston police lieutenant. Lundbohm lost his. He was probably the only one in the city who did not know Cox was wired. Certainly all the gangsters knew.

O'Sullivan, the Organized Crime Strike Force chief, was asked during a congressional hearing whether he did any investigations to stop Bulger and Flemmi who he described as murderers. He pointed to only two occasions: the Lancaster Street garage, Appendix G, and this time when Cox was wired. Both were total failures, the latter doomed from the start because of Morris's dastardliness.

Agent Orange, who is FBI agent John Newton. Boston police names I remember were a Gerry O'Rourke who got five hundred dollars and a sergeant called Louis who received two hundred fifty. Jim used to give Kevin O'Neil some envelopes to give out. Joe Lundbohm never got one.

I knew how much money was in the envelopes. I would sit with Jim Bulger at the table when he counted it out and stuffed it in them. He would give the gifts for the FBI agents to Connolly to deliver. He also gave the FBI agents cash. Most of the cash was for the Boston Police in South Boston and ranged in amounts ranging from one hundred to five hundred dollars.

I saw envelopes for Zip at Theresa Stanley's house. One time in the late 1980s or early 1990s I don't remember the exact year but it was the time Jim Bulger was going to Chris Nylan's house in Ireland over Christmas. Jim Bulger gave me two envelopes to give to Connolly. One labeled "Z" had five thousand in it and the other "Agent Orange" had a thousand in it. I don't have any records to help me remember the exact year. Criminals don't keep records.[148]

---

[148] Bulger called FBI Agent Newton by the nickname Agent Orange because he served in Vietnam. Weeks allegation that Newton received an envelope with $1000 from Bulger was known to the FBI a long time prior to the trial. Despite this Newton remained on active duty as an FBI agent. It was only when Weeks testified to this in open court that the FBI felt compelled to act. It suspended

The next day I gave the envelopes to Connolly at the store. It was at the South Boston Liquor Market. I went into the back of the store and handed to him. Connolly left and went to his car. He came back in with gifts for Bulger and Flemmi. They were books. I knew that at times Jim Bulger also gave books to Connolly. There were a lot of customers and police officers around the store at Christmas time. When Connolly was there and police officers came in, they would go over and talk to him. As far as Eric was concerned, Flemmi was his primary contact and he would give him the envelopes.[149] Eric got paid twice a year.

Mr. Bulger told me he had corrupted six FBI agents. One of them was Jim Ring. Ring got a Chelsea clock but generally I didn't know who got what. I knew what we bought but not who got them. Jim Bulger would buy a group of gifts. I was there when he gave the gifts to Connolly for the agents. It was done in the back parking lot of the liquor store. They would transfer a handful of gifts from trunk to trunk. There was not much

---

Newton because the public revelation embarrassed the Bureau. Had it not become public knowledge Newton would have been allowed to work despite the FBI's knowledge he had been accused by one of its star witnesses of taking gifts and money.

[149] This corroborates Schneiderhan's (Eric) testimony of his life long friendship with Flemmi. It gives further lie to that of Martorano who said he turned Eric over to Flemmi.

traffic behind the store because mainly the employees used it.

We kept our money in an X fund. When we made scores through extortion or a shake down, we would put a certain percentage in that fund. This was kept for our expenses. Once it had one hundred five thousand dollars in it. I would hold it and give it to Jim Bulger whenever he wanted it. Jim would decide who was to get money but would usually discuss with Stevie Flemmi how much to give. I never used it to pay off the cops, Bulger did that.

I would see Bulger every day. From the X fund we bought cars. We had group cars and personal cars. Our personal cars were Lincolns and Jaguars. We sometimes gave money from the X fund to families that came upon hard times. Sometimes we gave money to the food pantry. X fund money also went to twelve to twenty local cops. I kept the X fund from the mid-eighties until it ran out of money in 1997 when Flemmi told me to give the money to his lawyers. When I was arrested, there was no money in the X fund.

Jim Bulger sometimes complained to me that Connolly was too ostentatious. He said he was flashing too much cash. Zip had bought a 40 foot boat with a 9½ foot beam and twin engines.

An FBI employee, Denise M. Taiste, testified she put Connolly's pay check into the middle drawer of his desk one day at his request. She said she saw at least ten other pay checks in amounts of two thousand dollars that had not been cashed that were scattered around in that drawer.

Jim Bulger told me that Schneiderhan and Connolly were looking out for his welfare. Stevie Flemmi told me the same thing.[150]

Connolly retired in 1990. After that he'd come to the South Boston Liquor Mart probably about twice a month. When he came in, there was just small talk. He would ask "Is the other guy around?" referring to Jim Bulger.

In 1994 I knew about the investigation against Bulger and Flemmi. Stevie Flemmi told me he was on top of it. Information also came from people called to the grand jury, from press accounts, and from our connection in the state police.

I knew Frank Salemme. I was told that in the early 1960s Salemme and Flemmi were partners. Salemme associated with the Mafia. After Salemme got out of jail Flemmi began to meet him every other day. Jim Bulger did not like the association. He complained to Flemmi he was acting like a liaison with the Mafia. Flemmi said he wasn't going to join with Salemme. He was just keeping on top of things. I was with Jim Bulger twice when we met Salemme. Jim only gave him a cordial greeting.

On December 23, 1994, after three in the afternoon Connolly came to the South Boston

---

[150] No mention of Naimovich. Weeks will testify Connolly knew Schneiderhan was Stevie's source. It supports my theory that Connolly would never let Stevie's source in the state police be indicted.

Liquor Mart and asked for Mr. Bulger. He wasn't looking for me. He then said to me, "I want to talk to you, it's important." We went to the back of the store and into the walk-in cooler. We used the cooler to talk because it was wet and had fans so it would be difficult to bug. Connolly told me to get word to Stevie Flemmi, Jim Bulger and Frank Salemme that indictments against them were imminent. I previously testified he said they were pending. To me, imminent and pending mean the same thing.

Connolly said they were going to put the papers together over the holidays. He said FBI Agent O'Callaghan told him this and only four people knew. When Connolly left, I looked at the clock to see where Bulger would be. It was 3:30 p.m.[151]

I recall it was December 23 because it was a famous date, even though I don't recall the day of the week it was. But I know it was a weekday because Bulger usually got to the store about 4:00 p.m. and I was expecting him to come in. It's famous because it's the day Jim Bulger took off. He had been planning to be around and do a lot of

---

[151] This part of Weeks testimony I have great trouble believing. I believe Connolly told Whitey directly. Whitey or Connolly later told Weeks. The government didn't have Whitey's testimony. It needed Weeks to say this. If Weeks didn't, the statute of limitations would have run on the RICO statute. See Appendix B.

things over Christmas but he suddenly left. It was a clear cold day.[152]

I then went next door to the Rotary variety store and beeped Mr. Bulger. He called me back and said he was at Theresa Stanley's house. He came down to the store. I got into his car and we drove into Copley Square.

Theresa was in the car. Jim Bulger parked illegally in front of Neiman Marcus. Theresa Stanley went to stand in front of the store. We stood about five feet from the rear of the car. I told Bulger what Connolly said. We left the car because we didn't know if it was wired. We talked about 15 to 20 minutes. When we were done, Jim called Theresa back and spoke with her near the front of the car. I couldn't hear what was said. We then got back into the car and made it back to the store quickly. Jim was in a rush.

Theresa Stanley testified. She told several different stories. She knew Bulger for 37 years. She lived with him as his wife. She and Whitey returned from Europe just prior to December 1994. They planned to stay in Boston over the holidays. One day before Christmas they went to Copley Square. There Bulger told her to pack. They were going on a cross-country trip. She was unsure of the date they left, the directions they traveled, or how long it took them to reach their destination. She did remember being in New Orleans over New Year's Eve. She said they were on their way back to Boston

---

[152] The weather was nothing like Weeks said. See Appendix B.

193

driving through Connecticut when they heard Flemmi
was arrested. They turned around and left the area.
Some time later Bulger drove her back. Hotel records
introduced showed she and Bulger were in New Orleans
between December 26 and New Year's day.

I was dropped off at Prebble Street and walked back to the store. I figured I got back at four-thirty. Connolly called some time after that and spoke to Kevin O'Neil. He wanted to see if Mr. Bulger got the information. I don't think my times are off. It didn't take us that long to get to Copley Square and back. Did you ever drive with Jim Bulger? He's an aggressive driver. No, I don't say he can make the cars in front of him just disappear. But I will say Jim Bulger has made lots of things disappear.

Jim Bulger told me to get in touch with Stevie Flemmi. I knew Flemmi would show up at the store. I had no way to reach out for Flemmi because I did not have his beeper number. Since he regularly came to the store I planned to give him the information when he arrived. I wasn't that concerned with getting the information to him since Connolly said they were going to be working on the paperwork over the holidays.

Shortly after I got back to the store Flemmi came in. I told Flemmi that Zip was by and said the indictments were imminent. I told him they were planning to move quickly to pick up the three of them at once. Flemmi said he had his guy in there and he wasn't worried because his guy was on top of it. I told him Zip said only four people knew.

Flemmi stayed there a half an hour. He said Eric would have the information. A few days after Christmas I ran into Flemmi. I asked him why he was still around. I said, "Zip said four people knew. Jimmy's already gone." I told him to take off just for two weeks to protect himself

We had phone numbers and beepers put aside in case something like this happened. After Mr. Bulger fled I had no contact with him until January 5, the day Stevie Flemmi was arrested. About nine that night I was at the L Street Tavern in South Boston and Flemmi's brother Michael came in and told me Stevie had been arrested. He also told me that Kevin O'Neil, one of the owners of Triple O's, said Zip wanted to know if I got the information to the other guy, meaning Bulger.

After I got the news, I noticed a lot of people around the front of the L Street Tavern. It looked liked the cops were staking out the place. I went out the back door and called Jim Bulger. I told him that Flemmi was arrested. I said there was red all around the town. That's our code for danger or cops. Jim told me he heard it on the radio as he was coming back into the area and as soon as he did, he turned around and left.

Jim Bulger and Steve Flemmi were indicted on January 10. A couple of months later Jim came back to drop off Theresa Stanley. I drove his other girlfriend, Catherine Greig, to Malibu Beach where I met him. Jim left with Greig.[153] I kept in contact with Jim after he left. I was asked by an FBI agent in 1995 if I had contact with him. I lied to him and told him I didn't.[154]

I was not worried at that time about being indicted. The grand jury investigation was about the Jewish bookmakers. I didn't have anything to do with the bookmaking business. Even so when Flemmi was arrested I left the area for a short while in 1995. I did it because of an ounce of caution. I didn't expect to be indicted because Connolly only mentioned Flemmi, Bulger and Salemme.

Toward the end of 1994 Jim Bulger had been taking more vacations. We were no more concerned about surveillance at that time than at any other time because we were always concerned about surveillance. We always assumed we were being watched by the cops and acted accordingly. I usually knew when strangers were around. I lived in South Boston my whole life. My liquor store was between the Old Colony and Old Harbor projects. I was born and grew up in Old Colony. I knew just about everyone in the neighborhood.

I learned that Jim Bulger called Morris on the phone at Quantico. Jim told me that he called a lot

---

[153] 16 years later Catherine Greig would be arrested with Whitey in Santa Monica, California. Whitey's home parish when he lived in Old Harbor Village was Saint Monica's.

[154] Miner made much of this suggesting that rather than lie he should have taken the 5th Amendment. I'm sure the jury thought as I did that gangsters are expected to lie to FBI agents who ask them questions.

of numbers saying he was Mr. White until he got him. Jim blamed Morris for his indictment. He told Morris that if he goes down Morris will go down with him. He blamed Morris for a 1988 article in the Boston Globe that named him as an informant. Jim just wanted to kill Morris. He told me Morris created the problems with his lies and he was smart enough to straighten them out.

In late 1995 I told Connolly I had been talking with Jim Bulger and that Jim was doing good. When I told him about Bulger's call to Morris, Connolly laughed and said, "That must have been some conversation. Two days later Morris had a couple of heart attacks and almost died on the table in the hospital."[155]

After Flemmi's arrest I visited him at Plymouth jail. Flemmi asked me to be in contact with Zip and Eric. I did this between 1996 and 1998 on behalf of Flemmi. I called Connolly at work using the code name Chico. When Connolly wanted to reach me, he would call my brother Jack. He would ask Jack to have me call him. Jack would call me and say, "Your girlfriend is looking for you."

Kevin Weeks's brother John [Jack] testified and corroborated this. John's a Harvard graduate who owns his own company. He said Connolly would call him when he wanted to talk to Kevin. This happened

---

[155] I assume that during this period Bulger was in some type of contact with Connolly. This trial was not the place where one would learn if my assumption is correct.

sometime after 1994 or 1995. Connolly would say "Have your brother call me, please." After Connolly called he would call Kevin and say "Your girlfriend called".

Kathleen Orrick who worked as a secretary for Connolly at Boston Edison testified that around the time of Judge Wolf's hearings she began to receive calls from a person called Chico who called a fair number of times. Her caller-identification showed the prefix of the telephone number Chico was calling from was a South Boston number. She said Connolly wanted to be sure that she located him if any of four persons, aside from his family, called. These were the CEO of the company, the boss of his department, Billy Bulger's assistant, and Chico.

I met face to face with Connolly in Harvard Square at a bar in Cambridge called Finnegan's Wake and at the Top of the Hub in the Prudential Center Building where Connolly worked for the Boston Edison Company. I continually conveyed information back and forth between Connolly and Flemmi.

I would have conversations with Ken Fishman, Flemmi's lawyer. Connolly also spoke and met with Fishman. Flemmi was trying to get information on Guild Street where the Mafia induction ceremony was bugged. Flemmi asked me to get the names of the informants who ratted out the Mafia induction ceremony.

Flemmi knew who the informants were but he wanted proof of it. He wanted the names of the informants, the names that corresponded to some top echelon informant's file numbers, and the name of the FBI agents who were their handlers. In early 1997 Connolly gave me the names of the informants. He told me Bulger, Flemmi, Mercurio, and two others. Connolly said he was the handler for four of them. He said a major from Providence, Rhode Island handled the fifth. When I told him the names Flemmi said he knew it.

I asked Connolly to get the informant identification numbers. He could not get access to the numbers. He gave me the names of the agents' supervisors. Flemmi was trying to expose the names of the other two people. I didn't care about outing them. It was up to Flemmi to do it as he saw fit. I asked Connolly for Mercurio's informant identification number. Connolly never got back to me on that.

When I visited with Flemmi at the Plymouth House of Corrections, a large glass separated us but we could talk to each other on the phone. We knew the phones were monitored so we sometimes held notes up to the glass. Also by leaning close to the glass we could talk to each other and not be heard by others. The method we used depended upon the sensitivity of the information. I would do anything Flemmi asked me to do. At the time Flemmi was in the Plymouth jail along with Frank Salemme. Salemme was also told about the names of the informants.

Connolly showed me the book he was writing. He talked with me about the agent he had for the book. I saw some of the book. It was about the

1960s and 1970s. I didn't see any mention of Flemmi in it. I told Flemmi that Connolly was writing a book.

Flemmi told me that Morris told him he could do anything except commit a murder. I told Connolly that. Connolly said that was not what Morris said. Connolly said they were authorized to continue to do what they were doing. They were not authorized to expand into other crimes or else they'd be committing rapes and murders.

Flemmi wanted Judge Wolf to hold hearings so that the indictments would be thrown out. He planned to identify himself as an informant. I told Connolly of Flemmi's plan. I told him Flemmi needed his help. Connolly said he would write a letter to Wolf. One night near the time of the hearing I met Connolly at the Top of the Hub for dinner. After eating Connolly showed me a rough draft of the letter handwritten on a yellow legal pad. It said something about Frankie Dewan, about the bomb in Eddie Miani's car, it mentioned John Morris, and talked about gypsy wires. Connolly said he was going to send the letter anonymously as if from three disgruntled Boston Police Officers. I told him to add something to the letter about 'little lies'. Connolly wanted to send the letter on Boston Police letterhead so I used a connection to get the stationary. The letter was sent and hearings were held after the letter went out.

FBI Agent Richard Macko testified he searched Connolly's office and found in his file cabinet official

Boston Police Department, Boston Globe and Massachusetts State Police letterheads and envelopes. Witness Kathleen Orrick, Connolly's secretary, also said Connolly had Boston Globe and Boston Police Department letterheads in his office, the same as the letterheads on the letter sent to Judge Wolf.

Kathleen Orrick also identified the style of the letter as that of Connolly. She said he likes to highlight things using a lot of quotation marks and exclamation points. She also recognized the block format type as one Connolly would use.

Another witness, John Ford, who was a friend of Connolly's, testified Connolly gave him career advice and was responsible for him being a Boston Police officer. He never saw the letter that was sent to Judge Wolf but he did see another document that Connolly showed him. The language in the letter to Judge Wolf was also in that document. He remembered the information about Frank Dewan, a Boston Police detective. Ford testified that Connolly did not like Dewan because he was making derogatory comments about Connolly and his association with Bulger.

Flemmi planned on disparaging Morris in his testimony by saying Morris gave him a tape recording. At the Top of the Hub Connolly gave me a tape recording that Morris left behind. He told me to give it to Flemmi's attorney Ken Fishman. I did this. Fishman introduced it at the hearing.[156] Flemmi testified the tape had always

---

[156] Shortly after this case Fishman would be named a Massachusetts Superior Court judge.

been in his possession and used it to support his claim that Morris tipped him off. Connolly thought the tape would bolster Flemmi's defense.

When Connolly heard Flemmi would get on the stand, he became concerned. Connolly wanted to know if Flemmi was going to give up Eric.[157] He feared that Flemmi was going to say Connolly tipped him off. Connolly wanted him to say Morris tipped him off.

To help Flemmi prove Morris tipped him off we had to come up with a way to do it. Morris was out of town at the time he was tipped. Connolly told me to tell Flemmi that Morris told him he saw a pros memo when he was in DC. I gave the information to Flemmi. Flemmi testified Morris tipped him off. But Flemmi screwed it up when he testified. He called it some other type of memo.

Frank Salemme thought that Flemmi would testify that Connolly tipped him off. He was surprised when he said it was Morris. After that Flemmi and Salemme stopped talking.

After Flemmi was arrested I still continued my criminal activity. When Nick Murray, a friend of mine, had problems with Jimmy Flynn I said I would kill Flynn if I had to. With Jimmy Bulger and Stevie Flemmi out of the picture, I collected on the outstanding money that was owed to them. I continued my small loan business.[158]

---

[157] As noted in a previous footnote, Connolly knew Scheniderhan (Eric) was Stevie's source.

---

[158] Weeks had been on the stand all of one day and part of two others. I felt it would be difficult for Connolly to survive his testimony. His only hope was that the jury would decide that even if Connolly did everything Weeks said, it was just too much to ask it to convict a former FBI agent on the testimony of gangsters.

CHAPTER SEVEN

THE NOOSE TIGHTENS

FOUR WITNESSES WITH CRUCIAL EVIDENCE

Weeks finished his testimony on the seventh day of the trial, Thursday, May 16, 2000.[159] *Judge Tauro is in about three minutes before ten. He's wearing a dark blue shirt, red tie with thin blue stripes. His judicial robe is open as usual. There is a lengthy bench conference. Durham is gesturing with his right hand. He does most of the talking. Shepherd is doing more than I would expect. Boyle hangs back with an amused look on his face. The spectator section becomes quite noisy during the bench conference with almost everyone talking. The bench conference suddenly ends. Judge Tauro says, "Court's in session." The noise quickly ebbs.*

---

[159] As I wait to be allowed into the courtroom Connolly comes over to me. I speak to him briefly. I ask him how he is doing, half expecting him to say that he's reached a deal to plead guilty. At a minimum I expected him to be down after Weeks's testimony that ended the day before. He said he was fine. He mentioned something about J. Edgar Hoover and money. I didn't exactly catch what he said but in later readings about Hoover and the FBI it became clear.

JULIE MISKEL RAKES DAMMERS

STIPPO'S EX-WIFE

My name is Julie Rakes Dammers.[160]   I was married to Stephan Rakes who was called Stippo. When we were first married, we owned a mom and pop store. In 1983 we bought an abandoned gas station, secured a liquor license and opened up Stippo's Liquor Mart.   Shortly after that we received some phone calls relating to bomb threats.

On my last night at the store Jamie Flannery came in. He was a bouncer at Triple O's. He told me to get my possessions. I left with Flannery. We drove to my house. I saw Weeks, Bulger, and another person outside my house so I kept going past and drove around the block. I was scared. When we were heading back toward my house we passed Bulger, Weeks and the other guy who were walking away from my house. I was worried about my kids.

After checking on them Stippo gave me a paper bag full of cash. I took it to my parents' house to hide it. The next day Stippo, the kids, and I drove to Florida, to Disney World. We stayed

---

[160] I prosecuted Julie's brother for conspiracy to commit murder. He received 19 to 20 years in prison, the maximum. I was a friend of Julie's uncle Bobby Lundbohm who married my cousin Barbara.

there. Stippo left for a while but eventually came back. Then we drove back to South Boston.

I went to my uncle Joe Lundbohm, a police detective with the Boston police. I told him our lives had been threatened and we had to give up the store for cash. Our livelihood was damaged. Later we went back to my uncle to tell him that we were told to tell him to lay off the investigation.

My husband was later put on trial because of this. When I testified at that trial, I said I couldn't remember the conversations that I had with Joe Lundbohm which I have just testified about.[161]

JOSEPH LUNDBOHM

JULIE RAKES'S UNCLE

My name is Joseph Lundbohm. I was a Boston Police detective in homicide in the winter and early spring of 1984. I was on the Boston Police for twenty-four years and while a member I was

---

[161] Stippo was charged with perjury. Julie was called to testify against him. He was her husband at the time so she was motivated to protect him. He lost his business when the FBI did nothing about the extortion. Years later the Justice Department decided to go after Whitey so it wanted Stippo's testimony about the extortion. Stippo in fear of his life denied that the extortion occurred. He was then prosecuted for perjury and jailed. Somehow it doesn't seem right that the victim ends up being again victimized by the government.

convicted of a crime that had nothing to do with the present trial. The conviction was for two counts of obstruction of justice and one count for aiding a gambling operation. I did not take any money from the bookie.[162]

My niece, Julie Rakes, came to me to tell me that her business had been taken by force by Whitey Bulger. I took this information to John Connolly because he was on the FBI's organized crime squad. I met him in a coffee shop. I don't remember where but it may have been at Linda Mae's Coffee Shop in Dorchester.

Both sides agreed by a stipulation that Boston Globe Reporter Shelly Murphy and Boston Herald Reporter David Webber would testify that Connolly told them that Joe Lundbohm did approached him to complain about the taking of the liquor store from Stippo and Julie.

I told him that my niece Julie and her husband owned Stippo's. They had recently opened it. I told him that three men, Flemmi, Bulger and Weeks went to their house and said they were going to buy the store. They forced them to sell it to them. They didn't want to sell it but were told they had no choice. Stevie Flemmi put a gun on the table. As he did, Whitey Bulger picked up one of the Rakes' children and said you have a nice family here. They gave them sixty-seven thousand dollars for the store.

---

[162] Joe is my friend Bobby's older brother.

THE NOOSE TIGHTENS

Connolly asked me if Stippo would wear a wire. I said he wouldn't. I also told Connolly that neither Julie nor Stippo wanted to be witnesses. I mentioned to him that I wanted the meeting to be off the record. I just wanted to see if the FBI could do anything about it. I never asked Connolly to meet with the Stippo or Julie. I did not follow up on it. Connolly told me, "We'll figure out something."

After that I never heard from Connolly nor did I file a report with the Boston police with Rakes's information. I told the Chief of Detectives DiNatale what happened for intelligence purposes. I gave it to him to do what he wanted with it. I was not giving it to DiNatale to open an investigation nor was I reporting it as a crime. I was just giving it as intelligence of a crime. The Boston Police had an organized crime squad.[163]

---

[163] Connolly's defense seemed to suggest that he can hardly be faulted for doing nothing about Lundbohm's information in that it was from witnesses who would not wear a wire, nor testify and it was off the record. Lundbohm's testimony had a more damaging aspect to it. It showed Connolly received highly credible information that his informants were extorting people by threatening their children. His inaction shows he knew their ongoing criminal activity involved extortion through threat of death.

PATRICK PATTERSON

SPECIAL AGENT IN THE FBI

Leonard Boyle conducts the examination. As he's being sworn, in I hear someone behind me whisper, "He's holding up his left hand." I'm looking directly at him but do not notice this. Then I realize it's true. His left hand is held up high in the air as he takes the oath. I've never seen this before. Someone else notices and comments. Soon most of the spectators have seen it. A quiet chuckling breaks out. I pass it off as a witness who has never been in court before. I was really surprised when he said he was a special agent in the FBI.

My name is Patrick Patterson. I was a section chief at Quantico. I have been with the FBI since 1983. I have never handled Top Echelon informants. They are now called significant informants. I have supervised agents who had such informants. I am familiar with the FBI policy regarding informants.

Agents are not allowed to accept gifts from informants. If an agent receives a gift, the special agent in charge should be notified. The agent should not keep the gift and it should be documented in the file that it was received.

I came to Boston because Flemmi filed an affidavit stating he was authorized to commit crimes. I was assigned to determine how Flemmi had access to the confidential information he put into his affidavit. The files showed that from 1980 to 1990 Connolly was Flemmi's sole handler.

On July 16, 1997, I called Connolly at his Edison office to ask him some questions. Among the questions I asked him was "Have you been contacted by Flemmi's defense team?" Connolly said "No." I have no doubt that is what Connolly said. If Connolly had said yes, I would have followed up on it. Connolly's denial made us look at other people for the source of the confidential information leaks to Flemmi.

I did not record the conversation or make a transcript of it. I could not record the call because the special agent in charge has to approve such a procedure. I never let Connolly see my 302 report about the telephone call. I know of no case of a person reviewing what was written in a 302.[164] My purpose in calling Connolly was just to let him know we were in town and at some point we would be interested in interviewing him. I did not ask him if he was going to be a witness for the defense. I never named defense counsel by name.

---

[164] Judge Wolf, who will later testify, demanded as a condition of being interviewed that he be allowed to review the 302 and make changes where necessary.

THE NOOSE TIGHTENS

I later met Connolly face to face. The subject did not come up. I never showed Connolly the 302 reporting his denial.[165]

---

[165] The FBI investigated Norfolk District Attorney's office. Special Agent John Morris and another came to our office to interview the DA Bill Delahunt. Because I had had significant experience as a defense lawyer, I sat in on the meeting that lasted over two hours. Bill is a politician. Politicians don't give one word answers but ramble on and on. This was not a forum to do that. We didn't know what the FBI was looking for. We'd have preferred to know more about what the FBI wanted but were not told. We knew even though the request was supposed to be confidential that if we turned it down newspaper headlines would read: "DA REFUSES FBI INTERVIEW." My job was to make sure Bill answered the question as asked and without going into long explanations. I put on my defense counsel hat to remind him to do that. On more than a few occasions I reminded Bill, "That's enough. You've answered the question." I also needed to keep a record of the questions and answers. I did a lot of writing as fast as I could. I noticed the FBI agents were taking very few notes. I became convinced that they were wearing wires or recording devices. I was so certain of this that immediately at the end of the meeting I walked around outside our building looking for a vehicle they would have used to pick up the transmissions. Unless they had recorded the session they could not accurately reconstruct what was said. After they left I assume they returned to their office and filed a 302 on the meeting. What the 302 would contain was their recollections not actually what was stated.

THE NOOSE TIGHTENS

LYNN TREMAIN

SPECIAL AGENT IN THE FBI

My name is Lynn Tremaine. I have been an FBI special agent since 1986. I took five years off to work with the military in Germany. I graduated from a mid-western university and majored in German. I came to Boston in May of 2000.   I analyzed the telephone records, cellular, direct and calling card records that relate to the activity of

---

I eventually learned the FBI agents do not record interviews between its agents and others. They persist in this to the present day. I fail to comprehend why every encounter between an FBI agent and a target or a witness is not recorded.   The only reason I can see is the FBI adage if it is not in writing it doesn't exist. What a 302 contains is what the FBI agent believes the person stated, not what the person actually stated. When Congress under Title III gave the FBI the right to intercept electronic communications, it required that these intercepted communications be recorded on tape. It did not let the agents listen to the conversations and then file 302 reports about what they heard.   Experienced FBI agents have pointed to the recorded conversations on the tapes and stated that those are the best evidence because the people condemn themselves with their own words. If that is so, then why does Congress not require FBI agents to tape record all conversations with a person who is a target or a witness to insure that the best evidence, the person's own words, is preserved.   Congress must make recording the rule rather than the exception.

John Connolly during specific periods of time. I then put my analysis on the charts that I have with me.

The first chart shows telephone calls between Connolly and Weeks over a period between June 14, 1997, and September 26, 1999. Most calls lasted one or two minutes. One was as long as 18 minutes.[166]

The next chart shows calls between Connolly's telephones and those of Flemmi's attorney, Fishman, during the spring and summer of 1997. There were twenty calls to Fishman at his office and residence. One was a 68 minute call at 10:09 p.m. from a pay phone 3/10ths of a mile from Connolly's Cape Cod house which was made shortly before the call on July 16, 1997, by Agent Patterson to Connolly in which Connolly denied contact with the defense team.

---

[166]   I once wondered at Connolly's motive in aligning himself with Weeks to help Stevie. Did he do it out of sense of duty and obligation being so offended by the government's betrayal of his deal with Stevie that he felt morally obliged to help him? Or, out of fear, like Morris, believing that by protecting Stevie, he was protecting himself from Stevie turning on him? Or, had he associated so long with Whitey and Stevie he became like them? In reflecting I eliminated the first reason. Had he believed he had the right to authorize their actions he should have come forward and testified at Judge Wolf's motion hearing to that effect.

THE NOOSE TIGHTENS

Connolly used pay phones at the Hynes Convention Center right next to the Prudential Center where he worked and in the Prudential Center itself. We connected the pay phones to Connolly through the company calling card assigned to him.[167]

I have here another chart. This shows the dates Weeks visited Flemmi at the House of Corrections in Plymouth. This can be compared to the charts showing the telephone calls between Connolly and Weeks to show they were in touch around those dates.

On April 21, 1997, when there was a hearing on Flemmi's affidavit, Connolly called the South Boston Liquor Mart. These two other charts show a series of calls between Connolly and Weeks around the time of the filings of the affidavits.

The final chart shows calls surrounding the arrest of Flemmi.

---

[167] Any organized crime investigator as Connolly had to know any call he made on a telephone, cell phone or with a calling card assigned to him could be traced. It is the first thing done in such an investigation. Nevertheless Connolly left a well lighted trail of his doings. Did Connolly undermine himself because he was cheap? Some said his nickname Zip was because he was perceived as a tightwad. Or was it that Connolly having been an FBI agent thought he was above the law and never expected anyone would investigate him?

THE NOOSE TIGHTENS

On December 20, 1994, Boston FBI SAC O'Callaghan called to Connolly's office twice, once for under a minute and once for 21 minutes. On December 21, 1994, Connolly called to the cell phone of Kevin O'Neil, one of the owners of Triple Os.

On December 22, 1994, there was a meeting between the U. S. Attorney and the top people in the FBI over the issuance of the indictments for Flemmi and Bulger. On December 23, 1994, Connolly's cell phone was used to call the FBI switchboard at 1:23 p.m. That call lasted for two minutes. The chart shows later that day the meeting Weeks testified about when he said he met with Connolly at 3:30 p.m. at the South Boston Liquor Mart.

On December 24, 1994, at 9:44 am, Connolly called the South Boston Liquor Mart. On December 29, January 4 (twice), and January 5 Connolly called the FBI switchboard using his cell phone. I do not know whether the calls to the telephones that were listed as being one minute in duration on the cell phones were completed or not. I do not know whether the dialing of the number even if it is not answered counts as a one-minute call because of airtime use.

There is no way to tell whether the person using the call left a message. All I can say is the phones are listed to Connolly. O'Callaghan has a private line at the FBI that could have been called.

215

THE NOOSE TIGHTENS

There is no showing during this time period that Connolly called his private number.[168]

---

[168]   Agent Tremain's testimony concerning the telephone records cemented Connolly's involvement with Weeks's and Stevie's defense team.   It was almost impossible for the jury to acquit him of lying to Agent Patterson.   It hurt him by adding credence to Weeks's testimony about seeing the rough draft of the letter to Judge Wolf and to the December 23 tip off by showing a close relationship between them.   It gave the jury independent corroboration of certain events.

CHAPTER EIGHT

MEMORIES OF THE OLD DAYS

FRANCIS P. SALEMME

A MADE MAN, A KING'S MAN, AN OLD MAN

It's day 8 of the trial, Friday, May 17, 2002. At 9:55 am, Judge Tauro comes in and has a short bench conference. While I'm watching the bench conference. I miss the witness getting onto the stand. I glance over and see him sitting there. He's a slight, older guy. A couple of marshals stand next to him. There had been rumors that Frank Salemme is scheduled to testify. I ask the guy next to me who is from the Boston Police Department who the witness is. He confirms that it is Salemme. I watch him as he smiles and waives to someone sitting in the front middle section reserved for the police officers. He's in a white shirt, dark blue tie, graying hair, and thin drawn-in face.

As he begins his testimony, he appears more nervous than his fellow felons, Martorano or Weeks. He blows air from his mouth to relieve tension. His hands tightly clasp the arms of the chair. He looks real old. His mouth looks similar to those old codgers who have no teeth and smack their gums together. It looks like his long stays in prison have taken a toll on him. That is probably because he did a lot of that time in a state prison rather than a federal lockup..

Durham, as is his wont, carries Salemme through a lot of this material with his leading questions that are more like statements than questions. They only require one or two word

217

answers adopting the question's premise. When Salemme gives an affirmative answer, his head continues to shake up and down like those bobbing head dolls of sports figures and other celebrities. He has an involuntary tremor. His answers are mostly "There was" or "It did."

My name is Francis P. Salemme. I am 68 years of age. I grew up in Boston. I've spent some time in prison. I know Stevie Flemmi. He was a boyhood friend of mine.

I'm testifying pursuant to an agreement with the government. I was indicted on January 10, 1995 with Flemmi, Bulger, George Kaufman, Robert DeLuca, my son, and the two Martorano brothers. We were charged with RICO charges of running a criminal enterprise involved with extortion, loan sharking, and other crimes. I filed motions in that case that were heard by Judge Wolf.

In the fall of 1999 I decided to plead guilty. I knew at that time there were other investigations going on into my activities. I had been subpoenaed in December 1999 to the federal grand jury to testify. That had nothing to do with my decision to cooperate with the government. It was just that the subpoena made me think about what I wanted to do.

As I saw it, I had three choices. I could refuse to testify and be held in contempt. I wasn't going to do that since I didn't want to do any additional time in jail. I could testify and lie. I could testify and tell the truth. I wasn't going to lie. I could get ten years for perjury. I'm not interested in doing any more time at my age than I'm presently doing.[169]

218

My health's not that good. I've got internal injuries caused by gun shot wounds.

So thinking it over I decided to try to make a deal. The Justice Department wanted to know what I was going to testify to before it made the deal. I made a proffer and then signed an agreement. I executed a plea agreement on December 7, 1999.

I pled guilty to the January 10 indictment. I also pled guilty to the car bombing of the lawyer John Fitzgerald and to participating in the murders of the Bennettt brothers. I had an agreement that related to my grand jury testimony. I was to be asked no questions about the Mafia. I'd only testify about law enforcement officials and some other things.[170]

In the Mafia it is not sanctioned for anyone to testify against anyone else under any circumstance. I didn't seek the permission of the National Commission to testify.[171] I didn't send a message to

---

[169] Salemme did get out of jail not too long after he testified against Connolly. But in early 2004 he was back in jail again for perjury.

[170] Salemme is not required to testify about his knowledge of the Mafia or against any Mafia members. The Justice Department forfeited the ability to gain this important information yet it will assist this former Mafia boss in being released from prison earlier than scheduled

[171] Connolly's role in taking down the Boston part of the Patriarca LCN Family when it was run by Angiulo is in dispute. But few dispute he was instrumental in the bug at Vanessa's that took down the Boston Mafia group that took over after Angiulo. And when it tried to reconstitute itself, Connolly had three of the four informants for the bugging of the induction ceremony at Guild Street that

Gotti saying I was only testifying about cops and rats.

The Justice Department is going to do nothing for me. What I'm going to do is testify truthfully. All the Justice Department will do for me is to file a Rule 35b substantive motion. When Judge Wolf sentenced me to the time I am now serving, he gave me a sentence at the low end of the sentencing range.[172] The Justice Department made a recommendation closer to the high end. Under the Rule 35b motion Judge Wolf can adjust my sentence further downward and give me even less time.

There is no guarantee that the judge will do anything. The Justice Department hasn't yet filed the motion to lower my sentence. It is up to the judge to decide how much time I'll have to serve. I'd like the recommendation to be as low as possible. As it stands now, my release date is June 2005.

When I was first sent to federal prison, I had to wait a year or so to get to a prison with a good medical facility. I was held in a segregated housing unit. It's called a SHU. If I had my choice, I'd like to serve my time in general population and would do so in a minute. Since I can't get that, I'd prefer

---

destroyed the remnants of the Patriarca LCN Family. Salemme could justify his testimony to the Commission as a way for the LCN to get revenge against Connolly

[172] Some say Judge Wolf had a soft spot in his heart for the wise guys especially with Mafia connections. He is rumored to have had an Italian pastry party with some of them in his lobby.

to stay in the medical facility than going back to SHU. In FCI Lexington I was in the medical facility. That was because I had been shot. I had a growth in my stomach and I was in severe pain. I don't want to go into a witness protection program. What I want is to be allowed to go into general population.

In preparing my testimony I met with government agents ten times or so. I had around fifty telephone calls with them. I spoke to the government agents whenever they called. The Justice Department paid a $1700 phone bill I had when I was in jail in New Hampshire. These were for calls I made to my wife. New Hampshire jails charge exorbitant telephone fees so the Justice Department picked up my tab.

I've been involved in crime all my life. I forced a guy named Leo Schwartz out of business so that me and George Kaufman could open an auto shop. I had a reputation for not backing down. If I told someone to do something, they would do it.

I engaged in gambling, loan sharking, loaning money at high interest and collecting on loans through the use of threats. The first killing I was involved in was not gang related. It was In May 1964. I got a call to come over to a lounge. A sign on the door read "Closed for electrical problems." When I got there, I saw Stevie and Vincent Flemmi, Earl Smith, and Wimpy Bennett. Frankie Benjamin's body was on the floor. He had been killed by Stevie Flemmi.

I was an electrician by trade. They asked me to mess up the electric box so that it looked like there was a real electric problem. I did this. I made it look like there was an electrical fire. I helped wrap up Benjamin's body, blocked the alley, and acted as the crash car when we drove away. For a disposal operation to be successful you needed five men.

In the 1960s I was involved with Stevie Flemmi. I hung around with him, Edward Wimpy Bennett, and Peter Boulis. We had auto shops. We would switch car engines and other similar things to defraud insurance companies. George Kaufman was also involved with us. Part of our auto business was legal. We also got involved in the loan sharking and the numbers business.

At that time the Boston Gang Wars were going on. Initially we were not involved. The two gangs fighting were the McLaughlin group from Charlestown and Buddy McClean's group out of Somerville. We got involved in the gang wars when Stevie Flemmi's brother Vinny was shot at by Punchy McLaughlin. At the time of the shooting Punchy was in a car with Jimmy O'Toole, Stevie Hughes, and Connie Hughes. I had used machine guns and had access to them and other firearms.

I went after Punchy McLaughlin. It was kill or be killed. I made three attempts to kill Punchy. The first two times I was on foot when I shot at him. I hit him but he survived. He was moving fast. I finally figured out Punchy's moves and got him in West Roxbury at the Spring Street bus stop as he was getting out of his car. From my surveillance I knew he was going there and that's how I managed to get him.

I was involved in numerous shootouts on the Boston streets. Me and a friend killed Stevie Hughes who was with Punchy McLaughlin when he shot at Vinny Flemmi. At the time I killed Hughes I also had to kill Sammy Linden. But before killing Sammy I had to talk to Raymond L.S. Patriarca. Raymond L.S. was the head of the Patriarca LCN crime family in Providence, Rhode Island.

People referred to me as the general. I was good at making plans. I made the plan to get Stevie Hughes. It was a simple plan involving the use of illegal phone taps on his and Sammy Linden's phones. I learned how to do this from my studies as an electrician. It's easy to install the phone bug. The hard part is getting access to the location. I only tapped phones twice. In Punchy's case it helped, I knew exactly where people were going to be.

I spoke to Raymond L.S. about the war with Buddy McLean. I told him we were going to hit Stevie Hughes. We were going to take him out no matter what but I thought as a courtesy I'd tell the head of the Mafia gang in the area. The problem was that Hughes was Sammy Linden's bodyguard. He was always with Sammy. Sammy was involved with the T tickets, the illegal numbers that were played in greater Boston. He needed a bodyguard because he carried substantial amounts of money every day when he made his rounds picking up the bets.

I went to Raymond L.S. Patriarca two times telling him that Sammy was in the way. The second time Patriarca said I've warned him so do what you have to do. I got Patriarca's okay not because Sammy Linden was in the Mafia. He was an associate member but not a member. He could not be a member. Sammy Linden was Jewish. I didn't want to infringe on anyone's territory and that's why I told Raymond L.S. As I said, it's kill or be killed. So I killed both Hughes and Linden.

After that, the wars quieted down. I made peace with Jimmy O'Toole and Maxie Shacklefoot. They were with the McLaughlin gang.

In January 1967 Flemmi killed Wimpy Bennett who hung around with us. Wimpy Bennett's death was spontaneous. I was there at the time. It took place in Flemmi's garage. Flemmi was having a beef over money. Earlier that day, he was blaming Peter Boulis for the problem. Boulis denied he had anything to do with it. Flemmi then confronted Wimpy. They argued. Flemmi then shot him in the side of the face. I helped bury Wimpy in Hopkinton.

After we killed Wimpy we had to kill his brother Walter. He was drumming up support to go after Flemmi. Walter's demise was planned by me. Walter trusted me so I was able to lure him to the garage to have him killed. I helped kill him. We buried Walter's body at the same site in Hopkinton where we buried Wimpy. Then we had to kill another brother, Billy, because he was drumming up support to go after me and Flemmi.

We planned for him to be killed by two men in a car and then transported to the Bennett burial site. But there was a screw up. Billy fell or jumped out of the car after he was shot. His body ended up lying on the street.

Because of that I was indicted for his killing. But the case was dismissed against me by Chief Justice McLaughlin. The witness against me, Dadieco, would not show up to testify even though he was in protective custody.

There were a lot of people I knew who were killed but I had nothing to do with their killings. You know some may have been killed by the LCN. I really don't know. You're not supposed to know someone's a member of the LCN unless you are formally introduced.

I knew Thomas Hillary. He was an associate of my son. No one gave him no authorization to take three hundred thousand dollars of silk from the Chinese. One day I met him in a restaurant and told him to get out of town and stay out. If I wanted to hurt him, he'd never have left the restaurant. I called him a mush artist. He got a hellavah break he didn't get killed!

I don't know Richard DaVincent. If you tell me his nickname is Vinny the pig, all I got to say is I don't remember being in contact with any Vinny the pigs.

This comment made everyone in the courtroom chuckle. It was the way he said it. It was not intentional on his part to be humorous. His answer was one you'd expect from a dumb sidekick hoodlum in a 1930s gangster movie. When the laughter broke out, Salemme looked confused. He couldn't figure out why people were laughing.

When I had meetings with Raymond L. S. Patriarca, he'd talk about proposing me for membership in the LCN. Around that time, Raymond L.S. wanted John Fitzgerald killed. Fitzgerald was playing both ends. He was being a lawyer and also a gangster. Raymond L.S. thought he was going to be a witness against him. He gave a directive to Larry Zannino to wipe him out. Zannino was part of the LCN in the Boston area. LCN stands for La Costra Nostra. It is translated as "our thing."

Me, Zannino, Raymond L.S., and Flemmi decided the way to wipe out Fitzgerald was to bomb his car. It was Flemmi's plan. Flemmi designed the bomb. Flemmi had knowledge of explosives and had blown up another car. I could have done it but I didn't. A bomb is simply a two-wire procedure with a cap at the end.

We blew up Fitzgerald's car but he survived although he was badly injured. After that I learned there were arrest warrants out for me and Flemmi. I took it on the lam. I became a fugitive. I went to San Francisco with Stevie Flemmi and Bobby Boulis. We then went to LA, back to Boston, and then to New York City.

I stayed in New York City until I was arrested by the Bureau, the federal bureau. I was walking down the street in Manhattan. Connolly came up to me and pulled a gun. He did not throw me to the ground. He asked me to lie down on the street. He was with two other agents. I knew Connolly from "L" street.[173]

---

[173] L Street is a large bathhouse located on Carson

After Connolly arrested me I was brought back to Boston by two state troopers on an airplane. I remember thinking on the plane that I'd rather have been anyplace else than on that plane going back to the trial. At trial, I was found guilty and sentenced to 28 to 30 years. I served 16 years and some months. I was released in February of 1988.

After Fitzgerald's bombing Raymond L.S. owed me for that but he never gave me any credit nor did he ever give me any money when I was in jail. Some of the men in the LCN in Boston gave me some money. Even though the Mafia never gave me money when I was in prison it did pay for my daughter's wedding. But that was expected.

Flemmi was never convicted of the bombing of Fitgerald's car. Dadieco who testified against me wouldn't testify against him. The charges were dismissed. Flemmi didn't do no time.[174]

Beach in South Boston. It has facilities for exercise, lifting weights, and hand ball. It is the place where its members plunge into the frigid waters of Boston Harbor on New Year's Day. Its clientele spans the gamut of mankind: doctors, lawyers, my brother Billy and my cousins, teachers, preachers, gangsters, those on the dole, and everyone in between.

[174] When he said this, he smirked showing his recognition that at the time he was arrested in New York City Flemmi had been a long time FBI informant. Salemme now knew that Flemmi made a deal with the FBI to give the FBI Salemme's location in New York City so Connolly could come back to Boston to be Flemmi's and Bulger's handler. To get the deal FBI agreed to have the bombing charges against Flemmi thrown out. But now the worm had turned. It was Salemme time to deal.

When I was in prison, my first wife survived on welfare. I had some business on the outside that my brother would pick up for me. Bucky Barrett brought me some of the proceeds from the Medford Trust Company heist on one occasion. I got no money from loan sharking in prison. Any money I got went home to the family. I got furloughs from prison for 14 days over a year.

I had a list of approved people I could contact. I saw Flemmi a couple of times. I didn't run an illegal business while in jail. I saw my brother Jackie on furlough. He was engaged in criminal activity. In the early 1980s Jackie was indicted for George Pappas's murder along with Brian Halloran.

Of course, I wanted to help out my brother. But I didn't speak to Raymond L.C. about helping him. I never talked to Flemmi about killing Halloran. Bulger later told me about killing him. He said he made him look like Swiss cheese. I wasn't that happy Bulger killed Halloran. He was the only one who could clear my brother of the murder. My brother was convicted even though he had nothing to do with it. He was in jail for 2 ½ years before Chief Justice Liacos reversed his conviction. It didn't benefit me that Halloran got killed.

Raymond L. S. Patriarca was indicted in late 1967 for the murder of the Mafeo brothers. At that time, the case involving the Edward "Teddy" Deegan murder was pending. Joe 'the Animal' Barboza was the principle witness in both of these cases. I never had any dealings with Barboza.[175]

When I got out of jail in 1988, I went to live in Sharon. I started doing some legitimate work in the contracting business, building a condominium in the North Providence area. During that time George Kaufman kept beeping my son telling him to have me come to his auto shop to see Flemmi. I didn't want to do it because I wanted to stay out of trouble. But in May 1988 I decided to go to the garage. I had no car since I got out of prison so I went to see Kaufman who said he had found a car for me.

By the time I got out of prison Raymond L.S. Patriarca was dead. The Patriarca crime family was then being run by his son Raymond Joseph Patriarca, Junior. He was called Junior or Junior Patriarca. One day when I was working building condominiums in Providence, Junior Patriarca came over to visit me. He told me he wanted to sponsor me for membership in the Mafia. So in

---

[175] The Deegan murder case resulted in the conviction of four men. Barboza, an FBI informant and a main government witness, placed them at the scene of the murder. It took 30 years before FBI reports came out showing this was false and that these men were not involved. Two of them died in jail. Barboza lied and the FBI knew it. Even so Barboza was put in the FBI's witness protection program. While in it, he killed another person. FBI agents with Judge Harrington who will testify in this case for Connolly went to California to intercede on behalf of Barboza. Barboza was murdered a short time after that. FBI agent Rico of Wheeler murder fame was involved in it. When Rico was asked about it, he said he wasn't going to shed any tears over the incident. He felt that the four who went to jail were part of the mob so it didn't matter that they were innocent of Deegan's murder.

June, 1988, I went through the induction ceremony and I became a made man.[176] I was assigned to the head of the family, Junior Patriarca. The head of a Mafia family is considered a king. So I became a king's man.

He beamed with childish pride when he said he was a king's man.

When I became a made man, I took an oath to be loyal to the family at all times. I must be at the family's beck and call. The family is number one even above your own family. If they tell you to murder someone, you do so.

Within a year after that in 1989 I was ambushed and shot. My internal organs, my intestines, my liver and other internal parts are damaged. I wasn't armed at the time. I had just come from the gym. I was standing outside the Pancake House in Saugus. I was supposed to settle a dispute over some music contest. I was supposed to meet with Sonny Mercurio. He probably set me up. I never saw who shot me. They had masks on. I spent a long time recuperating from my wounds.

After I was shot I learned the FBI knew I was going to be shot. The FBI not only knew but it fomented the attack on me. The FBI shouldn't just let people get killed. It's got to inform a person if it knows he is going to be shot. Rather than doing that it fomented the shooting.   Connolly and James Ring were involved with the informants who knew about it. The Bureau should've informed me

---

[176] He's out of jail in February. He testified he wanted to stay out of trouble and do legitimate work. Four months later he's in the Mafia.

of this. I've blamed the Bureau in my pleadings and my testimony at the motion hearings for letting me get shot.[177]

I don't dislike Connolly because he arrested me in 1972. I don't dislike him because he didn't tell me I was going to be shot. It was the Boston FBI office I disliked. I never held it against Connolly. I also don't dislike him because he didn't come in to testify for me. I'm testifying because I just decided to tell the truth as I know it and to cooperate against Flemmi.

In June 1989 I became a capo in the Mafia. That's like a captain. There's the boss, the underboss, the consigliari, and the capo. Each capo had a degime, ten people under him. As a king's man capo, I had no degime. There was no one under me. I reported directly to the king. Maybe you could say my son who was also a made member of the Mafia was under me. As a capo, I was engaged in collecting rent, extortion, and also in the numbers racket with Flemmi. As a capo of a king, I could go anywhere I wanted in New England.

Capos should not take any money from their men. It's up to them if they do. The greedy ones do but the better ones have their own sources of income. The capos report to the underboss or

---

[177] Listening to Salemme complain I expect he'll be suing the Justice Department claiming it should have better protected him from being shot by other Mafia figures. If he did and recovered, the money should be escrowed for the families of those he killed.

231

the consiglieri. The Mafia is a financially successful organization.

In October 1989 Patriarca Junior held a making ceremony on Guild Street in Medford. I didn't attend it. I was still physically not in the best of shape. The government planted a bug there with the help of inside informants. Because of that in late 1989 or early 1990 most of the Patriarca family had been arrested and charged. By the summer of 1991 they were all in jail.

I think it's ridiculous that Patriarca Junior had an induction ceremony at Guild Street. He held it in someone's house. They had prosciutto and figs. Things have changed for the worse in the LCN. Back in the 1960s the LCN was much more stringent about who it let in. Back then no one knew when there was going to be an induction ceremony. You would just be pulled off the street or out of an alley and taken to some cellar. I'll tell you one thing for sure the quality and type of people they let into the Mafia now has really gone down. When Raymond L. S. invited me to join, that was the time when the LCN had a high quality membership. I was a high quality member.

If you want to know what I think, the Mafia should have stuck with men like me. In the '60s they were more selective about who joined the group. You can tell that by the Mafia's history.[178]

---

[178] He thinks he's a high quality member. Yet he's doing the same thing as the other Mafia rats testifying for the Justice Department to do lesser time in jail Perhaps its different since he's not testifying against Mafia figures and he's gaining revenge. But still he's turned state's evidence

In March 1990 Patriarca Junior was in jail. I was very close to Raymond L.S. Patriarca. I was not as close to Patriarca Junior even though he sponsored me for membership and made me his capo. I had access to the Patriarca home. I met Patriarca, Junior's wife, at his home. I also met her at the Lincoln Mall when Junior was being held in prison in Danbury, Connecticut, awaiting trial.

Junior was trying to get his sentence reduced by saying he was only a soldier in the Mafia. I told her to tell Junior not to say he wasn't the boss. Denying he was the boss was bad because he was revealing the La Cosa Nostra structure. I knew it would result in adverse consequences for him. It ultimately did. I was trying to warn him through his wife. But because Junior refused to act like a boss the Commission in New York removed him from the position of boss and struck his membership in the Mafia.

The Commission then asked me to come to New York City to meet with them. I met with the consiglieris of the three families that were still operating. James Ida, from the Genovese family, Frank Locasia, from the Gambino family, and Vincent Alloy, from the Columbo family. They knew the New England Family was in disarray. Bianco sent word to New York and I was told to report there. They made me the boss of the New England Family. People know you became boss when you go around and introduce yourself.

When I became boss, I took over the family. I took over the flock so to speak. There are no rival

---

to help himself.

factions in the family. There are disputes but no different factions. I did not settle disputes. That was done by the consigliore with the under boss. Except for Springfield, all New England was a closed shop and anyone wanting to operate there had to come to me for permission. I was involved in extortion, loan sharking, gambling, collecting rent, labor racketeering, and also getting rent from drug dealers.

It's absolutely false that I became head of the New England Crime family by tipping off the Guild Street induction ceremony so I could have those in front of me put in jail. After the induction ceremony was bugged a good number of the family was in jail and it was difficult for anyone not on the street to operate. I was one of the few members left standing. Flemmi never told me to stay away from the ceremonies.[179]

I could have gone to the ceremony but I didn't feel well enough to go. I was still recuperating from the gunshot wounds. If I went, I'd have to stay all day. If it were absolutely necessary, I would have gone. I would not have become boss if I had attended the induction ceremony.

When I became head of the Mafia in New England, the name of the group was changed from

---

[179] There's a good chance Flemmi did tell him to stay away. They were boyhood friends. They became close friends meeting every other day after Salemme got out of jail. We heard Weeks say that Bulger didn't like their closeness. They were planning to run a profitable numbers racket together. Connolly's book apparently made it appear that he was tipped off

the Patriarca crime family to the New England Crime Family. I didn't give my stamp of approval to everything. I told my capos, "You make the decision. Just make the right one. Just don't embarrass the family."[180]

As boss I killed no one. I authorized no murders. The Mafia was still a violent group but during the four years I was boss there were no murders committed by my people.

Once Natali Vittichi came and sat down with me. Vittichi wanted to open X-rated smut shops in New England. New York gave him permission to talk with me. Deluca and Guarino sat down with us. I told Vittichi that he already had one shop in Boston that was grandfathered in. I was not going to let him have any more. I didn't want him to have more because of the heat that would come on me if more smut shops opened in my territory. My conversation with Vittichi was intercepted by the government.

My son was involved in illegal activity in California. I never contacted the California Mafia to help him. The California Mafia is a Mickey Mouse Mafia. It's not as accomplished as the Mafia on the East Coast or in Chicago. I contacted the Las Vegas Mafia to help him. I had a discussion with Tally Vittichi, a Gambino family member who lived in Las Vegas for health reasons, to get approval for my son to work in Las Vegas.

My son was indicted in July 1992 for labor racketeering. He had never spent time in jail before that. I got no inside information about that

---

[180] See Appendix C on naming the book.

investigation. It wasn't investigated by the Boston FBI office. It was a Labor Department investigation. My son was never convicted. His case kept getting postponed because of his illness until he died.

My son and Bobby DeLuca earned their money from extortion. I earned about 16 to 29 percent of six million a year or over a million dollars a year from the numbers. They each earned from their extortion and loan sharking hundreds of thousands of dollars a year. It was a profitable business.

I knew a person named DiSauro. He owned a club called the Channel where my son was all the time. DiSauro could not implicate me in any criminal activity. I don't know if he went missing during the middle of the grand jury investigation of my son or if he is missing today.

In 1990 me and Stevie Flemmi formed a numbers business in Boston but we didn't get it going until early '91. We grossed about 120,000 dollars a week. We didn't come out ahead all weeks. Sometimes we were on make up. But on average, we were supposed to earn between 16 to 29 percent of the gross a year. Me and Stevie agreed to split the money fifty-fifty. Flemmi would split his half with his partner Bulger; I would divide the proceeds with Deluca and Charlie Fusina. I came to realize that over the time Flemmi was skimming money away from me. He took about 300,000 dollars of my money.

When we started the numbers business, Flemmi said he could provide some protection from law enforcement. Flemmi told me more than once they were paying money to Connolly. Flemmi was paying Connolly for the grand jury information. It was in June 1993 that I first became aware of the five thousand dollar payments to Connolly. Flemmi told me twice that they paid Connolly five thousand dollars. Flemmi also told me they were paying a state police officer in the Attorney General's office.

We set up an X fund from the illegal money we made. The Mafia had no cops on its payroll that I know of. I only had information about Connolly and a state cop. I didn't know what sources of information those under me had. I gave money to Flemmi to give to Connolly. The same amount was paid to the state cop. I didn't know the name of the person in the Attorney General's office who was the source of information. I only knew of Connolly. Flemmi knew the guy in the AG's office.

Some of the information that Flemmi told me he got from Connolly was that the grand jury was looking at the car bombing and the murders I did in the '60s to include those events as part of the RICO charges. In 1993 the numbers business wasn't doing as well as it had been. I continued to associate with Stevie Flemmi even though I knew from him that the grand jury was investigating us. I also knew what was going on with the grand jury from the witnesses who were going in to testify and generally from the word on the street.

In 1993 and 1994 Flemmi was giving me information. I learned in early 1993 I was under police surveillance. Flemmi would meet with my son and pass on the information. I was under constant surveillance since 1988.

I knew what a Title III was. Flemmi told me that if the government got a Title III it could use any sort of thing they wanted up to a battleship to surveil you. Flemmi told me Connolly said I was the subject of a court-authorized electronic surveillance. Later when the Justice Department told me that my conversations had been intercepted, I found out he was right

In 1994 I ran into Connolly. This was a chance meeting. I had driven into Boston from Sharon and wanted to use the telephone. I knew I was always under surveillance so I pulled into the underground garage at the Prudential Center to make a call on the pay telephone. I was on the phone talking to Bobby DeLuca when I saw Connolly coming up towards me. I told Bobby that he was coming right at me.

It was the first time I had seen him since he arrested me in New York. It wasn't awkward. Connolly extended his hand and said "Frank, Frank." He then said referring to the New York City incident where he arrested me, "I hope there's no hard feelings. I was just doing my job."

I said there were none. There were no hard feelings. Connolly had nothing to do with the car bombing. It was his job to arrest me. He said "How you doing?" - "What's up?" – "You're lookin' good." We chatted generally. He did not mention the book at that time. He told me he was working on the 30th floor. He invited me to come up for a visit.

Later I talked with Bobby DeLuca and my son about this. They figured I had nothing to lose. So I decided to see if I could keep up the relationship that Flemmi had established with Connolly. The next day or a couple of days later I went to his office. I went to see if Connolly was willing to share information with me. I knew I was under surveillance but it was pretty easy to slip it in the Prudential Center where there are thousands of people walking around. When I went there, Connolly was alone. His secretary told him I was there. We talked about different matters.

Connolly told me he was writing a book and had a chapter on me. I wasn't too happy to hear that. Connolly said two FBI agents from New York, Joe Pistone and Jules Bonefatala, had reviewed the book. They said to him that it looked like I had been tipped off by him not to go to the Guild Street induction ceremony. That concerned me.

Connolly knew who the informant was and it wasn't me. I wanted no association with being tied into being an informant for a bugging. No word ever got back to me that the people in the Mafia wondered why I didn't attend the ceremony. I asked Connolly if it was his intention to make me look like a rat. As a head of an LCN family, it would matter a lot to me if I was labeled a rat. Connolly also told me that the indictments were not out yet and he would let Stevie Flemmi know about it when they were coming down.

I made a second visit to Connolly. When I went in to see him, there was a gentleman standing there. His name was John. I thought he was an assistant district attorney in Middlesex County. I put out my hand to shake his when Connolly introduced us but John flinched back. He acted like there was a camera on him. When John left, I told Connolly I had been talking to my son. I told him I was worried about what he said that it looked like I was tipped by Connolly or Flemmi to stay away from the Mafia induction ceremony. I didn't want there to be any inference on the street that I was tipped.

Kathleen Orrick testified she remembered Salemme coming to the office without an appointment to visit Connolly. Connolly introduced him to her. She remembered the name because she typed the manuscript for Connolly's book and Salemme was mentioned in the book.

John was John Ford, a friend of Connolly's. He testified that in June 1994 he dropped by Connolly's office for a visit. He was sitting there talking to Connolly when Connolly's secretary came in. She said Mr. Frank Salemme was there. Salemme walked in. He quickly left the office and went back to his office. Ford said Connolly appeared surprised when Salemme showed up. Salemme was wearing a red tank top and gym shorts. After he got back to his office Connolly called him to express his surprise that Salemme showed up.

In the fall of 1994 I left the area for a while. The grand jury was ending. I thought the indictments were coming down. This was when Bobby DeLuca was indicted. No one told me DeLuca was going to be indicted in October 1994. I had no source that could give me that information.

Neither me, Stevie Flemmi or Bulger were charged in DeLuca's indictment. DeLuca had no connection with Bulger or Flemmi. I went to Florida for four to six weeks. After the trip I came back and went to see Flemmi who told me the indictments had not been handed down yet.

On January 5 I was home and getting ready to go to Boston. My son was very ill at the time and living with my ex-wife. I was with Joseph Ruggerio when I got beeped. I called my ex-wife. She told me to come to the house. I thought my son who has since died needed some attention. As soon as I entered, I walked into the kitchen. There I saw my son and Stevie Flemmi sitting at the kitchen table. Flemmi told me he received the word from Connolly that the indictments were coming down on January 10. He said Bulger had already left town. He was planning to take off over the weekend. Flemmi did not know the arrest teams were out that day. He got arrested later that day.

I took the information seriously. I first went to the Venetzia restaurant in Dorchester to gather my thoughts. Then I drove down to Federal Hill in Providence where I met Bobby DeLuca at Christina's. While there I got a call from my wife saying the house was surrounded by cops

Alice McLaughlin, Salemme's first wife, testified that she remembered one time when Salemme, Joe Ruggiero, Stevie Flemmi, and her son were in the home at the same time. She did not remember the date. She said Flemmi only came once.

I took off for Florida where I stayed until I was captured in August, 1995. What happened was that on January 5 arrest warrants had been issued for us. We thought they were coming down on January 10. They threw us a curve.[181]

After I fled I had no contacts in Boston. I had people who I thought were my friends but weren't like Mercurio or Bobby Shanks. If I told you what was going on inside the LCN, you would see why I didn't tell anyone where I was. Once I was indicted, I had no contact with anyone in Massachusetts. I used for my escape the money I had stashed in Massachusetts and money I had on me.

I was brought back to Boston in August 1995. Once I was put in jail, I was no longer the head of the LCN. I was held with Flemmi at the Plymouth House of Corrections. I did not know Flemmi and Bulger were informants when I first got locked up. But I began to suspect it after I was jailed.

Stevie Flemmi believed there was no way that the government would disclose the identity of the informants. Flemmi told me it was Connolly's idea to file the motions to seek disclosure of the informants. After a while the defense teams came up with a strategy to learn the identities of the

---

[181] The indictments did issue on January 10. The arrest warrants issued on January 5. Stevie didn't know this and was arrested on the fifth. He had been relying on his source who apparently told him the tenth. Weeks didn't know the tenth date. He said Connolly told him it would happen after the holidays. The FBI participated in the arrests on the fifth. It seems Connolly did not know of the issuing of the arrest warrants.

informants. If the informants were part of the indictments charging conspiracy then they were government agents. If they were government agents, the indictments couldn't stand because you can't be charged with conspiring with the government. If we could force the government to identify the informants, we figured we would get the government to dismiss the indictments.

My lawyer filed a motion to disclose the identities of the informants. It was signed by DeLuca, Martorano, and me. Flemmi did not sign it. Flemmi could not disclose he was an informant and still get help from the FBI under the guidelines.[182] The day after we filed the motions Flemmi was called in the judge's lobby. We learned later he was told he could have a separate hearing or reveal he was an informant.

When I first learned Flemmi was giving information, I was not furious. I was upset, mad. It was a break of friendship that goes back to when we were kids. I was very troubled that Flemmi had been an informant for many years. Flemmi told me that he never gave the FBI anything of value. He said he was giving up garbage and getting back gold. I wasn't furious that Flemmi had been an informant all those years because there was nothing I could do about what had been done.[183]

---

[182] As noted earlier, an FBI informant was extorted into not disclosing his status because to do so would mean he would not get the FBI's help.

[183] Surprisingly, Salemme remained friendly with Flemmi even after he knew Flemmi had been an informant. Others like Martorano who wanted to kill him were not so

After the fact of Flemmi being an informant came out Johnny Martorano decided that he would cooperate. Johnny always tried to make himself into a capo. His brother Jimmy was a made member who was involved with the Gambino family in an enterprise he had going on in Atlantic City involving the hotel linen business. I approved of him going there. Jimmy was indicted in 1992 in New Jersey. I knew he was indicted but not much more. I never provided any funds for him.

Stevie Flemmi kept telling me that Connolly would come in and help us break up the indictments. We got FBI 209s before the public hearings. It was then I learned that Flemmi was giving information out about me. On May 23, 1990, Flemmi gave information on me. The bulk of it was true. But I never said I visited John Gotti. I never said I was planning to take over Boston after their people were in jail. It never entered my mind I would be the boss of LCN. I never wanted the position. It was partially forced on me. It was a lucrative position but I didn't want it even though I didn't have to take it.

Stevie Flemmi sent Kevin Weeks out to try to identify the informants who gave the information about the Mafia induction ceremony at Guild Street. By that time I already knew Flemmi and Sonny Mercurio were informants. I don't remember Bulger's name coming up as an informant on Guild Street. We wanted to know the names because it was important that we get that bug suppressed. All the people involved in the

forgiving.

ceremony went to prison. In effect it destroyed the New England Mafia.

I saw Weeks with Flemmi in the visiting room when Weeks gave us the names of four informants. A visitor can either talk on the phone or lip sync through the glass. Weeks got the name of four informants: CS–1, who was Flemmi; CS–2, who was Angelo "Sonny" Mercurio, and CS-3 and CS–4. Connolly told Flemmi CS-3 was an informant. We also learned that through discovery. CS-4 was incarcerated at the time of the Guild Street ceremony. I suspected he was an informant. Connolly's information confirmed that. Even so the government didn't dismiss the indictments.

Weeks was getting the information he was giving to Flemmi from Connolly. Flemmi testified before Judge Wolf that he knew the precise date the indictment was to be returned. I had had numerous conversations with Stevie Flemmi up to that time about who gave him that information. He always said it was Connolly. Even in the elevator that morning going up to the hearing Stevie said to me that Connolly had told him about the indictments coming down. I believed right up to the time Flemmi took the stand that he was going to say Connolly tipped him off about the indictment.

When he testified that Morris told him, I was surprised. Before that I had never heard the name Morris. Actually I was furious. I didn't like the fact that Flemmi didn't put Connolly into the position I thought he would put him into. I didn't like it that Connolly did not come in to testify at the motion hearings. Flemmi told me Connolly was going to come in to help us. Flemmi had lied to me and cheated me out of money. I couldn't do anything about the past. I just wanted to get out of the position I was in.

Later in the court holding area I had a not-very-friendly conversation with Flemmi. He told me he had to say it was Morris. He said Connolly could hurt him and Jimmy Bulger. He could bury them. After Flemmi did what he did I had very little to do with him.[184] I made the decision to testify. I pled guilty and got an 11 year, 4 month sentence. I have a little less than three years to serve. If I lied here on the stand, I would be in trouble with this judge and Judge Wolf.

---

[184] Stevie, relying on Connolly's statements and actions, believed Connolly and the FBI would always protect him. He needed evidence that he was authorized by the FBI to commit his crimes so as to undermine the government's case. The best evidence would be Connolly. Connolly foolishly refused to bite the bullet and tell Judge Wolf what his deal was with Stevie. He tricked Stevie into saying Morris gave him the authorization hoping he could keep himself out of it. Stevie stupidly listened to Connolly and blamed Morris. Even Salemme knew that wouldn't work. All came a cropper when Morris denied the authorization to save his pension. Connolly's attempt to distort the truth ended up undermining not only Stevie but mostly himself. Connolly would have been so much better off had he not resorted to his trickery and deceit in this matter. After all if he said he was doing what was expected of him in handling these top level informants, he could have had a defense to the charges. He too relied on the FBI to protect him. We see how that turned out.

CHAPTER NINE

LIMPING TO THE END

A JUDGE AND FORMER PROSECUTOR
TESTIFY

Salemme spent most of Friday, May 17, 2002, on the stand. Late in the afternoon, the Justice Department offered some clean up witnesses to carry us into the weekend recess. I've previously included summaries of their testimony in areas relevant to it.[185]

On Monday, May 20, 2001, I'm reviewing my notes in the courtroom when Judge Tauro enters. I stand and glance at the witness stand. I see Judge Mark Wolf sitting there. He's the person most

---

[185] When court recessed for the day, I left the courthouse and strolled toward South Station where I planned to take a train to my home. Miner, Connolly, and her associate, Jay Tagney walking at a crisp pace came up aside me. Miner asked me what I thought. I said it's tough. I suggested she follow up on her opening and emphasize the sordid background of the gangster witnesses so the jury will disbelieve them. I said she made a good point in emphasizing Salemme 's deal that he was not required to testify against any members of the Mafia. Connolly started to talk to me. He expressed his disdain for Morris and I told him I didn't like him either saying Morris's story about being unable to give back the wine made no sense. Connolly said he never gave Morris any wine. He said he introduced Morris to the owner of Martingettis, a wine store. Morris always bought his wine over there. I said, "That's not the point, I'm talking about what Morris testified about. I'm saying his testimony in and of itself made no sense." We had reached South Station. Connolly stuck out his hand and said "Thanks." I said "Good luck."

247

responsible for this trial; the one who wrote the 661 page decision that blew the lid off the FBI's involvement with Bulger and Flemmi. [186]

He has thinning grey black hair. He will pull at his hair with his left hand when he reads some documents during his testimony. He's dressed smartly in a dark blue suit, blue and orange striped tie and white shirt. He wears thick glasses.

I have time to let my thoughts wander because Connolly is not in the courtroom. We wait for him. It seems like a long wait but whenever you come to the starting line and there's a delay, it always seems longer than it is. I start thinking of Connolly. He must be getting really nervous now that we're coming to the end. He's back in the courtroom. He looks fine, or as well as he could be given the circumstances.

MARK WOLF

FEDERAL DISTRICT JUDGE

My name is Mark Wolf. I am a sitting United States District Court Judge for the District of Massachusetts. I have been subpoenaed to testify.

I grew up in Newton, a suburb of Boston. I graduated from Harvard Law in 1971. I worked in Washington, DC, for the Department of Justice under Attorney General Levy. In 1981 I worked in

---

[186] The court house talk about him is that he has an acerbic disposition. A good word about him is as hard to find as a seat in the courtroom. I think if he weren't like, that we would not have penetrated into the depths of the FBI's infamous behavior. He demands a lot of himself and a lot of others. You take the good with the bad.

the US Attorney's office in Boston as Bill Weld's Deputy for four years. I then became a judge.[187]

Cases are randomly assigned to judges. In October 1994 I was assigned the DeLuca indictment. When the indictment of Salemme,

---

[187] I had met Wolf once when I went in to interview with William Weld for an assistant US attorney position. I remembered when he was appointed a judge. I thought he was very young to have been put on the federal bench. Earlier that morning while waiting outside the courtroom, I had been discussing with Tim Tanakos the necessity of life experience in making decisions. Tim is a screen writer and former medical student who came from LA to attend the trial, Tim told me a story of how he had to be tested for tuberculosis, TB, as a condition of working in one of his positions as a medical student. The test consisted of a scratch being made into the skin on his left arm. The next day there will be a reaction where he is scratched. The size and shape of it indicated whether he had TB. Tim's was done on a Thursday. The doctor who would look at it was not going to be back until Monday or Tuesday. Tim looked at the reaction a thousand times over the weekend and studied about it in medical books. It looked exactly like the pictures of people with TB and had the same measurements that would indicate he had TB. He was convinced he had it. In his mind he prepared for the worst. He would not get the job he was seeking and he would be isolated for a year falling behind in his studies. He lamented this cruel turn of fate. When the doctor returned, he went with trepidation to get the bad news. As soon as the doctor lifted up his sleeve he said, after a quick glance "You're fine" That was experience rather than books. I always thought it best not to appoint judges until they've practiced for over twenty years. I found those that had labored in the pit of the courtroom were the better judges. Yet there are always exceptions. Perhaps Judge Wolf is one of them.

Bulger and the others was returned, it was a superseding indictment to the DeLuca case so it remained with me. The pre-trial litigation went on for six years with a multitude of motions to suppress evidence and to dismiss the indictments. The motions to dismiss revolved around the claim that Bulger and Flemmi were authorized to commit the crimes, or that outrageous government conduct should defeat the government's ability to prosecute these defendants.

The latter is sort of an exclusionary rule argument. Under the exclusionary rule police misconduct will prevent evidence from being introduced at a hearing or trial. By extension outrageous conduct should prevent a trial. There were no hearings conducted on the outrageous issue.

In March 1997 there were closed door hearings dealing with the need to disclose the identity of informants. This closure was to limit public knowledge as to the identity of the informants. On March 11, 1997, counsel for Salemme asked to see me in the lobby seeking to learn if Donati, St. Laurent, Guarino, Bulger, and Mercurio were informants. The next day I held a meeting with Department of Justice officials without the defendants being present to discuss the issue about disclosing the identity of informants and the effect it would have on the case. I gave them time to decide whether to disclose or to dismiss the case.

On March 13 another hearing was held to decide whether the informants' identities should be disclosed and whether there should be live testimony about this issue. The next day I issued an order that the defendants file legal memoranda on the issue by March 31. The order was under seal. Only the lawyers and parties were to have access to it.

The initial motion for disclosure of informants was not filed by Flemmi. Flemmi's name was not included among the original informant names that the defendants sought to have disclosed. Defense counsel stated it had substantial information that the persons listed were informants. They wanted the government to confirm it. The government denied DiNardi was an informant. St. Laurent, Mercurio, and Guarino were brought to Boston to determine if they were informants. As to St. Laurent and Guarino, the issue about their status was never officially resolved. All I can say is that it was resolved to my satisfaction but I could not discuss it because the matters are not part of the public record. I'd say that as to one of the two individuals, it was not resolved.

The defendants' memorandum was filed on March 27. On March 31 I received a letter under the letterhead of the Boston Police Department from three anonymous Boston police officers.[188] The letter was received by deadline date during the time when all the matters were still under court seal. When I read the letter, I thought it was relevant. I ordered that copies of it be sent under seal to all parties. I was trying to conduct the

---

[188] This letter was written by Connolly as part of his plan with Flemmi.

251

hearings in strictest confidence so as not to jeopardize the identity of the informants.

The defendants were moving to suppress the Kaufman wiretap which was done during a joint investigation between DEA and the FBI. They argued that it was not properly authorized. This letter seemed to relate to that event. The letter made reference to Boston police officer Frank Dewan. I had never heard of him before I received the letter. The claim set forth in the letter was that Dewan had fabricated information that went to the judge who authorized the warrants. It also said Dewan had engaged in gypsy wiretaps, wiretaps done without court authority that are illegal, to get information and attributed it to informants. The letter also contained attacks on FBI Agent Morris.

I never accepted anything in the letter as true. That was the reason I had a hearing on it to determine whether it was true or not. I often receive letters from families, prisoners, and others. I do not recall ever receiving another anonymous letter. It is not my practice to give every letter I receive to all litigants. I do it on a case by case basis. If a letter has the potential to influence me one way or another relative to a matter before me, I will distribute it to others. Aside from the letter there was enough other information before me to hold the hearings on May 22.

If I had received the letter after the March 31 deadline, I still would have handled it the same way. There were a fair number of leaks of sealed information during the hearings. I ordered an investigation into them.[189]

I don't recall thinking when I received the letter that the sender of the letter had inside information on what was going on at my hearings that were closed to the public. I did not focus on that until April 18. The government argued that I give no weight to the letter because it was anonymous. There was a belief because of its relevance that it must have come from Flemmi especially because Flemmi's brother was a Boston Police officer. It seemed that there was a Flemmi influence in the letter.

On April 2 I ordered counsel under seal to address certain additional issues including the anonymous letter. Only some of the defendants had filed the motions regarding the informants. I noticed that Flemmi had not signed the motion. That was unusual because normally all defendants sign such a motion. In the middle of April I held hearings on the outstanding issues including those raised by the letter.

On May 22 I directed the Justice Department to confirm or deny whether Bulger, Mercurio, St. Laurent or Guarino were FBI informants. The order remained under seal for a week while the Justice Department made the decision whether to disclose the identity or to move to dismiss the case. During the month of June the Justice Department refused to obey my order. Motions were filed to

---

[189] Without knowing, I assume he asked the FBI to conduct the investigation. On one hand he's in a battle with the FBI, yet on the other he's asking for its help. It seems counterproductive to expect the FBI or even the Justice Department to investigate itself.

hold the Deputy Attorney General in contempt and to jail him for his refusal to act pursuant to the court order.

The Department of Justice never disclosed the identity of the informants. With respect to Mercurio I was forced to bring him into open court to inquire of him whether he was an informant. He admitted to being one.

I would not agree that there was just a fair amount of controversy at that time. I would say there was an enormous controversy concerning disclosing informants.[190] There were repeated discussions and orders. I had to bring Mercurio, St. Laurent and Guarino to court although I never put St. Laurent and Guarino on the stand. DiNardi was dead. The government said he was not an informant.

Later in the hearing the identity of other informants was brought to my attention. I have

---

[190] The Justice Department's actions still seem to rankle him. He seems to regret not having thrown the Deputy Attorney General in jail. To avoid the confrontation, he was forced to come up with a creative solution to avoid dismissing the case. When he said the Justice Department denied DiNardi was an informant, I detected in his voice a note of disbelief and frustration as if to indicate he knew he could never find out the truth. I felt that if he faces the issue again, he'll not hesitate to uphold the power of the court to reach the truth to his satisfaction. I wondered if his animus toward the Justice Department might not cause him to gain a degree of retribution by giving lighter sentences to criminal defendants as he did with Salemme. Unfortunately our laws reward criminals for government misconduct rather than punishing those engaged in the misconduct.

here a sheet of paper with two names on it. These individuals have been identified as informants C-3 and C-4 in the affidavit for the induction ceremony wiretap. I recognized C-3 and C-4 as named informants. I'd agree there was an awful lot of controversy from March until the end of June over the disclosure of informants.

From January to March 1998, I held hearings on the motions. Morris testified before me about the incident involving Eddie Miani that was referred to in the letter. Former US Attorney Gary Crossen and DEA Agent Steven Boeri testified about Dewan's information. I found the information in the letter about Dewan was unsubstantiated and untrue. The allegations against Morris in the Miani matter were true. The letter did impact the system of justice because a series of orders were issued concerning it. I had to write about it in my decisions and during the 1998 hearing it was the subject of some of the testimony.

I was required to answer two questions regarding the letter. First, I had to decide whether to order evidentiary hearings on the motion to suppress because the affidavits might have contained deliberate falsehoods; and also whether to disclose that any of the five named persons were government informants. To get an evidentiary hearing you need to meet a high standard called the Franks standard. A defendant has to show that false information was included in the affidavit and that it was material. If defendant can show that, he must show that it was put in there deliberately with disregard for the truth. The letter's allegations helped the defendants meet that standard and contributed to my decision to have the identities of the informants released.[191]

The FBI did conduct an interview of me. I would not allow the interview unless I could see a draft of the 302 that they were going to file. I saw the draft and made some minor changes. I saw other areas in the 302 that I thought I should flesh out. I took a couple of things out of the 302 and added other things in. Misunderstandings in conversations can happen at any time.[192]

---

[191] Wolf clearly showed the letter's adverse impact on the legal system. The prosecution is fixing on this. The letter is a significant piece of evidence. It is not tainted by a connection with a gangster. It cannot be explained away. Connolly's friend Ford identified a couple of paragraphs from it, his secretary recognized the type and style of the letter, and Boston Police Department stationery was found in Connolly's office. I thought the letter was Connolly's Achilles heel through which all the poisonous testimony from the gangsters might flow. I thought Connolly's goose was cooked. His misguided attempts to hide his relationship with Stevie and to own up to his actions are hard for me to understand.

[192] Judge Wolf received a special privilege of reviewing a draft of a 302 report and changing it. All others are told they can be interviewed or face a grand jury. If they are interviewed, they will not see the 302 nor have a chance to correct it. Judge Wolf arrogated to himself a right almost no other citizen can claim. If he is so suspect of the FBI's use of 302s, he should work for a change in the court's policy regarding their use to benefit everyone. Only when interviews are recorded will a citizen have the necessary protection from an FBI agent's mistakes, carelessness, or misinterpretation of a person's words, or as Judge Wolf testified, 'misunderstandings.'

LIMPING TO THE END

JONATHAN CHIEL

FORMER ASSISTANT US ATTORNEY

My name is Jonathan Chiel. I am a Harvard Law School graduate. I clerked for Judge Tauro and worked in the US Attorney's office as chief of the criminal division under Donald Stern. I knew Connolly when he became the FBI representative to the Organized Crime Drug Enforcement Task Force (OCDETF).

In the fall of 1990 I was supervising a matter called the 51 case. It was a DEA investigation into cocaine trafficking in South Boston. Boston Police Detective Frank Dewan assisted us. We were trying to find out whether Bulger was directly involved in the cocaine trafficking or whether he was collecting rent from these people. During 1987 and 1988 we did significant electronic surveillance in the matter. We put indictments together against 51 defendants in the fall of 1990.

Frank Dewan was quite aware of what was going on in South Boston. He knew Bulger had connections with law enforcement. Our investigation did not come up with sufficient evidence to indict Bulger because the case against him was compromised.

DEA was the lead agency in the case which was done mainly with the Boston Police. On the day we executed the arrest warrants Connolly called me. He had not been directly involved with the investigation even though it was an OCDETF case.

Rule 6E forbids the disclosure of grand jury matters until there is a public event. The grand jury is all about secrecy. Connolly called me and asked, "Jonathan, are you indicting Whitey Bulger?"[193] He said there are rumors from the Malone camp that Whitey Bulger is going to be indicted. Malone was running for a state-wide office at the time.

I didn't tell Connolly anything. Connolly's voice showed he was upset and frustrated by my refusal. I felt dismayed about the incident. At that time I did not know Bulger was an informant or that Connolly was his handler. I was not aware that Bulger ever gave information about illegal drugs in South Boston to the Justice Department. I'm aware that the FBI protected its informants.

In February or March 1989, Jeremiah O'Sullivan was appointed interim US Attorney. He succeeded Francis McNamara who had a short much criticized, tumultuous term in office. McNamara conducted an investigation of the so-called 75 State Street matter. He finished the investigation without bringing charges against anyone. One of O'Sullivan's first jobs was to review McNamara'a investigation into the 75 State Street matter. He reopened the investigation but I was not involved in it.[194]

---

[193] It is not a violation of the rule to share what is going on in the grand jury with investigating officers you work with. I thought Chiel was stretching the secrecy point. Connolly was not asking for grand jury information but whether arrest warrants had issued and whether arrests were being made which doesn't seem improper.

Around that time Connolly was continually calling me and pestering me to go to lunch. I finally agreed but only on the condition that the DEA representative from OCDETF, Gerry Franciosa, go along with us. As soon as I got into the car Connolly was driving. Connolly turned to me and said, "What's going on with that 75 State Street investigation?"[195] I replied, "Gee, John, I don't know I'm not involved in it. I'm just doing the drug cases in the office." Connolly said "The Senate President is a great man. This is crazy. I don't know what they are doing over there."[196]

At the end of 1994 the investigation into the activities of Flemmi and others was ready for indictment. As chief of the criminal division, I was involved. Shortly before Christmas I met with the FBI to tell them that we were going to indict Bulger and Flemmi. The meeting was arranged a few days before it was held. Present at the meeting were Stern, Jim Farmer and myself from Justice and Svenson, ASAC O'Callaghan, and Supervisor Ed Quinn from the FBI. At the meeting my concern was with Bulger being an informant because we expected the defense would raise the issue. I wanted the FBI to review Bulger's informant file.

---

[194] 75 State Street is covered in Appendix E.

[195] Connolly told me they didn't drive but walked the restaurant being a short walk from the building where they worked.

[196] This little encounter was magnified in the press. The media reported Connolly tried to interfere with the 75 State Street investigation on behalf of William Bulger. There was no basis for the press's assertions based on this one encounter but it showed the press's bias.

There were rumors about the FBI's conduct with Bulger that was why we wanted to see the files. I told them the indictment was going to be returned on January 10.

By the fifth or sixth of January the FBI still had not confirmed that Bulger was an informant. After that time we were told that both Whitey Bulger and Stevie Flemmi were long term informants who were closed in 1990. I was surprised that Flemmi had been used as an informant. I'd say when I heard this, it came as a kick in the head to me. The FBI later said that the review by their legal officer Callahan found no problems with the relationship between the FBI and Bulger or Flemmi that would adversely affect their being indicted.[197]

There was another meeting with others including Quinn, Farmer, and Tom Duffy of the Mass State Police. We talked about the arrests. We wanted to be sure to arrest Flemmi right away. He was in the wind. No one would know where to look for him if he took off. We had a fair idea where Bulger would go, a specific place in Canada or in Florida.

Prior to the arrests there were arrest teams and meetings planning the arrest. Surveillance had been done on the defendants leading up to the arrests. Bulger was not in the area a lot of the time. We had no idea of Flemmi's whereabouts.

A number of people were aware of the upcoming plan to arrest the persons to be indicted.

---

[197] This is another example of the futility of asking the FBI to review its actions. The FBI never finds a problem with what it does unless it becomes public.

You've asked me how many people knew about the arrest. You're showing me a list containing about fifty names. Some on the list may have known or others may not have known.

I talked to Farmer about the issue of a pros memo. Pros memos are routinely used internally within the US Attorney's office to lay out the legal theories and show the weaknesses in the governments case and the defendant's case. It is usually not shared outside the office. It would not surprise me if the pros memo went to DC even though I don't recall it.

Before a grand jury issues an indictment it will not receive any evidence from the defendant or the defendant's lawyer. When reviewing evidence for an indictment, I must review the evidence to see that there is evidence beyond a reasonable doubt before bringing an indictment. The evidence in the indictments against Flemmi and Bulger went back to the Sixties.

At this point Chiel ended his testimony. The prosecution then put in some minor documentary evidence such as the dates Connolly attended school at Harvard. These tie in pieces of evidence to conform to technical requirements of proof and help counsel in the final argument.[198]

---

[198] It was confusing listening to the publication offered out of context. It was clutter that had little if any chance of sticking in the minds of the jury.

CHAPTER TEN

THE CASE FOR THE DEFENSE

AFFIXING A SHINE TO A SNEAKER

DENNIS MICHAEL O'CALLAGHAN

RETIRED FBI AGENT

It is the afternoon of May 20 the ninth day of the trial when the defense starts its case. The first witness called is retired FBI agent Dennis O'Callaghan. His grayish black hair extends over his collar. Miner puts in O'Callaghan's testimony in the proper manner with limited leading questions allowing the witness to give the evidence.

Durham seems in a fury during his cross examination. He all but shouts his questions at O'Callaghan like an irate schoolmaster. He acts as if he takes a personal affront to the idea O'Callaghan dared testify for the defense..

Durham seems uncomfortable in the role of cross-examination. I watch him pick up a cup of water. His hand is steady. He's under control but I think his manner of questioning shows he's either in unfamiliar territory or deliberately putting on a show of revulsion toward O'Callaghan.[199] I figure

---

[199]   At the prosecution of Richard Schneiderhan several months later, Durham will cross-examine Schneiderhan in a calm methodical manner effectively destroying Schneiderhan's credibility. Then I realized Durham's rage and fury at O'Callaghan was a deliberate and clever strategy.

his shouting will play well to the press who have been vigorously cheering on the case against Connolly.

I will see that O'Callaghan is comfortable testifying. He remains calm and composed under Durham's angry cross-examination. Durham attempts to crack him by his blistering attack. I think he's doing himself a disservice with his yelling. After court ends I talked to the reporters. They loved it. As far as I was concerned, they were mistaking noise for progress but maybe I am wrong.

Early on in Durham's cross-examination Miner objected to one of his questions that appeared to have no relation to her direct exam. Judge Tauro made a surprising ruling stating he was going to let Durham conduct his examination as if on direct. In other words Tauro was going to let Durham go into any area that he wanted and not confine him to what was brought out on direct examination as is normally done. I saw this as a serious blow to the defense. How would Miner know what traps were contained in the FBI files about any of the witnesses she proposed to call? The Justice Department having gained such wide latitude I thought Miner must reconsider who to call as a witness.

My name is Dennis Michael O'Callaghan.[200] I graduated from Mount St. Mary's in Maryland. I have been an FBI agent since 1972. I started my career in Minneapolis. I have had a lot of

---

[200] O'Callaghan died a little over a year and a half later at age 59.

263

organized crime experience. I came to Boston as the assistant agent in charge, the ASAC, in September 1988. I first reported to James Ahearn then to Thomas A. Hughes and finally to Richard S. Svenson. When I arrived, I was one of two ASACs. When I retired there were three ASACs in the Boston office. The ASACs supervise the squad supervisors. During my time there were 250 street agents in Boston. As an ASAC, I had my own office and a direct dial telephone. Supervisors have the same set up.

The street agents sat in what we referred to as bullpens when I first came to Boston. After we moved to other office space they sat in pods of four desks facing each other. Usually agents need authorization to spend over twenty-five or fifty dollars. Generally speaking, if over twenty-five, they need a receipt. Expense reimbursement checks had the same appearance as the salary checks up until the late 1980s.[201]

I was in charge of eight squads that dealt with criminal matters including organized crime, drugs, violent crimes, and fugitives. Between 1988 and 1990 the other ASAC was James Ring. Our primary focus during those years was on the La Cosa Nostra. It was involved in gambling, loan

---

[201] This is the defense explanation for the checks in Connolly's desk. I believe it will have a negative or at best a neutral effect by bringing up the matter again. The witness who testified about them said they were in the amount of two thousand dollars. Hardly would they be expense checks.

sharking, extortion and corrupting government officials. The New York Commission consisting of the five New York crime families oversees the LCN in America. Sometimes other people are on the Commission. Angelo Bruno from Philadelphia was a member of it when I was an agent assigned to Philadelphia.

The LCN operates by the word Omerta – the oath of silence. It is difficult to penetrate. I knew of no successful case against the LCN without using a top echelon informant.[202] These informants provided information about the structure that you are investigating. They are critical in obtaining a Title III warrant. I cannot remember securing a Title III without such an informant. Getting a Title III is a tedious process. To get one you need a case agent to prepare the affidavits sufficient to convince the court of probable cause.[203]

There were no set rules from 1988 to 1990 about the amount of information needed for probable cause.[204] The general view was to always

---

[202] There were many such successful cases without informants. Those were in the days when the FBI did black bag operations breaking into places and planting bugs without court interference. When they could no longer break the law so openly, they turned to using informants giving some the right to live criminal lives as long as they rat out others.

[203] Getting a Title III is not tedious if you're not afraid of doing the work required. As far as obtaining a Title III against the LCN without a top echelon informant O'Callaghan, only had to look at the Lancaster Street case in the Appendix to see how it can be done.

present the strongest case possible. Electronic surveillance is a very intrusive technique so the courts are very demanding. The more informant information we have with a showing of prior reliability the stronger the affidavit.

Top echelon informants were critical to getting the bug into the house on Guild Street where the Mafia induction ceremony was being done. It was critical there as it was in all affidavits. This was a very successful Title III investigation. The bugging of the Guild Street location was the first Title III in Massachusetts where we had permission to use a roving bug. With a usual Title III you name a location where you want to do a wiretap but with a roving bug you name an individual to be intercepted and not a location. Getting a roving bug is even more difficult because it is very intrusive.

From the Guild Street investigation we learned the names of all the people there and the identity of the persons they reported to. We heard the actual oath and ceremony. As a result of that, we arrested and convicted a number of capos and the leadership of the LCN organization.

The capture of the induction ceremony is the single most important piece of evidence ever

---

204 This answer made me think he knew little about affidavits since it made no sense. There never have been "set rules" spelling out what is enough information to establish probable cause. You can establish probable cause with one page done right and not do it with twenty pages done wrong.

developed against the LCN in America. This was so because under a RICO charge you have to show membership in a group. The LCN defendants through their attorneys used to pretend there was no LCN. They would laugh at the suggestion. Once we had the tape, we had the proof of the enterprise. Listening to the tape of the ceremony was like the Godfather being played all over again. It was so important that the day after we recorded the induction ceremony we flew a copy of it directly to FBI headquarters at Washington, DC.[205]

Connolly never gave more information than he received. Working with informants you have to give out some information. When an informant is giving you information, you sometimes have to direct the conversation to find out what you are looking for. In doing this you are giving him information as to what you are looking at. If you ask an informant about a telephone number, the informant will know you're interested in that telephone. For the special agent to get accurate information from an informant he must give out accurate information.

Morris reported to me. Connolly was on the OCDETF. I learned right after I came to Boston that Bulger and Flemmi were top echelon

---

[205] The evidence showed Connolly played a major role in this investigation. The affidavit for the Title III of the Guild Street induction ceremony identified four Informants, C-1 through C –4. Three of these informants, Flemmi, Mercurio, and C-4, were handled by Connolly.

informants. The top echelon program was created in the 1970s to target made members of the LCN. The FBI needed people with access to the LCN leadership. All the top echelon informants were career criminals with a background of criminal activity.

Neither Bulger nor Flemmi were members of the LCN. To get them approved as top echelon one had to go to Washington, DC. To use any informant a street agent must propose his intent to do so to a supervisor. The supervisor decides whether to open the informant. He also decides whether to close one.

At times Connolly would interview Bulger and Flemmi together. Any information provided was joint information that could be attributed to either party. I never reviewed Flemmi's informant file to see what information he was providing. I did not review informant files in the usual course of business.

I don't know if Connolly provided the information on Castucci, Halloran, or Callahan. My knowledge is limited to the time I was in the Boston office from 1988 forward.[206] I did not know that Morris and Connolly tipped off Bulger and Flemmi about the Bahorian wiretap. I knew Sonny

---

[206] That would have put Callahan in the office for less than three years before Connolly retired. He knew very little about Connolly's actions between 1973 and 1988. I wondered how he could assert Connolly never gave out any more information that he received knowing so little about him.

Mercurio was one of Connolly's top echelon informants whose information was critical to getting the induction ceremony bug.

I knew of the Bahorian investigation that was done under John Morris. Bahorian was targeted along with Billy Silvesta. Morris had the authority to tell an informant to stay away from a location or a telephone. He could tell him not to visit a certain location or talk to certain people. If a top echelon informant is involved in an activity that is not approved, he can be closed. Morris never told me Flemmi was a target of the Bahorian investigation nor did I know that at the time.

Bahorian was investigated for gambling and paying for protection. It is not unusual to tell informants to stay away from locations.[207] They have given critical information so it made no sense to have them walk into one of our investigations. Informants are essential. An agent is not supposed to be giving information to informants about other investigations being conducted.[208]

I never authorized Bulger or Flemmi to commit crimes but I don't see that anyone did. There is no

---

[207] He is another high ranking FBI agent that thinks you can tell a criminal about a Title III wiretap without to some extent compromising it and undermining its validity. I'm surprised.

[208] O'Callaghan, an FBI organized crime veteran, agrees with Morris that an agent can tell informants about wires. He then adds that an agent is not supposed to give information out about other investigations. It's hard to reconcile these two statements.

written authorization in their files giving them permission. But clearly from reviewing the files you can see these persons are engaged in criminal acts. I knew Bulger and Flemmi were involved in criminal activity. They did more for us than just give information against their competition to get them off the street. The FBI did not authorize any extortion. An FBI agent should report up the chain of command if he learned his informant had engaged in an act that extorted the business from a person by putting a gun on the table in front of a small child.

One should be measured in the use of informants. The Attorney General's directives on the use of informants made good sense. It is important that agents tell the truth. A supervisor must rely upon the truthful reporting of agents. Things would be difficult if agents didn't tell the truth.

James Ring retired in 1990. Ring never suggested closing Bulger. Quinn took over for him. He came to me and said Bulger should be closed and targeted. I reviewed the file. Bulger and Flemmi had provided information for the induction ceremony but all the people they had information on seemed to be in jail. The LCN was in disarray.

The information we had been getting from Bulger and Flemmi was dramatically reduced. There were public allegations that Bulger was an FBI informant. Because of the speculation in the media Bulger's utility was less. I agreed that it was better for him to be closed and to see if we could target him.[209] Other agents and other agencies had information that made him better as a target than as an informant.

The US Attorney set up a task force with the Mass State Police, DEA, IRS, and other agencies to chase after Bulger.[210] There were articles about this in the newspapers. There was a lot of talk around town about Bulger and Flemmi being indicted. Connolly would call me up each time there was an article. He'd ask me what was going on. I would tell him I wasn't involved and that I could not give him any information.[211]

I recall the December 22, 1994, meeting with Donald Stern and others in the US Attorney's office. We were told that Bulger was going to be indicted. They wanted us to provide his informant file prior to indictment. We would neither confirm nor deny at that time for them whether he was an informant. Flemmi's name was never brought up at the meeting. I did not know that Flemmi was going to be indicted.[212]

---

[209] The true reason Whitey and Stevie were closed is because the FBI had no one who was able to or wanted to handle them. Agent Quinn would confirm this. They were never targeted by the FBI.

[210] The FBI was excluded, many others included.

[211] This seemed like a lame answer. Why is Connolly continually calling him to get the answer "I'm not involved"?

[212] Four people will testify about this meeting: Stern, Chiel, O'Callaghan, and Quinn, two Justice Department attorneys and two FBI agents. All agree the meeting was

I contacted headquarters to tell them the US
Attorney asked for access to an informant file. At
some point I asked the US Attorney to send a pros
memo to them. I don't know if they did or not.

A decision was made to issue a complaint and
secure warrants prior to getting an indictment.[213] I
was asked by Ed Quinn to provide agents for the
arrests.   Usually in joint operations the FBI
provided one man for each subject. I figured we
provided six, eight, or ten agents.   Between
December 22 and January 5 I had no conversations
with Connolly. I never told him Bulger was to be
indicted in the middle of January.

Flemmi was arrested in Boston. Weeks had
been put under surveillance. We were trying to
locate Salemme. He was not at his residence.
Weeks was at a bar in Southie where he was being
watched, but about 10:00 p.m. he bolted out of the
bar and we lost him.

On January 9, 1995, we advised the US
Attorney we were going to give them Bulger's

---

called to find out if Bulger was an informant. Both FBI agents
say Flemmi's name never came up; both DOJ lawyers say it
did. I believe it did come up. FBI agent Quinn said after the
meeting they requested their legal officer Callahan to review
the files of Bulger and Flemmi. Seemed strange they'd make
that request if Flemmi's name never came up. This shows how
faulty memories can be. I'm sure each man believed he was
telling the truth.

[213]   If O'Callaghan was the tipster as alleged he
would have told Connolly about the arrests warrant and it is
clear he never did.

informant file. We also told them Flemmi had been an informant. We discussed the procedure for reviewing the files. We wanted Callahan, the legal officer in Boston, to review the file. In it he found there were 12 instances of self-reporting of criminal activity by the informants. Both informants had tacit approval for that activity.

A memorandum of that meeting was prepared and sent to FBI Headquarters. We informed DC because it is unusual to let someone outside the FBI review an informant's file. I am well aware that Weeks testified that Connolly said I tipped him off about the indictments. I did not tell Connolly about those. I can state absolutely that I never gave confidential information to Connolly.

I knew about Joe Murray's allegations that Connolly and Special Agent Newton were taking money to tip off wiretaps. The initial allegation did not come from Murray but from his wife, Tina. Murray is now deceased.

I was aware of the investigation that my office did into those allegations. I remember that Ed Quinn and Ed Clark interviewed Murray. When Murray was interviewed, two supervisors did the interview because at the time the allegation was made Connolly was a supervisor. I heard Murray's allegation was unsubstantiated. When Clark wrote up the 302 of the interview on June 14, 1989, a Teletype was sent to Washington, DC. I was given a copy of the 302 of the interview.

302s are supposed to be complete, accurate, and truthful recollections of the agents. Agents keep notes during the interview and then they construct the 302s from their notes. There are no verbatim transcripts of the interviews. There was nothing in the 302 showing they asked anything about the allegations against Connolly and Newton. It is the FBI policy that an agent makes a record of things completely and accurately. I have heard the FBI adage that "If it's not on paper, it didn't happen."[214]

I had not seen the notes of the interview so I don't know if they contained any reference to Murray's allegation. I'll look at the notes if you have them. I've just spent four or five minutes reading through them and I can find nothing in them about the allegations against Connolly or Newton.

But 302's are just the agents recollections based upon his notes. The report of the Murray interview was just the recollection of Special Agent Ed Clark. Clark told me that when they first contacted

---

[214] Think of the absurdity of this incident. Murray alleges two FBI agents were taking money to tip off wiretaps. Two supervisors are sent out to interview him. They file a 302 report. There is nothing in the report about the reason they went out to interview him. The report is read by the supervisors and approved. No one is curious about why Murray made the allegation. This is why the first step in reforming the FBI is to require the recording of all interviews. If the FBI believes the only facts that exist are what they decide to reduce to writing, we're being poorly served as a people.

Murray to make certain that he would give them an interview he denied making the allegation against Connolly and Newton.[215]

I wrote the telex that went to Washington, DC. I wrote saying the allegations against Connolly and Newton were not substantiated. I later spoke with Ralph Rogatino who was with the FBI's Office of Professional Responsibility, (OPR). He told me to close out the case. This happened even though the field notes show that Murray was not asked about the allegation against Connolly.[216]

---

[215] There is no 302 report showing this.

[216] After initially appearing as a strong witness, O'Callaghan's credibility started to sink fast. He dismisses the value of a 302 as mere recollections based on notes. They normally are regarded as gospel as witnessed by the prosecution's reliance on the 302 of the agent who said Connolly lied to him. O'Callaghan would have us believe they are the equivalent of a grocery list.

Supervisor Clark was sent out by the Office of Professional Responsibility (OPR) to interview Murray because Murray said two FBI agents, Connolly and Newton, were taking protection money to tip off wiretaps. Later Weeks would make the same allegations. It is hard to believe that if Murray denied the allegation, not only would the denial be in Clark's report, but it would have been the banner headline. The only conclusion is Murray told them things not to their liking reminding me how Montanari could not remember what Halloran said about Connolly.

Only in a bankrupt organization is it conceivable that two supervisors sent on a mission to determine an enormously important fact could return and file a report with nothing stated about it. Only in such a group could all those in positions of responsibility above the supervisors from O'Callaghan up through the OPR accept the silence of the

Connolly and I are friends. Connolly was in the OCDETF position as a supervisor when I was here. When the career board recommended that Connolly not be made a supervisor, I was not in the office. A career board consists of a group of supervisors who make recommendations to the ASACs on filling positions. The ASAC is then responsible for making the recommendation to the SAC. The recommendation is non-binding. The SAC doesn't have to follow it as happened in Connolly's case where the SAC overruled the career board's decision. Headquarters at Washington, DC, makes the promotion to the position of supervisor.

Informants get credit if their information is used in affidavits. You might want to put informant information into affidavits so to be able

---

report as an answer to the mission. Ranalli confronted Clark over his failure to write about this in his report. Clark said to him, "I did what I was told to do. You weren't there, you don't know what it was like. You wouldn't understand." This incident had such an overwhelming odor of corruption to it that it prompted Ralph Ranalli to write 'Deadly Alliance' one of the best books written about these times.

How can anyone believe an FBI report? In 1997 a five week FBI investigation of the Boston FBI office by the FBI found nothing amiss. The leader of that investigation became the number 3 man in the FBI. Over and over again it is clear that the FBI cannot investigate itself.

I wonder if the burying of Murray's statements was the bargain that prompted Connolly to retire from the FBI letting him quietly slip out the door to avoid embarrassing the FBI.

276

to tell an informant about the ongoing investigation. I cannot think of any reason why Connolly would give Weeks information about four informants. Nor can I think of a reason why he'd give information to Salemme. I don't know whether there was electronic surveillance in the Bahorian case.

I know there were many papers in my office about that case but I didn't know if there was a wiretap. I doubt that Flemmi was a target of that case since I doubt a top echelon informant would be a target in a gaming or police corruption investigation.[217] As far as I am concerned, it would be proper to tell him if he were a target. The decision is up to the supervisor. Morris had the right to make that decision. No one ever told me Flemmi was a target. Wiretap affidavits are reviewed by supervisors. Morris would have reviewed the Bahorian wiretap papers. It was up to him to decide whether it is appropriate to warn an informant that a wiretap is about to occur.

I knew a person named Campbell. He owned a radio station in Plymouth. He provided free Red Sox tickets to Agents Montanari, McGeorge and others. I wasn't investigated because of this. I was suspended for five days for using a form without

---

[217] We learned from other witnesses that Flemmi was a target in the Bahorian wiretap. He was tipped off by Morris. That wiretap happened before O'Callaghan arrived in the Boston office in 1988.

headquarters approval. This had nothing to do with Campbell.

At the December 22, 1994, meeting only three agents were aware of the indictments. I had only an hour or two notice of this meeting. It was not until December 23 that Callahan was brought into the loop. It was then that four agents knew the indictment was coming down in the middle of January.

I talked to Connolly about once a month after he left in 1990. I wouldn't say that Connolly left the FBI on short notice. He didn't leave because he learned that the Guild Street transcripts had been leaked to the media and the OPR was going to conduct an inquiry. Connolly didn't retire from the FBI under the cloud of an OPR investigation. Connolly left because a change in the pension system made it a profitable time for him to leave. He would be able to get a lump sum type payment.

There was nothing unusual about Connolly leaving even though he had just made supervisor. I've heard the term "high three." It means an agent usually wants to work for three years after getting a higher appointment since one's retirement pay is based upon the highest three years of salary. Sometimes if there is a buy out it made better sense to take the buy out rather than waiting for the end of the three years.

I used to hear from Connolly whenever there was a newspaper article about the investigation. Connolly was not entitled to any information about the indictments that were coming down. At times Connolly would call me looking for information on various matters. I never provided any information to him or discussed any FBI investigations with him after he retired. I don't recall Connolly asking me whether an indictment was coming down. Now that you refresh my memory with my grand jury testimony I see I was asked back then if Connolly called me and asked what I was doing. I answered he was asking about the status of the indictments and when they were coming down. I do recall saying that before the grand jury. But don't forget the FBI was not involved in grand jury that returned the indictments on January 10, 1995.

I spoke with Connolly on December 20, 1994. It had nothing to do with indictments because the meeting with Stern had not been set up by that time. When Connolly called me, he'd use my private number. It would be unusual for Connolly to call the switchboard if he were calling for me. The two minute call to the FBI switchboard at the Boston office on December 23 at 1:23 p.m. could not have been made by Connolly to me because it is impossible for me to have a two-minute conversation on the telephone with Connolly. Look at the conversation I had with Connolly on December 20. It lasted 23 minutes. I never spoke to Connolly for just two minutes.

But now that you refresh my memory with the records of telephone calls between Connolly and me I may have misspoken. It seems that I did speak with him for a couple of minutes on occasion. Well I probably should say I not only had long calls with him but I also had short calls.[218]

I learned on the 22 of December that the Bulger indictments were coming down. Connolly would have no reason to give Weeks any information. I had no knowledge that he gave him any.[219]

---

[218] Ironically, O'Callaghan's lack of credibility and the stench of corruption emanating from the FBI may not hurt Connolly. A juror listening to O'Callaghan may accept that Connolly is being scapegoated to protect the rest of the den of deceivers. Perhaps I'm underestimating Miner's strategy. Maybe she knows exactly what she's doing. The more O'Callaghan and his cronies look like blink, wink, and nod buddies in a sea of stench the more the jurors will accept that Connolly as a small part of a corrupt culture is being unfairly punished for the sins of the whole group.

[219] When the trial ended for the day, O'Callaghan was in the middle of his testimony. I spoke outside the courtroom with LA screenwriter, Tim Tanakos. He asked me what I thought. I said I thought O'Callaghan helped the defendant's case. He didn't seem to think so. We went down in the elevator and walked outside. The day was still chilly. We ran into Dave Boeri from Channel 5. He thought that Durham had effectively destroyed O'Callaghan. I told him I didn't think he hurt him. The press as a whole thought Durham did an outstanding job in cross-examining O'Callaghan. I thought O'Callaghan came across as a good witness but as a little too anxious to help Connolly. When I came to court the next day O'Callaghan resumed his testimony. He finished his cross-examination. Miner then started her re-direct. I thought that was a mistake. It would give the government a second shot at O'Callaghan. Miner got little from O'Callaghan. Durham in his re-cross was less hostile yet extremely effective having had

THOMAS J. DALY

RETIRED FBI AGENT

Daly is not a tall man nor does he look like the typical FBI agent. His appearance and demeanor is in sharp contrast to the bigger than life voluble O'Callaghan who was obviously intent on helping Connolly. Daly seems intent on just getting through his testimony as quickly as possible appearing as a very unwilling witness. He holds things close to the vest, trying to be very accurate in his testimony and limiting his answers. Daly had evidence the prosecutors could have used but decided not to call him. I assume that he had a hostile attitude toward the prosecution.

My name is Thomas J. Daly. I am a retired FBI agent. I graduated from Iona College in 1967 and Western New England in 1998. I did no military service. I was a 29 year FBI agent from July 1969 to October 1998.[220]

---

the prior evening to prepare. When O'Callaghan left the stand his credibility had completely crashed. I then agreed with the others that he seemed totally unbelievable. His cavalier approach toward the truth made it seem he regarded truth telling as an inconvenience. I wonder about the damage he may have done to others with this attitude throughout his long FBI career.

[220] I wondered if Daly like Connolly who entered the FBI at the height of the Vietnam draft did so in order to avoid the service.

I arrived in Boston in September, 1970. In January 1971 I went to the organized crime squad. At that time there were two squads doing criminal business, one doing property crime and the other doing organized crime. In 1976 both Connolly and I were on the organized crime squad investigating the LCN and Winter Hill.

I was in the Boston office on the organized crime squad in 1975 and 1976 when Jim Scanlan was the SAC. I was Richard Castucci's handler. Castucci was a heavy better. I don't believe he was a bookie. I prepared 209s with inserts about Richard Castucci. Castucci was providing information on McDonald's and Simms's whereabouts over a period of a couple of months slowly pinning their location down to a specific area in New York City. He eventually told me they were located in the vicinity of Christopher and Gay Streets in the Village section. I was aware that there was an informant for the FBI in New York City who was giving more specific information on the location of McDonald and Simms than Castucci was providing.[221]

Informants can talk to other people about their activities and let things slip. I don't know if Castucci would do that. I don't think that Castucci was stupid enough to talk about his status as an

---

[221] I noted before that this exercise with Castucci was unnecessary because the informant in New York City was the one who secured the apartment. Its address must was known at least to the NY FBI.

informant. Although he was stupid enough to place past post bets.

Whenever I received information from Castucci, I would put it on the 209 inserts. These were disseminated into other files including the criminal intelligence file. That file was kept in the rotor. Everyone had access to it. There were thousands of reports in the rotor file.

We also had squad meetings among both criminal squads. The information given to me by Castucci was probably discussed at those meetings. These were informal meetings with the organized crime team where I would discuss Castucci's information. I have no recollection of discussing any of it with Connolly

Castucci's information was singular which means not many other individuals would know about it. From the specific nature of the information provided one may be able to determine the identity of such an informant. Castucci's information was very sensitive because of the high profile individuals he was squealing on.

I have no idea how Bulger would have been able to tell Martorano in 1976 that Castucci was an informant. Only the FBI had that information. It was not shared with anyone else. I don't recall Connolly ever asking me about the location of McDonald and Simms. I never told Connolly that Castucci was an informant nor did I give him his informant number. Connolly never showed any interest in Castucci.

Castucci was paying rent to Henry Tameleo.[222] I had some informants who were close to Castucci when he was alive. The word on the street from my other informants was that Castucci was past posting bets with the Winter Hill bookies. After Castucci was murdered we tried to figure out why it happened. The consensus was it occurred because he was past posting the bets with the Winter Hill gang.

The FBI had a representative to the Organized Crime Strike Force. Other agencies participated in the Strike Force. They would meet to discuss matters of mutual interest. On January 3, 1977, within days after the murder of Castucci the Strike Force met. I never participated in those meetings and did not attend. The report of the Strike Force shows most people believed Castucci was killed for either past posting bets or for borrowing heavily from loan sharks.

Connolly was at that Strike Force meeting. He told those assembled that he didn't think Winter Hill did the hit. He said it's not their MO. I don't know what Connolly meant when he said MO. I don't know what MO means. Well, as I give it more thought, it must mean 'modus operandi' or how they operate. [223]

---

[222] Tameleo was one of the four persons mentioned by Barbosa as having been involved in the killing of Teddy Deegan, the case where the FBI had exculpatory evidence but hid it.

[223] I thought Daly's initial denial of knowledge of the

My informants told me Winter Hill operated in the precise same manner as had those who murdered Castucci. They told me that Winter Hill put the body in a sleeping bag in the trunk of a car. That was how Castucci was found. I had no personal knowledge that Winter Hill would use a sleeping bag in conjunction with a hit other than what my informants told me. Contrary to what Connolly asserted I did think that Castucci's killing fit the Winter Hill MO.

I was the lead agent in the race fixing case. I talked to O'Sullivan about the defendants in that case. Connolly never asked me to protect Bulger or Flemmi. He never asked me to protect anyone.[224]

EDWARD F. HARRINGTON

SENIOR US DISTRICT JUDGE

My name is Edward F. Harrington. I am a Senior US District Court judge for the District of Massachusetts. I graduated from Holy Cross in 1955 and from Boston College Law school in 1960.

---

meaning of MO was another example of an FBI agent's cavalier attitude toward truthfulness.

[224] I had no idea why he was called as a witness. He added nothing to the case. My patient waiting to hear the true story of what happened in the race fixing case was not requited. I wanted to know how he felt when O'Sullivan decided not to indict Whitey and Stevie. I wanted to know whether O'Sullivan told him that they did not have sufficient evidence to indict them. Neither side is interested in going there.

I am a former law clerk for Chief Justice Reardon of the Massachusetts Supreme Judicial Court. From 1961 to 1965 I worked for the Department of Justice. From 1965 to 1969 I worked in the US attorney's office. Between 1969 and 1973 I was chief of the Federal Strike Force. Then in 1977 I became the United States Attorney for Massachusetts. I held that position until 1981. Between 1981 and 1988 I was in private practice. In 1988 I was appointed to the federal bench.

From 1977 to 1981 I was the United States Attorney. I had supervisory capacity over the Strike Force that was headed by Gerry McDowell and then by Jeremiah O'Sullivan. I had a close connection with both men.

From the time I joined the Justice Department in 1961 until the time I left in 1981 our priority was to use all the resources we had to eliminate the National Crime Syndicate, the Mafia. We believed the Mafia posed a serious danger to the United States. Our policy during that time was to use informants. There was a program for high echelon informants. They were necessary because you needed human intelligence about what was going on at the high levels of the Mafia. We wanted criminals with the access to the deepest secrets of the organization.

An informant relationship has two characteristics. First of all, the informant has to be a criminal.[225] Next, the relationship of the informant to the government must be an absolute secret. It is very dangerous if an informant's identity is disclosed. Not only because the informant may be killed, but also because no one would want to become an informant if his or her identity were to be disclosed.

As a prosecuting attorney and then as US Attorney in Massachusetts, I had to answer to the directives and to the policy of the national government as promulgated by the Attorney General of the United States. I had no right to disregard these directives and policies. It was my obligation to adhere to those rules and regulations. The Attorney General's guidelines are set out in manuals that set forth what can and cannot be done.

As United States Attorney, I never provided false information, covered up crimes, leaked sensitive information, or withheld relevant information. I followed the rules and in doing that I had some significant victories. Adhering to the rule of law is important.

A handler and an informant must be close. They can only deal if there is trust between them. A handler is not charged with the job of investigating his informant. In some cases an agent handler would not want to know as much about his informant as he should. It is important to adhere to the regulations of the Attorney General

---

[225] I assume he is talking about high echelon informants since not all informants are criminals.

but on the other hand you do not want to dry up sources.[226]

Information given to an agent in a hypothetical fashion does not have to be reported. If a person were to give evidence against Bulger, he would have to testify or wear a wire. In either event the person would have to be protected. Information obtained over a wire would make the case stronger.

The confidentiality of the identity of an informant has to be secret. I'm not sure why Connolly would tell a clerk in his office the identity of his informants. I'm not sure how things worked within the office of the FBI and who would have that information. I would not tell one informant the identity of another informant. That would put an informant's life on the line.

The handler of an informant understands that the informant is a criminal. If the person were not a criminal, then he would not be an informant. I would think that if an informant committed a crime and the agent knew about it, he would report it. Agents cannot conceal crimes committed by their informants. The guidelines do not allow informants to participate in acts of violence. Line agents are not authorized to let informants commit crime nor can they authorize any person to commit a crime. I'd state that if an agent knew a person's

---

[226] I didn't quite understand Harrington's suggestion. He said it is important to follow the Attorney General's guidelines he then suggests you sometimes don't have to do it.

business was being taken away by force, he would have to report it.

An FBI agent would not want to give out any more information than he received. If the identity of a cooperating witness were to be disclosed to an informant, the handler would be giving up more evidence than received.

As a general rule, gifts should never be given or received. Perhaps minor tokens of appreciation could be exchanged because the handler has to maintain a friendship with the informant. Some small gifts would not be violative of my rule but who knows. Neither a case of wine nor a cash gift of $1,000 would be appropriate. I'd say exchanging books may be all right. It would help maintain the relationship of trust and keep up the close friendship.

I know of John Connolly. I knew him through the attorney in charge of the Organized Crime Strike Force, Jeremiah O'Sullivan. I did not know him directly. I knew what Connolly was doing through information I received from O'Sullivan. Connolly never gave me any information. I knew Bulger was a notorious and vicious criminal.

Connolly was considered an organized crime specialist. The bugging of the LCN headquarters at 98 Prince Street was the most important case tried in the New England area in 40 years. It brought about the virtual decimation of the Boston Mafia, the Angiulo family. Between 1961 and 1981 the

Mafia had been virtually eliminated in this part of the country.

Connolly's contribution to the defeat of the LCN was significant. He developed high echelon informants. They were necessary to have if you were going to do electronic surveillance.

I was aware of Connolly's work on the Myles Connor case. Myles Connor's case was not an organized crime case. It was an important prosecution. Myles Connor was an important figure but not an organized crime figure. His case was a state case that was tried in Norfolk County. Connor was convicted. His conviction was overturned, and he was then acquitted. I did not know if Connolly had any informants in that case. Connolly vigorously assisted the district attorney in the prosecution of the case.[227]

I knew Francis Green only as an associate of Paul Tierney. Tierney supported me in my campaign for attorney general of Massachusetts. I did not know Green before that time. When I was in private practice in 1977, Green came to me. Green told me that he had been threatened by Whitey Bulger. Bulger was trying to have Green pay back some money he had borrowed. I told Green that if he didn't pay him back, Bulger would cut his ears off, gouge his eyes out, and stuff them down his throat. At that time, I did not know Bulger was an informant.

---

[227] See Appendix H for a discussion of Myles Connors case.

Green was very fearful. He knew I had been engaged in organized crime investigations in the past. He was seeking my help. He asked me what he could do. I told him he could pay the debt, report the threat to the District Attorney, or get out of town.[228]

EDWARD QUINN

RETIRED FBI AGENT

My name is Edward Quinn. I am a retired FBI agent. I graduated from Boston College High School and Boston College. I received my masters at Fairleigh Dickinson. I spent 3 ½ years in the Marines. I've worked in the FBI for 30 years, 3 months. I have been stationed in Seattle, Cincinnati, New York City, and Boston. For 9 years I was on the organized crime task force in Boston. For five of those years I was a supervisor. I am a friend of Connolly's.

---

[228] Green did come to the Norfolk DA. We turned him over to the FBI. It wouldn't tell us what was happening on the case. Apparently nothing did. Harrington became United States Attorney the same year Green came to him. Harrington apparently had no further interest in the matter after that even thought he knew Bulger would "cut his ears off, gouge his eyes out, and stuff them down his throat." Harrington also said he learned about Connolly from O'Sullivan. I wondered if in 1978 O'Sullivan told him that Whitey and Stevie were informants who he cut loose from an indictment.

On December 22, 1994 Svenson, O'Callaghan and I went to meet with Sterns, Chiel, and Farmer at the US Attorney's office. The call to set up the meeting came earlier that same day. They wanted to learn whether Bulger was an informant and wanted to tell us that an indictment would be coming down against him.

The only name discussed was that of Bulger. After the meeting we asked our legal advisor Callahan to review the files of Bulger and Flemmi. There was a later meeting with all of the same participants plus Steve Hyman of the US Attorney's office. At the later meeting Callahan revealed to the Justice Department that both Bulger and Flemmi were informants. We also discussed the question of whether Bulger would raise the authorization defense. We concluded that there was no reason to believe he would raise that defense.

The plans for the January 5, 1995, arrests were made among the Massachusetts State Police, the FBI and the DEA. We decided to make the arrests using a magistrate's warrant in order to limit the access to the information about the indictments. Applying for a magistrate's warrant rather than an indictment warrant is not an unusual procedure. Any experienced organized crime investigator would know we would probably take that route.

As far as I knew, there were only four people in the FBI who were told the indictments were coming down in January. I have no idea how

Weeks would know that only four persons knew that was to happen. There was some public information out about the investigation. But Weeks would not know from the public information that only four agents were part of the group who knew the date of the indictment and that one of them was O'Callaghan.

I worked organized crime with Connolly for many years beginning in 1978 and ending in 1986. Connolly had other top echelon informants in addition to Bulger and Flemmi. I personally had met Bulger and Flemmi once. I don't know if O'Callaghan had met them.

In 1990 Connolly was supervisor of the drug task force. After I took over as ASAC, I recommended that Bulger and Flemmi be closed as informants. I did this because Connolly had been their handler for a long time. He was their only handler. It would be extremely difficult to get another agent to handle them especially since they were top echelon informants and were highly visible. Also, their information was somewhat dated. They seemed to have no current information of value. To be frank since the early 1980s I did not believe Bulger or Flemmi were providing good information.[229] Connolly had said

---

[229] This is wrong. Flemmi gave considerable information in the mid-80s that helped destroy the Boston Mafia group that came into being after the Angiulo group and for obtaining the bug at the Mafia induction ceremony.

293

they were in semi-retirement. But I believed they were still involved in organized crime activity.

From early on I knew Bulger and Flemmi were informants. I was the case agent on the 98 Prince Street investigation of the Angiulos. I was in charge of the investigation and when I filed my first affidavit I tried to make it as complete as I could. I knew that the targets would be represented by highly competent counsel, that it would be a hard fought legal battle, and that my affidavit would have to withstand strict judicial scrutiny. Knowing that, I initially submitted my affidavit without any information from Bulger or Flemmi.

I withdrew that affidavit and filed a second affidavit in which I included Bulger and Flemmi. They provided substantial information. Flemmi obtained technical information. He went into 98 Prince Street to get the layout of the premises at the request of Connolly. This was a significant contribution. I only included Bulger's and Flemmi's information after Connolly asked me to put it in. There was no significant evidence from Bulger or Flemmi in my original affidavit. One of the reasons I omitted putting it in was because they were very visible. I feared that if I used their information, it would lead to their identification. It would be clear it came from them.[230]

---

[230] This is yet another example of FBI-gobbledygook-speak. Quinn justifies not using Whitey and Stevie in his affidavit in the first instance because he said he feared using

Bulger had no reason to know anything about what was going on at 98 Prince Street. Flemmi would be on notice that we planned to do something there because we used him to find out what the inside of the location looked like. During the bugging of 98 Prince Street we recorded conversations of people talking about Bulger and Flemmi. Larry Zannino, the consiglieri, said that if he needed to do so, he could use Bulger or Flemmi to kill people. I never heard Gerry Angiulo say that.

But on second thought now that you are showing me the grand jury transcripts of my prior testimony I see I did say there was a conversation between Zannino and Angiulo where on February 4, 1981, Angiulo made reference to Bulger and Flemmi killing someone for him.[231] The conversation was significant because it showed the cooperation that was going on between Winter Hill and the Mafia. We had no evidence other than that to show that Bulger or Flemmi were committing crimes for the LCN.[232]

I never exchanged any gifts with an informant. I had many successful organized crime

---

their information would lead to their identification. Then after being approached by Connolly he uses the information. His fears mysteriously evaporate. They were included solely for the purpose of protecting them and tipping them off about the wiretap. Quinn pretty much agrees Whitey added nothing.

[231] Yet the FBI still continued to protect and use them.

[232] What more did they need after hearing it from the local Mafia leaders?

investigations. One could still be a successful organized crime investigator without being a successful developer of informants.

In the 1970s and 1980s the La Costra Nostra was the primary target of the FBI. All agents were utilized against it. It was not until the 1990s that the agents started to work against the Asian and Russian gangs. The FBI had great success in going after the LCN. When I retired, Salemme was the boss of the LCN in New England. They were still in business of loan sharking and gambling in the Boston area.

I interviewed Joe Murray with Ed Clark. At the time I was the supervisor of the violent crime squad. The information we were getting came from Murray's wife, Tina. She reported the information herself to Bill Weld who was then head of the Attorney General's criminal division in Washington, DC. Her allegations were significant. She said Agents Connolly and Newton were getting money from Bulger and Flemmi to tip off wiretap investigations.

Supervisor Ed Clark was assigned to interview Murray by the Office of Professional Responsibility (OPR). I was a friend of Clark's so I decided to accompany him on the interview. Since Connolly was a supervisor two supervisors had to conduct the interview.

We interviewed Murray in the federal courthouse in Boston. One of the reasons for interviewing him was the statement that Connolly had been taking money for information. At the beginning of the interview we asked Murray about it. He laughed and said "She's crazy, there's nothing to that."[233] We never told him that his wife gave us the information. So when he immediately identified her as the informant and responded like he did, we believed him and went on to other matters. Clark wrote up the 302. He included in it information of a positive nature.[234]

The 302 is not supposed to be a verbatim transcript of everything that occurred. I don't know why Clark didn't put Murray's exoneration of Connolly and Newton into the 302. I assume that because Murray gave us no basis to believe the allegation against Connolly so Murray's allegation had no substance and therefore was not included.

Connolly retired to take a job with the Boston Edison Company. He had a good offer from them. He was not under any cloud. In all my years

---

[233] Murray was dead at the time Quinn testified having been gunned down by his wife. Had he exonerated the agents, as I noted before, it would have been the lead line in the 302.

[234] The more we hear about 302's the less reliable they seem. Now according to Quinn they are only supposed to contain information of a "positive nature." It is hard to know what that means but any reasonable interpretation of positive would include Murray's denial that he claimed Connolly and Newton were tipping off wires. It seems some major FBI witnesses skirted around the full truth. What is it about these men that they testify like this?

associating with Connolly he never asked me for any information about informants.

GERALD FRANCIOSA

RETIRED DEA AGENT

My name is Gerald Franciosa. I graduated from college in 1966 and joined the Drug Enforcement Administration (DEA) when it was established in 1973. I stayed with them until 1998. I worked with Connolly in 1987 when he was transferred to the Organized Crime Drug Enforcement Task Force (OCDETF) in Boston.

I had lunch with Connolly and AUSA Chiel at Joe Tecce's restaurant in Boston on one occasion. Going to lunch isn't a difficult job but this was not one of those two hour four-martini type luncheons. I remember that because I was not drinking at the time

The purpose of the lunch was to discuss the problems DEA and the FBI were having with other federal agencies who wanted to be the lead investigative agency in an OCDETF investigation. There were nine federal agencies in the task force including the FBI, DEA, IRS, ATF, Customs, Coast Guard, etc. To be funded, two or more agencies had to participate in an investigation. The FBI and DEA were fearful that agencies such as ATF and Customs would do their own investigations using the OCDETF money and would exclude the FBI and DEA. Chiel controlled OCDETF money.[235]

At no time at lunch was there any discussion of 75 State Street or of William Bulger as Chiel testified.   Connolly never asked me for any information about the investigation of nor did I ever discuss with him anything about William Bulger.

The luncheon didn't go too well.   Joe Tecce was well known for his prejudices. He made some anti-Semitic remarks when he was talking to us. Chiel, being Jewish, got upset at the remarks. I never saw Chiel prosecute a case. I suppose he's a person of integrity. I normally would not doubt his word.   But I remember what happened at the luncheon and it differs from what Chiel has testified to.[236]

---

[235] I learned early on in my career not to come between cops and grant money. The endless squabbling by law enforcement groups over the division of the spoils is very disruptive. OCDETF received huge chunks of federal money which could be spent in many ways including buying the latest law enforcement toys and paying overtime. More time and effort was spent in scheming to get or complaining about the distribution of the funds than in the fight against the criminals. It seemed at this meeting the FBI and DEA tried to convince Chiel to cut the other agencies out of the money.

[236] The Cheil/Franciosa tiff shows how easily a case can get side tracked. Franciosa's attempted to impeach Chiel by showing Chiel might have been mistaken about a small part of his testimony. Chiel's testimony in the first place shed no light on the charges against Connolly. His impeachment was basically meaningless to the case. This foolishness could have

AFFIXING A SHINE TO A SNEAKER

When Franciosa finished testifying we took the noontime recess.[237] *When court resumed at 2:00 p.m.,*

---

continued with the government offering witnesses to impeach Franciosa. Soon they'd be off trying a different case.

[237] At lunch I sat on the bench outside the court room. Connolly came over to me. We walked away from the bench. I asked him about the contradiction between Chiel and Franciosa. He said Chiel was always an arrogant person. He never discussed Billy Bulger with him at all. They did not drive to Joe Tecce's in a car but walked there saying it was just a short walk from the back of his office building. When they got there, Joe Tecce came over to their table. It wasn't what he said at the table that upset Chiel, it was when he took him into a private back room in the restaurant In there Tecce had some type of shrine set up honoring Mussolini. When Chiel saw that, he became upset.

I switched the subject recognizing I just heard a third recollection of an every day luncheon that took place a dozen years before. I figured each one believed his memory was correct but the truth lay somewhere within a combination of the three. It seemed the real purpose of bringing it into the trial was an gratuitous attempt by the government to throw William Bulger's name into the trial. It was quite successful. The next day it was spread all over the local newspapers.

I said to Connolly it seems one of the prosecution's goals is to get Billy Bulger's name mixed up into the trial. I noted that it looks like they are trying to convict you hoping that you'll give them something on Billy. He said, "What could I give them? I know nothing that he's done wrong. He's a man of integrity." He went on to say, "I didn't have to be on trial. They were willing to deal with me if I could give them someone above me." He added, "How could I do that since there was nothing to give? I couldn't lie about someone just to get myself off the hook. I'd have that hanging over my head the rest of my life. I couldn't live with myself if I did that."

Connolly went on to tell me about some of the people involved in organized crime activity in the North End. He told

300

AFFIXING A SHINE TO A SNEAKER

Judge Tauro told the jurors that John Durham and Tracy Minor were going to another office to work on some documents. The jury would be seeing a twenty minute training tape that Connolly made in 1983. This tape had been used to train FBI agents in the handling of informants.

The training tape showed a much younger Connolly and an older man sitting in hard back chairs facing each other in a nondescript room. They were about three to four feet apart. Connolly's dark hair was stylishly long, befitting of the early '80s. He wore a sports jacket and a tie. He did not talk boastfully. Rather he was soft spoken and restrained. He seemed to epitomize an ideal FBI agent and projected the message that if he could do this stuff any FBI agent could. But the presentation was slow and tedious. Not long into it

---

about meeting with this person and that person, names unfamiliar to me. He said he has several informants telling him what was going on there. He implied his informants, which I took to mean Whitey and Stevie among others were far from useless after early 1980s. They played a major role in the Vanessa wiretap where the next generation of Mafiosa was destroyed. Connolly then went on to tell about other things he did successfully in the mid to late 1980s. I couldn't follow what he was saying because he was throwing out name after name and incident after incident. I finally suggested to him to get some lunch saying his friends were probably waiting for him.

I sat back down on the bench. I thought to myself, "I hope he doesn't attempt to say anything about Billy Bulger if he's convicted. That will put me right in the middle as a witness." Of course, he never did. Instead it looks like he'll die in prison.

I thought that if it were to be shown after a big lunch in a hot room, then there would be few who would be awake to see its end.

DEFENDANT JOHN CONNOLLY

SPEAKING ON AN FBI TRAINING TAPE ABOUT INFORMANTS

An agent must first determine the needs of the office and then find informants who will fill those needs. Before approaching an informant an agent must know as much as can be learned about the person. The agent must realize the informant has a certain mindset about an FBI agent. Informants expect to meet a professional person. The agent should not try to outgangster a gangster. Always get out of the office and talk to the people. Try to indicate a friendship with different criminals but continually read and assess the person you are talking to.

By and large you won't get anything on the first conversation. It may take up to six months or a year. But you have to assess your progress all the time. Sometimes five contacts with a person might be too many because the person just won't be an informant. On other occasions fifteen contacts might not be enough. Judge the person's personality to determine how you are doing.

You want to meet with an informant with no one else around. But you want to meet in a place where if you are spotted the person you are talking to will have an out, a way to satisfactorily explain his speaking to you. I let my informants pick the place for the meeting. Limit phone contacts. It is best to meet in person. If you use a phone, use a pay phone to pay phone contact.

You have to recognize you are risking lives when dealing with informants. The rules and regulations provide that if you are paying money you have to have two agents present. The other agent should be somewhere in the distance.

I have 7 or 8 informants. I pay only one at Christmas time. When dealing with informants, you are dealing with criminals who might make an allegation against you. Some of my informants will not meet with anyone else except me.

If an agent is transferred, it is important that he find another agent in his office whose personality will match that of the informant. The informant is the most important asset of an agent. I had two or three informants too many. I had to introduce them to other agents. When I do that, I will see my informants again so they know I'm around. In shifting informants the secret of success is to find another agent who is tailored to handle the informant.

The Attorney General's guidelines deal with the agent informant relationship. Informants are criminals, we are professionals. Informants are criminals, we have a different mindset. The agent should be friendly. An agent can like an informant. But he must never forget that he is an FBI officer.

Make sure you don't authorize crimes, always be in the driver's seat, and be in control of the relationship. Informants are dangerous and are criminals. You have to watch out so that they don't burn you. Watch out for bizarre activity or unstable behavior. It takes work to develop them.

I've had 25 to 30 informants in my career, ten were top echelon informants. These organized crime informants never consider themselves to be informants. They usually want you to get someone they don't like.

The video ended. The television screen was moved to the front side of the courtroom. Stacey Miner prepared to go through some of the exhibits that she intended to offer. Miner presented the following items into evidence without objection by the prosecutor.

Flemmi's brother, Michael, has been a Boston Police Officer for 30 years.

The distance from Long Island, New York to New Orleans is 1350 miles.

A person who examined Connolly's computer would testify that nothing on it could be connected to the letter sent in March 1997 to Judge Wolf.

Durham will show the computer was manufactured on February 2, 1998, after the date of the letter.

FBI fingerprint analysis of the letter to Judge Wolf showed 16 prints on the envelope and paper. None of them belonged to Connolly.

A transcript where Flemmi testified that on August 20, 1998, he had words with Salemme.

AFFIXING A SHINE TO A SNEAKER

A statement that in 1987 it was revealed that Flemmi was an informant and that Flemmi had informed against Salemme.

Some other exhibits were entered and others kept out. None seemed to have much bearing on the case or likely to stay in the memory of a juror. At that point Miner rested her case. [238]

Judge Tauro told the jury he was going to start arguments on Thursday. He told counsel they could have as much time as they wanted. John Durham said he would need 90 minutes. Judge Tauro told him he could have more. Durham then said he may need up to two hours. Tracy Miner indicated she would need the same amount of time. Tauro explained to the jury he was going to give them Wednesday off. He indicated that counsel could use that time to prepare their final arguments. [239]

---

[238] Up to the point the defense rested without Connolly testifying the pundits debated the wisdom of his not taking the stand. Then I thought he would have been foolhardy to testify since Judge Tauro would let Durham have at him freely and I thought Connolly would lose control under his fire. Tracy Miner would recognize much of this. She had been with Connolly week after week preparing the case. I felt sure she'd advise him not to take the stand. I didn't know if he would follow her advice or not.

[239] This struck me as a great idea. Too often the judges force counsel into argument as soon as the case is finished. This is fine in a simple case that lasts for up to three days. But this case although tried in ten days had been tried under the Tauro's strong hand where no time was squandered. The three hour morning session had a ten minute break that

AFFIXING A SHINE TO A SNEAKER

was actually ten minutes. The afternoon session of two hours fifteen minutes was interrupted by a 30 second "stand up and stretch" break. There were only a handful of periods when testimony was not being taken. This puts enormous pressure on counsel to prepare for witnesses and to digest the testimony. Although the court may only be in session from shortly before ten to a little after four-thirty counsel must work late into the night and on weekends to keep up with the continually changing momentum of a trial. The extra day to put all of it together was surely welcome.

CHAPTER ELEVEN

CLOSING STATEMENTS

It's Thursday, May 23, I'm up at a little after 5:00. I decided to drive my car to Boston. I'm on the road a little after 6:00 for the ride hoping to avoid traffic problems. I think of how much easier it is to drive to the city outside the normal commute hours. Too bad I didn't think about this thirty years earlier when I worked in Boston. I pay my $7 to park and head into the court a little before 7:00.

I am the first one there. I take my place with my newspapers and book at the head of the line. I do not expect that there will be much of a crowd that day. I was never so wrong in my life. By 8:00 there were about a dozen people there. By 9:00 nearly one-hundred stretched out in a queue along the corridor.

Tony the courthouse denizen who traditionally occupies the front spot in line is next to me. He arrived about 7:15. I tried on a couple of occasions to talk to him but he acts toward me with disdain considering me an officious newcomer. He never says too much to the people sitting around him but perks ups and jumps up to talk to the press people who arrive. Also sitting on my bench are the mother and son of Tracy Miner. Some colleagues of Leonard Boyle sit nearby. A calm Boyle drops by to speak to them. They talk about having left home at a very early hour because of Boyle's warning to get to the courthouse as early as they could.

307

CLOSING STATEMENTS

I see my long time friend Brendan Bradley arrive. A retired Boston Police Captain he usually has an ear on the law enforcement talk of the town. I make sure my seat is safe and I go over to him. We talk. He's discouraged the line is so long. He asks Jack, a court officer, if he can bypass the line. Brendan tells him of his interest and his background. Jack says the chief is going to be there that day. He cannot help him. I go back to my spot at the head of the line. Brendan remains standing far down the hall talking to another court officer. Later I look and he's standing at the end of the line. Then when I look again he's gone. I feel bad for him. I know he wanted to see this part of the trial. I think he gave up any hope.

The press arrives. The crowd around the door has grown much larger than any time during the trial. Lawyers representing victims arrive and are let through the door. Tracy Miner comes out and brings her son into the courtroom. Her mother is left in the lurch. Tracy then comes back and rescues her. FBI agents and other law enforcement officers crowd to the front of the line and pass through the door. I'm beginning to worry that they'll be no seats left. Two or three court officers blocking the door start letting some of the press in one by one. Jack scans their faces and credentials. Those who have been there throughout the trial he lets in while he tells others to wait.

I walk forward while Jack is still outside. He's been there since the first day and knows me. He lets me in. The front row I usually sit in is filled. I decide to sit in the last row. I head toward my left to take a seat. I see Brendan already sitting there.

CLOSING STATEMENTS

I never saw him walk past me. He looks at me with a big smile noticing my surprise. He tells me that he ran into a court officer he knew and after some discussions he was brought in through the back way. He was quite pleased with himself. I couldn't blame him. We moved from the corner of the back row to where we could look straight at the podium where counsel would stand to address the jury.

The courtroom is packed to capacity. The press members who were initially excluded are allowed entry. I looked around to see if Tony who was second in line got in. I don't see him. He's been at the trial most days, arrived this morning at 7:15, and is shut out. Judges should insure that there are always some seats saved for people like him so that they don't get bumped at the end.

The court quiets when the judge comes in. He checks to see that counsel are in place, looks for and espies Connolly, and says bring in the jury.

Throughout the trial I've been scanning the jury to see if I could determine anything by looking at them. I can tell nothing. They seemed attentive during all of the trial. For the most part they sat back with little or no emotion showing on their faces or in their demeanor. I watched them throughout the argument to see if they paid attention to counsel.

Sometimes you can see in a juror's reaction to an argument that his or her mind is made up. The juror's aspect will show an indifference to one lawyer or the other. But here I see none of that. They all listen closely to counsel. Some lean forward at times showing a more intense interest.

CLOSING STATEMENTS

People have asked me throughout the trial what I thought of the jury. I tell them I've never been able to know what's going on in a juror's mind. I tell of the case I tried over two or so weeks. I was positive one juror was on my side. He looked at me with a smile as if approving of everything I was doing. He seemed to grasp each good point I made with a nod of his head. He smiled knowingly in agreement during my final argument. When the initial vote was taken in the jury room, it was 11 to 1 for my position. He was the one against me and held out for three days.

John Durham is first. He stands at the podium. He speaks in a quiet voice addressing the jury with his hands in his pockets. He starts with the usual litany used by many lawyers beginning their final arguments. He tells the jury it is its recollection of the evidence that matters and not what he tells them the evidence is. He asks them to disregard anything he says if it doesn't comply with their memory. He also reminds them Judge Tauro will be giving them the law of the case. He goes on to say that if he tells them anything about the law that conflicts with what Tauro says, they must disregard what he has stated. He refers to his notes while he stands quietly in front of them speaking softly.

The following are the highlights of his argument:

JOHN DURHAM

CLOSING STATEMENT TO JURY

CLOSING STATEMENTS

Connolly's defense is that he was only doing his job. But let's see what the case is about. First, let me tell you what it is not about. This case is not about whether informants are important tools, nor whether Connolly filled out the right forms, nor whether he followed the guidelines, nor whether he developed cases against the LCN, nor whether Bulger or Flemmi provided valuable information. Talking about that, remember what retired Agent Edward Quinn, Connolly's own witness, said. From the early 1980s he did not think Bulger and Flemmi were great informants. What did he do? When he could he shut them down. Remember that they were forced into the affidavit for the wiretap of 98 Prince Street. They did not provide much evidence for that investigation that could be relied on. So even though it is questionable that they provided valuable information the case is not about that.

Let me tell you what the case is about. The case is about Connolly's association with Bulger and Flemmi and others in a way other than as a normal informant relationship. The case is about whether Connolly had a corrupt relationship and the answer is that he did.

Connolly is charged with racketeering, that is he engaged in two or more criminal acts under the racketeering statute. There are fourteen racketeering acts alleged against Connolly. They involve accepting and giving bribes, extortion, and obstructing justice. There is also another charge that involves giving false information to an FBI agent about whether he was in contact with the defense team.

I'll explain the charge about the ring. The act of bribery has three parts. We have shown Connolly received something of value, the ring; that he was a public official, an FBI agent; and Connolly accepted the ring with corrupt intent to be influenced in his public duties.

Look at Martorano's testimony. Martorano confessed to many unsolved murders. Martorano thinks that as a result of that he received a sentence of twice what he would have otherwise received. Martorano made a deal to testify. You have to scrutinize his testimony extra carefully. Consider his demeanor on the stand. Consider whether his testimony was supported by other evidence and how well he recollected things. Although it may have been chilling to listen to him, he did not appear to hesitate. He had excellent recall.

Martorano said Winter Hill agreed to give Connolly a ring. Remember what Martorano said Bulger told him that Connolly was following Billy Bulger's request to keep my brother out of trouble. Connolly was engaged in continuing conduct to help Bulger.

Durham reads from the sheet in front of him as he proceeds through his argument with little show of emotion. He is comfortable standing behind the podium.

With respect to the ring Connolly's first wife testified she received the ring. How could

312

Martorano know about the ring if it didn't happen like he said it did? It's a memorable event to a criminal when he is successful in bribing a witness. Do you think Martorano was going to make that up? No way!

Connolly's corrupt intent is shown by his agreement to tip Bulger and Flemmi off about law enforcement moves against them or their friends. We saw that he did this. He told them Castucci was an informant.

Durham has lined up three cups of water on the desk behind him. He paused here to take a drink. His presentation lacks emotion. His matter of fact style is somewhat boring but he seems to have the jury's attention.

Remember how Martorano told Flemmi that I hope you're taking good care of Connolly. We know that they were doing that. Weeks told us of the concern they had about Connolly. Bulger told him that Connolly was showing too much money. He's doing this even though we know all his paychecks were sitting in his desk drawer. Weeks told us how he delivered the $5000 in the envelope to Connolly. Salemme testified that $5000 was paid to Connolly. All these show Connolly' corrupt intent.

Racketeering acts two to five involve the bribes given to John Morris. The difference between the elements of these charges and the first charge is Connolly is giving the bribe and not taking it. Three times Connolly directly gave the bribe to

Morris and on the fourth time he set up the meeting for the bribe to be given. Scrutinize Morris's testimony asking yourself what has he to gain from testifying. But he has a lot to lose. If he lies, he will be exposing himself to criminal prosecution for perjury.

Morris did not blame Connolly for his problems, he blamed himself. Morris did not overreach or avoid the issue. He put the request for the $1000 for his girlfriend squarely on himself.

Miner is sitting there looking at Durham as he talks. She doesn't take any notes. I notice throughout Durham's closing that she will not take notes. [240]

There were no inconsistencies in Morris's testimony. Morris took the gifts but he couldn't reciprocate. Morris's common sense told him that if he accepted anything of value, he was compromised. Connolly inveigled him into doing things he wouldn't have done by referring to Bulger and Flemmi and telling him the guys really

---

[240] It's apparently Miner's intention to stick to her script without trying any contemporaneous remarks. This has its advantages and disadvantages. There is school of thought in closing argument that you don't respond to particular arguments of opposing counsel but proceed ahead with your planned argument no matter what is said by the other side. The idea is to act as if there was nothing truly valuable in other counsel's presentation. The disadvantage is that there may be issues raised by counsel that you may want to specifically respond to at some point during your closing remarks. If you don't write them down, they may be gone forever

like you. Remember Morris testified there were two groups of people in the office, the older agents and the others. Morris belonged to neither group. Connolly convinced Morris to have Bulger and Flemmi come to his house and in the end corrupted Morris.

Now we get to the $5000 gift. Morris was having family problems. He had a child with special needs living with him. He went to live in a place in Florida owned by an informant. It would have been better if Morris disclosed the information about taking the place and money from the other informant. But that does not change the fact that Bulger and Flemmi must have learned about Morris's problems through Connolly. They then gave him the money to further compromise him.

Morris was corrupted because he leaked information to Connolly about Halloran's cooperation, he leaked information that the FBI knew the car that was used in Halloran's shooting, and he leaked information to Connolly in the Bahorian wiretap. We saw Connolly's tactics. He used the same pattern with Gianturco exchanging wines and gifts although there was no evidence Gianturco had the same weakness as Morris.

You heard from Julie Rakes and Kevin Weeks. Extortion is when you take something by the use of force or the threat of force and that was done here. Remember how one of Bulger's thugs told Julie to clear out of the store and how Weeks told about putting the gun on the table while Bulger was holding the Rakes' child.

This is the one part during his argument that Durham became more animated. He normally just talked with his hand in his pockets or with one hand out. Now he had both hands out emphasizing his points. Throughout his talk about this extortion he will show more emotion and concern before he lets himself slip back into his pedagogic manner of talking.

Connolly aided and abetted the extortion because he did not intervene in it. Remember what Weeks said Bulger told him afterward. He said "Thank God Lundbohm went to Zip." It was clear Connolly knew about the extortion. Connolly told Shelly Murphy of the Boston Globe that Boston Police Detective Lundbohm, Julie Rakes's uncle, had come to him about the threat but there was not much he could do about it. He made a similar statement to another reporter. Connolly doesn't report his knowledge of the extortion to anyone in the FBI. But he did tell someone. He told Bulger what was going on.

Racketeering act seven involved the cases pending against McDonald and Simms the fugitives. The evidence showed Connolly discussed this case with other people. Martorano testified that Bulger said Castucci was an informant and he was giving information on McDonald and Simms. How would Martorano know this if Bulger didn't tell him? There was no legitimate reason for Connolly to tell Bulger that Castucci is an informant. Recall how right after Castucci's murder Connolly said it was not Winter Hill's MO to kill people and wrap them in sleeping bags like the way Castucci was found. What did Connolly's witness retired FBI agent Tom Daly say? He said his informants told him that it was their MO.

The gist of racketeering act eight revolves around the killing of World Alai owner, Roger Wheeler. There was an ongoing investigation in Oklahoma about his murder. Connolly was aware of it from a Teletype that he signed off on. Morris told Connolly that Brian Halloran had implicated Bulger and Flemmi in it. Weeks told us that Bulger told him he learned from the FBI Halloran was cooperating.

Weeks spoke about how Agent Montanari was hanging around the club in South Boston. When Weeks asked Bulger what he was doing, Bulger told him he was investigating Wheeler's murder. He told him "Zip gave him the information" that Halloran was cooperating with the FBI. Then recall the meeting in New York City where Bulger told Martorano that he killed Halloran because he was giving information against Martorano. Now look at what Halloran said in January when he first went to the FBI. He told the agents that if Bulger, Flemmi, or Callahan knew he was giving up information, they would go to any length to kill him, his wife, and his family.

Moving to racketeering act nine, this involved Callahan's murder in Miami. Connolly is shown through the testimony of FBI Agent Montanari to be present at a meeting where the FBI had decided to target Callahan. It was the Bureau's plan to put the pressure on Callahan to implicate Bulger and Flemmi. Martorano met with Bulger and Flemmi in New York City. At the New York meeting Bulger and Flemmi told Martorano that Callahan was a huge liability. They said he had to be killed because he was being targeted by the FBI. How would Martorano have known that if Connolly had not told Bulger and Flemmi?

We see in racketeering act ten that Morris testified he spoke to Connolly about the Bahorian case. Morris told how Connolly went to Bulger and Flemmi then came back to Morris and said they want to hear it from you. Compare Morris's testimony to O'Callaghan's. Morris accepted the wrongfulness of his actions while O'Callaghan tried to justify the leak to Bahorian even though as ASAC he said he did not know about the Bahorian investigation. Do you really think you can tell a target about a wiretap?

Racketeering act number eleven involved leaking the indictment. There was a continuing grand jury. Connolly was passing information on. Salemme told about the meeting he had with Connolly. Salemme's demeanor was forthright, open and candid. Connolly told Salemme he would keep him advised when the indictments were coming down. In 1994 he told Salemme the grand jury was investigating things back to the

1960s. Salemme knew Bulger and Flemmi were paying money to Connolly.

Also, Weeks said Connolly showed up at the South Boston Liquor Mart. Connolly told him only four people knew the indictments were coming down and that the information came from O'Callaghan. How would Weeks have known this if Connolly did not tell him? Other evidence showed there were only four in the FBI who knew about it. Further proof that this happened is that Bulger fled. Bulger's girlfriend Theresa Stanley, told how they met at Neiman Marcus and then went out of town.

Tracy Miner turns around to look at the clock. It is 11:43 a.m. I think that like me she is also getting tired of Durham's steady but mostly unemotional presentation that has been going on for an hour and forty five minutes.

Racketeering act twelve involved Flemmi. Weeks said Connolly passed on the same information to Flemmi through Weeks. Flemmi told Weeks his guy is on top of it. Remember the meeting that took place at Salemme's house where Flemmi and Salemme discussed the indictment coming down on January 10.

Racketeering act numbers thirteen and fourteen involve the anonymous letter to Judge Wolf and Flemmi's testimony before Judge Wolf that Morris tipped him off about the indictment. Connolly knew the Wolf hearings were ongoing. Connolly showed Weeks a copy of the letter he was proposing to send. The formatting and the punctuation fit the usual way he wrote. Frank Dewan, the Boston police officer, was libeled in the letter. A computer expert would say the computer he examined that was seized from Connolly was manufactured after the day the letter was sent. It could not have a copy of the letter in it.

Connolly's letter was a cowardly act and a boldfaced attempt to impact the case. Connolly had identified informants so that the case against Connolly's associates would be dismissed. Flemmi identified Morris as the person who gave him the information. How would Flemmi know about such a thing as a pros memo? It is a rare event for it to go to FBI headquarters. This information had to be provided by insiders such as Connolly.

Then we have the count against Connolly charging him with making a false statement. Connolly denied that he had made contact with the defense team. He did this after being contacted by the Office of Professional Responsibility. After denying it Connolly then used the phone at 3:30 in the afternoon to converse for 45 minutes with Flemmi's lawyer, Ken Fishman. He did this from the public telephone outside of his house.

Give consideration to all the evidence. When you do, you will find Connolly guilty of all the charges beyond a reasonable doubt.

CLOSING STATEMENTS

It was 12:11 p.m. Everyone looked a little tired. Judge Tauro said that he would recess at that time until 1:00 p.m.

At 1:00 p.m. sharp Tracy Miner steps to the podium. She braces it with two hands, thanks the jurors for their attention.

TRACY MINER

CLOSING STATEMENT TO JURY

I'll tell you what this case is about. The case is about the defendant and his dealings with informants. It was Connolly's job to fight against the Mafia. Everyone told you how important it was to have top echelon informants. Everyone told you that to be a top echelon informant you had to be a top echelon criminal. The only way to have such informants is to build up a relationship of trust with them. Remember what Connolly said on the video, there is the necessity for trust.

Judge Harrington's testified about the Attorney General's guidelines. Remember what he said. He said that the black and white guidelines became gray in the field. Harrington said the job that Connolly did was a hard job. He was doing it because the government needed him to do it. The government needed him to have Bulger and Flemmi as informants because only through them could they reach to the top of the LCN and other high level criminals. Connolly got the government

321

the information it wanted and they used his information to good effect.

The government wants you to believe Connolly was corrupt and to prove it the government used stone cold killers to come in to testify against him. Recall Martorano's testimony when he said if he saw one of his associates talking to an FBI agent, he would kill him. Bulger knew that was how Martorano and the others would act. He needed his cover. He knew that some day he might be spotted talking to Connolly so he gave his gangster friends a cover story. He told them he was getting information from Connolly and not giving any to him. He told them Connolly was on the take. He told them Connolly was giving him things of value and he was giving Connolly nothing.

Bulger fooled his friends for over 15 years. One thing that is certainly known, Bulger was an excellent liar.

At this point in the argument Miner has a little more oomph to her than Durham showed. She is still behind the podium following her notes. She speaks in a quiet voice. She commands the attention of the jurors.

You heard about the ring. Martorano said it was a man's ring. Martorano has no idea what happened to the ring. He only knows what Bulger told him. For all you know if there were a ring, it ended up on Bulger's girlfriend's finger. A ring was given by Connolly to his wife in June 1976. It was not a man's ring and it had other stones in it than just the 2 carat diamond Martorano talks about. Remember also that Connolly had sold his house in South Boston and gained a $10,000 profit during the same year he gave his wife the $5000 ring.

No one ever put any cash in Connolly's hand except Weeks. The one thing clear from the evidence is that Bulger, Flemmi, Martorano, Salemme, and all the others they associated with were constantly lying and cheating each other. Flemmi stole $300,000 from Salemme his friend. Think how easy it would be for Flemmi to tell Salemme he was giving $10,000 to pay off cops while he was putting the money in his pocket. Remember how Martorano said he knew Bulger and Flemmi were stealing money from him. Bulger and Flemmi were continually lying to each other. How credible is anything they say about Connolly especially when it comes to money since they were constantly cheating each other.

Now let's talk about Weeks. He was a thug and nothing more than Bulger's driver. Do you think Connolly would approach a guy he knew as Bulger's flunky and pass information on to him? Do you think Connolly, an experienced and wily FBI agent, would take money from such a person as Weeks? Furthermore, how credible it is that Connolly would do these acts in a public place right in the middle of a store during the busiest season of the year. It's a plain out and out fact that Weeks is lying.

CLOSING STATEMENTS

Look at this chart. Weeks has to be lying. We know from hotel records that Bulger was in New Orleans on December 26, 1994. Bulger and Theresa Stanley were older people. It was unlikely they would be driving straight to get there. Stanley was sure she went to New York City after she left Boston. It was impossible for the meeting to take place on the 23rd of December, for Bulger to be in South Boston on the 23rd of December, in New York for three days, and then in New Orleans on the 26th of December. If he was really fleeing from an indictment, why would he have checked into the hotel in New Orleans under his real name? How did Connolly become his source in December and not in January?

None of Bulger's action was consistent with Weeks's testimony. I'd point out that if Connolly had O'Callaghan as a source in the FBI, he would never have told Weeks his name. Who do you believe, Weeks with the murders on his hands or O'Callaghan the FBI agent with years of meritorious service?

Four witnesses against Connolly were totally not believable: Martorano, the murderer of twenty people; Weeks, the braggart, who says he kills people who insult him; or Salemme who referred to the Mafia on the West Coast in a derogatory manner as the Hollywood Mickey Mouse Mafia. Salemme who would have you believe that when he was head of the New England Mafia, they did not engage in any violence. Imagine the government calling his testimony forthright.

And what about Morris? He's a serial liar. He set a bomb in a car in order to scare a person into becoming an informant. He was so bad he could not even tell us whether something he said was a lie or not. He lied about his mental state. He never told anyone about receiving money and a place to live from another informant. What did he say about not telling about that? He says the government never asked me!

Each of the four was testifying under a deal with the government. Morris gets a free pass for all the crimes he committed. Martorano gets a free pass doing about a year in jail for each of the murders he committed. The same applied to Weeks and Salemme. All the criminals will be getting out soon. They all made out very well. And look at what they forfeited: nothing! None of their assets were lost. Look at all the money they made over the years and when it comes to disclosing their assets to the government they're broke. It's just that their honesty in giving information did not go to their pocketbooks. Aside from the great deals they got for testifying they all had a pocketful of revenge they could gain from testifying. They couldn't get their revenge with their usual weapon the gun so they got it otherwise by coming onto the stand to testify.

Miner is now away from the podium walking slowly in front of the jury emphasizing her points with her matter of fact presentation with a steady voice somewhat similar to Durham's but more lively.

Castucci wasn't killed because he was an informant. The information that everyone had after his death was that he was killed for past posting bets. And with Callahan it didn't take Connolly to tell Bulger and Flemmi that he was going to be pressured by the FBI to cooperate. Callahan was right in the middle of any investigation of Wheeler's and Halloran's murder. Halloran told the FBI Callahan wanted to hire him to kill Wheeler. Anyone could figure out that he was a witness to these matters and would be approached by the FBI.

And Halloran, when he showed up at the FBI, he already had been targeted on two occasions by the Winter Hill gang for a hit. Connolly made an early threat assessment about Halloran that he was at high risk for being killed. For whatever reason he was killed it certainly was not something that originated with Connolly informing Bulger and Flemmi that he was informing on them.

It was Connolly's job as a handler of Bulger and Flemmi to get information from them. Page after page of criminal acts of Bulger and Flemmi were reported by Connolly on his 302 forms. The FBI did not want to know about their acts but the FBI knew they were doing them. It helped them in their fight against the LCN. The decision to keep using them as informants was made above

Connolly. It was not Connolly but the higher ups who wanted to use them.

There is no evidence that Connolly had anything at all to do with the liquor store extortion. Detective Lundbohm went to meet with Connolly at a coffee shop in Dorchester. He told Connolly he wanted to keep the information off the record. He said the Rakes would not testify, would not wear a wire, and would not be interviewed. Durham said Connolly should have reported it to the FBI so they could do something about it, yet on the other hand he tells us how vicious Bulger is to people he believes are informing on him. He'll cut off their ears, gouge out their eyes, and stuff them down their throat. It was not credible to believe Connolly knowing this would tell Bulger to lay off them because if he did and something happened to them, he would have been blamed for telling him. Recall what Judge Harrington said when he was approached by Frank Green who was being pressured by Bulger to pay back a loan. He told him all he could do was either to pay the money, get out of town, or go to the DA. The choices weren't that great.

Miner is walking back and forth in front of the jury.
She looks at the ground as she speaks and then looks at
the jurors.

There were no bribes given to Morris. Morris didn't testify that he made any agreement to do anything for the gifts he received.   There was no quid pro quo for the gifts. Nor did Morris ever do

327

anything in return for any of the money or wine that he received. There was no corruption. The wine was part of a reciprocal giving. It was nothing more than gift giving, an exchange of gifts.

The story Morris and his friend Debbie testified to was plainly incredible. At that time Morris and Connolly were on the outs with each other because Morris tried to stop Connolly from going to school. Why in that situation would Connolly be interested in helping him out?

O'Callaghan testified that it was in the power of an FBI supervisor to warn a target of an investigation who was a top echelon informant to stay away from a telephone. It was Morris who told Connolly about the planned wiretap. What did Connolly do but tell Morris that he should tell Bulger and Flemmi himself. Connolly didn't want to be put in the middle by telling them about a wiretap. He did not have the authority to do so. But Morris did. He was a supervisor. So Connolly told Morris to tell them.

Then consider the comment Morris said he made to Bulger and Flemmi that he did not want "another Halloran". It made no sense. Halloran was informing on Bulger and Flemmi. Bahorian was not an informant. He was the target of an investigation. It made no sense to think Bulger and Flemmi would want to kill a person who is a target.

No one in the FBI thought Flemmi would raise it as a defense that he was an informant of Connolly's. The FBI was publicly embarrassed when he stepped forward with his assertion. Then Flemmi reached out to Connolly who was his handler. Flemmi believed the government had authorized him to commit the criminal acts that he did. The government said he was not authorized to do any of those acts. Flemmi believed Connolly was going to come in to testify for him. He held off the wrath of Salemme and Martorano by telling them Connolly would come in and save them. But when Connolly refused to testify that Flemmi could do anything he wanted Salemme and Martorano got irate and decided to cooperate with the government to get revenge on Flemmi and Connolly.

But the bottom line is the government was embarrassed that it was known by all that they had two of the top gangsters in the Boston area Bulger and Flemmi as informants for over twenty years. The government wanted to shift the blame from itself. It had to find a scapegoat. All they wanted to say was this only happened because there was a rogue agent. The Department of Justice would wash its hands of the matter and move on by blaming Connolly for what they all did.

Connolly did not need to tell Flemmi who the informants were for the Mafia induction ceremony on Guild Street because he and his co-defendants already knew who they were. They sat through weeks of hearings in front of Judge Wolf where all of these items were discussed behind closed doors.

Now consider the anonymous letter to Judge Wolf. There is no physical evidence Connolly wrote the letter. There was nothing found on the computer. If the computer was not the one the government was interested in, why did they send it to be analyzed? If anyone sent the letter, it was Michael Flemmi a Boston police officer of 30 years.[241]

Let's look at the cell phone calls that went back and forth between Connolly and Weeks. Connolly did not want his family to know who he was talking with. At the time of those calls Connolly was a private citizen having left the FBI. Judge Wolf refused to be interviewed unless he could review the 302 that the FBI agents who interviewed him filed. When he did, he had to change some things and add others.

Look at the 302 that Agent Clark filed about his interview with Joseph Murray and how as

---

[241] I wrote in my notes "bad move." I thought the evidence of the letter was too strong to overcome. I thought the best tactic was to concede this and hope this would be the only bone the jury would chew on. But I did not know what went on between Miner and her client. He may have insisted that he did not send the letter, or if he did, would not let her concede the point. She then had no choice but to take the chance to somehow disassociate it from Connolly. But I thought it was a particularly bad idea putting it on Michael Flemmi who there was no evidence against. The chance Miner took in doing this may adversely affect her overall credibility if a juror remembered in her opening she blamed Weeks for sending the letter.

Agent Quinn said he had failed to include the most important point. This shows the overall inaccuracy of 302s. The agent referred to his 302 to say Connolly denied being in touch with defense counsel. Remember Connolly never got to review his statement in the 302. The agent refreshed his memory from the 302. He may have been in error.

Remember that Connolly had been a good FBI agent for 20 years. He was the top rated agent for recruiting top echelon informants. Remember that he did the job the FBI wanted him to do and that he is not guilty of any of the offenses charged.

Miner had gone for about an hour and fifty minutes. Immediately after she finished, Durham got up for his rebuttal. Judge Tauro told him to keep to the ten minute time limit. Durham went through several minor points he had jotted down on his sheet such as reminding the jury that Judge Harrington said an agent could not take money. It seemed he was not even half way through this rebuttal argument when Judge Tauro said "Time's up."

The jury left the courtroom for a quick break before Tauro began his charge. Tauro told Durham he gave him more than ten minutes. Durham countered and said that some of the people with him said he only had eight minutes.

When the jury came back in, Judge Tauro began his charge which is an explanation of the law as it applies to the case.. He told the jury he would give them a copy of the instructions to take with them into the jury room. In a little over an hour, he instructed then on various aspects of the law setting out one legal concept after another and explaining the legal elements of the crimes charged. As a lawyer experienced in this area, it was difficult for me to remember all he said. I imagined how much harder it would be for a juror to keep in mind his instructions. I thought it wise to give a copy of the instructions to them. He then sent the jury off to decide whether to begin deliberations that day or Friday. The jury returned. It decided to start on Friday at 9:00 in the morning.

CHAPTER TWELVE

AFTERWARDS

The jury was out. I had time to consider what I thought of the trial. I thought of the minor differences I had with counsel as you would expected from another trial lawyer. However, I recognized my disability. I did not have the information counsel had in making decisions. I did not have access to counsels' files to see where the traps might be hidden. I feel uneasy suggesting counsel may have done something differently. I never liked people who did not get into the ring but who felt justified in criticizing what others were doing. I think of the poem *"It's Not the Critic Who Counts."* Even so, I thought it best to tell the tale of the trial as I saw and thought about it.

It did seem to me there were strictures imposed on counsel. At one point prior to trial according to the press reports, Judge Tauro indicated that he was not going to let in any of the government's evidence about the murders. This may have been a tactic on his part to force the government into shortening its case in some areas. I don't know what Judge Tauro and counsel agreed about using leading questions or excluding evidence of certain other areas such as Connolly's display of wealth or his conversations with other FBI agents.

333

AFTERWARDS

Aside from the limitations in my ability to fully appreciate counsels' dilemmas and restrictions, I am able to say both the government and Connolly were well represented. The case was fully and fairly tried. I believe Tracy Miner faced greater disadvantages especially if she learned for the first time during trial that counsel for the government would not be limited in his cross-examination of her witnesses. As I indicated, I had no idea of what transpired between Tracy Miner and John Connolly. In recent years much of what any defense counsel can do has to be done within the strictures approved by her client.

I considered the charges against Connolly. He was charged in a racketeering complaint that had alleged 14 acts. Durham said if he proved any two, he would have a conviction of Connolly under the statute. Connolly was also charged in four other substantive complaints. These related to actions he took long after he had retired from the FBI. A significant aspect of the case is that most of the RICO charges would be beyond the statute of limitations if Weeks's story about Connolly going to the South Boston Liquor Mart and telling him to warn Whitey and others that the indictments are coming down is not believed.[242] The only charges that would then remain would be those that related to Connolly's actions around the time of the motion

---

[242] See Appendix B for my take on his story.

hearings when he got himself involved in his futile attempt to assist Flemmi.

On Tuesday, the day following Memorial Day, May 28, 2002, I received a call in the early afternoon from my son, Teddy. He heard on the radio the verdict was coming in. I turned on the television and flipped among the channels looking for local news. I could find nothing. A little while later he called to say Connolly was convicted of some counts and acquitted of others.

I again turned on the news. A television reporter was giving out the verdict. The best I could determine was he was guilty of sending the letter, having Flemmi testify that Morris tipped him off, and a couple of other charges. The jury had not believed most of the gangster testimony.

Gerry O'Neill of the Globe called me. He asked me if I heard. He said Connolly was guilty. I mentioned that he was not guilty of the major charges. I told him I thought the jury had done a good job in not believing Martorano, Salemme and Weeks. He told me they did believe the Weeks testimony that he visited the store on December 23. I was surprised since I didn't know that. We talked some more. He hung up because another call was coming in. I knew O'Neill wanted Connolly convicted.

Later Congressman Bill Delahunt called me from Washington, DC. He had heard from his staff that Connolly had been convicted. I explained to him as well as I could what I knew. He wanted to know what sentence he would be facing. I told him I did not know at that time since I did not know the breakdown of the verdict. Shortly after talking to him, I learned more about it.

Here are the charges he was facing. The ones he was convicted of are underlined and in bold:

A: RACKETEERING BY:

Bribery - receiving a diamond ring from Whitey Bulger

Bribery - giving $1000 to Morris's girlfriend for a trip to Georgia

Bribery- Giving Morris A Case Of Wine With $1000

Bribery - giving Morris a case of wine

Extortion – taking the South Boston Liquor Mart from the Rakes

Obstruction of justice - failure to report the extortion

Obstruction of justice - leaking that Castucci was an informant

Obstruction of justice - leaking that Halloran was an informant

Obstruction of justice - leaking that Callahan would be questioned

Obstruction of justice - leaking information on Bahorian wiretap

Obstruction Of Justice - Telling Bulger Indictments Were Coming Down

Obstruction Of Justice - Telling Flemmi Indictments Were Coming Down

Obstruction Of Justice - Sending Anonymous Letter To Judge Wolf

<u>Obstruction Of Justice - Causing Flemmi To Testify Before Judge Wolf</u>
<u>B: Making False Statement To An FBI Agent.</u>
<u>C: Obstruction Of Justice By Telling Of Planned Indictment.</u>
<u>D: Obstruction Of Justice By Causing Flemmi To Testify Falsely.</u>
<u>E: Obstruction Of Justice By Sending Letter To Judge.</u>

Connolly was acquitted of the most serious racketeering indictments involving the obstruction of justice charges that revolved around the murders and the extortion (A5, A6, A7, A8, A9, A10) and all the bribery charges except one. Except for the case of wine with the thousand dollars in it the rest related to actions by Connolly after he left the FBI. In other words had Connolly left the FBI and settled peacefully and happily into his new six figure job he may never have been convicted of racketeering.

The jury failed to believe the gangster testimony when it related to Connolly doing his job as an FBI agent. Weeks testified that Connolly, when an agent, took money and gifts, was involved in the Halloran and Callahan murders, and with the extortion of the liquor store from the Rakes. Connolly was acquitted. He testified to his actions after he had retired from the FBI about Connolly coming into that store to tip him off about the indictments and helping Flemmi's defense with the letter and the magnetic tape. He was convicted of the indictments relating to these latter matters. The jury believed Weeks on some matters but did not on others. The difference is that the jury believed what Connolly did as an FBI agent he was doing pursuant to his job's requirement. Didn't Miner argue that "Connolly did the job the FBI wanted him to do."

That is the only conclusion that makes sense to me. Martorano testified to Connolly's knowledge of and involvement in the Castucci, Halloran and Callahan murders and the ring. The jury may have believed this but accepted Miner's argument that whatever Connolly did in relation to them it was part of his job. The jury refused to cloth him with the same protection after he left the job. Even though Connolly may have felt a continuing obligation to help his informant Flemmi the jury did not buy into it. Yet had Miner argued that Connolly's obligation to protecting his informants from charges that related to the time they were providing information to the FBI was continuous and ongoing she may have convinced the jury of this. She may have prevailed on all the charges. Doing this was risky because she'd have had to admit Connolly did those things. For all I know, Connolly may not have been willing to let her gamble like that.

In her argument she did not concede anything so she denied Connolly tipped off Bulger and Flemmi to flee, or he sent the letter, or otherwise assisted Flemmi. Maybe that was the right thing to do.   Maybe no one would have ever conceived or argued that Connolly's duty to his informants ran to advising them to flee, to writing a letter to a judge, to helping persons testify falsely and the like.   One can only wonder had that type of argument been used to this jury which seemed to recognize an FBI agent can do things that are forbidden to other people how it would have worked out.   The jury gave Connolly a pass for almost everything he did as an agent.   Connolly was almost totally vindicated in his performance of his job while he carried his FBI credentials.   It only believed Morris on the case of wine with the money in it.

The initial speculation in the newspapers after Connolly's conviction was that he would seek to make a deal with the government.   I thought that was wrong.   He had nothing to offer.   The government didn't want to bring charges against another FBI agent.   One sacrifice was enough to satisfy the public outcry.   He told me he had nothing on Billy Bulger, the only other deal he could have made.   He quickly squelched that when he gave Boston Globe reporter Shelly Murphy an interview telling her like he told me he had no intention of making a deal since he had nothing to deal.

Then the letter writing campaign for Connolly began.   People were solicited to write letters supporting Connolly to Judge Tauro urging him to give Connolly a lenient sentence.   Many former FBI agents wrote. The pitch most of the more than 200 letters put forth was that John Connolly was only doing his job. In trying to defend him, they were condemning the Bureau.

The most controversial letter came from Judge Edward F. Harrington, one of Connolly's witnesses. It is improper for a judge to write such a letter to another judge. Judge Harrington had to withdraw it. He was later admonished by a higher court for sending it.

I was asked to write a letter but refused. I had no reason to believe Connolly was not rightfully convicted. But even though properly convicted I nevertheless wondered whether he deserved leniency.

Thinking about this I was especially bothered by Connolly's letter to Judge Wolf. Not so much because he was trying to help Flemmi but because he was willing to drag Boston police detective Frank Dewan's name through the mud and impugn the integrity of other law enforcement agencies. It seems what Connolly did was consistent with FBI practice. He thought whatever he did as an FBI agent was fine, whatever his informants did was fine, but what people did contrary to the FBI or his informants was wrong.

Connolly may have thought he was doing his master's bidding. He may in fact have been doing that. But stripped to its bare essentials it seemed to me that he had joined up with two gangsters. Maybe it was his job. No one in the FBI objected to it. He did it according to an FBI program. Even if many others deserved to be standing next to him in court, that didn't mean Connolly should not have realized that he pushed the envelope too far.

No, I couldn't write a letter for Connolly. He had these two gangsters as informants. He tried to subvert other investigations. He endangered the lives of others by his ongoing association with them. Even if he was required to do that by his job, I could not say anything nice for him.

But I had to consider what the appropriate punishment should be.

Throughout the period from his conviction to his sentencing I was asked what sentence I thought Connolly would get. I tried to figure out how Judge Tauro felt. I recall that he made a remark when the jury returned the verdict that had Connolly been convicted on the more serious obstruction of justice counts, those involving the cases where people were murdered, he would have revoked his bail. This indicated to me that Judge Tauro considered Connolly actions very troubling so I expected he'd get between eight and twelve years especially since he tried to undermine the cases pending before Judge Wolf. That action which is an assault on the integrity of the judicial system is not taken lightly by the judiciary.

On an early September morning Connolly stood silently before Judge Tauro. After listening to counsel for both sides, Judge Tauro imposed a sentence of 210 months, the top number on the probation sentencing guidelines.   Connolly was taken out of the courtroom in handcuffs to begin his sentence.

Over ten years later Connolly is still in prison. He has wrapped up his federal time. He has been convicted in Florida on pretty much the same facts the jurors in Boston acquitted him of relating to the Callahan murder. He is looking at spending the rest of his life in a Florida prison.

Three serial killers, Martorano, Weeks, and Salemme have been released from prison and are living among us. Martorano is the protagonist in a book in which he brags of his killings. None of his past murders bother him. He tells us he has made his peace with his Lord and is forgiven. He has shouted to the world at the end of his book, "I'm back!" That should provide a lot of comfort to the families of his victims.

Weeks wrote a book overflowing with braggadocio. Salemme got out, was quickly back in, but even he's out again.

Governor Perry of Texas has executed 235 persons over the last ten years. None of them have done anything like these three who testified against Connolly.

It seems to me there is something very wrong about the outcome. The head of the New England Mafia and two men who committed between them twenty-five murders and brag about them are free. These three men dedicated their lives to violent crime.

AFTERWARDS

An FBI agent of 20 years who acted openly with the approval of his superiors battling against such criminals was convicted for a murder committed by two men, Martorano and McDonald, he never met. He was convicted as an accessory to murder on the convoluted theory that he told a partner of one of these men, Whitey, that a potential witness (Callahan) would never stand up to the FBI pressure (something Whitey had to know in his bones without being told).

Putting things in perspective Connolly was convicted by the federal jury of bribing his supervisor Morris with a case of wine and a thousand dollars and of several non-violent actions after he retired. A Florida jury convicted him of abetting the murder of John Callahan by suggesting he would fold under pressure.

Weigh these crimes against Mafia boss Salemme's admitted involvement in the murder of three brothers and his ancient conviction of setting a bomb in an attorney's car seriously injuring the attorney; or against Martorano's actions of killing at least twenty people including an ordinary businessman at a golf course and a friend who lent him money and the use of his condo; or against Weeks who helped Bulger in at least five murders and beat and extorted his way through life; or even against Morris who told Connolly Halloran was informing on Whitey and told Stevie the FBI was doing a wiretap on his friend Bahorian or who tried to have Whitey and Stevie killed by revealing to the

Boston Globe their identities as informants or who took great pride in telling how Whitey said that he had a Machiavellian mind.

In the end Morris proved much smarter than Connolly. Morris, ASAC Fitzpatrick, every other ASAC or SAC had power to stop Connolly's interaction with his informants. They all walked away without spending an hour in jail.

I have great difficulty understanding how a state can put on trial a federal officer for actions he did while doing his job. Not only was the Supremacy Clause not invoked to prevent this, a Department of Justice attorney participated in his prosecution.

I wonder what we accomplish by keeping Connolly in jail. The Florida jury convicted him of the same actions on which the federal jury in Boston found him not guilty. The federal jury convicted him mostly on his actions after he retired. He deserved to go to jail for those actions. It did not convict him of any offense relating to his involvement with informants while he was active.

He does not deserve to die in jail. This is so because there is little clarity over what actions the FBI has the power to authorize its agents to perform and whether his actions were performed pursuant to this power. Until those are clarified, it is fair to say John Connolly has not had his day in court. I discuss this and other things related to the trial more fully in the Appendix.

CHARTS

Appendix A:
THE CHARTS:

THE FBI	—	THE MAFIA
↕		↕
THE DIRECTOR	—	THE COMMISSION
↕		↕
SPECIAL AGENT IN CHARGE	—	THE BOSS
↕		↕
ASSISTANT SPECIAL AGENT IN CHARGE	—	THE UNDERBOSS
↕		↕
SUPERVISOR	—	CAPO
↕		↕
STREET AGENT	—	SOLDIER

APPENDIX B:

WEEKS'S WEAK TALE

Of the three gangsters Weeks's testimony was the most compelling. Even so, the jury did not believe most of it. They did believe his story about the December 23, 1994, meeting at the South Boston Liquor Mart between him and Connolly. That part is the most unbelievable to me. To start with it is difficult to corroborate. What little we can corroborate from other records or experience gives lie to it.

His story in brief is that Connolly showed up at the liquor store sometime after three o'clock on December 23, 1994, looking for Whitey. He then wanted to talk to him. They entered into a walk-in cooler. Connolly told him indictments were going to be prepared over the holiday, only four FBI persons knew it and one was FBI Agent O'Callaghan who gave him the information. Connolly left at 3:30. Weeks went next door. He called Whitey who was due at 4:00. He waited outside for him until he came. The weather was clear and cold. They then drove into Neiman Marcus in Boston where Weeks told him the news. Whitey then fled.

Here's where I have problems with his story. To sustain the bringing of the RICO indictment against Connolly for actions he took while an agent the government had to show that one of his

346

criminal acts was committed within 5 years of the return of the indictment. By the time the government had the evidence for the indictment the only act within that time limit would be one that connected Connolly to Whitey's flight.

Weeks is an intelligent guy. He gained the nickname "Two Weeks" because he so hated jail that it took him that little time before he decided to turn state's evidence. He lusted for a quick key to the door of freedom. The best way to get that was to give the government whatever it needed. It desperately needed connecting Connolly to Whitey's flight. Weeks's motive to invent and the government's willingness to believe were great.

I look at the other evidence to see how his story stands up. On December 22, 1994, US Attorney Stern and his assistants met with three FBI agents including O'Callaghan to tell them indictments were coming down in January against Whitey. This information was given to a fourth FBI agent. There is a dispute over whether they said Flemmi was to be indicted.

On December 26 Whitey and his girlfriend, Theresa Stanley, signed into a hotel in New Orleans. They stayed there to New Year's Day. Whitey registered under his true name. It is unlikely he would have done this if he was on the run and expecting to be indicted. After January 5 when he learned the warrant was out for his arrest, he always used aliases.

On January 5 the FBI and other agencies secured arrest warrants after filing complaints against Whitey Bulger, Stevie Flemmi, Frank Salemme, and others. They did not wait until January 10 when the indictments were to be issued.

On January 5 Stevie was arrested in Boston; Salemme called his wife from Rhode Island and learned the house was surrounded by cops so he fled to Florida; Whitey was driving back to Boston when he heard on the car radio of Stevie's arrest. He turned around and drove away. Weeks contacted Whitey after ten that evening. He told him about the arrest but by that time he already knew.

Whitey left for New Orleans on or before December 24. He was returning to Boston after the holidays. Weeks said Whitey left because he told him the indictments were coming down after the holidays. It doesn't seem to fit. Would Whitey be returning to Boston right into the teeth of the most dangerous time?

It seems obvious Whitey and none of the other gangsters had prior warning the arrest warrants were to be issued on January 5. The best that can be said is that they expected it would happen on January 10. FBI agents knew about the January 5 date. O'Callaghan knew but he did not pass it on to Connolly. We do not know whether Connolly knew of this or not. But we do know that if he knew he did not pass it on.

Weeks had no information about warrants coming out on January 5. Weeks first knew of the warrants at about nine that night when he learned Stevie had been arrested. Weeks did not know January 10 was the date for the indictments. Stevie told Salemme his source knew of the January 10 date. His source did not know the arrest warrants were issued. Stevie's source had to be someone outside the FBI agents involved in the arrest. It had to be someone who knew about the grand jury. It could not have been Naimovich who had died by that time.

These known events cast doubt on Weeks's story. The actors were not performing in conformity with the information he said he passed on to them. There is more to make me disbelieve him.

Prior to December 23 Weeks and Connolly had no interactions with each other. Weeks testified that one time Connolly walked into the liquor store and said, "What's going on?" This benign statement so bothered Weeks that he complained about it to Whitey.

The best that can be said about the extent of contact between Weeks and Connolly up to that December date was they exchanged pleasantries. Weeks testified that Connolly and Bulger never spoke in front of him. Connolly knew him as Whitey's strong arm guy who worked in the store for Whitey. Weeks was as close to a stranger as one could be when it came to Connolly.

Connolly is a highly skilled FBI agent. He handled a dozen or more top echelon informants. He had taken down the Boston Mafia twice if not three times. He knew the system in and out. He knew the cardinal rule of not unnecessarily exposing himself. He taught other FBI agents how to deal with informants so that they didn't put themselves in compromising positions.

Weeks never said he was a go between for Connolly to contact Whitey. He did say that they had independent ways to contact each other. They always communicate face to face.

The information Connolly allegedly possessed was not of an urgent nature. Nothing was going to happen until ten or so days later. Connolly could have gotten it to Whitey in his usual manner of contacting him.

Weeks would have us believe that Connolly who had no prior relationship with him in a situation where there was no need for immediate action threw all caution to the wind and exposed confidential and incriminatory information to him. We also had to believe Connolly had no other way to reach Whitey. To me it beggars belief.

Put that aside and assume Connolly thought the only way to get a message to Whitey was to go to a crowded liquor store after three in the afternoon two days before Christmas. Weeks said they went to the back of the store and into the walk-in cooler with fans so they would not be overheard. We assume from that Connolly is highly cognizant that he is passing on highly confidential and compromising information. In that state of mind Connolly needed to say nothing more than, "Tell Whitey indictments are going to be prepared over the holidays."

If Weeks testified to that, it is possible though unlikely it could have happened. But Weeks expanded on that. He testified that Connolly told him things that are totally unnecessary for him to know namely, only 4 FBI agents know about it and Connolly said he got his information from O'Callaghan.

Why would Connolly say that? Is he trying to impress upon Whitey how singular the information is? If that were the case he would not be passing it on through a stranger. He could always tell the details of how he got the information and who knew about it to Whitey later if he needed to do that. All he had to say to Weeks was that the information is confidential.

Connolly trusted Bulger. He had no reason to trust Weeks. Connolly knew how the system worked. He knew crooks like Weeks once caught always trade off information for deals. He had flipped hundreds of them himself. At this time with Whitey about to be indicted Connolly had to know that he too was no longer absolutely immune. It is inconceivable he would trust a person he considered a strong arm thug with information that could be used to compromise him.

The prosecutor argued to the jury that Weeks could not have known that information if Connolly did not give it to him. Perhaps, but that does not mean Connolly gave it to him that day. He could have given it to him much later when they became co-conspirators meeting in restaurants trying to help Stevie thwart the indictments.

The most likely scenario is that it was much later that Connolly gave the information directly to Whitey. Whitey was upset he came so close to being arrested and at some point asked Connolly why he didn't let him know about the indictments. Connolly told him he didn't know about them but found out later from O'Callaghan that only four FBI agents knew about it. Whitey then passed the story on to Weeks about what happened at that time. Weeks maintained continuing contact with Whitey for years after his flight keeping him posted on the events and meeting him in Chicago and New York with fake identification papers. He had countless opportunities to learn this from him.

The predicament Connolly faced in exposing the falsity of Weeks's story was that it did him no good. He gains nothing by showing he would not have given that information to Weeks but rather directly to Whitey. The thing that hurt him was he gave it out, not who he gave it to.

Another circumstance that shows Weeks' story does not have the ring of truth is the existence of surveillance. Stern testified that the surveillance on Whitey and Stevie had been increased around this time.   If Connolly was so on top of things, he would have known this so he would not want to be seen at the liquor store.

But there is a more fundamental reason to disbelieve Weeks.   He testified that he clearly remembered December 23, 1994, as a *"clear, cold day."* That would be what one expected at that time of year.   When he said it, in my mind's eye I could clearly see him standing outside the South Boston Liquor Mart in his heavy jacket trying to keep warm while waiting for Whitey.   The store was located at the rotary on Old Colony Avenue.   It occupied the same area as the Stop and Shop supermarket which was there when I was a child. I remembered back to the days before Christmas as being bitterly cold.

Curious, I thought to find out how cold it actually was. I Googled that days' weather. The answer I came up with on the internet seemed wrong. I thought the best source would be a local newspaper. I went to the public library to check the Boston Globe for Friday, December 23, 1994.

On the front page of the Friday morning Globe was a picture of a man wearing shorts and sitting shirtless on a bicycle.   Above it was the notation "Summer Rerun."   An article about the weather on Thursday said the temperature at Logan International Airport hit 61 degrees shortly before noon, just one degree shy of the 1990 record, 23 degrees above normal."   It was 61 on Thursday. What was it on Friday?

WEEKS'S WEAK TALE

The forecast for the Friday was for rain developing during the afternoon, high in the 40s. Saturday's Globe for December 24, 1994 had the information about the weather on Friday. It wasn't cold. The high temperature in Boston on Friday was 47 degrees and the low was 37. It was 11 degrees above normal. It was hardly Weeks's cold day.

Neither was the weather clear. The article about the weather said, "Cape Cod and the rest of south-eastern Massachusetts bore the brunt of a roaring coastal storm yesterday that packed hurricane-force winds and heavy rains." There were 81 miles-per–hour hurricane-force winds at Nantucket at 6:00 p.m. and 72 mph winds in Chatham. In Weymouth, just a couple of towns south of Boston, a Weymouth police officer is quoted as saying, "The weather conditions were ferocious." In Quincy, the city adjacent to Boston, the police reported downed power lines. In a section of Boston known as Jamaica Plain trees were blown down. In East Boston a cap on a pickup truck blew off.

Weeks had the power to make up almost everything about what happened on that day because there was no witness who could contradict him although perhaps there are surveillance reports in existence. The one independent witness who could verify his story, the weather, proved that he was not leveling with the jury. Weeks was so wrong about the weather that even without the other internal incredulities in his tale of that day his whole credibility must be doubted.

Ironically, Connolly made a tactical and deadly error in not gladly accepting Weeks's story. Had he, then he could have changed what was perceived as a criminal act into an act that was performed pursuant to an obligation he had to Whitey. Morris testified the FBI's deal with Whitey was to give him a head start. No one claimed Connolly had no right to make that deal.

The FBI gives itself the right to allow informants to commit criminal acts and to protect them. It surely has the right to tip them off that they are going to be indicted as part of its quid pro quo. If Connolly acted to preserve a lawful obligation incurred while an FBI agent, he could not be charged with that act. If the action is not criminal, Connolly is not engaged in a criminal conspiracy. He should not have been charged with the racketeering counts.

APPENDIX C:

THE TITLE OF THE BOOK

The title for the book came to me during the trial. The seed for it was implanted in my mind by Connolly's defense counsel, Tracy Miner. She used two charts during her opening statement to the jury: one showing the structure of the FBI and the other the structure of the Mafia. (See appendix A) Both had starkly similar hierarchical structures.

The FBI is controlled out of Washington, D.C. under a Director; the Mafia out of New York City under the Commission. Each group divides the country into separate geographical areas. In each area there is a person in charge: the FBI a Special Agent in Charge (SAC), the Mafia a boss. Under that person is an executive: the FBI had an assistant agent in charge (ASAC), the Mafia had an under-boss. Under these the FBI has supervisors, the Mafia capos. Under those are the street workers: the FBI has its special agents and the Mafia its soldiers, the "made men."

Looking at the charts and thinking of my experience with these groups other similarities came to my mind. Each group is a male dominated, old boys' network. To join you have to meet certain qualifications, pass a test, and go through a ceremony. The final Mafia ceremony was to burn a sacred image. The final FBI ceremony was to shake hands with the exalted leader, or at least it was when J. Edgar Hoover was boss.

There was a pride in membership. Each group demanded an inordinate degree of loyalty from its members that engendered and encouraged suspicion of outsiders. The FBI is notorious for its refusal to fully trust and cooperate with other law enforcement people. The Mafia is wary of other than its own people.

Honoring the code of silence, Omerta, seems required by all the members of each group. It is as unlikely for an FBI agent to betray a fellow agent as it is a Mafia soldier to betray another "made man." The code is broken only when one may gain a great benefit from doing it such as being an informant or a spy, or avoiding heavy jail time. Each group operates behind a high wall of secrecy imposing strict discipline on its members. The Mafia by necessity operates in the nether world hiding public disclosure of its evils; the FBI operates in its private world similarly obscured from public view.

There are of course some differences. The biggest is that the FBI continues to grow in strength and influence abetted by the national treasury whereas the Mafia has become a shadow of itself because these same enormous public funds were used to destroy it. Another difference is the Mafia runs most of its operation outside the law whereas the FBI runs only a part of its operation outside the law. The Mafia enforces its rules and protects itself by violence and threats of violence whereas the FBI uses the power of the federal system including its courts to protect itself. Finally, unlike the Mafia, the FBI has recently let women and people of color into its ranks.

These similarities and dissimilarities were in my mind as I listened to the testimony of Frank Salemme. He proudly described himself as a "made man" in La Cosa Nostra but beamed with delight when he noted he was also a "king's man". He rose to the top to become a king himself when he was made the boss of the New England Crime Family. He talked like an old Marine reflecting on the good old days. He lamented the demise in the quality of the soldiers who were lately being brought into the LCN.

Salemme testified that during his rule as boss no one in his New England Mafia Family murdered anyone. Asked how he knew that he said he knew what every member in the Family had done because he relied on the capos to control the men. He said he told his capos they could allow their men "to do whatever they want but don't embarrass the family" apparently meaning if you're going to follow the traditional Mafia line of business of murdering people, don't get caught.

When he said "don't embarrass the family" it was like a bulb was lighted. The motive behind the trial suddenly fell into place. For twenty or so years the FBI allowed Special Agent John Connolly to do whatever he wanted. It relied upon the images of Ephraim Zimbalist and its finely tuned public relations apparatus to shunt aside any adverse public comments. Unfortunately, despite all of the Bureau's power, pelf and friends Judge Wolf's hearings unexpectedly brought to light some sordid facts that severely damaged the FBI's image. It was highly embarrassed. Someone had to be sacrificed for this.

Then and there I decided on the title. I'd learn in reading and research after that trial that J. Edgar Hoover's first and greatest commandment is, "Thou Shalt Not Embarrass the Family." An FBI agent could do just about anything he wanted as long as it was kept in house. John Connolly's actions became public so he had to take the fall. Whether his actions were committed with the full concurrence of the Bureau or not no longer mattered. It was the reputation of the Family that was important not the innocence of the agent.

It would have been best for all if Connolly recognized his sin, confessed and offered to do penance. Connolly did not understand this. He thought that because everything he did was known by the Bureau and authorized by it he should not be punished. He failed to comprehend the immateriality of an individual's innocence in the face of a scandal affecting the Family. He never understood an individual did not matter in such a communist type organization.

The FBI and Mafia did differ in its final handling of an embarrassment. The Mafia, if it could get its hands on the person, simply cut out the cancer through a disposal operation. The FBI had to be more discreet. It feigned surprise at Connolly's treachery. It worked to bring RICO charges against him. In this way the public is supposed to believe a renegade agent brought about the scandal and it had nothing to do with the FBI itself.

An example of this is Special Agent John Newton. He worked with Connolly in the Boston FBI office. He jumped at the opportunity Connolly offered him to hang around with Whitey and Stevie. The FBI had knowledge from its debriefing of gangster Kevin Weeks that Newton had received money and gifts from Whitey. The Bureau continued to let him work as an active agent in the Boston office despite this knowledge.

It was not until Weeks testified at Connolly's trial about the money envelopes that were earmarked for Newton under the pseudonym "Agent Orange" that the FBI acted. It suspended Newton. Had Weeks not mentioned it in a public forum the FBI would have let Newton work unmolested. Nothing had changed except the knowledge became public.

On April 30, 2003 an article on Lexis in the *Bulletin's Frontrunner* was headlined, "Veteran FBI Agent Says She's Being Fired For Exposing Ground Zero Theft." The article was about Agent Jane Turner. Her interview with NBC's Lisa Myers was to broadcast that evening. It noted that after Agent Turner saw in her FBI office a damaged tiffany crystal globe that had been stolen by FBI agents from the site of the September 11 terrorist attack on New York City. She reported it to her bosses in the FBI.

The FBI began an investigation into the theft by its agents. It was still ongoing a year later. It is typical of the FBI, as we have seen when it is investigating itself, to delay and obfuscate until time erases the malignancy of the agents' actions. We face the same situation as I now write. Marc Rossetti a Mafia capo in 2011 was a Top Echelon Informant for the Boston FBI. The FBI was asked how this could be? It said it would investigate to find out. Over a year has passed and no answer has been forthcoming.

However, in the 9/11 situation it did act quickly in one respect. It was not against the agents who pilfered the goods. It was against the agent who exposed the other agents' turpitude which caused the family embarrassment. The article reported that the FBI within three weeks of learning of Agent Turner's complaint gave her a "scathing evaluation" charging "she has tarnished the FBI's reputation" by revealing the theft. Agent Turner was put on leave and her reputation began to be undermined by the FBI network of witting agents. She said the FBI was taking steps to fire her. The article ends with Agent Turner's quote, "The bottom line is you do not embarrass the Bureau, and I had embarrassed the Bureau."

THE TITLE OF THE BOOK

Many of the books by FBI agents tell the same story. In his recent book the former ASAC during Connolly's days in the Boston office, Robert Fitzpatrick, tells of his service in the FBI. It is replete with the notion that it is the FBI's belief that the worst thing one could do is to embarrass the Bureau.

APPENDIX D:

THE AUTHOR

I am a trial attorney. I have defended and prosecuted criminal cases of every type. I have had personal involvement with some of the people and events surrounding the Connolly case. This experience and knowledge allowed me to discuss matters to make them more understandable for those not familiar with the case.

In 1976 when I was appointed as an assistant district attorney by Bill Delahunt, the Norfolk County District Attorney, I was one of the first full time prosecutors in the Commonwealth of Massachusetts. For the prior 200 years those prosecutors worked part time. The investigative work was left in the hands of full time police officers. They investigated a criminal case from its inception to the issuance of the charges. Often they had substantial input in it right through to its end. Part time prosecutors were mostly concerned with earning a living through their private legal practice and picking up a small stipend and experience for prosecuting cases. They left the investigations to the police officers.

During the 1960s and into the mid 1970s the rights of criminal defendants were greatly broadened. The *Gideon* decision in 1963 required defendants be represented by counsel in serious cases. As of 1976 the rights and procedures we now accept as routine were still working their way into our system. The criminal law became ever more complex.

Skilled full time defense attorneys were pitted up against part-time prosecutors. The cops insisted on doing things the way they had always done despite the new mandates. Defense attorneys became adept at discovering errors in investigations that resulted in the exclusion of vital evidence at trial. Criminals who were clearly guilty were being set free to prey on society because of unnecessary errors of these prosecutors and police officers.

I was a criminal defense attorney between 1968 and 1976 at a small four person Boston law firm that had a very active practice in all areas of the law. DiMento & Sullivan. The firm represented organized crime figures and handled every type of case from murder, rape, arson on down the felony scale. I was involved in one degree or another in most of them. We took full advantage of these changes for our clients.

I recall one potential client, Digger. He came to my office with the following story. He had broken into a building and was in the process of jimmying open a strong box with his burglar tools when the police arrived. They walked up behind him and arrested him as he worked hard at his trade. I concluded that it was an open and shut case with no defense to the charges. He would plead guilty. I'd do my best to work out a deal for him.

I explained this to him. He seemed impatient with my advice. He kept shaking his head. I thought he was inwardly chastising himself for his stupidity in carrying out the crime the way he did. I was about to tell him there was a chance I could keep him out of jail when he said, "You didn't ask me the right question."

I was confused. Apparently it was not his regret at his crime but a failure on my part that had him shaking his head from side to side. "What right question?" He replied, "You didn't ask me if they gave me my Miranda rights." I said, "Okay, Digger, did they give you your Miranda rights?" He said, "No, they forgot." He leaned back with a big grin on his face believing that meant the case against him would go away.

He was quite crestfallen when I explained Miranda only applied if a person's admission or confession were to be used in court against him. Here the police caught him red handed. They didn't need to give him a Miranda warning.

He said something to the effect that he heard otherwise. He left my office disgusted with me in search of another lawyer. In the air at the time with all the wise guys was the idea that one slip up by the police meant they would not be punished. The courts seemed to concur with that idea.

As they adjusted to the Warren Court's holdings the judges searched every nook and cranny for police error. The criminal defense bar happily provided more and more novel theories aiding in the search. For a while the balance in the criminal justice system moved drastically in favor of the criminals. It wasn't just in the courts but in society at large in the late Sixties and early Seventies things felt a little out of kilter.

To counterbalance this trend a need for apt prosecutors arose. At the urging of a former state legislator and the then Norfolk County District Attorney, William Delahunt, the state legislature passed a law calling for full time prosecutors. I became a prosecutor shortly after that law passed. I quickly found myself in a fight not with the criminals but with the police officers.

They did not want to relinquish any power. The veteran detectives held a stranglehold on important criminal investigations. They resented being told how to do things by us newly appointed and much younger prosecutors. They persisted in doing things the way they had always done them. Cases were being jeopardized.

The fight to wrest control from police officers took place outside public view. It was intense, bitter at times, and personal. I was out front in the battle. At an office party in the early days a state police lieutenant told some of my associates he'd like to shoot me. It took years in my county to fully gain the ascendancy over the important criminal cases.

THE AUTHOR

My greatest interest as a prosecutor was doing investigations. These required that I work hand-in-hand with the best and most aggressive police officers. For the first half dozen or so years this was always a challenge. I had to prove myself over and over again. They kept expecting me to vanish like the prior part-time prosecutors or take my knowledge to the defense side. Things ran more smoothly when we reached the point where we hand picked the police officers to work with us.

I developed an expertise in the field of searches and seizures including the use of wiretaps. Year after year I would do more wiretaps than all other state and federal law enforcement agencies in the Commonwealth combined. We rented a small town house apartment to set up our wiretap plant. At times I'd be overseeing three active wiretaps on different groups with different police units.

Title III which gave the states the right to do wiretaps required that they be done under the oversight of a prosecutor. By overseeing I mean I was at the plant during most times the interceptions were occurring. We were very imaginative in securing wiretaps. We did not have informants for all of them but relied on tough, time consuming investigative work. We never told an informant we were doing a wiretap. Even if one were caught up in the tap there were ways to insure he would not be prosecuted and his identity remain secret. As I mentioned previously when the FBI tell their criminal informants about their Title

III, they are giving the criminal some control over the contents of the interceptions.

A Sunday Boston Globe reporter on April 24, 1977, wrote about my involvement in preparing to raid 15 gambling establishments:

"The 70 lawmen listened as Assistant District Attorney Matthew Connolly assigned the detectives to teams. He briefed the detectives on what they may expect to find in the different locations and the persons who were named in the warrants.

Connolly who has headed the lengthy probe was pale, his face drawn, as he spoke in a military manner with quick, short sentences. The 34 year old Connolly, a Boston Law School graduate and former Marine Corps lieutenant, was trying to outline every action a defense lawyer could take to derail the case if the detectives didn't follow constitutional guidelines."

I tried to insure that no police search was undertaken in our county unless the paper work for the search was first reviewed by an assistant district attorney. We had an unblemished record in upholding our searches. I oversaw hundreds upon hundreds of searches and wiretaps. None were ever found to violate the law. Most importantly, none of the police officers were ever injured or found to have violated anyone's rights. We showed that the tools available to law enforcement were sufficient and could produce effective results with the proper work and dedication.

Even some feds recognized our competency. A report I received from Detective Lieutenant Dave Rowell written on June 19, 1983 spelled out how Whitey and Stevie were responsible for many murders, maiming, and extortions. They ran a gaming empire and were broadening into drug trafficking. He wanted to target them directly. He wrote that AUSA Jerry O'Sullivan said he would help if a case could be made against them. He quoted O'Sullivan as saying that I should be used "as the prosecutor if the case involved electronic interception because of his expertise."

Aside from doing the investigations I tried jury cases at the major felony level from murder down the scale of felonies. For a while I did nothing but difficult arson cases. They seemed to always result in trials because so much was at stake and the evidence was circumstantial. Arson prosecutions seem to have died down. I don't hear much about them anymore. I had upwards of six arson cases under indictment at one time back in the late seventies and early eighties. Perhaps the rapid increase in real estate prices made them unnecessary. A small number of cases that came as a result of wiretaps went to trial. Most of them ended up in plea bargains because the evidence was quite solid.

THE AUTHOR

I brought this experience to the Connolly trial. I picked much that went on during the case others may not have grasped. During the trial the names of persons I knew as a teenager came up. Tony Veranis who was killed by Martorano was one. Two Boston police detectives Peter McDonough and Joseph Lundbohm were others. Peter, who we called Luke, and Joe were the older brothers to my friends Paul "Wimpy" McDonough and Bobby "Luzzy" Lundbohm. Our neighborhood had so many kids in one's age group you hung around mostly with kids your age. You knew their siblings but not well. What I knew of Pete and Joe was they were easy going, somewhat reserved and friendly to us younger kids.

I mentioned that Joe told me he was going to be acquitted which he wasn't. I never talked to Luke about his case.

Luke was implicated in the Baharian wiretap. Baharian worked for Whitey and Stevie. Morris told them about the wiretap. Once that was done all the evidence intercepted is tainted. By disclosing to criminals a planned wiretap on another criminal the FBI loses control of the wiretap to the criminals. When Whitey and Stevie knew Baharian was going to be intercepted they first thought of protecting themselves. That means they may have advised Baharian not to say anything over the telephone about their relationship and they may have told other associates not to call him. Once Baharian knew, he may have told others. We don't know what the others did or who they told.

Baharian then could direct the conversations one way or the other. He could have set up Luke and let other cops slide. There are a huge variety of events that could be imagined once the gangsters know of a tap. For Luke to properly defend himself, he should have known the wiretap had been compromised.

In Joe's case he professed his innocence to me. He testified in Connolly's case he never took any money from bookies. What we do know about his case is that a Boston police lieutenant Cox was caught by the FBI doing something illegal. To save himself he agreed to wear a wire. Whitey and Stevie knew he was wired. Weeks testified when Cox came to the liquor store Whitey reminded Stevie to be careful.

Cox became desperate to get himself out of the jam that he arranged to meet with Joe. They had both grown up together in Savin Hill and were lifelong friends. Cox was able to turn the conversation so that Joe said something that was used to incriminated him. What it was I don't know but when the wise guys have been tipped off that a police lieutenant is wired then the outcome is not going to be what it would have been otherwise.

The FBI investigations during this time period seem less than legitimate. They seem to have been directed by Whitey and Stevie through Connolly and Morris for the purposes of insuring their

371

criminal enterprise grew and flourished. Whitey and Stevie's interest was to protect their criminal friends and to put any potential enemies, like honest cops, out of business. It's an unsettling feeling knowing that was happening.

APPENDIX E:

WILLIAM 'BILLY' BULGER

THE POWER TO MAKE THE INNOCENT GUILTY

Full Disclosure:

I spent the first ten years of my life residing on O'Callaghan Way in Old Harbor Village a government housing project in South Boston. At that time Billy and Whitey also lived there on an adjoining street. I did not know Billy back then. I think I knew of Whitey.

When I was about seven or eight year's old, I had a great fear of an older kid who lived in our project called Whitey. My friends and I heard that he'd grab us kids and give us a whack or two if he could catch us. I vividly recall playing with these friends in the courtyard next to my house when a playmate came running around the corner yelling, "Cheese it. Cheese it. Here comes Whitey!" Hearing this we scattered off for the safety of our homes. Whether this was Whitey Bulger or another Whitey I cannot state with total certainty other than noting I never heard of any other Whitey living among us. That was the closest encounter I ever had with Whitey.

Over the years I heard about Billy. He was often mentioned during political discussions among members of my extended family whose roots were in South Boston. I was involved as a lawyer representing the Boston School Committee in the school desegregation case during the years 1972 to 1976. Billy was a prominent figure in the opposition to the force busing of children. Surprisingly, I had no interaction with him during those days.

The first time I recollect speaking to him was around 1977. I was prosecuting one of his clients for a minor felony. We dealt at arm's length. I don't think he knew I was from Old Harbor. He was very professional and easy to deal with. He impressed me with his presence in the courtroom, his grasp of the facts and the law, and his keen ability to present an argument on behalf of his client. I recall thinking he would have been a formidable trial lawyer because of his intelligence, natural oratorical ability and charm.

I saw him some more at parents' nights at Roxbury Latin School where our sons went to school. We'd talk briefly. It involved no more than light bantering. He had the gift of telling a quick little story apropos the topic of the day. I always left him with a smile on my face.

I probably met him on the streets in Boston two or three times. Even though he seemed busy he would stop and chat briefly and offer a quip or two. On one occasion in the early Nineties I was induced by my neighbor and close friend to attend a St. Patrick's Day dinner in Boston put on by an Irish group. Billy was being honored as man of the year. I asked Boston Globe photographer Bill Brett to take my picture with Billy. He did. I've never seen it.

In the mid-nineties I spoke to Billy on a piece of legislation pending in the Senate. I worked in the Norfolk DA's office. Bill Delahunt, the Norfolk DA, was pushing the bill. Billy had the power to stop this bill dead in its track. I'll talk more fully about that later. Billy never inquired into anything that I was doing. He never asked me to contribute in any way to his political campaigns nor sought my attendance at any of his political fundraisers. I never did. Only once did he ever ask me for anything and it was indirectly.

It was in late 1996. DA Delahunt had been elected to Congress and was out of the office in DC preparing for his new job. I was running the office. A new DA would be coming in after the first of the year. Because the governor was Republican we expected that sometime in January he'd appoint a Republican DA. ADAs served at the pleasure of the DA. Some young ADAs anticipating the new DA may change the prosecution staff left our staff for other jobs. We had holes to fill. This was difficult because all we could offer any prospective candidate was a job for no more than a month or two.

Billy's administrative assistant Jimmy Julian called me. The Julians were also from O'Callaghan Way. I didn't know the caller. My only prior interactions with him were when I was attempting to meet with Billy. He kept brushing me off.

He asked if we had any openings. Billy's son had just become a lawyer and was looking to get some experience. I explained our situation saying I'd be glad to interview him if he were interested but he'd probably lose his job when the new DA came on board. After the interview I checked with the DA. He left it up to me. I hired him.

That's pretty much my total interaction with him. I saw him at the 2001 funeral of Joe Moakley in South Boston where he gave the eulogy in the presence of President Bush, former President Bill Clinton and former Vice President Al Gore. Again, I saw him at one of the Congressional hearings. I did not speak with him on either occasion.

I want to talk of what I know about him from my own experience and personal knowledge. He never exercised any influence or tried to exercise any influence over any state or local law enforcement agency to prevent it from pursuing or investigating Whitey. Also, he insured legislation passed that allowed the district attorneys to professionalize their staffs so that they would be better equipped to go after criminals such as Whitey. He did this even though the district attorney who initiated the request was from Norfolk County who according to all reports Whitey despised.

Billy as Perceived by Investigative Officers:

When Peter Gallagher first brought me to the Quincy police sub station and showed me the chart that prominently featured Whitey up until the time I left the DA's office over twenty years later I knew Whitey was involved in organized crime. I had made extensive efforts against him and his group of criminals. Whether our failure to get evidence against Whitey came because Whitey was being protected by the FBI or because Whitey operated so close to the vest or because we missed some good leads is difficult to tell at this time. We did have in mind Whitey's status as an arch criminal during all those years and acted against him when we could. There was never any thought or suggestion, not even in jest, that Billy had anything to do with Whitey.

For over eight years prior to becoming a prosecutor I was an associate in a small law firm that represented the top Mafia and other organized crime figures. I left that firm to become a prosecutor. Throughout these times Billy, the prominent politician, and Whitey, the notorious criminal, were well known.

I worked closely with organized crime investigators doing well over a hundred organized crime wiretaps, listening to thousands upon thousands of intercepted conversations, and participating in hundreds of other investigations of organized crime people, drug dealers and other felons. I never heard even the vaguest suggestion that there was an illicit association between the two men or that Billy was involved in any wrong doing with Whitey or any other criminal or that somehow their relationship impeded law enforcement.

The plain truth is this. Billy's name never came up when we discussed Whitey. The people whose job it is to know these things and who aren't bashful about holding back their opinions never suggested any hint of a wrong doing between Billy and his brother. I can't be any clearer than this: their relationship did not affect anything we did as law enforcement officials.

This great falsehood that Billy's position as senate president inhibited the law enforcement officers in Massachusetts who were targeting Whitey. This is simply mendacious. It is a malicious untruth defaming the law enforcement community with which I worked which consisted of state police and local police. You don't have to take my word for it. Look at the actions of our police agencies. It was the Massachusetts State Police who did the Lancaster Street operation (Appendix G) that was aimed squarely at Whitey. It was the Quincy police that were continually after him to the extent it bugged his condominium and car with DEA.

Billy never did anything that I know to protect his brother, Whitey, nor has anyone ever shown that he did. Had he done the slightest thing in that way, I feel quite sure I would have heard it. It would have spread like wild fire among the cops.

Billy's reputation has been unfairly damaged when it comes to this point. Books and articles

378

have been written by people outside law enforcement wrongly asserting he influenced or interfered with law enforcement investigations against Whitey. The unvarnished truth is I never heard anything about Billy protecting Whitey until the late nineties when people in the media started to bring it up. To this date no one has supported this bald allegation with evidence nor has anyone found any credible law enforcement action that was hindered.

When I first heard it, I thought it was invented out of whole cloth by radio entertainers clever enough to understand you don't keep an audience listening to you unless you stir up the pot. The best way to do this in Massachusetts is to go after the Democratic politicians who have controlled the state for years. I'd eventually learn, as I explain later, that the genesis of that untruth may have first arose in the files of the FBI.

Billy Acting on Behalf of the District Attorneys:

I've noted elsewhere that Whitey had a particular hatred for one District Attorney, Bill Delahunt. Connolly's 302s mention Whitey's complaints that Delahunt was out to get him. The DEA report of an encounter with Whitey when they went to retrieve their listening device has Whitey complaining to them about Delahunt. I was Delahunt's right hand man charged with conducting the wiretaps and other organized crime investigations. Whitey hated Delahunt because of the actions taken by me and the cops I worked with in going after his operations.

The Massachusetts district attorneys had a problem. Experienced prosecutors would leave their offices for the private sector after working for five or so years becoming highly skilled in investigations and in the trial of complex criminal cases. DA Delahunt thought a way to remedy this was to improve the pension plan for assistant district attorneys. With the support of the other DAs he had legislation filed to do this. He asked me to take the lead in this endeavor.

The bill slowly moved through the House of Representatives finally arriving at the Ways and Means committee. At a meeting with Chairman Thomas Finneran attended by all the district attorneys and their first assistants I spelled out the reasons why the legislation was important. Finneran indicated he was inclined to support it but thought the Senate would not go along with it.

The legislation was languishing in the Senate, the body over which Billy ruled with an iron fist. To get the bill through there it would be necessary to get his help. I arranged for an appointment to see him. When I talked to him, he was familiar with the bill. He, of course, knew Delahunt was behind it and that it would benefit the district attorneys. To be absolutely candid, as I think back to that time, the idea that Billy had anything to do with Whitey did not even occur to me.

Billy treated me with courtesy and respect. He listened to my argument pointing to importance to the Commonwealth for it to keep the best prosecutors. He must have been persuaded. The legislation passed.

I speak only to this one piece of legislation because I was intimately involved in it from the beginning. His action here gives lie to his alleged animus toward law enforcement. Had he had the slightest wrongful connection to Whitey, who would have done anything to undermine Delahunt, the bill never would have passed.

There are two other conclusions relating to Billy I arrived at considering these events. One being that there is no evidence he ever committed a criminal act despite a full blown federal effort to find something against him. The other is that the entity most responsible for the unfair suggestion that Billy used his influence to help Whitey is the FBI. The person in that Bureau in large part responsible for that was John Connolly, Billy's friend.

Billy as Involved in Criminal Activity:

It seems to me the proof of Billy's rectitude is simple. I've told how he seemed very much on the mind of the government during the trial with Durham's slip of the tongue, Morris's story about leaking information on Billy to the Boston Globe, Martorano's story about Connolly saying Billy wants him to look out for Whitey, and the utterly unnecessary testimony of former AUSA Chiel. I mentioned how I told Connolly that I thought the federal prosecutors were more interested in Billy than in him.

Other actions showing the federal disdain were the leaking of grand jury information by the DOJ of Billy's grand jury testimony about his relationship with Whitey and Congress switching an investigation from the FBI's use of murderers as informants over to whether Connolly helped Billy. I had little doubt the federal prosecutors were highly intent on finding some type of case against Billy.

Despite this no gangsters have creditably implicated Billy in any wrongdoing even though the government would provide a munificent largesse. All the mobsters who have turned state's evidence apparently have nothing believable to offer. Whitey's partner Flemmi, or Whitey's right hand man Weeks, despite the goodies they could have gained failed to implicate him. The treacherous John Morris had nothing to use to ease his plight. None of the many FBI agents who interacted with him suggested any wrong doing. Hundreds of other felons who could have received a golden ticket from the DOJ offered nothing that resulted in charges against him.

The countless hours of grand jury testimony, the countless interviews of people associated with Billy, and other investigative steps have come up with nothing. Even with that there is usually some type of income tax or obstruction of justice charge that can be brought. Nothing has come down against him. When the federal prosecutors coupled with the FBI go after you full bore and find nothing then that tells me there is nothing there. But that doesn't stop the media and others from proclaiming otherwise.

The FBI role in libeling Billy:

It would turn out that the first mention of Billy helping Whitey that I am aware of was in a FBI 302 report. Connolly filed it. It is ironic he would be the first one to allege such an activity since he was supposed to be Billy's good friend.

Connolly was on the hot seat having been accused by Colonel O'Donovan of the state police of having told Whitey of the Lancaster Street bug. In October 1980 to defend himself he fabricated a story. He wrote that the state police believed he told Billy about the bug so that he could pass it on to Whitey. This was absurd. The state police believed Whitey was Connolly's informant. They did not think he had to use an intermediary to get information to Whitey. They believed Connolly dealt directly with Whitey, not through Billy.

What was in Connolly's mind when he wrote this can only be surmised. Did he think by throwing Billy into the mix he'd cause everyone to back off? Did he realize he was planting a seed that would take on a life of its own to the detriment of his friend?

Every FBI agent who read that 302 had to wonder why the state police thought Billy was passing information to Whitey. I have no way of knowing how many other FBI 302s had similar outrageous suggestions as that. But I do know from other 302s I have read that the connection is implied.

For example, Special Agent in Charge of the Boston FBI office James Ahearn wrote to the FBI Director who was inquiring about Whitey. He made it a point to note that he's the brother of Billy, the Senate President who is "an extremely powerful political figure in this State."

An illicit relationship between Billy and Whitey became so established in the minds of FBI agents without a scintilla of evidence that it warped the thinking of some agents. A former ASAC in the Boston office Robert Fitzpatrick, who like Morris leaked to the Boston Globe that Whitey was an informant, had a chance to meet with Billy.[243] His story about the meeting is very strange.

In 1981 he had a very unpleasant meeting with Whitey. He wrote that after that he filed a two page report suggesting Whitey be closed as an

---

[243] Fitzpatrick in his book *Betrayal* does little to restore one's faith in the FBI or himself. For instance, he takes credit for destroying the Angiulo Mafia group while he continually denigrates AUSA Jeremiah O'Sullivan. But the truth is O'Sullivan brought down that group doing lengthy wiretaps and grand jury hearings. All Fitzpatrick did was serve the arrest warrants that came about as a result of O'Sullivan's effort.

informant.[244]   He also wrote that at that time his FBI unit was doing a corruption case that was targeting Billy.

He notes that during annual inspections "it was common practice to introduce the . . . brass to "important" people in Boston . . . . "   A month after his missing memorandum where he said that he recommended Whitey be closed, an inspection was ongoing. Connolly offered him a chance to meet with Billy. He takes a sinister view of Connolly's invitation saying, "I knew he was bringing me to see Billy Bulger as the guy who posed a threat to his brother and, perhaps, to him by connection. Or, maybe, I thought, Billy had requested the meeting so that he could get a look at his nemeses." He goes onwriting, "His taking me to Billy Bulger carried with it an implicit threat in the form of the political connections I'd be up against if I continued to press my case against Whitey. There was no doubt in my mind that Billy had already been briefed on the fact that I was the guy who wanted to close his brother as an informant, subjecting Whitey to arrest by O'Donovan's State Police and Billy to endless public embarrassment."[245] He offers no evidence to support his fantasy. Unintentionally, he points out that the state police were not intimidated by Billy.

---

[244] He kept no copy of it and it has not been found.

[245] Fitzpatrick's surmise that Billy would be subject to endless embarrassment if Whitey were arrested is puerile. It was hardly a secret Whitey was a top criminal.

After reading what he thought about the invitation you figured Fitzpatrick as Connolly's boss wasn't going to be lured into that trap. He's allegedly in the middle of a corruption investigation targeting Billy and he's expecting Billy to put pressure on him. He can avoid the meeting with a simple "no thanks." Inexplicably he doesn't do that. He decides to go into the lion's den and meet with a target despite all his forebodings.

In Fitzpatrick's mind whatever happened at the meeting would inure to Billy's detriment. He writes, "Billy couldn't have been warmer or more gregarious." He writes that when Billy shook his hand that "was just part of his con." Going on he says shaking his hand made him feel as he did when he met Whitey. (Whitey by the way refused to shake his hand.) He wrote that, "The specter of arrogance never once rose in our carefully worded, yet cautious exchange." But Fitzpatrick was not a man to be fooled by this civility. He continued that he "caged the rest of the meeting in a framework that Billy, too, was a con man used to getting what he wanted and taking whatever action was necessary when he didn't."

His description of the meeting is that Billy treated him respectfully like he'd treat any other guest in his office. The only odd things that happened were his mental processes where he had already condemned Billy because he was Whitey's brother. I can never figure out why he went to meet with him.

He said walking back to his office he thought, "Billy Bulger was a bully using power in place of his fists. And he wanted me to know I was alone, helpless against powerful forces I could neither control nor fully comprehend." The sad thing is Fitzpatrick went to see Billy of his own free will without any pressure being exerted on him. Without an adverse thing being said he leaves feeling like some Don Quixote figure fighting the whole world.

Here's the telling point in all this. Billy's evil is a figment of Fitzpatrick's imagination. How is it possible for an FBI agent to think "I was alone, helpless against a powerful force" when he meets with a state senator? He thinks this without a scintilla of evidence to justify this. Fitzpatrick never pointed to anything to show Billy had any illicit connection with Whitey but feels free to defame him.

About that corruption investigation we don't hear another thing. Surely if such an investigation existed it would have been leaked out by now. There is no record showing such a 1981 investigation. Fitzpatrick seemed to have invented it. He assumed the worst of Billy even to the point imagining he was conducting a corruption investigation of him when he wasn't.

Here's the irony of all of this. Billy was a state official with power over state law enforcement. He had no power over the FBI. Yet the FBI was intimidated by him. The state agencies had no fear. Fitzpatrick said they were looking to arrest Whitey.

Another irony is that Billy went out of his way to meet with FBI agents and graciously offered to assist them get another job after they retired. All the while some FBI agents were attributing sinister motives to his actions. If ever there was a situation of damned if you do, damned if you don't, Billy was squarely in it.

Connolly's 302s, Fitzpatrick's conjuring of malicious motives, and Ahearn type memos about Billy based on false or imagined connections between him and his brother poisoned the air against Billy. There is not one solid fact supporting any of it. The FBI was the fertile field where the rumor that Billy used his position to help Whitey grew. The rumor spread within the Bureau and eventually to within the attorneys in the Department of Justice.

It brings to mind U.S. Supreme Court Justice Anthony Kennedy's recent question to the Obama administration's lawyer during the hearing over Obama's health care bill. He inquired: "Can you create commerce in order to regulate it?" Here, I wonder "Can you create a crime in order to investigate it?"

How Did Billy Become so Reviled by the Media:

A politician similarly astute as Billy, Tony Blair, testifying at an inquiry at the Royal Courts of

Justice in London concerning Robert Murdoch's media enterprise said: "If you're a political leader and you've got very powerful media groups and you fall out with one of those groups, the consequences is such that you . . . are effectively blocked from getting across your message, . . . I'm being open about the fact that frankly I decided as a political leader, and this was a strategic decision, that I was going to manage that and not confront it. And we can get on to whether that was right or wrong at a later stage, but that was the decision I took."

Contrast this to what Billy wrote in his autobiography, *While the Music Lasts.* "I have no quarrel with journalists who fault me, as so often they do, for denying interviews, ignoring questions, refusing to be accountable to the press. What they say is true. Wise or unwise, it is the path I have chosen. I do not commend my style to others; it is a matter of choice. But I am still here."

At the time Billy wrote his autobiography he was riding high. He was still the president of the Massachusetts Senate. He was about to become the president of the University of Massachusetts. After the relentless attacks upon him in the media since the Connolly trial his name has been blackened. His influence and power is a shell of what it was when he wrote. The road Billy took was one where he treated the media with disdain and disrespect.

The media's hostility arose because of how Billy handled his power. It would be easy to say it happened because of his relationship to Whitey. It's true had Whitey not existed Billy may have served 17 years or more as the president of the University of Massachusetts rather than six. He'd still have his enemies as every prominent politician has but those issues would be the sort of inside politics games that never become widely circulated. But it was more than that, much more because others in high political office have not been sullied by bad siblings to the extent their reputations became badly damaged.

Billy had been in the forefront of the fight against forced busing which didn't endear him to the media but it didn't hurt him too badly. After that he was elected Senate President in July 1978. He still had an edge endemic to those growing up in the rough and tumble of the courtyards which belied his hail fellow well met exterior. It became more prominent as he sat in this heady position. He began to make enemies giving short shrift toward some people feeling he could do so because he had the power and the ways and the means to keep it. People had to come to him and little got done without his imprimatur.

Billy in his seat of power explained why he refused to be accountable to the media for his actions. In his autobiography he came up with an odd theory. He noted the media "were of necessity in the business of making profits." He then said its "guardianship of the public interest" is less than its desire to make money. He on the other hand felt accountable to the public and not to private industry. He wrote, "I see no purpose in cooperating with *that* enterprise other than to sell papers and improve ratings, neither of which is my concern. "(Billy's emphasis)

He goes on, "Each a time a press query was addressed to me I asked myself: *"Cui bono?* For whose benefit?" The answer that came to me often, so very often, was "Not for the public good, but for the benefit of the media." So – just as often – I thought silence the better course." He continued by adding that he was confrontational and "to blame for my strained relationship with the press. Often I exacerbated matters by being brusque and even cutting, . . ." and noted "I have been guilty of baiting the media." He suggests that "It was a self-righteous manner that did me no credit . . . ." After spelling out all this hostility and disdain for the media out of the blue he drops this, "However imaginary my bellicose attitude toward the press may be – and it is pure fiction as far as I am concerned – it has become accepted as a fact."

I had difficulty trying to juxtapose his litany of hostile actions and attitude toward the media with his suggestion his bellicosity is a fiction. Whether a fiction or not the press corps believed he was hostile toward it. Justifying his refusal to answer questions from the media because the media made money seems unsupportable. If that were a

391

universal prescription, then all government actions would be cloaked in secrecy which is definitely not in the public good. Justice Brandies said, "Sunlight is said to be the best of disinfectants."

Billy sought to work in the dark shadows disdaining media coverage and the ability of the public to know what he was doing in his high public position. It was an approach designed to make enemies. It explained why there was such a little reservoir of good will toward him at a time when he needed it. It was an approach I have difficulty countenancing. As a public officer, I believed the media kept us on our toes. It is the life blood of our liberty. Without a free media the public would have even less knowledge about the happenings in the government than it does now.

The media would eventually get its revenge. The Department of Justice to its discredit baited the press by bringing Billy's name into the trial unnecessarily. The hyperbolic coverage that took place each time his name was mentioned during the trial told that it was payback time. Billy was painted as a demonic figure knee deep in everything evil in the Commonwealth. Everyone piled on. Eventually a Congressional Committee would join in the free-for-all.

The 1988 Boston Globe Spotlight Article on Billy and Whitey:

In the thoroughly researched Boston Globe 1988 Spotlight article there is not the slightest suggestion that Billy had done anything at all that appeared to be wrong, never mind criminal. The article described Billy as one who: "can be a petty despot, but also a masterful conciliator . . . a doctrinaire conservative on social issues but a tax-and-spend liberal on anything involving the urban poor; . . a reserved man who is transformed by a microphone into a stand-up comic; . . . an urban populist who champions the arts and education; . . . as compassionate with elderly constituents as he is vindictive with State House opponents; . . . feigns indifference to press criticism but never forgets a slight and remembers it by name."

The Globe quoted George Bachrach who Billy Bulger stripped of his committee chairmanship for challenging him. He said, "I think Bill Bulger is probably the smartest, most charming, most resourceful leader I've known." It also quoted Michael Dukakis, former governor and Democratic presidential nominee saying of Billy that, "There has never been any question about the integrity of the Senate since he has been president."

The Globe Spotlight said, "The streets taught Bill Bulger you give and get loyalty from your friends and you never take an insult." The part about friends is true, the rest isn't. The first lesson taught is to be respected. The next and equally important is as the Bible and the streets teach there is a time and place for all things. You learn there are some insults you walk away from and others you don't. You learn you can fight someone, lose, and still be respected; and you can fight another, win, and be ridiculed. You know some fights end quickly but others never end. You're taught friends are important and to never make unnecessary enemies.

Street people understand that pride comes before the fall. They know there's always someone better than them or the person they know when it comes to handling fists, tossing a ball, shooting hoops, using wits, figuring things out or being meaner than a junk yard dog. They understand when their head hits the pillow at night they may be champion but they may not be the next time they put down their head. I was introduced to this lesson as a very young boy walking down Southie's Mercer Street with my uncle Bobby. He was educated on the hard knock Southie streets and was as street wise a Southie wise guy as every existed. "Always, remember, Matty," he said, "the bigger they are the harder they fall."

Billy's use of his power became his undoing. The greatest purgative to remembering that being king of the hill is ephemeral is power. Billy wasn't corrupt or evil. His sin was once in power he forgot that you never make unnecessary enemies like he did with the media which always has the last laugh.

75 State Street Affair and Billy's Autobiography:

75 State Street has been Billy's bane. It is mentioned by most who write about him. It was

brought up during Connolly's trial even though totally irrelevant to the issues. It is thrown back at me whenever I say I believe Billy is a good man.

75 State Street is an address in Boston where Harold Brown, a man who had wealth estimated between $500 million to $1 billion and who had been indicted for giving a bribe of $1,000 to a city building inspector, planned to build a new high rise building. Looking for every edge he could find, Brown made an initial payment of $500,000 to Billy's law partner Tom Finnerty for legal assistance in securing the necessary approvals. Billy received almost half of that $500,000. Billy said he thought the money he received was an advance on a fee he had coming. He said he did not know it came from Brown but when he found out it he returned it. Some alleged Finnerty extorted the money from Brown. Others that after Billy returned the money he took it back again.

It was investigated by two US Attorneys and the Massachusetts Attorney General. None found any crimes had been committed. To get into it more deeply than that would be like what happened at trial when the defense used a witness to contradict a government witness on an aspect of his testimony far removed from the issues of the trial.

For months the media carried 75 State Street stories. *Black Mass* and other books have been written about it and discuss it in great detail. Wherever the truth lies the result was that Billy's good reputation was severely stained and on the way to becoming irreparably damaged.

I mentioned Billy's autobiography. My opinion is that he'd have been wiser not to have written it. There's an old saying that the art of politics is pretending. You never reveal your true feelings. You never let people know what you really think of them. Truisms like "don't write it down if you can verbalize it"; and "don't verbalize it if you can indicate it otherwise as with a nod or a wink" exist for a reason.

Apparently heeding Dylan Thomas's admonition not to go gentle into the good night Billy's book dripped with triumphalism. Gracelessly he skewered his enemies, demeaned other people, and spread tales of the foibles and failings of some poor souls in a mean spirited manner holding them up to ridicule. Reading it brought to mind the admonition my uncle Bobby gave me.

Billy took no prisoners. He left no one who crossed him unscarred. Those who had been willing to let bygones be bygones had old wounds reopened. The people and the friends of those people he spoke ill of had no doubt of his feelings toward them. Again, like he did with the media he made unnecessary enemies.

Examples of the Attack on Billy:

In July 2011 the Boston Daily, a Boston Magazine blog had an article by Alan Dershowitz.

It was introduced with the words, "As those who follow Boston politics well know, there's no love lost between Billy Bulger and Alan M. Dershowitz, the Felix Frankfurter Professor of Law at Harvard Law School." Dershowitz wrote, among other things, the following:

> When Billy was the most powerful political figure in Boston, corruption permeated every aspect of public life, from the FBI, to federal prosecutors, to the state judiciary, to Beacon Hill, to building inspectors, to the State Police. Everyone — from governors, to justices of the state's highest court — kowtowed to "The President," which in Boston meant Billy Bulger. And everyone knew that messing with Billy was messing with Whitey. Even more important, everyone knew that messing with Whitey was messing with Billy. Billy believed his job was to protect Whitey and to keep him out of prison. Without Billy there would not, in my opinion, have been a Whitey — at least a Whitey who could persist in his murderous rampage for so long.

> Not only did John Connolly — who's now serving a long prison sentence — keep the mass-murdering Whitey out of prison and in business for decades, but he also tried to keep

Billy out of prison. Billy was suspected of extorting a quarter-million-dollar bribe from the Boston developer who was building a skyscraper at 75 State Street. Business as usual! According to an assistant U.S. Attorney who testified at Connolly's trial, during the 75 State Street extortion investigation, Connolly improperly lobbied him to drop the scrutiny of this "special person." Connolly also tried to milk the prosecutor for confidential information about the probe. It turned out, moreover, that the Chief Federal Strike Force Prosecutor in charge of investigating Billy Bulger's corruption happened to be Whitey's handler, Jeremiah T. O'Sullivan. The entire "investigation" of William Bulger was a scandal.

Poor Felix Frankfurter, a man known for clear thinking and writing, would be rolling in his grave if he read such a diatribe. Dershowitz's article is full of gross exaggerations. He impugns the integrity of just about every public official in the Commonwealth.[246] He doesn't stay his hand being solely motivated by his black hate for Billy.

---

[246] Dershowitz elsewhere wrote: "[T]he real villains of this tale of mass murder and massive corruption are the 'good' people who knowingly facilitated the bad brothers – the Dukakises, Whites, McCormacks, Cardinal Laws,

As far as everyone "kowtowing" to Billy and everyone knowing "messing with Whitey was messing with Billy" nothing is further from the truth as I explained. Dershowitz totally distorted Chiel's testimony about his one meeting with Connolly. Chiel's testimony was that Connolly did no more than ask what was going on in the investigation of Billy and expressed his opinion Billy was a great man. He didn't "improperly lobby him to drop the scrutiny" nor did he try "to milk [Chiel] for confidential information" for as Chiel explained he had nothing to do with the investigation of Billy. Also O'Sullivan was not Whitey's handler which Dershowitz should know since US Attorneys do not handle informants.

Dershowitz is an outsider to law enforcement. He has no conception of the work and effort put in to catch Whitey. The picture he paints of corruption everywhere is based upon his notorious animosity toward Billy. What is a true scandal is a person like Dershowitz will be believed by others who may think he knows of which he writes and are unaware of his unremitting hostility toward Billy. Dershowitz in all fairness should make full disclosure before he writes any article about Billy

---

O'Sullivans, Welds, Moakleys, and Silbers. Also guilty were the cowards who appointed Billy Bulger president of UMass instead of indicting him for extortion and taking bribes, and the reporters for *60 Minutes* and *The New Yorker* who glorified Billy and romanticized Whitey. "

and note that just hearing his name throws him into a tantrum.

Billy, when asked whether he intended to sue Dershowitz for his libels told the Harvard Crimson, "The law is all weighted against the plaintiffs. It's expensive. It's time consuming. It's almost impossible to win victory. It's very difficult for a public person. So it isn't worth it." He's right. The US Supreme Court make public officials easy targets.

Billy and His Brother Whitey:

In his autobiography Billy writes that he could not write "an honest memoir and ignore the subject." True to his word he doesn't. He promulgates a defense of Whitey in two parts: one Whitey is not really as bad as they say; the other the evidence against him is bought or fabricated.

W. Somerset Maugham gives us an insight into this. In his book *"The Summing Up"* he wrote after a lifetime of keenly observing people, "I think what has chiefly struck me in human beings is their lack of consistency. . . . It has amazed me that the most incongruous traits should exist in the same person . . . . I have often asked myself how characteristics, seemingly irreconcilable, can exist in the same person. I have known crooks who were capable of self-sacrifice, sneak-thieves who were sweet-natured, and harlots for whom it was a point of honor to give good value for money."

Billy sees a side of Whitey that has been hidden from the rest of us. That view colors his perspective. It is far from uncommon for family members to refuse to believe a member of their family could commit a heinous crime. Several years ago a doctor in my county was charged with murdering his wife. His three highly educated adult children, also doctors, refused to believe their father could kill their mother despite the compelling evidence showing he did. They stuck by him throughout his trial. As far as I know they still believe his innocence despite his conviction. Many people close to an accused absolutely refuse to believe the evidence against him. Most experienced prosecutors have encountered this.

The Final Blow:

A Congressional Oversight Committee was formed to investigate the Boston FBI office relating to events surrounding a 1968 murder of Teddy Deagan.[247] Six people were convicted for that murder based on testimony of an FBI cooperating witness Joseph "the Animal" Barboza. Four of the six may have been innocent. It appeared Barboza perjured himself at the trial and the FBI withheld exculpatory evidence that may have affected the outcome of the trial.

---

[247] The Committee issued a report entitled: *Everything Secret Degenerates: The FBI's Use of Murderers as Informants,* 108th Congress, 2nd Session, Report 108-414.

The committee in its report harshly condemned the FBI actions from the lowest level up to its then director J. Edgar Hoover. It also berated the present leadership of the FBI for the lack of cooperation it received from it during its investigation. Unfortunately, it bleated out the mandatory apology for its criticism by noting the FBI is "the finest federal law enforcement organization in the world," pretty much undermining its findings that the evils were systemic.

It seemed to be common knowledge that the committee really had no desire to do anything about the FBI so no one bothered with its efforts. They were treated with a big ho-hum. That was until the committee changed its focus.

Committee wrote it did this because Connolly had Whitey as an informant and may have done so "to advance or protect" Billy Bulger. It was a naked assertion. No evidence was adduced to support that supposition. Having come up with a theory, it decided "to take testimony from William Bulger regarding his knowledge of the relationship between the FBI and his brother." The relationship of Connolly and Whitey had not been a subject of the hearing until that point.

The media was delighted with the news that Billy was subpoenaed to appear. The committee was delighted with publicity. Billy was an easy target because the members of the committee had the full backing of the media. Billy's fall from grace and public esteem was shown when the Congressman from his own home town of South Boston joined in the questioning of Billy. Speaker McCormick and Chairman Moakley must have had their eternal rest disturbed by one of their own joining this charade.

A fair statement is that the committee was not looking to find out what Billy knew of his relationship with Connolly. It was immaterial to the matters before it.[248] The committee sought publicity. It hoped that somehow it could entrap Billy into providing evidence against himself that would allow him to be prosecuted.

Billy answered the subpoena in December 2002. He took the Fifth before the committee. He knew or was told by his lawyer, Tom Kiley, that the committee had turned its legitimate investigation into a witch hunt.

The benefits of the Fifth Amendment are available to one in a high public position of trust. As with the right of free speech, it is protected and guaranteed to us by the Constitution. What is not guaranteed is that there will be no downside to exercising it. The position of university president demands a showing of absolute personal probity which is determined by public perception. Taking

---

[248] No reliable evidence has ever been brought forward showing that Billy knew that Whitey was Connolly's informant. Billy denied having that knowledge. The evidence tends to show Billy had no idea that he was since he condemns people who inform in his autobiography.

the Fifth gave the media a chance to pounce upon Billy's character and twist and darken his reputation in the public's mind. No one spoke of the good works he had been doing at the university. The public only perceived that a university president had something to hide.

In June 2003 Billy was given a grant of immunity and forced to testify. He knew the long knives were sitting on the laps of the congressmen. He had to be extremely cautious testifying about events that happened thirty or so years before. He knew that the government was hoping he'd say something that it could prove may not have been true so it could indict him for perjury. Unless he was absolutely certain about these ancient matters, he answered by saying he could not remember. It wasn't his finest hour nor would it be anyone's realizing the slightest slip up in a memory about long past events would result in criminal charges.[249]

The trustees of the university continued to express their full confidence in him. It would not be enough to save him. Governor Romney expressed his displeasure. Threats were made to remove the trustees and to add such persons as Dershowitz to the board. Within weeks Billy gave up and tendered his resignation. His dream of

---

[249] The Committee truly was after the slightest thing. It sent investigators to Boston after his testimony to see if it could prove Billy lied when he said he didn't help Connolly get his job after retirement; or that he had no involvement in legislation aimed at certain state police.

leading the university to greater heights was dashed.

After Billy's testimony the Committee was left to express its concern with two trivial areas in his testimony: whether the FBI waited six years before contacting him regarding the whereabouts of his brother; and, whether Billy told his lawyers that Whitey called him shortly after he fled.

The Committee did a follow up investigation of Billy's testimony sending investigators to Boston to plough through government records and to interview people looking for something, anything, that it could use to fault his testimony. This search for the most part confirmed that the material part of his testimony was true.

One FBI agent recalled having a short conversation with Billy within a week or two after Whitey had fled. The gist of the conversation was disputed but that was the only contact by the FBI with Billy in six years after Whitey's flight. On the other issue it was unclear what the attorneys did with the information Billy gave them about the call from Whitey. The Committee spent about one sixth of its report discussing Billy. Nothing came of its hearings other than Billy's job loss.

CONCLUSION:

I can only speak of my own experience as a professional prosecutor. All the evidence I have seen shows there is no evidence of an illicit connection between Billy and Whitey or that anyone was intimidated by their relationship. The only entity that seemed concerned about it was the FBI.

I always thought Billy knew or heard very little about Whitey. You have to understand the culture we come from. People don't say negative things to you about your family. They are simply off limits. No one, even close friends, ever said anything that was other than complimentary to me about my brothers or sisters.

I cannot see an outsider talking to Billy about Whitey or see Billy talking about Whitey other than within his family. That's my gut telling me how it would be in an Irish family from the project. I was taught as a very young boy that you don't hang your dirty laundry in public. What happens in the family, stays in the family.

I cannot put myself into Billy's shoes to decide how I would act if my brother was accused of being a murderer of at least 19 people including two young women.[250] I know how one sees those close to him is not the same how they may appear to society at large. I don't find anything wrong with him standing by him.

Billy has been condemned for not being more helpful in the hunt for Whitey. Billy felt he had no

---

[250] I have difficulty believing Stevie's story that Whitey killed the two Debbies. It was Stevie who was sexually involved with these girls. One planned to leave him. The other to reveal that he abused her when she was a child. What motive would Whitey have to kill them?

obligation to do that. Society recognizes a right of a brother to aid a brother knowing the brother committed a crime without consequences.[251] Billy has made a public showing of support of Whitey by attending court when he has been brought here from his jail cell.

I never believed nor do I now that Billy had anything illicit to do with Whitey and their relationship was no more than that of brothers. I had no personal knowledge Billy did anything wrong in relation to him, I never heard anyone I worked with suggest it, and the extensive scrutiny under which he has been put by the federal prosecution agencies and the Congressional investigators proves it. Harry Truman would say if it is there then "Show me!"

But in reality that no longer matters other than saving Billy further aggravation. Malcolm X wherever he is must be nodding knowingly. A long time ago he said: "The media's the most powerful entity on earth. They have the power to make the innocent guilty and to make the guilty innocent, and that's power. Because they control the minds of the masses."

Like a pack of wild dogs the media tore away at Billy's reputation. Voices raised in his defense

---

[251] Massachusetts General Laws Chapter 274, Section 4 which sets out the punishment for an accessory after the fact to a felony states that if a person charged with aiding an offender after his felony is a brother of the offender that shall be a defense to the prosecution.

were shouted down by the clamor. Congress and the prosecutors fell in line. No one said "Show me the evidence." The Queen of Hearts told Alice, "Sentence first. Verdict afterwards." The media and prosecutors in Billy's case tell us, "Conviction first. Evidence afterwards."

APPENDIX F:

JEREMIAH O'SULLIVAN

THE MAN BEHIND THE MASK

Jeremiah O'Sullivan, a former assistant US attorney, was chief of the Federal Organized Crime Strike Force in Boston and then interim US Attorney for Boston. He was closely involved with many of the happenings during the days Whitey and Stevie were being protected by Connolly and the FBI. I had contact with him off and on during this time. He had an excellent reputation and presented himself as a forthright prosecutor who was not intimidated by others. For most of the time I believed he had done an outstanding job up until the time Naimovich was arrested when I found he was not what he appeared to be. He testified before the congressional committee investigating the FBI on December 5, 2002. He revealed a different side of him.

75 STATE STREET:

Asked about his role in the 75 State Street investigation he explained he was appointed as interim US Attorney upon the resignation of Frank McNamara. One of his first orders of business was to cause that investigation. It was carried out by two top assistant US attorneys in his office without input from him. At the conclusion of their investigation they found nothing that was criminally wrong. O'Sullivan said it was a case of nothing more than power brokering.

He said that because the case had received so much notoriety he held a press conference to announce the findings of his assistants. He admitted this was unusual but pointed out so was the extensive media coverage. He said the attorney general of the Commonwealth also conducted an independent investigation of 75 State Street and arrived at the same conclusion.

BRIAN HALLORAN:

O'Sullivan said he refused to let Brian Halloran into the Witness Protection Program because he was under indictment for first degree murder in Suffolk County. Tom Mundy, the top ADA, was prosecuting Halloran. He needed Mundy's approval. Mundy wanted to prosecute Halloran for the murder and refused to consent to him being accepted into the program. Mundy was one of the toughest and best prosecutors in the Commonwealth. He would want to put Halloran in prison for life. What weighs against O'Sullivan's story that Mundy was hot after Halloran is that Halloran had been out on bail on the murder charge which is not normally the case. Also, it runs contrary to what he told other people at earlier times.

First, Mundy died a young man and was not alive when O'Sullivan made this statement which no one reported hearing earlier. Also, Detective Michael Huff of the Tulsa police department met with O'Sullivan in 1982. O'Sullivan told him Halloran was a coke freak, would not give information against Howie Winter, and was a liar. He didn't mention Mundy.

FAILURE TO INDICT WHITEY AND STEVIE FOR RACE FIXING:

Inquired about his decision not to indict Whitey and Flemmi in the race fix case he first talked about a Winter Group and a Winter Hill Group. I had never heard this before. Later I learned that some people referred to Howie Winter, Joe McDonald and James Simms as the Winter group.

Winter Hill is a section in Somervillle, MA where Winter owned an auto repair garage called Marshall Motors. When Whitey, Stevie, Martorano and other hang around types joined with Howie Winter it became the Winter Hill Group because they did their business out of his garage.

O'Sullivan agreed that Connolly and Morris approached him asking him not to indict Whitey and Stevie. He admitted he knew both Whitey and Flemmi were vicious murderers at the time he decided not to indict them. He stated their request had no effect on his decision since he had already decided not to indict them. It got interesting when he set about to explain his decision.

First he said the only evidence against them came from Fat Tony Ciullo. He had no corroboration. Because of this he decided not to indict them. He pointed out he had indicted 21

411

other people in the case. Asked if he had corroboration for all 21 people he said all but one.

The committee members seemed skeptical. He offered an alternative reason for not indicting them. He said he already had 21 people and did not want more.

When this fell flat, he changed his story again. He said he thought they were not in the leadership of the Winter group. Then he agreed they were in the leadership of the Winter Hill group.

O'Sullivan's alternative answers did nothing to allay the committee's skepticism. Being pressed he returned to his original answer that he lacked sufficient corroborative evidence.

At that point counsel for the committee produced a statement O'Sullivan had submitted to Washington, DC when he was preparing the case for indictment. In it he stated that he did have sufficient corroborative evidence to indict them. Hearing this he conceded that may have been the case.

I was left with the belief that he did not indict Whitey and Stevie because he was asked by Connolly and Morris not to do it. He was reluctant to admit that. I can only assume that it would make him look bad to admit that he did not indict two vicious thugs who he knew were stone killers because a couple of cops asked him not to do it.

98 PRINCE STREET INVESTIGATION:

The Committee sought to learn whether the information from Whitey and Stevie was necessary to the probable cause for the wiretap on Angiulo's headquarters at Prince Street in Boston's North End. O'Sullivan was emphatic in stating that their information was not necessary. He said he had plenty of probable cause without them.

O'SULLIVAN'S AND THE FBI:

O'Sullivan said he met with some FBI informants and knew the identity of others. This is highly unusual. The FBI traditionally did not disclose the identity of its informants to anyone outside the Bureau.

The most surprising part of his testimony came when he discussed the time SAC Sarhatt decided not to terminate Whitey and Stevie as informants. O'Sullivan protested that he had nothing to do with Sarhatt's decision. When someone told him it said otherwise in O'Neill's and Lehr's book *Black Mass*, O'Sullivan said he did not read anything that dealt with these matters. A member of the committee pointed to a report stating that O'Sulllivan did have input into that decision.

SAC Sarhatt filed a memorandum on December 1, 1980 that he spoke to O'Sullivan on the phone. Sarhatt said O'Sullivan told him that it is "crucial" that the FBI not discontinue Bulger as an informant because, "the information he is currently furnishing is crucial to a Title III application of LCN members in Boston, Massachusetts." SAC Sarhatt went on to say, "O'Sullivan stated that he did not feel there was any improper conduct on the part of the FBI by

413

continuing the Informant relationship with [Bulger]."

O'Sullivan somewhat upset shot back that the 302 report by Sarhatt was wrong. He said it was Sarhatt who did not want them terminated. He said Sarhatt was yelling and shouting at him when the topic came up.

I suggest the evidence supports O'Sullivan. Agent Quinn testified he had already written the affidavit without input from Bulger before he was told by Morris to put them in. Morris didn't do this because the information was "crucial" but rather because by doing this he could let Whitey and Stevie know about the wiretap. Basically Sarhatt dissembled so to keep Whitey as an informant by putting it on O'Sullivan. It also shows you never know what untruths the FBI agents are writing.

O'Sullivan went on to say it was very difficult dealing with the FBI. He was afraid of the FBI agents. He said they had great influence that could adversely affect him in his job. This really opened my eyes. I pictured O'Sullivan as a feisty, stand-up guy, who was a tough prosecutor who no one pushed around. After all he was responsible for prosecuting many of the top Mafia figures. His fear of crossing the FBI showed he had abdicated his job as a prosecutor for that of a toady to the FBI.

O'SULLIVAN AND LANCASTER STREET:

O'Sullivan said the state police came to him with the Lancaster Street investigation. They did not want to work with the FBI nor did they want the FBI to know anything about what they were doing. He arranged for them to get the help from the Suffolk DA Newman Flanagan. The ADA assigned to help the state police had no experience in doing electronic surveillance. O'Sullivan agreed to assist him in getting the surveillance order to plant the bug in the Lancaster Street garage.

In his prepared statement to the committee, O'Sullivan talked about the leak writing, "The source of the leak has publicly been identified in other proceedings. Flemmi testified before Judge Wolf in 1998 that the tip came from an FBI agent who had consulted me. That is categorically untrue. Judge Wolf's opinion, which questions the accuracy of Flemmi's assertion about me, is correct in doing so"

My analysis as set out in Appendix G shows Flemmi is telling the truth in this one instance. Wolf found that the leak was Trooper Naimovich, who O'Sullivan had indicted and who was acquitted. Wolf had no evidentiary basis to support that finding. Wolf has the misimpression that Naimovich had been convicted. Wolf had worked in the US Attorney's office with O'Sullivan and may have had a personal relationship with him. That closeness may have made him unable to accept that O'Sullivan was a leak.

When asked who he thought tipped off Whitey and Stevie about the bug at Lancaster Street, rather than going along with Judge Wolf, he contradicted his finding. He quickly answered the FBI. No one followed up on his statement. It is a pity. He should have been asked what made him think that.

THE UNRELIABILITY OF FBI REPORTS:

Sarhatt wrote that he talked with O'Sullivan about the leak in the Lancaster Street investigation. He said O'Sullivan "indicated that it was his impression that the MSP [Masssachusetts State Police] had problems on electronic coverage from the beginning of their operation . . . . O'Sullivan indicated he was very supportive of Supv. Morris and had no reason to believe that Supv. Morris had leaked any information out to the criminal element concerning the MSP's undercover operation."

Sarhatt's memorandum is impressive. The only problem is that O'Sullivan says he never said those things. O'Sullivan's bottom line is the Boston FBI SAC filed fictitious reports about conversations with him, the strike force chief. This is easy to do. The subject of an FBI report never gets to read what is written about him. There is no check on the agent and no one to verify what he puts down. A report may not see the light of day for years. What is put in writing even if it never happens becomes the reality. The FBI has created this alternative reality that has no relation to the truth.

That would be fine if the FBI was a child of three or four living in a pretend world. It isn't. Its work is too important to be left to the vagaries of an agent desirous to cover his butt or to a SAC trying to make his agents look good and save the FBI from embarrassment. What is written may come back to hurt other people. One can only wonder how many people are in jail because of false FBI reports. When the person denied what was contained in the report, he was faced with a perjury charge. Or, more likely, a report was used to tie the person to a crime he did not commit or to defame someone an agent did not like.

CONCLUSION

O'Sullivan painted a frightening picture of how the FBI ran rough shod over the US Attorney's office in Boston during his era. It was sad to hear him testify. He was in a position where he was supposed to be in charge of investigating organized crime but he portrayed himself as doing little more than trying to please the FBI so he could hang on to his job. This did not fit my portrait I had of him nor his reputation.

When I interacted with him I had a great deal of respect for him up until the time of Naimovich's arrest. When I read the minutes of his presentation of evidence to the grand jury that indicted Naimovich, I saw that O'Sullivan never disclosed that bookie Francis McIntyre, the main witness against Trooper Naimovich, was an informant for Naimovich. The record of conversations between them was portrayed as something sinister. I had also told O'Sullivan that I authorized Naimovich to return a "cuff list" to a bookie named Katz yet he put in evidence to the grand jury as if this was a wrongful act.

There were lots of things in the prosecution of Naimovich that seemed very underhanded. O'Sullivan seemed determine to avoid presenting a true picture of Naimovich solely for the purpose of getting an indictment and to have little concern with the truth. It was only when I heard him testify about how terribly afraid he was of the FBI and his fear that they could easily destroy him that I understood. He was going to do whatever the FBI wanted whether it was right or wrong.

APPENDIX G:

THE LANCASTER STREET GARAGE

A LEAK UNCOVERED

As a prosecutor, in order to convict a person of a crime I had to prove to a jury beyond a reasonable doubt he committed the act charged. In many cases, especially in the arson area, I did this using circumstantial evidence. In the same manner I'm able to show how the leak at Lancaster Street happened.

Circumstantial evidence is used as a supplement to or instead of direct evidence. Suppose I have a long term relationship with a woman called Maria who rises very early every morning and goes to the gym. Most mornings I see her get into her Porsche in our driveway and drive off. That is direct evidence that she did that.

But today I slept late because the game didn't end until long after midnight. I wake up and drag myself out of bed. I see Maria has left the house. I look out to the driveway and see her Porsche is gone. I figure she has taken it and driven off to the gym. I didn't see her do it but the circumstances make me as certain that she did as if I had seen her. For someone to understand why I arrived at that conclusion I would have to explain the full picture as I just did.

Others have made conclusions about Lancaster Street. They didn't consider the full picture. Judge

Wolf in his extensive findings got bogged down in the avalanche of facts and testimony and missed it. Colonel John O'Donovan of the Massachusetts State Police arrived at the right conclusion more by gut feeling rather than a full picture analysis. Strike Force Chief O'Sullivan believed the FBI compromised it but did not explain how he knew that.

Jack Webb on the old TV show Dragnet used to say. "The facts ma'am, just give me the facts." Here they are about Lancaster Street.

Whitey and Stevie moved their headquarters from Winter Hill in Somerville to a garage on Lancaster Street in Boston's North End, the section of the city where the Mafia also had its headquarters. This is a narrow street close to the old Boston Garden where the Boston Bruins and Celtics play their home games. It was a perfect location because it was extremely difficult to surveil.

It is said that quite by accident in the spring of 1980 State Trooper Rick Fralick, who knew the organized crime actors, noticed some of them outside a garage on that street. He told his boss Sergeant Bobby Long who decided to follow up. With his small tight knit group of state police he began a relentless investigation that involved spending countless hours in a cramped, cockroach and vermin infested apartment across the narrow street from the garage doing tedious surveillance and much photography. They did their investigation the old fashion way. They planned each step, they fought off tedium and ennui, they were highly aware one misstep would undo their whole operation, and they maintained the high degree of discipline and the enthusiasm of an elite group insulating themselves from others and operating on a need to know basis.

For months they operated over this treacherous landscape disguising themselves as street people. Nothing went awry. Without the benefits of informants but merely through tiring hard work they put together enough evidence to establish probable cause that not only Whitey, Stevie, and their Winter Hill associates were conducting their criminal activities from the garage but they were doing it in conjunction with the top Boston Mafia figures Larry Zannino and the Anguilo brothers.

The head of the federal strike force Jerry O'Sullivan accepted that it was going to be a big case. He would not concede that had the operation come to a favorable conclusion it would have been the biggest New England organized crime bust ever. One reason is that having spent so many years as a federal prosecutor he could never concede that a handful of state troopers were on the brink of accomplishing more than dozens of FBI agents were ever able to do.

But it was more than this. At the same time the state police were doing their investigation, O'Sullivan and the FBI were in the middle of investigating the same Boston Mafia group. The state police investigation would have eradicated

421

the leadership of both the Winter Hill gang and the Boston Mafia. O'Sullivan's plan would only take down the leadership of the Boston Mafia. O'Sullivan not only had no intention of taking down the Winter Hill leaders, Whitey and Stevie, but he worked to protect them.

On January 9, 1981, O'Sullivan and the FBI installed listening devices in the locations where Anguilo and Zannino ran their criminal enterprises. They began their interceptions. O'Sullivan would eventually be highly successful in his endeavor.

It would be otherwise for the state police. Their investigation would come a cropper six months earlier in the summer of 1980. We go back to that time to look at the full picture.

The state police had developed enough evidence to establish probable cause that criminal activity was taking place in the garage. Bobby Long went with that evidence to Colonel John O'Donovan. These two men decided to get a court warrant to put a listening device (bug) into the garage.

At that time O'Sullivan was actively working with John Morris's group putting together the evidence needed to secure the warrant for bugging Anguilo's and Zannino's headquarters. Morris was directing the operation. FBI Agent Quinn was writing up the affidavit.

To understand the significance of what O'Sullivan was doing, we should understand the attitude of the FBI toward the Mafia and the importance it put on O'Sullivan's planned operation. Judge Harrington testified that between 1961 and 1981 the Justice Department's priority was to use all its resources to eliminate the Mafia or as the FBI referred to it, La Casa Nostra (LCN). FBI agent O'Callaghan testified the FBI's primary focus was on the LCN. FBI agent Morris testified, as supervisor of a group of fourteen agents that their overwhelming effort was to target Gerry Angiulo's LCN gang. FBI agent Gianturco testified that the investigation of the LCN was the number one priority mandate from the United States Attorney General's office.

Morris filed a memorandum on April 1, 1981 supporting the continuation of Whitey as an informant. He wrote "These affidavits [that Whitey provided information for] are in connection with two of the highest priority organized crime matters under investigation in the Boston Division. One of these two cases, [98 Prince Street] is one of the *highest priority organized crime cases in the FBI* today and involves what has been characterized by [FBI Headquarters] officials *as one of the most important* and successful Title IIIs to have been conducted by the FBI in the past ten years." (Emphasis added.) The FBI was devoting all its organized crime resources for the purpose of taking down Angiulo and his Boston Mafia group. FBI headquarters was closely watching. This was to be a very big FBI day.

O'Sullivan knew that the FBI would be very unhappy if the state police took this glory away from it. He also knew that if he had anything to do with the state police success the full force of the FBI's ire would be directed at him. O'Sullivan was afraid of the FBI on every day matters. This is shown by the following interchange between him and two congressmen.

Congressman Meehan asked him what his testimony told us about the FBI's culture. O'Sullivan replied, *"It tells you that the FBI if you go against them, they will try to get you. They will wage war on you. They will cause major administrative problems for me as a prosecutor. That's what it tells us."*

The Committee Chairman Dan Burton brooded over that answer. A short time later he jumped in.

Mr. Burton. *"Let me follow up. I might have missed what you said just a minute ago but did you indicate that the FBI said — you can put it in your own words — that if you caused them problems, that they wouldn't cooperate with you in an investigation or something?"*

Mr. O'Sullivan. *"Yes."*

Mr. Burton. *"Can you tell me in your words how you said that?"*

Mr. O'Sullivan. *"During the Lancaster Street Garage aftermath, the SAC of the FBI, Lawrence Sarhadt (sic) called me and asked me to come over to his office and berated me up and down, swearing at me, yelling as loud as he could about how I should never have associated myself with the state police and gone against FBI informants."*

Mr. Burton. *"So you felt that they were not going to cooperate with you unless you worked with them?"*

Mr. O'Sullivan. *"That's what he told me."*

To set that table, in the summer of 1980 the FBI is deeply committed to taking down the Boston Mafia. O'Sullivan is working with it to do this knowing that one misstep might cost him his job. Without O'Sullivan's or the FBI's knowledge the state police have a jump of about six months on the FBI. The state police have just decided to seek court permission to put a bug in the Lancaster Street garage.

Up to this time this had been a state operation that had run smoothly. To get the bug, it would be necessary to go to a state judge. The expertise and equipment to do this was available on the state side.

I had done upwards of twenty electronic surveillance operations by that time some that included the use of bugs. I had purchased all the necessary equipment to do this so I did not have to go to any other agency to seek its help. But O'Donovan would not use my expertise. We were in the middle of a turf battle.

I had been doing my wiretaps with the state police, Metropolitan police and local police. O'Donovan believed it was the exclusive domain of the state police. He visited me at my Bridge Street office one day. He demanded that I stop using other than state police. I refused to do that. He responded by saying he would not let the state troopers in his elite units do electronic surveillance with my office until I changed my position.

O'Donovan figured he'd get help from outside the state system. He sought out the assistance of O'Sullivan. O'Donovan and Long laid out their investigation to O'Sullivan. This was the first time O'Sullivan was aware the state police were on the cusp of undermining his big act. O'Sullivan knew that under no circumstance was the FBI to know what the state police were doing. He knew O'Donovan was convinced that Whitey was an FBI informant. O'Donovan believed the FBI would never let the state police target its informant.

What O'Donovan did not know which would come back to take a large chunk out of him was that O'Sullivan lived in terror of the FBI. He also did not know he was telling O'Sullivan that the state police troopers were about to plunge a dagger into months if not years of a total commitment by FBI agents working on what it considered one of the highest priority organized crime cases in America.

It is not difficult to imagine what O'Sullivan was thinking as O'Donovan and Long set out their facts. He had to be in a state of sheer panic when he was handed this time bomb. State police success spelled his doom and the end of his career. That was a terrible burden to put on one man and expect him not to weaken under it. It was more so when we know of O'Sullivan's morbid dread of the FBI.

O'Sullivan had no choice but to undermine it. He could not walk away from it since he had the information. He could not tell them he couldn't help them lest he tip off what the FBI was doing. He could not tell them Whitey and Stevie were FBI informants who he was protecting. He couldn't say he was targeting the same Mafia targets and that the state police investigation was about to run over his own investigation. He could not suggest they cooperate with the FBI since the state police already said they didn't trust the FBI and the FBI had no intention of letting anyone else share in its expected triumph.

O'Sullivan's inability to do other than to undermine the state police investigation makes one think of the legal definition of insanity. O'Sullivan had an uncontrollable impulse to do this. He had to do it to survive in the FBI world. He knew the FBI's fury if it were bested by a half dozen state cops with his assistance. He knew the FBI would view his part in a state police success as the ultimate treachery.

The bugging of Lancaster Street was authorized by court order on July 24, 1980. It took a couple of days to get the bug in. The state police quickly knew it had been tipped when the conversations they intercepted were discussions of what a good job the state police were doing patrolling the Massachusetts turnpike. Months of secrecy were destroyed after the state police reached out to O'Sullivan.

On August 1, 1980, the FBI disclosed that it knew about the bug. That was the Friday evening when Morris met Boston Police Sergeant Bob Ryan at an after work cocktail party. Ryan said Morris asked him "Do the state police have a microphone in the Lancaster Garage?" Ryan said he got the opinion that the wise guys knew about it.

Ryan called Suffolk DA Newman Flanagan who called O'Donovan with the information. O'Donovan, knowing the bug had been compromised, now knew the FBI knew about it. He called for a meeting of all the law enforcement people involved. O'Sullivan attended. The FBI ASAC Wendal Kennedy also attended. He was assigned to ferret out the truth.

He interviewed Morris. Morris reportedly said in a rambling answer that a month ago a source told him there were a lot of "new faces" in the North End who were not Boston cops or FBI agents because the latter are known to the wise guys. He then heard that a Boston police SKIP unit was told to stay away from the Lancaster Street garage. He said he put two and two together and figured the state police had a microphone in the garage. He mentioned it to Sgt Ryan because he figured if his sources knew something was up there then he should pass it on.

This, of course, was a nonsensical fable that fell apart upon a closer examination. New faces in town, SKIP being told to stay away from the garage adding up to the conclusion of a state police microphone being in the Lancaster Street garage is farfetched nonsense. If new faces were seen, any number of other law enforcement groups aside from the state police could be involved. Even assuming it's the state police the assumption that a bug was in the Lancaster street garage is a great reach. An extremely few investigations involved bugs. All saw it as a transparent falsehood because it had one enormously huge problem. He used it to explain how he figured out the bug was in the garage. It did not explain how the gangsters came to the same conclusion at the same time. Morris would later change his story.

O'Sullivan worked closely with Morris on the same targets as the state police. Morris lies about it how he obtained the information. The circumstantial evidence clearly indicates when looking at the big picture that O'Sullivan told Morris who told Connolly who told the gangsters.

Unfortunately O'Donovan again made a big mistake in thinking that the FBI was interested in finding out how the gangsters knew of the state police bug. The FBI was happy that it had been compromised It protected its informants and kept the Mafia in operation for them to target. It began its disinformation operation.

ASAC Kennedy in his report to the SAC found nothing wrong with Morris's puerile story and pried no further. Instead, in order to protect Morris and the FBI, he turned the tables on the state police. He added to his report slanders and speculations that had nothing to do with the Lancaster leak:

> "As you are aware, the C-3 Squad has been extensively involved in several investigations during which

429

allegations have been made that certain members of the State Police, Major Regan and Lt. Masuret, if not criminally liable are professionally liable for substantial misconduct with regard to their handling of informants. More specifically, in certain instances, there are indication that these two individuals furnished information of an extremely confidential nature to certain members of the criminal element in the Boston area.

It occurs to me that the stage has now been set with regard to this current investigation that if for any reason the investigation falters or is not successful with regard to the Lancaster Street Garage, that the State Police is now in a position to make allegations that the FBI and more specifically, John Morris and members of the C – 3 Squad have furnished information of a sensitive nature to organized crime elements in the Boston area."

Incredibly at the time he wrote his report ASAC Kennedy knew the investigation had faltered and was not successful and those allegations had already been made. He pretends that hasn't already happened. He then maligns the state police who naively called the meeting with the FBI hoping to get redress for their grievance. He twists

430

their legitimate concern to some type of revenge motive against the FBI. It almost makes one want to cry out in despair. There was no attempt to get at the truth. There was only an attempt at a cover up and a willingness to defame others.

Later SAC Sarhatt would report that "O'Sullivan indicated that it was his impression that the MSP had problems on electronic coverage from the beginning of their operation . . . ." O'Sullivan testified that Sarhatt's reports contained things he never said. Whether he said what Sarhatt wrote or whether Sarhatt just followed the usual FBI procedures of writing down his wishful thinking is anyone's guess.

To top it off Connolly would report on October 30 that either Whitey or Stevie "learned from their state police source that the Lancaster Street Garage was loaded with "bugs" and that there may have been anywhere from eight to ten of them installed." He doesn't say how Morris knew about this. One can only think the FBI files are filled with deceit, deceptions and untruths seeing this criminal and tawdry performance.

The state police had a 100% secure operation until it goes to O'Sullivan. It gets compromised. The state police accuse the FBI of compromising it. The FBI investigates itself and ASAC Kennedy infers, SAC Sarhatt invents and Connolly lies that the state police compromised their own investigation. The cover-ups run deep and wide.

A November 21, 1980 FBI memo noted that the state police believed that information about its

431

Lancaster Street Garage investigation was "filtered by Supv. Morris or at his direction to the subjects of the Lancaster Street Garage." At trial Morris said he first learned of the bug from Connolly who learned about it from Whitey. He invented a new reason for why he talked to Sergeant Ryan. He said he was concerned with the safety of the state police officers. Morris knew there was absolutely no risk to any state police officer.

It was well known that a year or two before O'Donovan heard that someone in Winter Hill had threatened one of his men. Packing a brace of handguns he went to the Marshall Motors garage and confronted Whitey. He told him what he could expect if anyone dared do that. Whitey properly took him very seriously. He promised him there would never be any retribution by them against a state trooper.

Whitey and Stevie knew O'Donovan didn't bluff. They knew that any action by them against a state trooper would be the end of their careers, if not lives. Martorano testified they killed one of their associates because he planned to hurt a police officer. He said they did not want that type of heat to be brought down on them.

Further, if Morris were concerned for the safety of the state police as he testified, shouldn't he have gone directly to the state police rather than blurting out the information at a cocktail party to a Boston police officer? Why not pick up the telephone and call O'Donovan during working hours? It had to be that Morris, or as Whitey

432

called him, Vino, was in his cups at the Friday party and he became indiscrete. The wine he consumed prompted this friendless man to try to impress Sergeant Ryan with his inside knowledge. Without the wine abetting his need to be a big shot he would not have disclosed this.

Had Morris learned of the bug from Whitey as Connolly would have us believe he would have stated that to Kennedy in the first instance. A straightforward response would have been, "You know an informant told us the wise guys found out that a bug was planted in the garage. I wanted to let them know their bug was compromised."

Stevie testified the leak came from O'Sullivan who told Connolly and Morris. Judge Wolf said the leak came from John Naimovich based solely on Stevie's testimonial lie that Naimovich was his informant. Wolf also said that Naimovich was convicted of corruption which was wrong. There is no credible evidence Naimovich knew about the bug at Lancaster Street. There has never been any evidence connecting Naimovich with Whitey or Stevie or any other Winter Hill member.

All the other explanations about the Lancaster leak do not hold water and seem easily refutable because they don't explain how Morris and Whitey and Stevie knew about the leak at the same time. More importantly, and this is crucial, they don't explain that if the gangsters discovered it and told the FBI, how they knew it was a state police bug rather than a bug planted by DEA, Boston, Quincy, or some other agency or even the FBI. The gangsters knew it was a state police bug because they started talking about the good job the state troopers were doing on the Mass Turnpike. Morris knew because he told Ryan it was a state police bug.

Some suggested Stevie's source in the state police, Schneiderhan, tipped off Stevie. He worked in the Attorney General's office from 1968 to 1977. Schneiderhan had no direct involvement in the planting of the bug in Lancaster Street. He might have learned about it but it is extremely unlikely. Only one of the troopers who helped install the bug was known to have worked with Schneiderhan. That trooper was not friendly with him. He had transferred out of the Attorney General's office to get away from him.

O'Sullivan suggested that the state police used an outside consultant on the bugs who also did work for the Mafia as the person who may have been the leak. I worked with him and found no problems. But as with anything there are always other possibilities.

That's the one downside to circumstantial evidence. It only goes so far. Take my earlier example of Maria and the Porsche. Suppose while I slept Maria found the Porsche did not start so she had it towed to a garage and arranged with a friend to drive her to the gym. When I got up I'd see no car in the driveway and my conclusion about how it left would be totally wrong.

Circumstance evidence does not provide for absolute certainty. But even direct evidence lacks that. A witness could be lying or mistaken as to her direct observations. In life however we continually operate on circumstance evidence. That is why to convict a person of a crime we do not need absolute certainty but proof beyond a reasonable doubt. There is always some doubt in our dealings.

Whether O'Sullivan wanted to destroy the state police investigation or just share his knowledge with Morris because he did not want to carry this burden alone is hard to tell. We do know that O'Donovan held the meeting to discover how the leak happened. O'Sullivan also attended. He remained silent. Apparently it did not concern him. He knew for sure then that he could continue targeting the Angiulo's Boston Mafia without any interference from the state police. O'Sullivan would later testify that he believed the leak came from the FBI.

For me there is no reasonable doubt that this state police investigation was compromised by O'Sullivan's disclosure of its existence to Morris. I approach almost certainty when I factor in Morris's lie to ASAC Kennedy, Stevie's assertion that was the case, and O'Sullivan's testimony that the FBI leaked it. Then the frosting on the cake is shown by Sarhatt's outburst against O'Sullivan where he berated him up and down for his assistance to the state police even though his assistance accomplished nothing.

When you come down to it, O'Sullivan had no choice. He had to protect his job. He had to protect the FBI's ongoing investigation. He had to protect their two top echelon informants. Had the state police investigation not been compromised he would have undermined himself, highly embarrassed the FBI and endangered the darlings of the FBI, Whitey and Stevie.

APPENDIX H:

MYLES CONNOR

A LIVING LEGEND

Judge Harrington testified Myles Connor was not an organized crime person and that Connolly received a commendation for working on his case. Morris testified that Whitey and Flemmi helped Connolly in that investigation. Most people did not seem to notice that the FBI was using its organized crime agents and two top echelon informants to go after a run of the mill criminal. A few might wonder how Judge Harrington who was then U.S. Attorney in Boston knew about this.

I knew of Myles Connor. I've never met him. I first heard about him from his father, a Milton police sergeant, who was a police prosecutor in the Quincy court. I was a young defense lawyer representing a client charged with a Milton crime. He was representing his town. He was a nice friendly guy. He treated me kindly unlike the way other salty police prosecutors treated young criminal defense attorneys. We spent a good deal of time talking prior to resolving the matter.

He relayed to me a story about Myles. I can't vouch for its truthfulness; all I can do is repeat it. Myles's father told me had recently gone through a bout of serious illness that prevented him from doing his job. His doctors were baffled. Eventually they conducted a battery of blood tests. These showed he had large amounts of arsenic in his system. At first he could not figure out how this was happening. Eventually he discovered his wife and son, Myles, were flavoring his morning coffee with arsenic. It was a strange story one does not easily forget. [252]

At that time I had never heard of Myles. He had been a big name locally in a rock 'n' roll. An article in "The History of Boston Rock & Roll" states, "He played with the best of them, headlining over the Beach Boys, gigging with Sha Na Na and more." Myles's band in the early 60's was called "Myles Connor and the Wild Ones." The more appropriate name might have been "Myles Connor the Wild One." He'd spend much time in prison.

20 year old Myles, when locked up in Maine, escaped by using a gun fashioned out of a bar of soap. In 1966 he got in a gun fight with Massachusetts State Police Colonel John O'Donovan who was then a corporal. O'Donovan took a bullet in the gut. Myles took four back. Both landed in the hospital. Lore has it that his first words after his capture were, "How's the cop I shot?"

After years in prison Myles made a musical comeback billing himself as the "President of

---

[252] In 2009 Myles wrote his autobiography, *"The Art of the Heist."* He does not mention this incident in his book. My recollections of Myles and his dealings are based on my personal knowledge although I refreshed my memory slightly after reading his book.

Rock." It was brief. He stole several Andrew Wyeth paintings in Maine. Trying to fence them he was arrested by the FBI in a sting and charged with federal crimes. While out on bail needing a bargaining chip to mitigate any federal penalty, he hoisted Rembrandt's 'Portrait of Elizabeth Van Rijn' from Boston's Museum of Fine Arts by boldly walking out with it in broad daylight.

This received much publicity. The Boston police and FBI immediately began investigating. They were coveting the favorable publicity that would happen if they were able to recover it. Myles should have made a deal to return the painting through them and allowed them to preen in the glow of the media at their success.

Myles knew this. But for some reason, whether he didn't trust the FBI, didn't like them, or an inner perversity that made him live on the edge, he thumbed his nose at convention. He made his deal through State Police Major John Regan incurring the everlasting hatred of the FBI which in its fury sought to destroy him. Regan would later be maligned by ASAC Kennedy in his report on Lancaster Street for doing this. But that was nothing compared to what would happen to Myles who underestimated the fury of scorned cops.

Myles popped into my ken when I was at the DA's office. It was in the early fall of 1977. I read in the papers that DA Delahunt had found the burial site in Northampton, Massachusetts of two 18-year-old women, Susan Webster and Karen Spinney. They had been murdered in our county by Tommy Sperrazza. Myles had helped the DA locate the burial site.

Myles was a friend of Sperrazza. Sperrazza and John Stokes shot Ralph Cirvinale outside a Roslindale Tavern in the company of the two young women. Because the women witnessed Cirvinale's killing, they were taken to a Quincy apartment and murdered. Prior to that Sperrazza had killed an off-duty Boston police officer Donald Brown. Sperrazza would brutally murder his buddy John Stokes in prison according to Myles.

Sperrazza had at least five murders to his name. He would sign his letters from prison "Manson" fashioning himself as the new Charles Manson. It is not surprising the expression, "Once you've kill one person the rest are easy," has been attributed to Sperrazza.

Delahunt had become DA in 1975. Being new to the prosecution field he relied heavily upon his friend Major John Regan for advice and assistance. Myles was serving prison time at Walpole with Sperrazza. Regan had made one deal with Myles so he made another deal. Myles and another associate Ralph Petrozellio would get out of prison about a year early if they'd tell where the young women were buried. They told Sperrazza they'd help him escape from prison if he told them the location of the bodies. He did. They would try to break him out at a later time.

This event of unearthing the bodies received much news coverage. There was little joy in FBI land or among certain Boston police officers at again seeing Myles and Regan basking in the warmth of the media lights. It was a bad time to cross the FBI. In *Black Mass* Lehr and O'Neill wrote about that time, "By and large, the media sided with the FBI, mostly on the strength of John Connolly's personal ties with reporters at the *Boston Globe* and the *Boston Herald* and with some television reporters."

Delahunt accepted the deal believing that it was important to recover the bodies of the young women to bring closure for their families and knowing that with the bodies Sperrazza could be charged with their murder. Delahunt's office convicted Sperrazza of first degree murder in June 1978. He was sentenced to prison for life without the chance of parole.

Myles used his lawyer Marty Leppo before dealing with Regan. Leppo a highly skilled criminal lawyer saw no danger to Myles in dealing with Delahunt and Regan. None of these men believed he had anything to do with the murder of the young women. If they did, they could have provided legal protection to him by immunizing him and forcing him to provide his information before a grand jury.

Where they made a mistake was failing to appreciate the FBI's intense desire to destroy Myles not for any crime but for the insult. By pointing to the burial site Myles had linked himself to the murders. The FBI and Boston cops could sate their thirst for revenge against him.

The road for doing this ran straight through the despicable and sadistic Sperrazza.[253] The Boston police had evidence that implicated his wife and in-laws with Sperrazza in the murder of Donald Brown. The ground work existed for a grand scheme to link Myles into the murders of Spinney and Webster through the cooperation of Sperrazza with the help of Whitey and Stevie.

Sperrazza was approached by FBI seeking his help. No deal is too sordid to slake the FBI's hurt feelings. Sperrazza was told that if he linked Myles to the Brown, Spinney, and Webster murders and a Norfolk bank robbery he'd be put in the FBI's witness protection program, his family would be given financial benefits, and charges against his wife and in-laws dropped. As John Camp, an investigative reporter for a Boston television station wrote, "Sperrazza's decision did not require a lot of deep thought."

Sperrazza dutifully spun his tale. The FBI dug up Doreen Weeks who was in its witness protection program under the name Dianne Wazen. She was facing charges for 22 counts of larceny which she committed while in the program.

---

[253] By now you must understand that no police agency is happy at another's success especially if the other is solving something that did not fall under their jurisdiction in the first place. This is especially true of the FBI who had a whole department set up to provide publicity and had an irrational fear of letting others take credit for things it thought it should have done. The FBI only cared for solving crime if it got credit.

The young women were murdered in her apartment. She'd help the FBI and herself by testifying that she called her apartment while the young women were being murdered and heard Myles's voice.

Myles was charged in three cases based on their evidence. The Feds charged him with a bank robbery of a Norfolk county bank. The Suffolk DA charged him with the murder of Donald Brown. A special prosecutor was appointed to indict Myles for the murder of the young women.

Judge Harrington, then the US Attorney, assigned his top assistant to prosecute the bank robbery charges against Myles. The FBI plan according to an article by Boston attorney Harvey A. Silverglate,[254] was to try to convict Myles of a bank robbery charge, have a stiff sentence imposed on him, and then gain the "necessary leverage . . . to turn him into a full-fledged informant against Delahunt and Regan." Myles was going to be the road to ruin the lives of two good men because they bettered the FBI in solving crimes.

Sperrazza was a witness in the Norfolk bank robbery case as was Dianne Wazen. The testimony offered at the trial was so incredible that the jury took only six hours to acquit Myles and his co-defendant of all the charges.

---

[254] The article printed in the Boston Phoenix on March 24, 1981, beginning on page 8, was entitled *Briefcases, The strange case of Myles Connor.* It tells in great detail the sordid dealings of the FBI and Harrington's office in their actions against Delahunt and Connor.

The second case tried involved the great tragedy of two young women being brutally murdered. Its weakness aside from having the murderer testify was ascribing a motive to Myles. It made no sense for him to participate in the murders of the women. The prosecution alleged that because Sperrazza had no idea how to finish off the women after stabbing them he turned to Myles for instructions. Myles's motive was that the young women heard his voice so they could put him at the scene of their killing. Myles didn't testify. The jury convicted him.

After this conviction he went to trial on the Brown murder. The same line up of incredible witnesses testified. The jury was out an hour and a half before acquitting him.

The verdict in the young women's murder case was appealed. The conviction was reversed. When Myles was retried, he did testify. He was acquitted. The three cases against him mainly based on the testimony of Sperrazza had failed miserably. But because DA Delahunt and Regan had worked with Myles it did not end.

Harrington would find another way to go after them. Connolly was deeply involved in abetting Harrington in his misguided and incomprehensible quest. Connolly had as his allies Whitey and Stevie.

My final involvement with Myles involved dealings I had with his attorney Marty Leppo, a fellow Marine. He had encouraged me to accept Delahunt's job offer when we were both defense counsel. I had a handful of cases with him over the years. He was a formidable opponent, a latter-day Damon Runyon.

He represented Myles who claimed ownership of certain rugs and weapons that had been seized by us. The detectives in my drug task force executed a warrant for drugs in a second floor apartment in Dorchester without any idea Myles was connected to it. While searching it, they came upon a bordered up closet. They broke into it and found what appeared to them to be stolen items including Native American rugs and antique weapons. These were seized.

Also in the closet was a large piece of parchment paper which had been considered of no value and tossed aside. The detectives carried out the evidence and were ready to secure the search. Just before leaving they sent one of the group back upstairs to insure nothing was left behind and to lock the door. He saw the parchment lying on the floor. He picked it up and sauntered over to the second floor window. Waving the parchment he yelled down: "Do we want this?" Someone yelled, "Leave it." Someone else then yelled, "Yeah, throw it down."

He did what he heard last. It landed on the sidewalk and someone flipped into the back of the van. The next morning we did the inventory of the items at an undercover office in a Quincy office building. One of the ADAs who lived in Quincy dropped by to see what was happening. He picked up the parchment and recognized it. It was the first page of the original charter of the Commonwealth of Massachusetts, an invaluable historical treasure that had been stolen from the state archives several years earlier.

We held a press conference (as you'd expect) announcing our great achievement in recovering this. We allowed people to think that we knew what it was immediately upon setting our eyes on it and that we treated it with the care and respect it deserved. When I learned Myles was asserting a claim to the items in the closet, it figured he was holding the charter as one of his bargaining chips.

Myles would end up doing more time in the Midwest. In his autobiography he prides himself on his skill at stealing from museums, his cleverness as a bank robber, and his life as a musician. He tells of his involvement with Sperrazza and other criminals. He claimed he was never one for violence even though he twice fired a gun at cops during his escape attempts. When I left the DA's office in 1997, Marty Leppo was still trying to get the goods back. I don't know how it worked out.

APPENDIX I:

CROSSING THE FBI

A TRAGEDY AVERTED

In Appendix H I noted the feds hoped to convict Myles of the bank robbery charge to gain the "necessary leverage . . . to turn him into a full-fledged informant against Delahunt and Regan." Delahunt's naiveté about the ways of cops and their jealousies made him totally oblivious of the pot that was seething in Boston because of the hatred Myles had engendered. Connolly along with his two gangster friends was hip deep in the muck and mire stirring the pot and turning up the heat.

Whitey and Stevie pushed Connolly. Connolly pushed Judge Harrington, who was then US Attorney. Harrington expressing outrage at Myles's deal went after DA Delahunt and Major Regan. Harrington had his own history of dealing with criminals. He had worked closely with FBI agents Paul Rico (who had lined up Wheeler to be killed) and Dennis Condon, his partner, both men will be Connolly's mentors, to use Joe "The Animal" Barboza, a mob hit man as a witness. They got him into the FBI's witness protection program. While there, Barboza murdered a man. Harrington, Rico and Condon flew to California to testify on his behalf in his trial. Nothing Myles was ever accused of came within a mile to what Barboza had done.

Barboza was a vile killer. The Mafia boss Raymond Patriarca used him to kill people. Agents Rico and Condon used him as a witness in a case against others knowing he was committing perjury. His testimony resulted in innocent men being sentenced to death.

Harrington announced he was impaneling a grand jury to look into Delahunt's relationship with Myles. During this time I was operating out of a satellite office. I knew nothing of the matters relating to the prosecution of Sperrazza or the dealings with Myles other than what I read in the newspapers. I was busy doing wiretaps against organized crime groups. When I learned that the US attorney was investigating Delahunt, I was totally flabbergasted. My concern was heightened by the knowledge a prosecutor can indict a banana peel.

I was brought over to the main office. I tabled my pursuit of organized crime groups to concentrate on defending Delahunt and our office from these implausible charges that were being circulated against us. That's when I put on my defense attorney hat.

In the realm of things a county district attorney has few tools with which to fight back against the federal government. We could not subpoena agents to the grand jury nor could we find out what evidence the FBI had. Unfortunately in that era no one would believe the FBI was acting with malice. We were at its mercy.

We could not make sense of the rumors nor of the reason behind the attack on us. What was happening had never happened before. A US Attorney sought criminal charges against a state prosecutor because he did not like the deal a state prosecutor made with a criminal. Harrington was attempting to criminalize the discretionary acts of a state prosecutor because he disagreed with them.

What we did was less than the FBI and US attorney did on a daily basis in their dealings with their informants or cooperating witnesses. We arranged for Myles and another prisoner, Ralph Petrozellio, to get out of prison 10 months early in exchange for them providing the location of the bodies of two young women murdered in our county. It was a sad spectacle seeing the US Attorney going after a DA. The pursuit became ludicrous when we learned in later years Harrington was being helped by two top gangsters who had a grudge against the DA.

I recall feeling we were alone in a fox hole. It seemed everyone in law enforcement abetted by the FBI lackeys in the media was lobbing shots at us. The FBI's word was considered gospel. The media worshipped at its altar of propaganda. No one dared stand up against it.

We may have all gone under at that time except for the assistant US attorneys who handled the grand jury, George McMahon and Janis Berry. They were straight, ethical and not swayed by FBI influence. They followed the evidence and found there was nothing at the end. It is difficult to imagine how they withstood the FBI pressure especially after hearing what O'Sullivan said of the pressure the FBI uses.

I believe if O'Sullivan handled the case there would have been indictments. Not because any crimes were committed but in doing this he would have pleased the FBI. I saw how he manipulated a grand jury reading the minutes of his presentation against John Naimovich. He could easily have secured indictments.

After what seemed like forever the grand jury that had been investigating Delahunt terminated with no indictment. *Black Mass* correctly noted, "Delahunt had limped away from the bruising encounter with the FBI over using Myles Connor as an informant, chewed up in the FBI public relations maw." The FBI having lost at that attempt would continue its goal of impugning the integrity of Delahunt.

We learned this years later when a few of the secret FBI's 302s surfaced. ASAC Kennedy in his investigation of Morris's involvement in the undermining of the State Police operation at the Lancaster Street Garage officiously maligned two state police officers, Major John Regan and Lieutenant Bob Masuret, who worked in our office. He wrote in August 1980, "Certain members of the State Police, namely, Major Regan and Lt. Masuret, if not criminally liable, are professionally liable for substantial misconduct with regard to their handling of informants."

The specter of Myles circulated in the minds of FBI agents. Regan handled Myles. The substantial misconduct was Myles not going to the FBI with the stolen art. Unfortunately these libels take a life of their own through the secret 302 files as they circulate among the naïve FBI agents who assume the truth of them.

On October 30, 1980, Connolly wrote that the state police were looking to impanel a grand jury to investigate the failure of the Lancaster Garage bugging operation. He further wrote that he would be the prime target of the investigation because of his involvement in Myles's case. He said Attorney General Bellotti is a close personal friend of District Attorney Delahunt and that Bellotti hates Senate President William Bulger. He said, "Bellotti could embarrass Senator Bulger and SA Connolly with this investigation, which would please both himself and District Attorney Dellahunt. (sic)"[255]

This was absurd on its face. Connolly had no qualms defaming the state police, the attorney general and a district attorney. It is tragic to think that Connolly had the ears of Harrington into which to pour his venomous lies.

On January 21, 1981, Morris wrote that Whitey thought the state police had put a pen register on his home telephone with view to developing

---

[255] Delahunt so hated Billy that he authorized me to hire Billy's son.

information for a wire tap. Whitey lived in Quincy in Norfolk County so it would have been done in conjunction with the Norfolk DA.

On October 17, 1984, a report by James Ring[256] to SAC Greenleaf stated, that Whitey and Stevie "knew they were under intense physical surveillance and had observed Quincy Police officers in South Boston. They knew from their sources that District Attorney William Delahunt had specifically targeted them as subjects and they further felt that Colonel Jack O'Donovan of the Mass. State Police had a vendetta against them and concluded that the state police would also participate in such an investigation."

Also in this report, as is the FBI wont, Ring maligned the Norfolk DA's office. Without setting out any facts to support it, he maliciously adds that from his conversation with Whitey and Stevie he assumes their sources of information are in the "District Attorney's [Delahunt's] office." This is an example of how evil is spread. Ring knew the truth was the total opposite.

I controlled the wiretap operations in our office. They were done with a very small group of people. For years, one trusted secretary, Sheila Craven, did all the typing (before the word processor), copying and paperwork. Knowledge of our actions was closely restricted. We worked

---

[256] Whitey referred to Ring as "Pipe" since he was always smoking a pipe. Weeks said Whitey bought pipes and gave them to Ring as gifts. Ring denied this.

from a satellite space. After borrowing the equipment from the attorney general's office a couple of times I purchased our own more sophisticated equipment so we would not have to rely upon any outside sources to do wiretaps. We trained our own people into doing the technical work. Other DA offices used the equipment of the Attorney General where Stevie's source Schneiderhan worked.

Our office had not been penetrated by either the FBI or the gangsters. We used different groups of investigators. We did our wiretaps with State Police, Metropolitan Police, local police officers or a combination of them. This was one enormous threat to Whitey and Stevie because they seemed to have sources everywhere else except in our office. It seemed clear that was why they wanted to destroy us.

Ring's malicious fabrication demonstrates how FBI agents think and write. Ring, a close friend of Connolly's and O'Sullivan's, couldn't stop his deceitful hand from writing a total falsehood in an attempt to undermine our reputation. SAC Greenleaf was quickly told not to trust us. Again and again we see the unreliability of FBI 302s and their ability to destroy others.

On November 1, 1984, Connolly wrote to SAC Greenleaf that Whitey and Stevie realize they have been under investigation by the state police. They called this "a continuing vendetta." The report noted that much of the activity against Whitey and Stevie involves the Quincy police. Whitey and

Stevie said "They are not sure of the motivation for the increased attention; they believe it has its inception in Quincy which means District Attorney Delahunt to them!"

On February 25, 1985, Connolly wrote to the SAC that his source "has noticed current coverage on them and believes that this is a continuous "vendetta" against them by the Massachusetts State Police and Bill Delahunt's Quincy cops." Only in the FBI world is trying to stop two arch criminals from running a murderous criminal empire considered a vendetta.

On March 11, 1985, when drug enforcement agents went to retrieve a bug that Whitey found in his car Whitey said to them, 'The fucking Quincy cops and Delahunt have been out to get me."

These are only a few of the reports that I have seen. I assume there are many more that have been put in the FBI files without our knowledge that wrongly blackened our name and hindered us. Its agents were encouraged to look upon us with distrust. Connolly's warped world view turned inside out, up became down, black turned into white, bad was good, and trying to bring to justice two vile criminals a vendetta.

Connolly was motivated by his fear that somehow behind our impenetrable walls we were endangering Whitey and Stevie. They were deeply involved in the gaming and in the illegal drug operations in our county. We were constantly nipping at the heels of their operations. They were at a continuing risk. The one time we intercepted them I was required by statute to notify them. I did this but the notice did not say anything other than we identified them as aggrieved parties because we had intercepted their conversation. They must have gone to Connolly to find out what was happening. He had no way to get the information.

Connolly knew he had no way to protect them from our office. He apparently decided he would try to use Harrington to shut down our operations. What was difficult to fathom is how Connolly convinced Harrington that Delahunt was involved in criminal activity. Harrington had already been duped by FBI agents in the Barboza matter. They never let on to him they knew Barboza perjured himself in the Deagan trial. They continue to use him to help Barboza and he didn't see it. They probably figured it would be easy to use him again. Helped by Whitey and Stevie and their underworld contacts, Connolly dredged up every bit of imagined scandal to feed Harrington a witting believer.

I sometimes get a shiver thinking Connolly and the FBI's pursuit of Delahunt may very well have come out differently. If the case had gone to O'Sullivan he would have tried to please the FBI. If Myles been convicted for the robbery, would he have received an offer he couldn't refuse, freedom and a bag of goodies for his testimony against Delahunt, state cops and whoever else they disliked? The FBI and Myles could have imagined many criminal acts to toss on Delahunt's shoulders. It would have been easy to find other jail birds to corroborate them after all they had Whitey and Stevie out tilling the field. The stars above were positioned just right with a willing and gullible U.S. Attorney already convinced of Delahunt's criminality; an omniscient and omnipotent FBI at the height of its power; and a credulous and craven Fourth Estate.

An indicted Delahunt would have never been elected to Congress. The FBI, Whitey and Stevie would have quickly accomplished their goal of shutting down our investigations. Delahunt and others charged with him may have been incarcerated for years. Even if acquitted, their reputations would be destroyed and their lives shattered. It would not have been until 20 years later, if ever, that the truth may have come out to show that the prosecution was rigged.

Had exoneration eventually come I suppose a congressional committee may have asked the FBI what it thought of such an injustice. I imagine its response would be the same as FBI Agent Paul Rico made when asked to justify the false imprisonment of four men, two who died and the others who spend 30 years in prison: ``What do you want, tears.''

Nothing ever surfaced to indicate Delahunt or our office engaged in any type of wrongdoing.[257]

---

[257] The natural fallout from the FBI attack on our office was our refusal thereafter to do business with it. We found we could be quite successful without its help. Payback time came in 1994 when John Salvi murdered two women at a Planned Parenthood Clinic in Brookline. The FBI wanted to

Yet the FBI tried valiantly to destroy our reputations. Many Boston police officers thought we were corrupt. Protecting ourselves from the frivolous investigation took us away from going after organize crime people. When Harrington's investigation fizzled, we slowly picked up pace. We'd continue to be a source of trouble for Whitey and Stevie and needless to say their protector Connolly.

They didn't sit back. They later came up with another scheme. They caused the indictment of State Trooper John Naimovich who worked closely with me. He was making plans to move from the SSU to my office so we could work together to go after the OC types They alleged he was leaking information to organized crime people. Naimovich's indictment was Connolly's swan song. Naimovich was acquitted but the stigma of being corrupt remained. So did the lingering distrust of our office for the FBI.

---

take over the investigation and prosecution. I turned it down. Its agents were welcome to assist but we would maintain the full control. There were a lot of unhappy agents.

APPENDIX J:

THE PROSECUTORS

TRIAL TACTICS AND DEALS WITH WITNESSES

Billy Bulger in his book called the actions of the prosecutors unethical. He said they were purchasing testimony by giving deals to people who would say anything to get them. He's wrong about them being unethical. He's right that they are purchasing testimony. Tradition has dictated that prosecutors have an exemption from the prohibition of purchasing testimony. But to use this testimony a greater burden must be imposed on a prosecutor. He or she must insure such a witness testifies truthfully.

The Cross-Examination of a Witness Testifying After a Deal:

When a prosecutor offers a witness a benefit in exchange for testimony, especially such nefarious witnesses as in this case, the prosecutor should not be able to sit back and let the witness play dodge ball with the defense counsel. A prosecutor is obliged to make a criminal trial a search for the truth. A prosecutor must insure a government witness does not fabricate.

Several times Tracy Miner asked questions of the government witnesses and received deceitful answers. Martorano was always trying to be cute with his answers. When he was asked about how

458

much he paid for his house in Florida he said he really didn't know. Miner had to chase after him to finally get the answer and the best she got was somewhere in the thirty to forty thousand dollar area. Often Miner had to ask several questions of him to get a simple answer. This same routine happened with Weeks and Morris both of whom ran on and on avoiding answering.

Not once did I see the DOJ lawyers step in to stop their witness from skirting around the truth. They sat back throwing the total obligation on Miner to ferret it out. This may be all right for counsel in a civil suit but it should not be with a prosecutor using a benefited witness. Such attorney is obliged to insure that its witness not lie or obfuscate. The witness should be totally candid and the DOJ attorneys must be ready to correct the record if the witness offers any material information that contradicts what that attorney has in his file.

Obviously this is difficult. Doing it may affect the credibility of the witness. However failing to do it aligns the government more closely with the underhandedness of the person it has made a deal with and put forth as a witness. The prosecution of a person is not a game to be won or lost. The DOJ prosecutor acts on behalf of the people of the United States in whose name the charges were brought. Winning must be secondary to insuring that the whole truth is not withheld from the jury by a slippery or less than forthright witness.

The Forfeiture Deals with the Cooperating Witnesses:

This is in a sense an offshoot of the first point. At some point prior to the testimony of a cooperating witness the defense attorney was provided with a statement setting out the deal the prosecutors entered into with the witness. A part of this statement contained a list of the things the defendant forfeited. More often than not the things listed as being forfeited are a chimera. Weeks was reported to have forfeited his interest is several businesses when it turned out he had no interest in them. Martorano forfeited things he had no interest in.

The government knew very little was forfeited but made it appear otherwise. If someone does not forfeit something of value, it should not be listed as having been forfeited. The exact value of the items forfeited should be set out. I couldn't get over the feeling that the prosecutors were trying to pull a fast one.

THE DEALS:

Initially I had great difficulty with the deals the prosecutors made with its witnesses. I thought it was not right putting three serial murderers on the street for the purpose of convicting Connolly. As I write in 2012, Connolly is still in prison. The others have been out for years.

Connolly has done more time in prison since the trial than Weeks, Martorano and Salemme combined, three people who put bullets in other people's heads or stood by while they were murdered. Connolly now over seventy years old is in the early stages of a 40 year sentence for allegedly suggesting that Callahan would not stand up to FBI pressure. He will die in prison unless things change. I am not a fan of Connolly's but to keep him in prison any longer for an act which may have been condoned by his job is plainly wrong.

It is a difficult decision a prosecutor must make knowing the type of crimes Weeks, Martorano and Salemme committed to deal with them by offering them a great benefit for their testimony. Without making it in their interest to disclose their knowledge they won't do it. Yet the idea behind getting information and making a deal is so that the person who committed the crime is punished. Better not to recover a body if it means not punishing the murderer. But here the murderers were not punished. They received sentences which were less than the prosecutors could have given them for the crimes that were provable. They were rewarded for their murders. They used them to get lighter sentences than they otherwise would have received.

Is it wrong for the prosecutors to deal with three men responsible for perhaps killing a half a hundred people to get a bad FBI agent? Absolutely. There's no doubt about it if that is the goal.

Upon reflection though I recognized I was looking at the actions of the prosecutors too narrowly. They did not make the deal to get

Connolly alone. It was much more. They wanted to gain evidence against the masterminds behind these murders, Whitey and Stevie. That made the decisions more acceptable except perhaps for the inclusion of Salemme.

The Frank Salemme deal:

All DOJ really got from dealing with Salemme was a headache. It made no sense to me to deal with a Mafia leader even though the bargain only saved him a couple of years in jail. Durham in recommending a reduction in his sentence told Judge Wolf that Salemme was critical to the investigation and conviction of Connolly. I suggest it was the reverse. Listening to his testimony and seeing the outcome of the trial I tended to think he helped Connolly by adding to the sleaze of the government's case.

Salemme knew little having viewed the world from behind bars until 1988 throughout the period Connolly, Whitey and Stevie wreaked havoc. He hit the street just in time to catch Connolly's successful bugging of the Mafia induction ceremony. Salemme's bias alone made him a bad witness.

Connolly arrested him in New York City which led to his 16 year incarceration in Walpole state prison; he believed Connolly knew he was going to be gunned down and let it happen; and he thought Connolly was making him look like the FBI informant for the bug used in the Mafia induction ceremony in a book he was writing. Any

462

one of those incidents was a good reason to hate Connolly. The three together made it irresistible. Add in that Connolly helped destroy the Mafia in Boston and Salemme as a Mafia don could get retribution for his LCN buddies by destroying Connolly.

Salemme's one bit of relevant testimony is that Connolly told him he would tip him off about his upcoming indictment. This seemed like so much rot because he was never tipped by Connolly. On January 5 the day he was to be arrested Stevie told Salemme that the indictments were coming down on January 10.

The deal was bad because the government vouched for the veracity of a multi-murderer, hardened jailbird, head of a Mafia family felon who had a big grudge to settle against Connolly. No one believed him. He may have undermined the other criminal witnesses. Using him was a huge mistake.[258]

The John Martorano deal:

Martorano confessed to murdering one person in 1965, two in 1966, three in 1968, two in 1969, five in 1973, two in 1974, two in 1975, one in 1976, one in 1981, and one in 1982. Of these two were contract killings and a handful of others either

---

[258] An FBI report released after Salemme's testimony tells of information it received from a confidential informant who said Salemme told him he was prompted by the government to testify a certain way and that he was testifying to get revenge on Connolly.

government witnesses or innocent persons. We have no way of knowing how many people he actually killed.

Assuming it was only twenty, just pause and think of it for a second. Twenty murders! More than Charles Manson, Richard Speck, Jack the Ripper or many other notorious murderers. Since 1977 when the death penalty was officially reestablished in the United States almost 1,000 people have been executed. The great majority killed only one or at the most two persons.

Durham tried to mitigate Martorano's actions by pointing out that none of those murders were solved and that no charges had been brought against anyone on account of them prior to Martorano telling of them. But what good does it do to solve them if the perpetrator avoids punishment for them. I'd think it would bring little solace to a family to know a murderer explained how he killed their kin and in exchange he was going to be rewarded for it.

Martorano received an astounding deal. The initial RICO charge in the January 1995 indictment exposed him to a sentence under the sentencing guidelines of 24 to 30 years. An additional fugitive charge may have added to that time. After dealing with the DOJ he served half the time he faced if he had been convicted under the initial RICO charges. He served 146 months or 12 years.

U.S. Attorney Sullivan in his June 24, 2004 press release explained why Martorano deserved the deal. He said he told of his role in the murders.

Normally when you tell cops about your involvement in murder plots it is called confessing, not cooperating, and you don't get praise for it. Sullivan also said he was instrumental in the convictions of John Connolly, Richard Schneiderhan, and Stephen Flemmi who had pled guilty in October 2003.

Martorano was not instrumental in Connolly's conviction. His evidence was rejected by the jury. He did not testify at Schneiderhan's trial as agreed. The information he gave about Schneiderhan may well be false. As to Flemmi, I'm sure Martorano's cooperation played a large part in his decision to plead guilty.

I hope it took much courage and many sleepless nights by the prosecutors to make the deal. They should have understood that to tear down Whitey and Stevie's house of murder and corruption it may appear they were indifferent to justice. Even though the deal was bad for the Connolly case, overall it was good. It proved important in bringing about the destruction of Stevie.[259]

Now we will have the opportunity to see its true worth. Martorano has made himself less credible. He worked together with a newspaper columnist to publish a book telling a sordid and

---

[259] It could be argued it also helped cause Weeks to begin cooperating. I think that would be wrong because Weeks was motivated to cooperate as soon as the jail door locked on him.

bragging story of his life. Whitey's competent defense counsel has weeks of devastating cross-examination material. He'll also be able to bat around the newspaper columnist if need be.

Martorano is not a likeable witness. He thinks he is but he comes across on the stand as the wise guy gangster he is. His testimony has already been rejected by one jury. He is now in a worse position. Another jury likewise may be totally revolted by his noxious testimony and turn on the government for vouching for him. He may be the key to Whitey's acquittal on all the murder charges, including those in Florida and Oklahoma where Martorano was the one who pulled the trigger.

The Kevin Weeks deal:

One cannot look at Kevin Weeks and fail to think that crime pays. Weeks was arrested in November 1999 on a 28 count racketeering charge including extortion and money laundering, He faced twenty years or more in prison. He implicated himself in five murders and a multitude of extortions and other criminal acts. Weeks received 6 years. He did about 5, less than one quarter of the time he faced under the original charges. He goes scot-free for abetting all the murders and the multiple extortions.

He testified he had never been in jail before and all things considered he'd like to get out as soon as possible. Weeks testified Whitey told him Morris tipped him off about the FBI knowing the plate on the car used to kill Halloran. Whitey said,

466

"Thank God for Beck's beer." Weeks testified when Whitey learned Lundbohm went to Connolly about the Rakes extortion, Whitey said, "Thank God he went to Zip." Weeks must now think, "Thank God for Whitey."

Whitey made Weeks a young Southie tough, a somebody. He lived the good gangster life, fat with cash, fancy cars and fast women. When his world tumbled down, he cashed in his Whitey ticket because he can't do time.

Weeks cooperated not from remorse but from self interest. Weeks gave value for his deal. He's a telling witness. The jury accepted his story of the December 23 meeting which opened the door to Connolly's racketeering convictions. It rejected other parts such as those relating to the South Boston Liquor Mart extortion.

Weeks told the cops where he buried the bodies. He revealed caches of illegal arms. He gave evidence against Stevie, gave up Stevie's brother Michael and Stevie's state police source Schneiderhan. He is very important if Whitey is to be convicted.

He, like Martorano, has damaged his credibility. He wrote a book in which he shows no repentance but bragged much about his criminal exploits. Whitey's lawyers will have a field day with him.

Whether the deal with Weeks was worth making will depend on how he stands up against Whitey. I could not get over the feeling listening to him testify that he still admires Whitey who he calls Jim, Jimmy or Mr. Bulger. The government might be in line for a double cross from him. After all the Southie project connection is still there and now he has to face his old boss. No longer can he hide behind the word that was on the street in Southie that Weeks had been given the OK by Whitey to testify against Connolly.

The John Morris deal:

Morris accomplished what he set out to do when he started his career as an FBI agent. He got through it so as to retire with a comfortable FBI pension. He left with little honor. The FBI was not a good fit for him. He was a small man among bigger than life men.

He was portrayed as a friendless man unnerved and overwhelmed by the voluble Connolly; a little gray duckling nesting with the pruning swan; the retiring boss of the bigger-than-life subordinate; the small silent type buddied-up with the big windbag. It was a clever ruse by him assuming this persona. But it does not square with reality especially when we remember that the dean of criminal intrigue, Whitey, thought Morris was Machiavellian.

The prosecutors had to deal with either Morris or Connolly to rebut Stevie's assertion that he had been given carte blanche by them to commit any crime he wanted except "to hit someone." There is no doubt Morris helped the Whitey and Stevie reign of terror to proceed apace. He was in a position of authority. He should have stopped it.

468

He didn't, rather he abetted it. He was in love with his secretary, good wine and himself thinking he was admired by two top organize crime guys.

He knew full well every step he took. His testimony that he didn't understand his actions is absurd. He is masterful in presenting himself as a victim of Connolly when the opposite was the case. He was much smarter than Connolly something Whitey spotted early on.

It remains if Connolly is culpable for the Halloran and Callahan murders so is Morris. Morris could have stopped Connolly. He didn't.

CONCLUSION:

The prosecutors and their investigators held their noses and did what they were compelled to do. They followed the evidence, made their best judgments, and brought about as just a result as imaginable given the immensity of the undertaking before them.

They made deals fraught with peril. Whether their boldness pays off is still up in the air. Whitey has yet to be convicted.

I know of no one who doesn't think this is a done deal. I happen to believe Whitey thinks he's can beat the rap. He knows the only evidence of his involvement with murders come from gangsters who will admit their participation in them and then tell of the great deals they got from the government. He knows they aren't a particularly believable group. They weren't believed by the Connolly jury.

469

On the other hand Whitey must know that he'll never get out of jail. If he wins here he must face murder charges in Florida and Oklahoma. He could be interested in striking a deal. The best way to do this is to pretend that is not the case. The deal would involve him pleading guilty to everything including the out of state murders. The sentences for all the crimes would be combined together so he'd serve life in prison. This would please the judges who wouldn't have a year or so of their time taken out of their schedule, the federal prosecutors who will have caused Whitey to be sentenced to the maximum and can walk away with a compelling win, and especially the FBI.

Whitey's motivation would be his ability to get a few more things. Of course he'd avoid the probability of being executed but he'd figure at his age he could draw out that date until he died of natural causes. Some say he'd do it to save his family from being embarrassed. There is hardly any more embarrassment that could be put upon his family than it has already suffered. To do a deal his one big demand would be that he be allowed to tell his own story and to finish out his life in a cushy federal penitentiary like the playground in Pensacola.

A request like that would appear to be beyond the pale. But Whitey has a big thing working in his favor, the FBI. It would give him anything it could to avoid having the great embarrassment of its dealings with him again exposed to the public.

470

As I see it there is one big overriding consideration which would prevent Whitey from pleading guilty. Whitey does not want the story of his life to be told by people who have ratted him out or written by newspaper people who abhorred him and his family. He'll want to tell his own story. His lawyer says he's obsessed with telling the truth and the true story, which has not been told. It remains to be seen.

APPENDIX K:

THE FBI

SELF ACCOUNTABILITY IS NO ACCOUNTABILITY

The environment will determine the outcome. A swimming pool left covered and unattended under the sun will quickly be overgrown with algae. The longer it festers the more dangerous it becomes. Given time it will produce dangerous and deadly amoeba. At some point it is beyond redemption.

The FBI is such a pool. Connolly swum freely but his actions were not exposed to the public sun light. They were open and obvious to his fellow swimmers from whom he hid nothing. He had no reason to. He knew no one would expose him by taking off the cover.

His life style earned him the nickname Cannoli because he appeared more a gangster than a fellow agent. He bedecked himself in gold, clad himself in expensive hand made suits, and hung around with gangsters. He traveled with the Bruins, dined with the famous, drank expensive wines and passed out gifts. He owned a 45 foot yacht, had a home on Cape Cod as well as in Southie, lived large on his uncashed FBI pay checks which his fellow agents cashed and just managed to get by.

None of what are supposed to be America's most skillful investigators saw anything wrong. If any did, none had the integrity or gumption to do something about him. All seemed bound by the code of Omerta.

For years what is right was smothered by a federation of programmed men living like a cloistered order of religious in the Middle Ages. They believed their first and only obligation is to protect their FBI and their fellow agents. They had no other. Truth was not a welcome guest in their monastery.

The Director knew, every SAC and ASAC knew, the file clerks knew and everyone in between knew Whitey and Stevie were informants. They knew these two men continuously committed vicious and deadly criminal acts. No one thought it wrong for the FBI to associate with them. No one complained about protecting them. No one stopped it. It was business as usual working hand in hand with violent killers.

Morris admitted knowing in 1974 that Stevie was believed to have killed a government witness. Agent Tom Daly filed reports saying Whitey and Stevie's group, Winter Hill, killed an FBI informant. Two men were implicated in killing government witnesses and FBI informants were protected and not prosecuted.

In doing this the FBI went on to become their silent partners in crime. It is hard to think this is an isolated incident since so many knew of it and accepted it as normal. We will never know how many other Whiteys and Stevies the FBI has allied itself to in the past or how many they are allied with now. We do know the practice continues because no one dares stop it.

ABOVE THE LAW:

After Connolly was convicted, his prosecutor AUSA Durham held a press conference at which he crowed that the verdict "should tell the public there is no person who is above the law." When I heard that I laughed thinking that the case showed the exact opposite. Hadn't he just presented a case where several people were above the law? Doesn't Durham understand the FBI believes it is above the law?

In the summer of 2011 long after Connolly's case Shelley Murphy of the Boston Globe wrote a front page story. It was about a Mafia leader named Mark Rossetti. He is an FBI informant with an FBI telephone who continues his Mafia activities. He is being protected by the FBI. Nothing has changed. Rossetti is above the law because the FBI protects him and allows him to continue his criminal ways.

So was the man referred to as Mr. X, identified by others as Sammy Berkowitz, who for 25 years was Morris's informant.

Boston Magazine in June 2002 described him thusly:

> "The wheels for permits and
> land sales were greased by fresh
> C-notes, while the fire department

paid unlimited sick leave to officers who hadn't worked for years. At the center of it all was bookmaker Sammy Berkowitz, who sat on his perch at the Grub 'n' Pub, where he smoked Pall Malls and played endless games of gin rummy while bookies and friendly vice cops paid their respects."

Whitey and Stevie for many years were above the law. They were top echelon informants who were involved in ongoing criminal activities and protected by the FBI. All the hundreds of FBI top echelon informants from the past and those now providing information are above the law.

That no person should be above the law should be a core American value. Unfortunately, that is not the case. The FBI arrogates to itself the right to sanction some people to live lawless lives. It protects one person's bookmaking operation while destroying his competition.

The FBI's ability to permit some criminals to act with impunity has caused many innocent people to suffer greatly. In my old neighborhood of Savin Hill one of its informants ran an all-night entertainment club. He attracted the usual criminal types keeping the neighborhood awake by the continual noise. He couldn't be stopped because he had a deal with the FBI that allowed him to do this.

An informant is a lazy cop's tool. Dealing with one should be done with extreme care and under strict guidelines. No carte blanche can be given. Innocent people cannot be hurt. One must be closely supervised and limited to a one time targeted act that terminates the relationship upon its culmination. The idea of a blank check puts the person above the law.

The FBI's approach to crime solving is to cozy up to hardened criminals but to come down hard on those new to the crime business. A person who commits one bank robbery by himself has nothing to offer so he's out of luck. Another person who has committed a string of bank robberies with others has a lot of bargaining chips. The FBI will want him as an informant. Those more heavily steeped in crime have a better chance to avoid jail than the one time criminal.

The FBI uses extortion tactics to silence its informants. If an informant gets into trouble, he is told he must keep his status as an informant quiet. If he doesn't, the FBI won't help him out but will try to increase his sentence; if he does remain quiet, it will help him and try to lower it. That is why the FBI never thought that Stevie would expose his status as an informant.

The judiciary has joined in. It allows the FBI to influence its sentencing of these criminals. The FBI's ability to do this has resulted in the great abuses. Some we have seen in this case.

LOYAL ONLY TO ITSELF:

The Connolly trial showed that the first loyalty of an FBI agent is not to the United States nor to us citizens but to the Bureau. No one outside the FBI knows its cadre of informants because the FBI operates behind opaque curtains with no oversight or checks and balances. Sitting through the Connolly case made me realize the FBI operates like the East German Stasi or the KGB by employing the most unsavory people to spy on others.

The idea it is under the Department of Justice (DOJ) is a chimera. Whenever the DOJ entered into a struggle to gain ascendancy over the Bureau, it has lost. The FBI's huge size in money and manpower, its loyal alumni and alumna, its well-place allies in the press, its web of connections, a timid Congress, and an indifferent president ensures the DOJ remains subservient to it.

AUSA O'Sullivan said it was political suicide to cross it. It had cowed him. It has only grown stronger and more insulated since his time.

Not only does the executive branch lack control of the FBI so does the judicial branch. Judge Wolf was frustrated in his attempts to get information from it. At one point he had to threaten to hold the head of the DOJ's criminal bureau in contempt for defying his orders. Even he failed to go after the FBI's top brass. The defiance never stopped. He had to find another way to get his answers. The FBI forced him to back down.

477

Likewise Congress has no control over it. I watched a congressional hearing into the FBI's failures to properly analyze intelligence information before the September 11 attack. Former director Louis Freeh was testifying. He repulsed any attempt to blame the FBI for any failures. He scolded the Congressmen who were meekly questioning him. He said it was Congress's fault the FBI had not done its job. It had not given the FBI sufficient money and agents. It's a perfect Catch-22. When the FBI blunders, it's because it has not received sufficient resources. Therefore, as long as the FBI asks for more money, equipment and other resources than Congress is willing to give it, any screw ups fall at the feet of Congress. It's never because it just isn't doing the job. It is because Congress refuses to do its job.

We thought the FBI was doing its job during the Connolly years but now we see how it fooled us. Still criticism of the Bureau is muted. Members of Congress who speak against it do so timidly and even then they chant the obligatory phrase that, "Most of the FBI agents I know are fine and outstanding persons" or "the FBI is the finest law enforcement group in the world". That may be the case but how is the Bureau controlled by such a small number of not-so-nice people and able to do what appears to be a lot of less than fine actions.

FRAUDULENT 302 REPORTS:

302s are supposed to contain the information conveyed to an agent during an interview. Frank Salemme was interviewed by counsel for the Congressional Committee after receiving a grant of immunity. He went through much of what he testified to and elaborated more on things that happened forty years ago especially his involvement with FBI Agent Paul Rico. One part of this transcript stood out.

Salemme had fled from the Boston area when he was charged with the bombing a lawyer's car. He always denied his involvement in it. He was arrested by Connolly in New York City and brought back for trial. The main witness against him was a person named Daddeico.

Salemme said the FBI also wanted Daddeico to testify against Angiulo, the local Mafia head. Daddeico refused. The FBI agents said they would subpoena him and force him to testify. Daddeico said if you do, "I'll tell how you people made me frame Frank Salemme"

Salemme went on to say that the FBI agents that interviewed Daddeico never filed a 302 about that. He asked, "How can you go, an FBI agent, two FBI agents, how can you have an interview like that and not have a document on it? That's my understanding, there's no document, and that's what stunk about it, . . . "

Joe Murray was interviewed by the FBI. William Weld, the Deputy Attorney General, received telephone calls from Joe's wife saying that Murray had information that two Boston FBI agents, Connolly and Newton, were taking money to tip off wiretaps as well as information on murders.

Weld asked the FBI to look into it. It was given to the Office of Professional Responsibility (OPR) which contacted Boston. Joe Murray who was in custody was transferred to Boston to be interviewed. Two supervisors in the Boston office, Ed Clark and Edward Quinn, were sent by ASAC O'Callaghan to interview him. They conducted the interview and filed a report. The report contained nothing about the reason why they were sent to interview Murray and nothing about the murders. Clark explained to Ralph Ranalli, "I did what I was told to do. You weren't there. You don't know what it was like. You wouldn't understand." ASAC O'Callaghan approved the report and sent it to OPR which approved it and closed out the investigation. As Salemme would say that from top to bottom, "That's what stunk about it!"

Allegations of serious misconduct by two FBI agents are swept aside by the local office and the OPR. It's as if someone at FBI headquarters asked Boston FBI to investigate terrorists planning to blow up the Copley Square Library and received a report back talking about the squirrels on the Boston Common.

Roger Wheeler was murdered on May 27, 1981. Shortly after that and again at the end of August

480

1981 the FBI in Boston was requested to assist the police in Tulsa in their investigation of the murder. Incredibly Morris assigned the request to Connolly. Not surprisingly Connolly did nothing. The requests were marked closed as if something had been done.

The FBI has an adage that "If it's not on paper, it didn't happen." In other words, an FBI agent can create facts to fit his own world view. When Daddeico told two agents the FBI made him frame Salemme, or when Murray told two supervisors Connolly and Newton were taking money, the FBI mindset is that by not writing down what they said then they never said it.

It is frightening to think of the unreliability of FBI reports when its agents pick and choose what to include in them. It is frightening to think that FBI agents live in a culture where they are taught they control reality by what they decide to write down. That 302 reports are notoriously unreliable is common knowledge.

Judge Mark Wolf was asked to be interviewed by the FBI. He agreed on one condition. He wanted to review the 302 that would be filed as a condition of being interviewed. Wolf is an experienced gutsy judge yet he had reason to fear that it would not contain the full truth. He doesn't understand he is taking advantage of his position to protect himself while at the same time he does not protect the rest of us who lack his clout. We have no idea what the FBI agent who interviews us is writing down. It could have no relationship to anything that came from our mouths.

In a footnote Judge Wolf quoted Edwin O. Guthman a former press secretary of Attorney General Kennedy who said: "You can have a conversation with an agent, and when it is over he will send a memo to the files. Any relation between the memo and what was said in the conversation may be purely coincidental. You would think you were at different meetings."

IN-HOUSE FICTIONS:

On February 10, 1989, the SAC in the Boston FBI office, James Ahearn, wrote to the Director of the FBI, William S. Sessions, one of the most outrageous and warped reports ever written.[260] It concerned a "DEA Boston Investigation of James 'Whitey' Bulger." Ahearn learned the DEA and Suffolk Country DA Flanagan were conducting a joint investigation 18 months after it began when the Boston DEA chief sought the FBI's help. He was told the FBI was being deliberately excluded

---

[260] Kevin Cullen of the Boston Globe wrote how in 1988 the Globe's Spotlight Team under O'Neill and Lehr wrote that Whitey has a special relationship with the FBI: He said, "The FBI vehemently denied the Globe's contention that Whitey was an informant. Jim Ahern, the FBI's special agent in charge in Boston at the time, angrily demanded a meeting and a retraction. We met with him at the Globe, but when we said we couldn't retract something we knew to be true, he was furious."

and that he could not share the information about it with others in his office. He was miffed.

His report begins by him saying he will provide the background of Whitey's relationship without examining any open or closed files because that "might seem unusual and might raise the attention of office personnel." Right off we see he doesn't trust the people in his office. That alone speaks a great deal of what the FBI is about.

Ahearn writes that Whitey is "The most important Organized Crime informant for many years." Within a year it will be determined that he is of no value and he will be closed out on its books.

Ahearn goes on to say Whitey is the brother of Billy, the Senate President who is "an extremely powerful political figure in this State." He infers thereby that Whitey must be handled with kid gloves. Ahearn continues that he is not aware of any interaction between Billy and Whitey or any allegations regarding an illicit relationship having just indicated the opposite by noting their connection.

I've told how on the state side we never gave one thought to the idea of Billy being related to Whitey. It looks like it consumed the thoughts of the FBI agents. It is absurd to tell someone of a connection between two people and then tell the person there is no reason for mentioning the connection.

But it is not absurd to think that Connolly was abetted in his dealings with Whitey by ASACs, SACs and other agents who were either fearful of Billy's wrath or planning to curry favor with him. We in the state who could have been harmed by Billy had no fear yet the FBI over which he had no control seemed terrified. I don't understand it.

Ahearn notes Connolly then a supervisor has been operating Whitey as well as numerous other top echelon informants. He adds, "Connolly is also well-known for his long-time association with Senate President Bulger going back many years to the neighborhood from which they both came." Again he is suggesting the FBI director take Billy into consideration. It seemed the FBI made its decisions based on political considerations.

Ahearn praised Connolly's "outstanding reputation as an informant developer." He said he had a well known reputation. I don't think he was referring to Connolly's daily parading through his office clad in gold.

Then Ahearn resorted to FBI form. He went into typical FBI spin and smear. He impugned the motives behind the DEA investigation. I can see Connolly standing over his shoulder as he writes. He goes far afield. He says DA Delahunt was publicly embarrassed by an investigation started by Connolly some years ago and that Delahunt is a close ally of DA Flanagan.[261]

---

[261] This is all nonsense. Delahunt was not a close ally of Flanagan. Their relationship was arms length. Delahunt

He moves from that to say resentment still remained from the Lancaster Garage investigation where Whitey discovered the bug. He notes "older DEA and MSP officials" believe the "FBI 'tipped off' Whitey." Ahearn disingenuously says a prior SAC "exhaustively" investigated that allegation. By exhaustive he meant an interview of Morris. Ahearn writes that the allegation that the FBI tipped Whitey was found to be "groundless." He didn't stop there. He added that "we have, in fact, indicted an MSP officer [Naimovich] in an unrelated matter who was advising OC figures of the location and identify of FBI wiretaps."[262] It seemed Naimovich was going to serve as the convenient scapegoat for the FBI wrongs.

Ahearn adds "Because of jealousies, rumors and unfounded distrust, DA Flanagan chose to not involve the FBI" and his motive as you might expect is not to protect the investigation from leaks it is "with the purpose in mind of public embarrassment to the FBI." Ahearn tells how he told DEA Administrator Coleman he was "deeply disappointed" that DEA did not trust the FBI.

He then resorted to the now common FBI tactic of maligning Flanagan saying he "has proven to be an ineffective local prosecutor on any matters

---

was not involved and knew nothing of the investigation. It has the shades of Connolly's Delahunt/Bellotti hating Bulger type thinking.

[262] This was again a false statement. The information on FBI taps was never charged to Naimovich.

relating to organized crime or public corruption." As we've seen, Flanagan has no idea he is being slandered. Ahearn then adds "[t]his is but one of a lengthy series of allegations over the years . . . all others have proven groundless and SSA Connolly is held in extremely high esteem."

He then talks about Morris who he called, "The long-time Supervisor and close associate of SSA Connolly's for many years and who also suffered from some of the verbal abuse and rumors mentioned herein. SSA Morris is one of the most highly regarded Supervisors in the Boston Field Division . . . ." At the time Ahearn is writing the memorandum Morris is leaking information to the Boston Globe hoping to get Whitey killed.

The memorandum demonstrates the FBI mindset. It had at least two agents in its office who undermined state police investigations. Its investigations of itself are a sham as is shown by Ahearn's report that was filled with scandalous lies. Attempts by other law enforcement agencies to do their jobs caused the FBI to malign them. Imagine the FBI SAC indicating that a successful investigation by the Suffolk DA and DEA would only serve to embarrass the FBI. He never for an instance bothers to consider that they had good reason to distrust his agents when he himself as he wrote couldn't examine Whitey's files because it might cause suspicion.

Year after year from the FBI's viewpoint no one had a valid reason to question it. Those that did were corrupt, jealous or engaged in vendettas and may be targeted. AUSA O'Sullivan stated that reports to the file by SAC Sarhatt were fabrications. Ahearn writes to the Director similar type fairy tales. Neither DA Flanagan or DA Delahunt know about them. DA Flanagan who had a stellar reputation remains oblivious that he has been labeled by the Boston SAC as one who is "an ineffective local prosecutor on any matters relating to organized crime or public corruption." It is not only that it is totally false, it is something he knows nothing about so he is unable to defend himself and may have had the potential to adversely affect him.

Fortunately it didn't. Flanagan would go on to head the National District Attorneys Association. He escaped the unwarranted venom of the FBI.

FRAUDULENT 209 REPORTS:

The 209 is supposed to contain information that an informant has provided. Connolly was the past master of filling them with information that slandered other people. He used them in a childish "them against us" manner reporting once that State Police Colonel O'Donovan said some bad things about the FBI. Connolly over and over again used them to prejudice his fellow agents against outside agencies. Few agents would trust DA Delahunt, DA Flanagan, Attorney General Bellotti, Colonel O'Donovan, the state police or the Quincy police after reading his tales which may have come from

487

the mouths of his informants or more likely from his fertile imagination.

Morris told Connolly that Halloran was a FBI informant and that he was providing information against Whitey and Stevie. Connolly passed it on to them. He then began to implicate others in the upcoming death of Halloran. He blamed the Mafia on April 23 saying Whitey said "the outfit" continues to be interested in killing Halloran because it knew he was dealing with the FBI. It considers Halloran a weak person and is concerned he may make a deal with the DA's office to give up Salemme.

Brian Halloran was murdered a little over two weeks later on May 11, 1982. Two days later Connolly reported that Whitey said the word on the street was that Halloran was killed because he was cooperating in the Pappas murder. Connolly then tossed about various theories for other FBI agents to chew upon: "the outfit" (Mafia) killed him to protect Salemme's brother; Jimmy Flynn thought Halloran was informing on him; Halloran had been robbing coke dealers at gunpoint; Halloran was extorting money from other people. Connolly ended by suggesting the most likely source of the hit was the old bugaboo, the Mafia. Nothing was mentioned about Whitey even though the location of the murder in Southie and Whitey knowing Halloran was ratting on him points to Whitey as the person who most likely killed Halloran.

In a cute twist Connolly added at the end of the report that the information "is singular . . . and should not be disseminated outside the Bureau without first contacting the writer." There was nothing singular about the collage of rumors. Making it singular put Connolly in the position of learning what the other agents were doing if they were gullible enough to go to him.

On May 21 Connolly filed a report that Whitey said Jimmy Flynn did the hit on Halloran and other people from Charlestown were in a back-up van. It's easy to imagine Whitey and Connolly smirking as they conspired to file these reports. Connolly added that people suspected Halloran was wired up (there were FBI reports from other agents stating it was common knowledge on the street Halloran was wired).

Connolly took another shot at Colonel O'Donovan writing Whitey got word that Halloran was cooperating with O'Donovan. How despicable can he be when he had told Whitey that Halloran was cooperating with the FBI which he never mentions.

In early July he continues his mission of deceit stating Whitey told him the state police are saying the FBI got Halloran killed but the "People from Charlestown say it was the state police who let the cat out of the bag . . . [because] Halloran was talking to Colonel O'Donovan and Trooper Fralick." Then blatantly spitting in the face of truth he writes "[s]ource pointed out that no one had any information that Halloran was cooperating with the FBI until it appeared in the paper after his death." It's not hard to see why one of the detectives investigating the Wheeler murder said after a conversation with Connolly that he felt Connolly had become part of the Winter Hill gang. He was following in the footsteps of his mentor FBI Agent Paul Rico.

More significantly false 209s can be used to undermine investigations and destroy reputations. They can condition the FBI true believers to turn against people who are really working for justice. They can attribute criminal acts to innocent people as Connolly did to Flynn who was indicted for Halloran's murder. They can be a source of unending misinformation.

OBSERVATIONS:

The problem with dealing with the FBI mess is that agents from the earliest days are bred into its culture. These agents are slowly drawn down year after year until totally immersed in the idea that the most important thing is not to embarrass the Bureau and that everything be kept in house. The Catholic Church severely damaged itself when it preferred that road to the right road. The similarities are eerie especially when you see the punishment for doing wrong is a transfer to another post.

An endless line of men with a sprinkling of a few women are fed with that idea although some women agents seem to resist the old boy mentality. Agents enter one door and twenty or so years later pop out the other stamped with the belief that nothing is more important, not even the truth, than protecting the FBI. The federal judiciary are witting agents in that endeavor.

FBI agents easily disassociated themselves from the truth when testifying in court. Daly's suggestion of not knowing what MO meant, Montanari's failure to remember what Halloran said about Connolly, Quinn's attempts to justify Clark's report about Murray's interview, O'Callaghan's many half-truths, and Morris's inability to tell the whole truth show a pattern of conduct.

The type of thinking that truth is subservient to propaganda seems endemic to the FBI. Its leadership and upper level management all have been brought up to share that perverse value dutifully clinging to the mindset of don't embarrass. No doors are open to the outside so that a breath of fresh air in the form of new blood can penetrate this atrophied entity where ideas have petrified.

This may have been all right when the FBI was just chasing the Mafia. Most of us could avoid becoming entangled in situations or relationships that would bring us in contact with the underworld. But the times have changed. We now look to the FBI to protect us from an ongoing serious terrorist threat.

Unfortunately the September 11 attack may have insulated the FBI even further as it received extraordinary new powers to combat terrorism. It has the right to examine bank documents using a letter, a practice already shown to be abused. It participates in wiretaps that are not court authorized. There is no check or balance on it other than what it decides it should do. It hides behind a closed door and the little opening provided by Judge Wolf that let light into its darkness is not reassuring.

Self accountability by the FBI is no accountability. The FBI is the Wizard of Oz standing behind the cloth screen. Unlike Dorothy we have no way to get behind the screen to find out who is really turning the knobs and pulling the strings. Frankly we don't know what the watch dog is doing nor do we have any way of finding out. That is not good for a democratic society.

In March 2007 DOJ's Inspector General revealed that the FBI "seriously misused" and improperly—and often illegally—abused that broad authority to secretly obtain information about citizens. Louis Wolf, founder of Covert Action Information Bulletin, stated: "[The FBI] have been using 9/11 as this case demonstrates very clearly as a cover for massive abuses. In fact, the FBI's own records of the abuse were so slipshod, according to the audit report, that the agency did not even keep a count of the number of national security letters which were issued. I think this latest scandal is indicative of a leadership-kind of culture within the FBI which they claim they dispensed with after [former FBI Director J. Edgar] Hoover, but it still survives very strongly."

Shelley Murphy's August 2011 article in the Boston Globe spoke about a Mafia leader Mark Rossetti being used as an informant. She wrote that the codefendants of the Mafia leader "are seeking to have charges dismissed based on Rossetti's relationship with the FBI. According to the documents, they argued that any evidence obtained in relation to Rossetti should be dismissed because his relationship to investigators was not disclosed to judges who approved wiretaps and search warrants."

It's as if there were never any problems in the Boston FBI office. The culture that gave us Connolly has not changed but lives on.

HUMBLE SUGGESTIONS:

I don't know if the FBI can be reformed. It is difficult to change a culture where people believe they enforce the laws but do not have to follow them; where people believe they can let certain people commit crimes with impunity; and where people are upset when others in the law enforcement community are successful. I hope that it can be reformed. I have a few modest proposals to make.

No group can be an effective organization when those who find in-house problems must be quiet about them or be labeled as trouble makers. This is a pool where evil will thrive. A corrosive conspiracy of silence makes all truth its victim. Only through vigorous self examination and by openly airing its problems will the FBI become a law enforcement agency worthy of our trust. We trust the FBI is doing a rightful job but as President Reagan noted trust is not enough, we must have a mechanism to verify that is happening. There are a few simple changes that can be made immediately that may start it on the road back into our confidence because they will minimize the abuses we have seen.

1: **Record Interviews:**

Require that all interviews between FBI agents and others be recorded and preserved. Only allow exceptions in an extremely limited number of cases and require a SAC or ASAC to sign off on any decision not to record an interview and to specify the specific reasons. The failure to record must be the rare exception. Prevent any FBI agent from testifying about what s/he was told by a person if this mandate is violated. If the agent is concerned the presence of a recorder may intimidate the person being interviewed, a hidden recorder can always be used.

Under Title III, FBI agents are required to record all intercepted communications. We do not trust them to listen to them and then reduce them to writing. The best evidence is a person's own words on a tape. All the problems with the 302s will cease if the full conversations are recorded and preserved.

2: Review Filed 302s:

As to any 302s based on interviews or conversations that are not recorded, the person interviewed must have the right to review what is written down. Allow the person to correct any errors or to add any additional comments.

3: Better Informant Control:

i/ Time Limits: Forbid the FBI from authorizing either in writing or by acquiescence anyone to commit crimes for an extended period of time.

ii/ Review: Require all reports from within the FBI or from other law enforcement agencies that show an informant is engaged in criminal activity to be reviewed by a SAC who will be required to put in writing his findings about the future handling of that informant.

iii/ Crime Limits: Require that informants be advised they cannot commit crimes without FBI approval of each specific act. Any violation of this automatically ends the relationship forever.

iv/ Assistance Limits: Forbid FBI agents from going to other law enforcement agencies when their purpose is to help informants who have committed new crimes.

v/ Trickery Limits: Stop the system of closing out informants on the books while keeping them active as informants. Insure that once an informant is closed out he or she can never be reopened.

vi/ Eliminate Top Echelon Informants: The top echelon informant is a criminal with a violent past and ongoing criminal activity. He should not be empowered by the FBI to commit his crimes while being protected by it.

4: Independent Authority To Review Informants:

Establish an independent authority to review the informant files of those in that status for a year. Require written approval by the independent body to continue such an informant and yearly written reviews thereafter. Make it a dismissible offense to have an informant "off the books."

5: Real Punishment for Wrongdoing:

Have real punishment for substantive violation of the FBI rules or criminal laws. Publish them to all agents so that they are aware of the consequences of any wrongful actions. No agent should be promoted or transferred after being found to have violated certain of these rules. Stop the practice of transferring and promoting agents to keep them quiet.

6: Change the Culture:

Destroy the mentality of "if it is not in writing it doesn't exist." This encourages a culture of deception. Make sure that everything is in writing and is truthful if it is relevant. We should strive to have honest FBI agents telling the whole truth. We should have a system where derogatory information about other law enforcement officials is vetted to insure its truthfulness.

7: Better DOJ Control:

Make the FBI responsive to the DOJ. The FBI is a law enforcement agency. It must aggressively pursue criminals or terrorists. The DOJ must insure the pursuit is done in accordance with the law and done fairly across the board. Make it impossible for the FBI to undermine the actions of DOJ attorneys or put DOJ attorneys in fear.

8: Right To Review:

Require all 302 reports that are put into FBI files concerning interactions between FBI agents and attorneys for the DOJ be forwarded to the DOJ attorney for his/her review and comments.

9: In-House Discipline:

Make the failure to file required reports a serious matter that will adversely impact the career of an agent. Require agents to file a report of any gratuity they receive from an informant above a certain dollar value. Make failure of those in leadership positions to carry out their duties of properly supervising the agents under them also a serious matter.

10: Real Punishment:

Put the agent's pension at risk for misconduct that is committed during the time the agent is performing his/her sworn duties. Make it mandatory and not subject to plea bargaining the loss of a pension for serious misconduct.

11: Fresh Air:

Bring in people from the outside at middle levels of management who are not bred in the culture. Give such people an opportunity to make the FBI a career. Let them be instruments of change and fonts of new ideas.

12: Strive for Greatness:

Encourage agents to experiment with new ideas. Stop trying to make everyone think and look alike. Chase away the myth and become the best investigative agency in the world but do it right.

13: Insure Proper Convictions:

Require that anyone indicted on evidence obtained through electronic interceptions be notified if any persons outside the law enforcement community were made aware of the electronic surveillance.

14: Minimize Intrusions on Privacy:

Limit intrusions on the rights of the people. Stop watering down the rules and make them more stringent. The rights of privacy are serious matters that must require at a minimum a document in writing establishing probable cause (or some lesser standard depending on the intrusion) presented to an independent authority with a requirement of notice prior to examining a person's personal effects. It also happens to be a Constitutional right of the people. If the government needs to intrude on our privacy, we must receive notice of that intrusion at some time after it occurs. Any delay in notice must be approved by a court.   It is just too tempting for an FBI agent who can secretly access emails without notice not to be curious about what family, friends or associates are saying to each other.

15: Get Rid of the Fear:

Accept embarrassment. Change the culture so that any actions by agents or other employees that may embarrass the FBI can be reported in a public forum. Stop hiding the problems. Recognize that by facing embarrassing events openly and working to insure they won't reoccur is better than hiding them. One product of working hard and doing good work is accepting embarrassment. Hiding embarrassments, you only encourage a comfort with deception.

499

FINAL WORD:

I worked in the field of organized crime investigations for many years. I worked with all the restrictions that have now been loosened. I know that effective law enforcement work can be done on the up and up. All that it requires is a little hard work, a good deal of integrity, and recognition that you sometimes make mistakes. It is better to suffer the embarrassment of that than to cover it up.

APPENDIX L:

JOHN CONNOLLY

Villain or Victim

How I Look At This Matter Prior to Trial:

I went to Connolly's trial with hardly any idea of the evidence the government intended to present or the deals the government made. As best I can recall my feelings were: an unhappiness that the FBI allowed Connolly to use Whitey and Stevie as informants; satisfaction Whitey and Stevie had been indicted; the highest respect for the accomplishment of Fred Wyshak and his team of US Attorneys, the Massachusetts State Police, DEA, and other agents involved in the case; a belief Connolly was doing what he had been paid to do; that he was taking the hit to protect others in the FBI which I told him on the first morning of the trial; and an overall feeling the FBI was doing an adequate job despite its obvious disdain for other law enforcement agencies.

What I learned at the trial, what I knew from my own experience, what I learned from FBI documents I have examined, and from readings I have done since the trial I have arrived at the following conclusions.

How I Look At Connolly at this time:

I still am unhappy the FBI abetted, encouraged and empowered Connolly to use Whitey and Stevie as informants. I understand more than I originally did that knowledge of these actions was widespread as was the knowledge of their evilness. Long after Connolly retired Whitey and Stevie were continually protected by the FBI leadership in the Boston office.

I am pleased that Whitey is in jail and I hope that Stevie will never get out of jail. My respect for Fred Wyshak is still high but some of his actions have me puzzled. In his relentless pursuit of only Connolly he has turned a blind eye to the clear showing that his activities were known by others in the FBI and encouragement by them from the highest levels. I do not understand why he does not see that the pernicious Connolly was but a small cog in the FBI wheel. Connolly could have been removed and replaced at any moment.

Wyshak knows that memoranda exist showing that the highest levels of the FBI knew the murders of Wheeler, Halloran and Callahan were connected. He ignored this and dropped everything on Connolly's shoulders. I am bothered by Wyshak's participation in the State of Florida murder trial.

Durham, the timid attorneys in the Justice Department, and the pusillanimous Congressmen were all content to stop at Connolly for fear of taking on the FBI. All settled for the idea in the face of compelling evidence to the contrary that the horrors of Whitey and Stevie resulted from the act of one man. We have seen that is untrue. It is wrong that one man take all the blame for the failure of the Bureau and that he be condemned to die in prison for the sins of the many in the FBI.

My respect for the investigating officers remains high, although it was severely buffeted by their actions. Seeing them acting as a cheering section for the gangsters, I sensed they had let themselves get too close to them. Martorano boasted that if he needed anything he just call them and they'd come running; Salemme told how they picked up his expensive long distance telephone bills and gave him money. In a way it reminded me of Connolly and his informants where the handlers become the handled. Just because the gangsters are working for them they seem to have forgotten they are still gangsters. If a gangster could make life easier on himself by turning on an investigator he'd do it in a New York second.

I still believe Connolly was doing what he was supposed to do but there's no doubt he became too close to Whitey and Stevie if Morris is to be believed when he says they traveled everywhere together when going to meetings. He seemed less like their handler but more like their associate warding off any bad things that may happen to them. He closed his eyes to their numerous criminal activities which were obvious. Although in fairness, many of the murders we now know about he had no way of knowing about them. He filed numerous false reports to cover their crimes sowing dissention between the FBI and other law enforcement officers. The question that remains is whether this is part of an FBI agents job.

Connolly operated to the applause of the FBI. It gladly preened itself to the public eye when his actions gave it arrests to brag about. Sadly, many of his actions were done in an underhanded and wrongful way. Does the FBI have this right?

I no longer believe the FBI did even an adequate job. Hoover's idea of "don't embarrass the Bureau" still rules and the FBI culture.

The Problem I Have In Dealing With Connolly's Culpability:

I believe Connolly engaged in some dastardly and heinous acts. Some certainly were criminal when viewed by a normal standard. What I do not know is whether they were criminal when done by an FBI agent in Connolly's position.

We need the full picture to determine this answer. One difficulty with obtaining this is that the FBI is a pretend organization. It pretends it is one thing when in fact it may be the other. No one knows which it is because it has hidden its ongoing operations behind its impenetrable walls because of its inordinate fear of embarrassment.

Another problem is Connolly's silence on the matter. As the hearings before Judge Wolf were taking place, Connolly conspired with Flemmi to blame Morris for tipping him off the indictments were coming down. I do not understand why he sought to remove himself from the situation. If Connolly believed his relationship with Whitey and Stevie was proper, he should have owned up to it and not tried to hide it. By taking the Fifth and sitting silently at his trials, Connolly played into the hands of those trying to destroy him.

Maybe he disabled himself from testifying because he knew his gangster-like actions after leaving the FBI could not be justified. His fate was sealed on those charges whether he testified or not. Had he a compelling and proper reason for those actions he should have owned up to them.

He had the right to remain silent. So did Billy Bulger have that right. But in exercising it, you have to remember that Constitutional protection does not protect you from adverse consequences.

Even without testifying he could have constructed his defense to give the jury an idea of the environment in which he operated and what was expected from him. He failed to do this. He did not expose the FBI operations for all to see. If as Connolly asserts his actions were authorized and approved by the government, he failed in his obligation to demonstrate that.

Here's The Overall Problem I See With the Case:

I've talked previously about circumstantial evidence. I showed that one must see the whole picture to make any valid deduction from the circumstances. In Connolly's case, both in the federal court in Boston and in the state court in Miami, the jury got to see only a small part of the picture. The great part that was missing was evidence concerning the powers, rights and duties of an FBI agent. Not only what is contained in the manuals, but what happens in everyday life in an FBI office. A jury must know what is sanctioned from the highest levels down through the SACs.

One custom I read about goes like this. One makes a request from headquarters for a certain thing. If nothing is heard back then it is considered all right to do the thing. The idea is that you can do it but don't expect anyone up in headquarters to give you permission in writing to do it. There is the other thing I've already mentioned the idea that if it is not in writing it doesn't exist.

These customs and many others in the FBI matter. An agent who operates in accordance with the customary procedures, rather what is written down, should be judged by what is expected of him by custom not what is written down and ignored by everyone from the director down until dusted off to avoid embarrassment.

William F. Roemer, Jr., a long time FBI agent who was in the lead in taking down the Chicago Mob told how FBI Director J. Edgar Hoover was pressuring his office to get evidence against that group. He said the only way to do that was to break into private areas and plant bugs. Before they could go ahead they had to insure Hoover that the target was significant, the plan was well thought out, and the operation could be done without any embarrassment to the Bureau. He wrote that embarrassment was Hoover's greatest concern. His policy was, "Do the job, by God, but don't ever let anything happen that might embarrass the Bureau."

He summed it up by writing:

"The Bureau's policy on all operations of this type, the so-called black bag jobs, was that if we got caught, we were not to identify ourselves as FBI agents, and we were to attempt to escape without being identified. We were to carry no badge or credentials, no gun, nothing to connect us with the FBI. But, heaven help us if we were

apprehended and it eventually came out that we were employed by the FBI; then the Bureau would denounce us. We were "rogue," carrying out an unauthorized operation."

I'm sure that there were instances when the Chicago police caught some FBI agent breaking into someone's office. They'd quickly let him go when they learned he was doing his job. When Roemer writes about it becoming known they were FBI agents, he means know by the public and the media.

But assume the most unlikely happening. An FBI agent did get arrested and was prosecuted for breaking into a building. Shouldn't he be able to explain to a jury the full picture: that he was acting against the mob pursuant to the directives of the FBI director?

That what is lacking in the Connolly case. Most basically the jury was not told what the powers of an FBI agent are when it comes to high level informants. The jury was not told that when FBI chicanery or criminality is publicly exposed, the FBI will label and agent "rogue" even though he was doing the things the FBI expected him to do. The jury heard that agents are not supposed to let their informants commit crimes, while at the same time hearing, sometimes from the same person, that all informants commit crimes, especially high echelon informants. The jury should have been told that Hoover instituted the top echelon informant program for the specific purpose of hiring and protecting top level gangsters who agreed to give the FBI information in exchange for the FBI giving protection to his business.

The juries have not been provided with answers to the simplest questions: Can an FBI agent tell his informant he can commit certain crimes and not be prosecuted? Can an FBI agent tell an informant he can commit any crime he wants as long as he does not hit a person? Can an FBI agent tell an informant that in exchange for information he will give him a "head start?" Can an FBI agent tell his informant that he believes a certain witness will not stand up under FBI pressure? These are a few of the multitude of questions about the rights and duties of an FBI agent handling informants that remain unanswered at Connolly's trial. If they can't be answered, how is a jury to make a judgment on his conduct?

That is the great difficulty I faced in trying to understand this case. What is to be the standard I should use for considering Connolly's actions. Does he have the right to do more than an average citizen can do? The standards of what an FBI agent is allowed to do were not considered. If I do not know what an FBI agent can do, how then can I judge Connolly's actions? If a jury does not know, how can a jury judge him?

Do you think that firing upon and killing four unarmed persons, two being pregnant women, who are not involved in criminal activity but are sitting on a fishing boat on a river is a crime? Suppose the shooter was working with DEA agents in a helicopter who mistakenly thought they were transporting contraband. Do we apply different standards in that case?

As an FBI agent Connolly had certain powers beyond those of a regular citizen. He could make deals with criminals which if done by anyone else might be considered a criminal conspiracy. In making deals for information Connolly and all other agents dealing with Top Echelon Informants are authorized to enter into a certain quid pro quo. What was Connolly authorized to offer or do for Whitey and Stevie in exchange for their information against the Boston Mafia? That was left unclear at his trial.

Stevie alleged that his deal with Connolly was that he could commit any criminal act as long as he did not hit (murder) anyone. Was that a permissible deal for Connolly to make with Stevie? It would be nice to know the answer to that.

Morris testified that was not the deal. He said even though he was Connolly's supervisor he asked Connolly what deal he had made. That suggests any FBI agent has wide latitude and discretion in making deals. Morris testified that Connolly told him that all he was obliged to do was to give them a head start, which is to warn them if any charges were coming down against them so that they could flee. Was that a permissible deal for Connolly to make with Stevie and Whitey? If so, why was Connolly charged with obstruction of justice for telling Whitey to flee?

If an FBI agent is offered money by an informant and he feels to decline it will impair their relationship, what should he do? Should he take it and report it? If it is not reported does that make the acceptance of the gift a crime or is the failure to report just an administrative matter? If it is a crime, what did the agent do for the gift that he would not otherwise have done?

If an FBI agent has the right to protect his informant and he receives payments from an informant to do what he was going to do anyway is that a crime? How far can an FBI agent go in protecting an informant? Most seem to agree he could tip him off about a wiretap. Can he tip them off if someone is squealing on him? Can he tell him who is going to be called before the grand jury to testify against him?

The written FBI guidelines testified to by Agent Thomas Powers had more holes than Swiss cheese. An agent must tell his informant that being an informant will not protect him from criminal prosecutions *"unless the FBI determines otherwise."* The informant is to engage in no violence or other criminal activity *"without approval."* If an informant commits a serious crime FBI headquarters *will decide whether or not to notify* the state authorities. Even the written guidelines are vague and mushy. The customs, the ways of doing business that are accepted and practiced by all from the director to the street agents, are even vaguer.

They are left purposefully vague when they should be crystal clear. What did an FBI agent mean in 2011 when he was overheard on a state police wiretap telling his Top Echelon Informant, a Mafia capo, that "my job is to keep you safe"? Is that his job? Was that Connolly's job? If so, what must they do to live up to that obligation?

Assume Connolly had the right to make a deal with Whitey that in exchange for information on the mob he'd give him a heads up if any indictment was coming down against him. Connolly's action in following through on that agreement would not be construed as criminal. That would mean that if Connolly tipped off Whitey that the indictments were coming down after the holidays then he was doing what he was bound to do by his agreement. He should not have been charged with that act. It is not an obstruction of justice, it advanced justice being part of a proper agreement. If that is the case, then Connolly should not have been charged with any of the RICO offenses because the statute of limitations would have run.

Connolly did not make this argument at trial. It goes back to my dilemma regarding Connolly. He should not have remained silent but have defended himself if he felt he acted properly. Even so, if his action is not a crime then he need not have brought it up. One cannot be convicted of a crime if no crime was committed.

How I Look At The Witnesses Against Connolly:

Morris:

I initially felt he got in over his head and enjoyed the camaraderie of being on the gangster merry-go-round being led around by the nose by Connolly. But that doesn't square with Whitey saying he was Machiavellian. I wonder what he did to make Whitey the master criminal think that of him.

It's hard to shake the feeling that Morris is quite clever and devious if he impressed Whitey that way. There's much more to him than the picture of the insipid man in the gray suit that the prosecution presented.

He knew or should have known Whitey and Stevie were involved in the murders of Wheeler, Halloran, Callahan and others. He didn't care. He protected them, took gifts from them and tipped them off about investigations against them until he thought they may be recording him after he took the five thousand dollars.

He knew if that were the case and either man was arrested then he'd be a get out of jail free card. To prevent this he then worked harder than ever to undermine other investigations. He finally came up with a plan. He went to the Boston Globe to reveal to the reporters that they were informants. He hoped to get them killed by outing them.

He began to put distance between himself and Connolly. He did not want him to attend Harvard. Early on as one with what Whitey recognized as Machiavellian tendencies he began to paint the picture of Connolly as the bad agent while he was a dupe. He opposed his promotion to supervisor.

Morris was in it for Morris. His portrayal as being subservient to Connolly was false. He was his own man. I could not convict Connolly on anything Morris said. I look at it this way. Morris got a pass on his actions, he was the supervisor and very much in charge, so I wouldn't punish

Connolly while Morris who was most culpable skates free

Martorano:

He is a truly despicable man who brought a stench to the prosecution. I had no confidence that I can tell what part of Martorano's testimony is truthful or what part was filled with self-serving lies. Lying for a man who admits to murdering twenty people, mostly unarmed and shot from behind, without a good reason, comes as naturally as blinking his eyes.

On top of that Martorano never met Connolly. His testimony consisted in telling about what others said to him by answering yes or no to leading questions. The people who were giving him this information were also hardened criminals or convicted perjurers who likewise lied as often as they took a breath. We're asked to find a kernel of truth from the mouths of two liars. How does one believe what one hardened criminal said another hardened criminal may have said to him especially when the one talking has been showered with gifts beyond belief by the government to tell a story the government wanted to believe?

Martorano was not in the Boston area during almost all the time at issue. He fled at the time of the race fixing indictment in 1979 and did not return until 1995. Seeing this crude man enjoying himself after spelling out his twenty murders turned me against the government's case. The in-court adulation of him by some of the police officers reinforced that feeling. Like the jury, I credit nothing of Martorano's testimony.

Weeks:

Weeks was Mister Ice, a smooth slick witness. I marveled at his ability to keep his eyes on Connolly's lawyer all through her cross-examination like a tiger preparing to pounce on its prey. Most of his testimony had a ring of truth to it yet I had no doubt he manufactured his role in the December 23 meeting with Connolly at the South Boston Liquor Mart. I thought that he came across as still being loyal to Whitey.

He hurt Connolly in three respects. He provided the evidence to get the government past a statute of limitations problem on the RICO charge; he put Connolly in continuing contact with Stevie after he left the FBI; and he tied Connolly to the letter that was written to Judge Wolf.

I would have convicted Connolly on Weeks's testimony only to the extent his testimony was corroborated as with the letter, the jail visits, and his involvement with Stevie's lawyer.

Salemme:

Little of what he said I believed. Most of it was inconsequential. It should have been obvious to him that Stevie ratted him out to Connolly when he was in New York City. He was arrested and then spent 16 years in prison for a crime that on the one hand he admits to committing but on the other says he didn't. When he gets out of prison he immediately goes back into business with Stevie who set him up in the first place. The man seemed to lack the ability to understand what is going on around him. I don't see what he brought to the trial.

How I Look At The Specific Crimes Charged Against Connolly:

These are the the obstruction of justice charges under the RICO charge. First let me say I don't believe the evidence that Weeks gave about the meeting on December 23, 1994. As far as I am concerned the statute of limitations ran on all these charges and there should not have been a conviction on any.

Castucci's murder

Connolly's assertion that the way Castucci was stuffed in a trunk did not look like the MO of Winter Hill especially in light of his later 209s covering up Whitey's actions is suspect. It was contradicted by Agent Daly who said his informants told him that was their exact MO. Weeks testified that seemed to be the way they handled the people they killed.

Connolly seems already too close to Whitey at this early date in 1976. He is protecting him by throwing curves at the investigators. Is giving out disinformation part of his job in protecting his informants?

Castucci was the man who carried the money back and forth between Winter Hill and New York City. Winter Hill owed the New York Mob

$150,000. Winter Hill figured they could save that money for themselves. They killed Castucci.

When the New York Mob came to collect they said that they gave the $150,000 to Castucci and whoever killed him has the money. The NY mob could not prove otherwise. This cleared their debt.

Castucci was not killed because he was an informant. I don't see Connolly's hand in it.

Halloran's murder:

I am unable to believe anything the gangsters testified to beyond a reasonable doubt without corroboration. The corroboration for Weeks's testimony that Whitey killed Halloran is Montanari's testimony that Halloran was implicating Whitey in the murder of Roger Wheeler, by Morris's testimony that he passed this information to Connolly who later told him that he told Whitey, by Halloran's killing in Southie shortly after that information was given to Whitey, and by Morris telling Whitey after he leaked to him information about the Bahorian wiretap that he "did not want another Halloran," among other things not the least is Weeks's story that after his killing, possibly that night, Connolly, Morris and Agent Newton got together with Whitey and discuss the murder over a few beers, "Thank God for Beck's."

Connolly started filing 209 reports shifting the focus of any investigation away from Whitey and onto others. He knew full well these reports did not accurately reflect the truth.

Connecting Connolly to Halloran's murder is dependent upon me believing Morris. Montanari told Morris Halloran was informing on Whitey, him. If Whitey was told, it is as likely Morris did it as Connolly.

It also means I have to close my eyes to what seemed to be common knowledge among the wise guys that Halloran was talking to the FBI according to FBI 209's and Morris's unit providing protection for Halloran. Because Morris was a likely as Connolly to have told Whitey about Halloran and because Whitey had many other ways to find out that Halloran was cooperating with the FBI, I could not find Whitey guilty of this. Making it more difficult was that within weeks of Halloran's killing Morris was asking Whitey for money to fly his girlfriend down to Georgia.

Callahan's murder:

Agent Montanari told Connolly and Morris he had targeted Whitey and Stevie for their involvement in Wheeler's murder. He told them that Halloran had met both men at Callahan's place where they solicited him to kill Roger Wheeler. I assume whatever Montanari told Connolly he passed on to Whitey.

Connolly knew Montanari was pressing Callahan. Connolly met with Callahan to assess Callahan's ability to withstand FBI pressure. Callahan faxed Connolly a statement denying any knowledge of the Wheeler murder. Two months later Callahan is murdered.

I have no doubt that Connolly kept Whitey apprised of Montanari's investigation. It reached the point where Montanari had to hide his file in ASAC Fitzpatrick's office. Connolly complained to Fitzpatrick about that. It was eventually resolved by ASAC Fitzpatrick in the strangest manner. He required Montanari to tell Connolly what he was doing in the investigation of Connolly's informants, Whitey and Stevie, with respect to the Wheeler and Halloran murders.

Martorano testified Whitey was told Callahan would not stand up by Connolly. He said Whitey then arranged for him to to kill Callahan. I can't believe any of that so I limit my consideration to Callahan being killed two months after Halloran without knowing the circumstances of the killing. I can assume Connolly and Whitey discussed Callahan. I can assume Whitey knew without discussing it with Connolly that Callahan would not stand up. Without Martorano's testimony I cannot make a link to Connolly and could not convict him. Here again, if I could, I would have to decide whether he has the right as an FBI agent to give information to a Top Echelon Informant that a person is giving information against him and that person may not stand up to the FBI pressure.

Rakes's Extortion:

No matter how you want to slice it any deal with Whitey, Stevie and Weeks with the display of a gun on one side and a person with children on the other is an extortion. Suppose Stippo Rakes is the worst person in the world, as some allege, and suppose he sought to sell his liquor business as others allege, the idea that those three gangsters didn't use force and threats of violence to take advantage of him is preposterous. Stippo was so afraid of them he left his family in Disney World to fly back to Southie to stand on the sidewalk waving to passersby because they demanded he do this.

Weeks's story was corroborated. Connolly admitted to two reporters that Joe Lundbohm told him about it. Lundbohm testified that he did. The issue is not so much whether there was a prosecutable case but Connolly's knowledge. He knew his informants were extorting property from legitimate business people. He wrote no reports about it. His clear knowledge and acquiescence in their criminal activities cannot be gainsaid.

Some defend Connolly saying that Stippo was a criminal. The logic of that is that it is all right to commit criminal acts on other criminals, even murder. That makes little sense to me.

At a minimum Connolly should have reported this or referred it to another FBI agent to handle. He did not intend to do anything about it. In a sense he was hiding his informants' wrongdoing and preventing it from being investigated. I believe in the big picture this is an obstruction of justice. I would have convicted him on this unless he was authorized by the FBI to do this.

Bahorian wiretap:

Laying this at the doorstep of Connolly is not right. Morris had the information. Morris said he wanted to protect Stevie because he believed if he fell he'd be brought down with him. I suggest it was more likely that Morris told them because he needed some more money from them and knew they would be grateful.

Morris said this was a tough time for him going through a divorce and living in his girl friend's apartment. He said he ran to Connolly with the information but Connolly told him to tell Whitey and Stevie himself. He told them and received five grand. This was Morris's gambit. Connolly gets a pass.

Advising the felons the indictments are coming down.

There is no showing that Whitey, Stevie or Flemmi knew before hand that the complaint warrants were going to be issued or did issue on January 5. If Connolly had a source in the FBI keeping him posted on events he should have known this. He obviously didn't. Whitey who had been in New Orleans over the holidays was driving back to Boston on January 5 and that day Stevie was telling Salemme that January 10 was the day things were going to happen.

Weeks's story about the meeting in the freezer I didn't believe. Durham asked how he would have known only four FBI agents knew the indictment was coming down if that meeting did not occur. The answer to that is easy. When Weeks and Connolly were scheming to help Stevie, Connolly may have outlined the whole thing to him. Salemme called Connolly a windbag. O'Callaghan said you never talked for just two minutes with Connolly. Dick Lehr and Gerry O'Neill in their book *Black Mass* tell how Connolly met Lehr on the street and very indiscreetly talked and talked about a wiretap investigation they had just completed.

Weeks also had many conversations and meetings with Whitey over the years between the date of his flight and the time of his arrest. He could have learned it from Whitey at any time in that period. Although it would not help Connolly's trial defense to argue he did not pass the information through Weeks but directly to Whitey.

I would give Connolly a pass on this because the gangsters did not know of the issuance of the complaint warrants and Weeks's story is invented. What gives me great doubt is that Flemmi told both Weeks and Salemme that he had his own source who was keeping him advised.

The anonymous letter and false statement to the FBI agent:

I've talked about these before. Connolly had no defense to them. They happened. The anonymous letter was so significant that additional court hearings took place because of it. The false statement though minor was also made. He was rightfully convicted of these charges. I doubt an FBI agent's right to obstruct investigations continues after he no longer is in active service.

The ring:

Martorano testified about a five grand diamond ring Connolly gave his wife. Martorano said he got it from Bulger who got it from Joe McDonald. A subsequent investigation showed that she had been given one by Connolly. Durham asked how Martorano knew about that ring if he didn't learn it from Bulger.

ASAC Fitzpatrick in his book talks about the diamond ring Connolly said he received from Bulger. He said he wore it around the office. He said it had engraved on it the words, Fidelity, Bravery, and Integrity.

No one else said anything like that. I'd suggest Fitzpatrick heard about the ring from others. He did not know that it went to Connolly's wife so he put it on his finger and made up the story about the engraving.

The answer to Durham's question is that Connolly was a braggart. He probably told everyone in the office about the ring he gave his ex-wife. I'm sure that during their marriage Connolly paraded her around at various FBI functions through the years to the consternation of other agents whose wives flamed red with jealousy.

Martorano probably picked up the story from the people questioning him and added his own flavor to it. I'm just unwilling to convict Connolly on anything testified to by Martorano.

My Conclusion About Connolly:

When Wheeler was murdered the FBI in Oklahoma asked for help in its investigation of the murder. It was assigned to Connolly. A subsequent request from them was also referred to him. He did nothing other than mark the matter closed.

Connolly was assigned to deal with Callahan. He knew that Halloran said Callahan, along with Whitey and Stevie, had tried to recruit him to kill Wheeler. Connolly interviewed Callahan and received a letter from him denying any information about the Wheeler murder. Callahan was murdered in Florida. Connolly did not bother to investigate of this.

These sinister actions that were done by Connolly that are known without taking into account input from the gangsters. Connolly over the years filed false reports protecting Whitey and damaging the reputation of others. He failed to file reports of his close relationship to him such as their dinners or giving gifts to others. He did not file reports that may have put Whitey under suspicion of being involved in criminal activities. He knew Whitey and Stevie were involved in ongoing serious criminal activities but he continued a close association with them, never once questioning his actions as an FBI agent empowering the mayhem they were sowing.

Here are just a few of the other things that I know can be attributed to Connolly. He actively undermined other investigations of Whitey and Stevie. He was involved with Morris in destroying the state police investigation of Lancaster Street. He wrote false derogatory statements about the state police causing mistrust among law enforcement agencies. He had a prominent role in causing the investigation of the Norfolk District

Attorney's office which was chasing after Whitey. He set the mindset for FBI agents to believe Billy Bulger was operating to protect his brother Whitey. His actions made other federal and state agencies refuse to work with the FBI. He was involved in the baseless investigation of Trooper Naimovich who was acquitted. He compromised other FBI agents by bringing them to dine with Whitey and giving them gifts from Whitey.

To defend him by saying he had the right to do what he did brings into disrepute the whole FBI. We must ask does the FBI have the right to do any of those things that Connolly did? It is a troubling question because almost all of Connolly's actions were condoned or at a minimum were known throughout the FBI yet they were not stopped.

The problem I have is that the only one held accountable for it is Connolly. I think of the incidents with the Catholic priests. The blame did not stop at the priests causing the harm but went to those who could have stopped them. The same standard of blame should be applied to the FBI. Those who had the power to stop Connolly should likewise be accountable

The one big difference is that it is clear no one in the Catholic Church had the right to authorize its priests to involve themselves in criminal behavior. With the FBI the situation is less clear as the line is blurred. The FBI has some leeway in this area. It can allow its agents to commit crimes when they are acting in an undercover role. It can authorize its informants to engage in criminal behavior by protecting them. A bright line has not been established and followed. The failure to do so will allow the problems we've seen with Connolly to fester and continue.

Connolly was instrumental in destroying the Boston Mafia, men as sinister as the ones he befriended. The FBI gained great publicity from Connolly's activities and our society benefited. Keep in mind that other partners of Whitey and Stevie such as Martorano, Weeks and Salemme, people whose lives were devoted to crime and who have participated in many murders, received less time in prison for their actions in these matters than Connolly has already served. It is also important to remember that the deal with those men that gave them the easy sentences was not made to get Connolly but to get Whitey and Stevie. It could not have been justified if it were made to get Connolly.

The thing that most bothers me about Connolly is not the Boston trial reproduced here but the Florida case. To date, the Florida appeals courts have refused to write a decision on his appeal from his conviction. That seems wrong.

It is not so much that which is wrong, consider this: Connolly was put to trial in a state court for actions he did as a federal agent. The Supremacy Clause of the United States Constitution exists to protect federal officers from state charges for actions taken pursuant to their duties. It should have been invoked by the Department of Justice (DOJ) as was done a few years back in the Ruby Ridge case when an FBI agent was charged by the state. Connolly's actions that resulted in the murder charge in Florida resulted from his dealings with his Top Echelon Informants. As I've noted what is permissible for an FBI agent in those situations is enshrouded in thick federal fog.

It is not a matter that a state should decide. It had already been decided by a federal jury in Boston and he was acquitted of that charge. Not only did the DOJ not intervene to protect Connolly, it sent members of the DOJ to prosecute him. I can find no precedent in the United States history for such an action.

I find it difficult to have anything but disdain for the FBI's and Connolly's actions in these matters. What Connolly did was in the open. He could not have done what he did without the concurrence and assistance of other men in the FBI who are perceived as good and who have walked away unscathed.

I am deeply bothered that he will die in prison. Fair is fair, he has suffered enough. He should be immediately released.

The best thing to do is to learn from him. We should insure that the FBI can never again allow any of its agents to do what Connolly did. We should never allow it turn on an agent because it is embarrassed. Sadly, the FBI appears to have already forgotten Connolly. It is back doing the same thing again and probably never stopped. We are so much the lesser for it.

We direly need a mechanism outside the FBI to insure that innocent people will not suffer because the FBI has joined hands with a murderous criminal.

23515593R00282

Made in the USA
Lexington, KY
15 June 2013